MOUNTAINTOP
MORNINGS

MOUNTAINTOP MORNINGS

ALYSA VANDERWEERD

XULON PRESS

Xulon Press
2301 Lucien Way #415
Maitland, FL 32751
407.339.4217
www.xulonpress.com

Unless otherwise indicated, Scripture quotations taken from the English Standard Version (ESV). Copyright © 2001 by Crossway, a publishing ministry of Good News Publishers. Used by permission. All rights reserved.

Scripture quotations taken from the New American Standard Bible (NASB). Copyright © 1960, 1962, 1963, 1968, 1971, 1972, 1973, 1975, 1977, 1995 by The Lockman Foundation. Used by permission. All rights reserved.

Scripture quotations taken from the Holy Bible, New International Version (NIV). Copyright © 1973, 1978, 1984, 2011 by Biblica, Inc.™. Used by permission. All rights reserved.

Scripture quotations taken from the New King James Version (NKJV). Copyright © 1982 by Thomas Nelson, Inc. Used by permission. All rights reserved.

Scripture quotations taken from the Holy Bible, New Living Translation (NLT). Copyright ©1996, 2004, 2007 by Tyndale House Foundation. Used by permission of Tyndale House Publishers, Inc.

Printed in the United States of America.

ISBN-13: 9781545620366

Also by Alysa VanderWeerd:

Life.

I dedicate this book to my family.

So thankful for all of you.

Praying Matthew 5:3-16

and Psalm 112 for you.

Love you so much!

"Your word is very pure; therefore Your servant loves it."
Psalm 119:140

"Your word is a lamp to my feet and a light to my path."
Psalm 119:105

"The works of the LORD are great, studied by all who have pleasure in them."
Psalm 111:2

AUTHOR'S PREFACE

God placed the idea of *Mountaintop Mornings* on my heart years ago when I was serving in the Jr. High ministry. The youth loved going to the mountains for retreats. They couldn't wait to get away to be in God's presence; to spend time reading His word, and worshipping their Lord and Savior. When they left the mountain, they were on fire for Jesus Christ. Then a couple of weeks would go by, and the fire would dim a little. They had stopped reading God's Word. They had stopped seeking Him as diligently and passionately as they had when they were away on the mountain. I would tell them, "You can still have that mountaintop experience every morning when you read God's word, sitting in His presence."

And then a couple of years ago, I had given my Daily Light away to a patient at work who was struggling. The Daily Light is an amazing classic published in 1794. Pure scripture. As I was talking with this patient, I knew Jesus Christ was the answer to her problem. I kept the Daily Light devotional in my purse to read on my breaks; I quickly grabbed it and offered it to the patient. Thanking me, she took it and left. At this time in my life I could not afford to buy another Daily Light, but I wanted a devotional that was pure scripture. So, one morning when I was struggling, instead of writing out my prayers in my prayer journal as I sat before the Lord, I began to find scripture verses that relayed my heart in the moment as well as what the Lord was speaking to me in regards to my situation. I searched the word wanting to hear God's heart and began piecing these scripture verses together into devotionals.

Searching God's heart is addicting.

I love that our conversation with Him never ends, but will continue right through eternity. There are times in our life, though, when we need to stop talking and truly sit and listen to what He has to say about the specific situation we are dealing with. Treasured moments—listening. God is our Defender always—**Psalm 59:9**; the Perfect Encourager—**1 John 3:20**; and the Best Exhorter—**Hebrews 12:5**.

This devotional is different than the Daily Light as each devotional ends in an "Amen." During this season, the Lord was also teaching me how to pray His Word; recognizing His authority over all. I love to talk to Him and I absolutely love praying. I don't always have the right words to pray; but true power is found in His Word that never returns void—**Isaiah 55:11**. The best prayer to pray is "Not my will Lord, but Yours be done"—**Luke 22:42**.

God's will is God's word.

No other book will be able to take the place of the Bible. This devotional is simply a tool that points people back to the Word. And maybe, you too, will run into someone one day who is struggling; and you can offer them this devotional so they will see that the answer to their problem is found solely in Jesus Christ, the Word made flesh—**John 1:14**.

::Alysa VanderWeerd
2017

INTRODUCTION

*The power in prayer is found in God's Word, not our voice;
it's God's voice, not our words.*

God's word is timeless. It meets every need. It is the power of the Holy Spirit moving and breathing here on earth in the lives of God's children. God's word is an invitation to everyone to enter into a sweet relationship with Himself. He wants to speak to you. He wants you to hear His voice speak into your specific situation as you cry out to Him. When you pray God's word, mountains move effortlessly. Your heart is aligning with God's heart in a perfect position to battle.

So often, we believe we have to physically get away to a mountain to be refreshed, recharged, or renewed to tackle what God has placed before us. We want to meet with God. We want God to meet with us. We need His presence. We need His voice so clear. Yes, God meets people on the mountain when they seek Him. Yes, when people get away from distractions they hear God. However, we all can have a mountaintop experience every morning when we read God's word, seeking to hear His clear voice. God wants to talk to you every day. He wants to hear your voice every day. He desires a dialogue, not a monologue. When you talk to God and read His Word, you enter into a conversation that transforms your heart—**Romans 12:1-2,** and gives you peace of mind—**Philippians 4:6-7.** And then when you begin praying His word, you show your submission to His Sovereign plan. God is all knowing. He knows what is best for every situation. Trust Him!

Mountaintop Mornings is a devotional that is pure scripture. Every devotion ends with an "Amen," as each devotion is a prayer; praying through scripture. It is my prayer that as you pray through scripture you will hear God speak directly to your heart. Whatever is concerning you right now, God has a word for you. He wants to comfort you, encourage you, and exhort you to right living. He loves you so much! It is also my prayer that we would be a generation that seeks to hear God's voice over man's voice. Who doesn't love a good word found in a prayer journal? There are a lot of wise people that seem to spout gold all day long. However, the BEST journal is God's journal—the story of redemption proclaimed in the Bible. God redeeming mankind from the destructiveness of sin through Jesus Christ's death and resurrection. He says it the BEST! All wisdom comes from God's word; wisdom "is a tree of life to those who take hold of her, and happy are all who retain her"—**Proverbs 3:18 NKJV**. The wisdom you need, God has supplied. You simply need to seek Him—**Jeremiah 29:13**, and ask—**James 1:5**.

READER'S GUIDE

There are many ways you can utilize this devotional as a tool to grow closer to God. The goal of every Christian is to know God—to know God's heart, to live His heart, and to share His heart with others. His heart is His word.

1. You can pray the Scripture verses each day.

> "Because of Christ and our faith in Him, we can now come fearlessly into God's presence assured of His glad welcome."
> **—Ephesians 3:12 NLT**

Every day you can enter God's presence knowing He wants to hear from you. He absolutely loves you and He loves those you care about. You don't have to fear. Jesus Christ's death on the cross forgave the sin that separated you from God. He rose again and is now seated at God's right hand; Jesus is praying for you specifically. He lives to intercede for you—**Hebrews 7:25**.

When you pray God's word, you are aligning your heart with His heart for whom you are praying; saying, "Not my will Lord, but Yours be done"—**Luke 22:42**.

You can pray the verses for:

Your church
Family

Friends
Yourself
Nation
Spiritual Leaders
Workplace
Co-workers
School
Community Group
Or anyone else God places on your heart

2. You can study each verse provided for on the given day.

   a.) Pray and ask God by the power of His Holy Spirit to illuminate His truth to you.

     "All Scripture is inspired by God and is useful to teach us what is true and to make us realize what is wrong in our lives. It straightens us out and teaches us to do what is right. It is God's way of preparing us in every way, fully equipped for every good thing God wants us to do."
     —2 Timothy 3:16-17 NLT

   b.) Take one verse at a time.
- What is the main concept of the verse?
- What is God speaking to you personally?
- How can you apply that verse to your life? How can you live this word?
- Who does God want you to share this word with?

   c.) As you read all of the verses, ask how they connect with each other?
- Do some verses provide a greater depth of meaning to the first verse?
- Is there a consistent theme in all of the verses?
- What is the overall take away truth?
- How can you live this truth?
- Who can you share this truth with?

3. A 3-year Journal is provided within the pages.

At a glance, you will be able to see what God has spoken to your heart over the years. It is healthy to look back at your steps in history to see what choices brought you to today. Remembering those moments God called you to obey, ignites your heart with passion; while, recalling His deliverances affirms your faith.

God loves you so much! Every day matters. Your decisions today affect your tomorrows; they affect your family and all those around you. So, when you sit before the Lord, it is always good to ask Him to search your heart; to point out anything within you that offends Him—**Psalm 139:23-24**. Our thoughts affect our emotions, which in turn affect our actions. God is so faithful to correct our wrong thinking by directing us to His Word and right thinking. We then repent of sin and leave transformed, submitted to His Word—**Romans 12:1-2**.

But so too, the Lord comforts the afflicted and encourages the downcast with a right word at the right time. He strengthens us when we are tempted—**Hebrews 2:18**; He corrects us with right discipline—**Hebrews 12:5**; He provides for all our needs—**Philippians 4:19**; He keeps every promise—**Romans 4:20**. God is faithful—**2 Timothy 2:13**!

Life is purifying. We are all in the Refiner's fire, going from glory to greater glory—**2 Corinthians 3:18**. But there is One who stands with us in the flame, never leaving us alone. With our eyes on Jesus Christ, the Great Shepherd of the sheep, we can endure until the end.

Patient endurance is what you need right now so that you are able to continue to do God's will—**Hebrews 10:36**. He is with you. He knows you. He loves you!

Do you desire to know Him on a deeper level?

Learning never ends; every day it sharpens your mind,
preparing you to see Jesus Christ face to face.

KNOW GOD

God knows you. He loves you—**John 3:16**. He created you in your mother's womb—**Psalm 139:15**. Every day of your life was written in His book, the days yet unseen—**Psalm 139:16**. With perfect knowledge, God is perfect love—**1 John 4:8**. He loves you so much that He allows you to choose the details of your life—**Deuteronomy 30:19**. He loves you so much that He allows you to choose whether you want to know Him. He doesn't force Himself upon you. Do you want to know God? It's up to you.

This is the way to have eternal life—to know God, the only true God and Jesus Christ—**John 17:3**. He's given you His Word, infallible; He's offered you redemption, unchanging. However, there is no redemption apart from repentance. You need to recognize the sin in your life and repent. The truth in God's Word is valid; He will never change—**Malachi 3:6**, and His offer of redemption is steadfast. So, what is holding you back from complete fellowship with God?

Sin stains a pure complexion. It mars a soul. It separates you from God on High—**Isaiah 59:1-2**. God is so holy and just that He cannot look upon sin. So yes, He allows you to choose the details of your life; but your choices separate you from Him or draw you close.

He knew you needed a rescuer. He knew you would be trapped in your sin. For all have fallen short of the glory of God—**Romans 3:23**. No one is perfect this side of heaven. Everyone misses the mark. The unspoken sin in your heart, He hears. What's in the dark, He sees. Nothing is hidden from Him. Yes! He knows you perfectly. And He absolutely loves you! The Good News is: "For God so loved the world that He gave His only begotten Son, that whoever believes in Him should not perish but have everlasting life"—**John 3:16**. Born of a virgin, perfect in holiness, Jesus died the death you deserved. For the wages of sin is death but the gift of God is eternal life in Christ Jesus our Lord—**Romans 6:23**. Thanks be to God! Jesus is the indescribable gift that rescues us from our sin—**2 Corinthians 9:15**. He offered up His life, suffering a cruel and torturous death, taking all of our sin upon Himself—**2 Corinthians 5:21**. In that moment, His perfect connection with God the Father was broken as God turned His face away from sin. The greatest sacrifice. Jesus endured separation from God so we could enter God's presence fearlessly, assured of His glad welcome—**Ephesians 3:12**. For by that one offering, Jesus forever made perfect those who are being made holy—**Hebrews 10:10**.

He was buried, but He didn't stay dead. He rose again on the third day—**1 Corinthians 15:3-4**, and He is now sitting at God's right hand—**Hebrews 1:3**. Jesus stood in the gap for you, providing a way for you to stand justified in God's sight, just as if you never sinned.

When you repent of your sin and turn to Jesus Christ, asking Him to come live in your heart, you are set free from the bondage that holds you down—**John 8:36**. When God looks at you, He doesn't see you in your sin; He sees you as pure, holy and righteous solely because of the death and resurrection of Jesus Christ. Your sin is cast as far as the east is from the west—**Psalm 103:12**. You're forgiven because your Savior paid the ransom for your sin with His precious lifeblood—**1 Peter 1:19**.

Who is a God like this? Who has compassion that moves Himself to action? His mercy and grace is unmatched. God set the standard of holiness and we fell short; so, He stepped in Himself covering where we lacked. God shows His unfailing love and faithfulness in His words and actions. He tramples our sin under His feet and throws them into the depths of the ocean—**Micah 7:18-20**; while speaking words of love, saying, "You are Mine"—**Isaiah 43:1**.

The One who knows you perfectly, owns it. For by grace we have been saved through faith in Jesus Christ; you can't take credit for this. It's a gift from God—**Ephesians 2:8**. Salvation is not a reward for the good things we have done—**Ephesians 2:9**; it is deliverance from the power and effects of sin by Jesus Christ's death on the cross and His resurrection.

As we look to the Lord for His help, we can wait confidently for God to save us; God will surely hear—**Micah 7:7**. For some today, there is one prayer that God wants to hear uttered from their lips and that is a prayer of repentance. He is waiting so ever patiently; but there is a day when the waiting game ends—**2 Peter 3:9**. He knows your sin. He loves you. Will you repent today and experience the freedom found in Jesus Christ?

> "If we confess our sins, He is faithful and just to forgive us our sins and to cleanse us from all unrighteousness"
> **—1 John 1:9**

Today, if you want to receive Jesus Christ into your life as your personal Lord and Savior or if you want to make a recommitment to Christ, fully surrendered to Him, you need to:

Realize you are a sinner

—Romans 3:23

Recognize Jesus Christ died on the cross for you

—Romans 5:8

Repent of your sin

—Acts 3:19

Receive Christ into your life

—Romans 10:9.

You can pray a prayer like this one:

Dear Jesus, I know that I am a sinner. I believe You died on the cross for my sins and that You rose again from the dead. I repent of my sins, today, and confess You as my personal Lord and Savior. Please help me to follow You every day of my life. Thank You for saving me! Thank You for accepting me! Thank You for loving me! I pray this all in Jesus' precious name, Amen.

A CLOSE WALK WITH GOD

Do you love details? Do you want to know the secrets of God's heart? If you sit in His presence, abiding, He will tell you—**Jeremiah 33:3**.

In **Exodus 24**, God's glory hovered over the mountain. The beauty of holiness displayed; so awesome in majesty, mighty in power. Moral perfection. Truth.

The people saw God's holiness without being consumed. They experienced His presence; and yet only described what was under His feet. Blue pavement as clear as the heavens. What a privilege to be in the presence of the King!

And then God invites Moses to come up the mountain to meet with Him. A mountaintop experience. In God's presence, hearing God's voice speak regarding His law; receiving the tablets of stone.

A cloud covered Mount Sinai, and the glory of the Lord rested there for six days and on the seventh day God called Moses out of the cloud. At the foot of the mountain looking up, the Israelites saw an awesome sight; devouring fire covered the mountaintop showcasing God's glory. And then Moses disappeared into the cloud for 40 days and 40 nights.

The amazing Shekinah glory; the visible presence of a holy and righteous God. What a sight to behold!

At this time, Moses received God's detailed plan for the tabernacle and it's furnishing. He spent time with God, hearing God's heart regarding truth. God is so faithful to reveal to us the details He cares about.

Moses walked closely with God; so much so that the LORD spoke to Moses face to face, as one would talk to a friend—**Exodus 33:11**. So too, we all have a choice to make regarding how well we want to know God. He doesn't hide His heart. Do we hide ours?

Today, do you hear Him calling out to you, "Meet Me on the mountaintop in the morning. I want to talk to you and hear your heart"—**Exodus 34:2**?

THE EXAMPLE

How often do you step away from distraction and go to the mountain? The place where you are able to seek God diligently and passionately, enjoying His presence—praying, reading His Word, worshipping before Majestic Glory.

Jesus Christ would step away. He walked up the mountain. He walked down. A purpose with each step, absolutely aligned with God the Father in truth.

He is our example. His footsteps are the righteous steps to follow—**Psalm 85:13**. The path is already paved. Do we see it?

Those times on the mountain: He taught, people listened—**Matthew 5-7**; He prayed, God heard—**Matthew 14:23**; He was transfigured, and Peter, James, and John saw and God affirmed—**Matthew 17:1-13**. Times when He was surrounded by many, times when He was alone with God, and times when only a few of His disciples witnessed. For isn't that life?

Today, does your heart mimic the cry of the psalmist who said, "Establish my footsteps in Your word, and do not let iniquity have dominion over me"—**Psalm 119:133 NASB**? "For the word of the Lord is right, and all His work is done in truth"—**Psalm 33:4 NKJV**. With the understanding that as you abide in His Word, as His disciple, you will know the truth and the truth will set you free— **John 8:31-32**.

Do you know the truth?

Do you need to be set free today?

Jesus said, "I am the way, and the truth, and the life. No one comes to the Father except through Me"—**John 14:6 ESV**.

Do you hear God calling out to you, saying, "Seek My face"
—**Psalm 27:8**?

From the start, Jesus was face to face with God—**John 1:1**. He knew God; for "in the beginning was the Word, and the Word was with God, and the Word was God." He is the Alpha and the Omega, the Beginning and the End- **Revelation 1:8**; the Word made flesh—**John 1:14**. He is truth incarnate. When He taught, He shared Himself. And as Deity in the flesh—**Philippians 2:6-7**, people had an encounter with God when they encountered Him.

The multitudes were searching. A desire in them, so deep; but could they explain it? They followed Jesus. And when He saw them following, needing guidance, He walked up the mountain and sat down and taught the Sermon on the Mount. Jesus shared the heart of God, expounding the depths of the law to his disciples and the multitudes who were astonished at His teaching for He taught them as one having authority—**Matthew 7:29**. "Blessed are those who hunger and thirst for righteousness, for they shall be satisfied"—**Matthew 5:6 NASB**. The people were hungry for truth. They needed Jesus Christ. He delivered exactly what they needed to hear to live a life right in God's sight. God sees the heart. He sees what is hidden to the eye of man—**Psalm 139:1**. He knows every motive. Jesus' direct word reached every person. Eternal life is found in Him, alone, the narrow gate—**Matthew 7:13-14**. Following Him leads to life, but He makes it clear that it is not an easy road. A choice one makes every day: walking in the fear of the Lord, resisting temptation, and living in the light.

Descending the mountain, the multitudes followed Him still. A leper came before Jesus, worshipping Him, saying "Lord, if You are willing, You can make me clean"—**Matthew 8:2 NASB**. Jesus then lived the word He just taught, "Blessed are the peacemakers, for they shall be called sons of

God"—**Matthew 5:9 NASB**; as He reached out His hand and touched the leper saying, "I am willing; be cleansed"—**Matthew 8:3 NASB**.

After the feeding of the 5,000, Jesus sent His disciples off in a boat and the multitudes away; for the people wanted to make him king. He withdrew to the mountain to talk to God and to hear the heart of His Father—**John 6:15**. The people's actions were not in line with God's will; to protect them in their enthusiasm over the miracles, and their misunderstanding of what truly was to come, He stepped away from them. We don't know what He prayed at this time; and that is ok. Not every one of Jesus' prayers are recorded for us. What belongs to God, belongs only to God.

Time spent alone with God, abiding in His presence, clears away all confusion in the midst of chaos. Being able to share your entire heart with God, unfiltered, while hearing Him speak directly into your situation is essential to life and right rest—**Matthew 11:28-30**. He knows you. He understands you. He loves you. He is your shelter—**Psalm 91:1**; your rock of refuge—**Psalm 94:22**. People pulling on you in every direction, wanting something, is draining. Everyone needs to be able to step away to be alone with God to renew their mind, focusing on His word—**Romans 12:2**; for He alone provides peace of mind—**Isaiah 26:3**. He gives you direction when you need to see—**Psalm 32:8**. And during the storm that has everyone terrified, He stays your mind so you are calm—**Matthew 14:25-26**. So too, He is your source of nourishment, and apart from Him you cannot do anything—**John 15:4-5**. He fuels you to feed those in your midst.

Notice when Jesus left the mountain during the fourth watch of the night—**Matthew 14:25**. His disciples needed Him. Time on the mountain alone with God is fundamental; you need to talk to Him and hear His heart in His word. The exact time you set aside to meet with God is between you and God. But He will tell you when you need to descend from the mountaintop to go live the word He just showed you. It's being sensitive to His voice and obeying His call. People need you to share what you learned while abiding in His presence. People need you to step in to their life. You are a rescuer filled with the Holy Spirit. You are a divine intervention in a life, every time you take steps of obedience. Go in the name of Jesus Christ! And impact those in your sphere of influence. Share His word; for it just might be that perfect word for the person who steps into your path. So many people need to hear what God is currently speaking to you. Just mention Jesus' name and watch the burdens leave.

Jesus said, "Come to Me, all who are weary and heavy-laden, and I will give you rest. Take My yoke upon you and learn from Me, for I am gentle and humble in heart, and YOU WILL FIND REST FOR YOUR SOULS. For My yoke is easy and My burden is light"—**Mathew 11:28-30 NASB**

When Jesus calls you to Himself, He may want to invite you to witness something amazing. Your weary soul, once burdened, will be alleviated in a moment as you become an eyewitness to His majesty. His power. His love. So much so, years later you may find yourself sharing with people what happened, just as Peter did. As he said, "For when He received honor and glory from God the Father, such an utterance as this was made to Him by the Majestic Glory, 'This is My beloved Son with whom I am well-pleased'—and we ourselves heard this utterance made from heaven when we were with Him on the holy mountain"—**2 Peter 1:17-18 NASB.**

Jesus invited Peter, James, and John to join Him on the mountain—**Matthew 17:1-13**; and He was transfigured before their very eyes. Watching Him intently they saw His face shine as bright as the sun and His clothes become a brilliant white like the light. Without explanation Moses and Elijah appeared and began talking with Jesus. Peter, thankful he was there to witness this amazing sight, not wanting to leave the mountain, spoke; but God interrupted his very words, saying, "This is My beloved Son, with whom I am well-pleased; listen to Him!" Upon hearing God's voice, the disciples fell flat on their face. But Jesus came alongside them and said, "Arise, and do not be afraid." Lifting up their eyes they saw no one but Jesus; and while descending the mountain, they heeded His voice regarding the vision to not tell anyone until after He had risen from the dead.

Listen to Jesus on the mountain. Obey His voice regarding the vision. He is God—**John 10:30**. He alone is worshipped—**Revelation 22:9.**

Jesus' transfiguration in the presence of Moses, Elijah, the disciples, and ultimately God, along with God's affirmation of His Son, shows God's power in a life. For Jesus Christ is the end of the law establishing hearts in righteousness before God—**Romans 10:4**. All who call on the name of the LORD will be saved—**Romans 10:13**.

When you are in God's presence praying, worshipping, reading His Word, and sharing it with others you will shine as lights in a dark world. So friend, "let your light shine before men in such a way that they may see your good works, and glorify your Father who is in heaven"—**Matthew 5:16 NASB**

In this life, faithful obedience to the end ignites every day of life—your own and everyone around you!

"So be ready in the morning, and come up in the morning to Mount Sinai, and present yourself to Me there on the top of the mountain."

Exodus 34:2

JANUARY

JANUARY 1

This Book of the Law shall not depart from your mouth, but you shall meditate in it day and night, that you may observe to do according to all that is written in it. For then you will make your way prosperous, and then you will have good success. * Blessed is the man who walks not in the counsel of the ungodly, nor stands in the path of sinners, nor sits in the seat of the scornful; but his delight is in the law of the LORD, and in His law he meditates day and night. He shall be like a tree planted by the rivers of water, that brings forth it's fruit in its season, whose leaf also shall not wither; and whatever he does shall prosper. * No good thing will He withhold from those who walk uprightly. * Blessed are the undefiled in the way, who walk in the law of the LORD! * And blessed be His glorious name forever! And let the whole earth be filled with His glory. Amen and Amen.

Joshua 1:8 NKJV * Psalm 1:1-3 NKJV * Psalm 84:11 NKJV * Psalm 119:1 NKJV * Psalm 72:19 NKJV

JANUARY

1 . . . .

Why is God's Word important?

20 _____ *

_____

_____

_____

_____

_____

_____

_____

20 _____ *

_____

_____

_____

_____

_____

_____

_____

20 _____ *

_____

_____

_____

_____

_____

_____

_____

JANUARY 2

I will instruct you and teach you in the way you should go; I will guide you with My eye. * Whatever I tell you in the dark, speak in the light; and what you hear in the ear, preach on the housetops. And do not fear those who kill the body but cannot kill the soul. But rather fear Him who is able to destroy both soul and body in hell. Are not two sparrows sold for a copper coin? And not one of them falls to the ground apart from your Father's will. But the very hairs of your head are all numbered. Do not fear therefore; you are of more value than many sparrows. * Your ears shall hear a word behind you, saying, "This is the way, walk in it." * For we walk by faith, not by sight. * So Abram departed as the LORD had spoken to him, and Lot went with him. And Abram was seventy-five years old when he departed Haran. * You will show me the path of life; in Your presence is fullness of joy; at Your right hand are pleasures forevermore. * Righteousness will go before Him, and shall make His footsteps our pathway. * To Him be glory in the church by Christ Jesus to all generations, forever and ever. Amen.

Psalm 32:8 NKJV * Matthew 10:27-31 NKJV * Isaiah 30:21 NKJV *
2 Corinthians 5:7 NKJV * Genesis 12:4 NKJV * Psalm 16:11 NKJV *
Psalm 85:13 NKJV * Ephesians 3:21 NKJV

JANUARY

2 . . . .

Today, what is God calling you to do?

20 _____ *

_____
_____
_____
_____
_____
_____
_____

20 _____ *

_____
_____
_____
_____
_____
_____
_____

20 _____ *

_____
_____
_____
_____
_____
_____
_____

JANUARY 3

This was the place where Abram had built the altar, and there he again worshiped the LORD. * Then Isaac built an altar there and worshiped the LORD. * David and all the people of Israel were celebrating before the LORD with all their might, singing songs and playing all kinds of musical instruments—lyres, harps, tambourines, castanets, and cymbals. * And David danced before the LORD with all his might, wearing a priestly tunic. * When David returned home to bless his family, Michal came out to meet him and said in disgust, "How glorious the king of Israel looked today! He exposed himself to the servant girls like any indecent person might do!" David retorted to Michal, "I was dancing before the LORD, who chose me above your father and his family! He appointed me as the leader of Israel, the people of the LORD. So I am willing to act like a fool in order to show my joy in the LORD." * Shout with joy to the LORD, O earth! Worship the LORD with gladness. Come before him, singing with joy. Acknowledge the LORD is God! He made us, and we are his. We are his people, the sheep of his pasture. Enter his gates with thanksgiving; go into his courts with praise. Give thanks to him and bless his name. For the LORD is good. His unfailing love continues forever, and his faithfulness continues to each generation. * Praise the LORD, I tell myself; with my whole heart, I will praise his holy name. Praise the LORD, I tell myself, and never forget the good things he does for me. He forgives all my sins and heals all my diseases. He ransoms me from death and surrounds me with love and tender mercies. He fills my life with good things. My youth is renewed like the eagle's! * Blessed be the LORD God of Israel from everlasting to everlasting! Amen and amen!

Genesis 13:4 NLT * Genesis 26:25a NLT * 2 Samuel 6:5 NLT * 2 Samuel 6:14 NLT * 2 Samuel 6:20-21 NLT * Psalm 100 NLT * Psalm 103:1-5 NLT * Psalm 41:13 NLT

JANUARY

3 . . . .

Why do you worship the Lord with all your might?

20 _____ *

_____
_____
_____
_____
_____
_____
_____

20 _____ *

_____
_____
_____
_____
_____
_____
_____

20 _____ *

_____
_____
_____
_____
_____
_____
_____

JANUARY 4

Give heed to the voice of my cry, my King and my God, for to You I will pray. * The LORD has heard my supplication; the LORD will receive my prayer. * I love the LORD, because He has heard my voice and my supplications. Because He has inclined His ear to me, therefore I will call upon Him as long as I live. * Jesus spoke these words, lifted up His eyes to heaven, and said: "Father, the hour has come. Glorify Your Son, that Your Son also may glorify You, as You have given Him authority over all flesh, that He should give eternal life to as many as You have given Him. And this is eternal life, that they may know You, the only true God, and Jesus Christ whom You have sent. I have glorified You on the earth. I have finished the work which You have given Me to do. * Grace be with all those who love our Lord Jesus Christ in sincerity. Amen.

Psalm 5:2 NKJV * Psalm 6:9 NKJV * Psalm 116:1-2 NKJV * John 17:1-4 NKJV * Ephesians 6:24 NKJV

JANUARY

4 . . . .

What have you learned about God's heart?

20 _____ *

_____
_____
_____
_____
_____
_____
_____

20 _____ *

_____
_____
_____
_____
_____
_____
_____

20 _____ *

_____
_____
_____
_____
_____
_____
_____

JANUARY 5

I, therefore, the prisoner of the Lord, beseech you to walk worthy of the calling with which you were called, with all lowliness and gentleness, with longsuffering, bearing with one another in love, endeavoring to keep the unity of the Spirit in the bond of peace. * To each one of us grace was given according to the measure of Christ's gift. * For the equipping of the saints for the work of ministry, for the edifying of the body of Christ, till we all come to the unity of the faith and of the knowledge of the Son of God, to a perfect man, to the measure of the stature of the fullness of Christ; that we should no longer be children, tossed to and fro and carried about with every wind of doctrine, by the trickery of men, in the cunning craftiness of deceitful plotting, but speaking the truth in love, may grow up in all things into Him who is the head—Christ—from whom the whole body, joined and knit together by what every joint supplies, according to the effective working by which every part does its share, causes growth of the body for the edifying of itself in love. * Even so you, since you are zealous for spiritual gifts, let it be for the edification of the church that you seek to excel. * Let no one despise your youth, but be an example to the believers in word, in conduct, in love, in spirit, in faith, in purity. * Do not neglect the gift that is in you, which was given to you by prophecy with the laying on of the hands of the eldership. * See then that you walk circumspectly, not as fools but as wise, redeeming the time, because the days are evil. * Praying always with all prayer and supplication in the Spirit, being watchful to this end with all perseverance and supplication for all the saints—and for me, that utterance may be given to me, that I may open my mouth boldly to make known the mystery of the gospel. * Now to our God and Father be glory forever and ever. Amen.

Ephesians 4:1-3 NKJV * Ephesians 4:7 NKJV * Ephesians 4:12-16 NKJV * 1 Corinthians 14:12 NKJV * 1 Timothy 4:12 NKJV * Ephesians 5:15-16 NKJV * Ephesians 6:18-19 NKJV * Philippians 4:20 NKJV

JANUARY

5 . . . .

What does it mean to walk worthy of the call?

20 _____ *

_____

_____

_____

_____

_____

_____

_____

20 _____ *

_____

_____

_____

_____

_____

_____

_____

20 _____ *

_____

_____

_____

_____

_____

_____

_____

JANUARY 6

As He passed by, He saw Levi the son of Alphaeus sitting at the tax office. And He said to him, "Follow Me." So he arose and followed Him. * And He said to the man who had the withered hand, "Step forward." * He said to the man, "Stretch out your hand." And he stretched it out, and his hand was restored as whole as the other. * Now the word of the LORD came to Jonah the second time, saying, "Arise, go to Nineveh, the great city, and preach to it the message that I tell you." So Jonah arose and went to Nineveh, according to the word of the LORD. Now Ninevah was an exceedingly great city, a three-day journey in extent. And Jonah began to enter the city on the first day's walk. Then he cried out and said, "Yet forty days, and Ninevah shall be overthrown!" * The grace of our Lord Jesus Christ be with you. Amen.

Mark 2:14 NKJV * Mark 3:3 NKJV * Mark 3:5b NKJV * Jonah 3:1-4 NKJV * 1 Thessalonians 5:28 NKJV

JANUARY

6 . . . .

What is God calling you to obey Him in?

20 _____ *

_____
_____
_____
_____
_____
_____
_____

20 _____ *

_____
_____
_____
_____
_____
_____
_____

20 _____ *

_____
_____
_____
_____
_____
_____
_____

JANUARY 7

Brethren, pray for us. * Pray without ceasing. * Do not quench the Spirit. * Continue earnestly in prayer, being vigilant in it with thanksgiving; meanwhile praying also for us, that God would open to us a door for the word, to speak the mystery of Christ, for which I am also in chains, that I may make it manifest, as I ought to speak. * We give thanks to the God and Father of our Lord Jesus Christ, praying always for you, since we heard of your faith in Christ Jesus and of your love for all the saints. * For this reason we also, since the day we heard it, do not cease to pray for you, and to ask that you may be filled with the knowledge of His will in all wisdom and spiritual understanding; that you may walk worthy of the Lord, fully pleasing Him, being fruitful in every good work and increasing in the knowledge of God; strengthened with all might, according to His glorious power, for all patience and longsuffering with joy; giving thanks to the Father who has qualified us to be partakers of the inheritance of the saints in the light. * And let the peace of God rule in your hearts, to which also you were called in one body; and be thankful. * Let the word of Christ dwell in you richly in all wisdom, teaching and admonishing one another in psalms and hymns and spiritual songs, singing with grace in your hearts to the Lord. * Walk in wisdom toward those who are outside, redeeming the time. Let your speech always be with grace, seasoned with salt, that you may know how you ought to answer each one. * Take heed to the ministry which you have received in the Lord, that you may fulfill it. * Recognize those who labor among you, and are over you in the Lord and admonish you, and to esteem them very highly in love for their work's sake. Be at peace among yourselves. * And whatever you do, do it heartily, as to the Lord and not to men. * Brethren, the grace of our Lord Jesus Christ be with your spirit. Amen.

1 Thessalonians 5:25 NKJV * 1 Thessalonians 5:17 NKJV * 1 Thessalonians 5:19 NKJV * Colossians 4:2-4 NKJV * Colossians 1:3-4 NKJV * Colossians 1:9-12 NKJV * Colossians 3:15 NKJV * Colossians 3:16 NKJV * Colossians 4:5-6 NKJV * Colossians 4:17 NKJV * 1 Thessalonians 5:12-13 NKJV * Colossians 3:23 NKJV * Galatians 6:18 NKJV

JANUARY

7 . . . .

Why is it important to intercede for others?

20_____

_____

_____

_____

_____

_____

_____

_____

20_____

_____

_____

_____

_____

_____

_____

_____

20_____

_____

_____

_____

_____

_____

_____

_____

JANUARY 8

The LORD is my shepherd; I have everything I need. He lets me rest in green meadows; he leads me beside peaceful streams. He renews my strength. He guides me along right paths, bringing honor to his name. Even when I walk through the dark valley of death, I will not be afraid, for you are close beside me. Your rod and your staff protect and comfort me. You prepare a feast for me in the presence of my enemies. You welcome me as a guest, anointing my head with oil. My cup overflows with blessings. Surely your goodness and unfailing love will pursue me all the days of my life, and I will live in the house of the LORD forever. * Who may worship in your sanctuary, LORD? Who may enter your presence on your holy hill? Those who lead blameless lives and do what is right, speaking truth from sincere hearts. * Because I have done what is right, I will see You. When I awake, I will be fully satisfied, for I will see You face to face. * For to me, living is for Christ, and dying is even better. Yet if I live, that means fruitful service for Christ. I really don't know which is better. I'm torn between two desires: Sometimes I want to live, and sometimes I long to go and be with Christ. That would be far better for me, but it is better for you that I live. * May the grace of our Lord Jesus Christ be with you all. Amen.

Psalm 23 NLT * Psalm 15:1-2 NLT * Psalm 17:15 NLT * Philippians 1:21-23 NLT * 2 Thessalonians 3:18 NLT

JANUARY

8 . . . .

Are shepherds essential to the life of a believer?

20 _____ *

_____
_____
_____
_____
_____
_____
_____

20 _____ *

_____
_____
_____
_____
_____
_____
_____

20 _____ *

_____
_____
_____
_____
_____
_____
_____

JANUARY 9

You are my hiding place; You shall preserve me from trouble; You shall surround me with songs of deliverance. * Make Your face shine upon Your servant; save me for Your mercies sake. * O Lord my God, I cried out to You, and You healed me. * For this cause everyone who is godly shall pray to You. * You have turned for me my mourning into dancing; You have put off my sackcloth and clothed me with gladness, to the end that my glory may sing praise to You and not be silent. O Lord my God, I will give thanks to You forever. * Then I said, "I will not make mention of Him, nor speak anymore in His name." But His word was in my heart like a burning fire shut up in my bones; I was weary of holding it back, and I could not. * So, as much as is in me, I am ready to preach the gospel to you. * As it is written: "There is none righteous, no, not one." * For all have sinned and fallen short of the glory of God. * But God demonstrates His own love toward us, that while we were still sinners, Christ died for us. * Therefore, just as through one man sin entered the world, and death through sin, and thus death spread to all men, because all sinned. * For the wages of sin is death, but the gift of God is eternal life in Jesus Christ. * That if you confess with your mouth the Lord Jesus and believe in your heart that God has raised Him from the dead, you will be saved. * For whoever calls on the name of the Lord will be saved. * Now to Him who is able to keep you from stumbling, and to present you faultless before the presence of His glory with exceeding joy, to God our Savior, who alone is wise, be glory and majesty, dominion and power, both now and forever. Amen.

Psalm 32:7 NKJV * Psalm 31:16 NKJV * Psalm 30:2 NKJV * Psalm 32:6a NKJV * Psalm 30:11-12 NKJV * Jeremiah 20:9 NKJV * Romans 1:15 NKJV * Romans 3:10 NKJV * Romans 3:23 NKJV * Romans 5:8 NKJV * Romans 5:12 NKJV * Romans 6:23 NKJV * Romans 10:9 NKJV * Romans 10:13 NKJV * Jude 24-25 NKJV

JANUARY

9 . . . .

Today, who will you share the gospel with?

20 _____ *

_____

_____

_____

_____

_____

_____

_____

20 _____ *

_____

_____

_____

_____

_____

_____

_____

20 _____ *

_____

_____

_____

_____

_____

_____

_____

JANUARY 10

Do not worry about tomorrow, for tomorrow will worry about its own things. Sufficient for the day is its own trouble. * Be anxious for nothing, but in everything by prayer and supplication, with thanksgiving, let your requests be made known to God. * "Lord, save me!" * "Why are you fearful, O you of little faith?" * The fear of man brings a snare, but whoever trusts in the LORD shall be safe. * He who trusts in the LORD, mercy shall surround him. * Trust in the Lord with all your heart, and lean not on your own understanding, in all your ways acknowledge Him and He shall direct your paths. * Hear my prayer, O LORD, and give ear to my cry. * And do not lead us into temptation, but deliver us from the evil one. For Yours is the kingdom and the power and the glory forever. Amen.

Matthew 6:34 NKJV * Philippians 4:6 NKJV * Matthew 14:30b NKJV * Matthew 8:26 NKJV * Proverbs 29:25 NKJV * Psalm 32:10 NKJV * Proverbs 3:5-6 NKJV * Psalm 39:12a NKJV * Matthew 6:13 NKJV

JANUARY

10 . . . .

What worry do you need to leave with the Lord?

20 _____ *

_____

_____

_____

_____

_____

_____

_____

20 _____ *

_____

_____

_____

_____

_____

_____

_____

20 _____ *

_____

_____

_____

_____

_____

_____

_____

JANUARY 11

You can make many plans, but the LORD's purpose will prevail. * We can make our plans but the LORD determines our steps. * These older women must train the younger women to love their husbands and their children, to live wisely and be pure, to take care of their homes, to do good, and to be submissive to their husbands. Then they will not bring shame on the word of God. * And you yourself must be an example to them by doing good deeds of every kind. Let everything you do reflect the integrity and seriousness of your teaching. Let your teaching be so correct that it can't be criticized. Then those who want to argue will be ashamed because they won't have anything bad to say about us. * Commit your work to the LORD, and then your plans will succeed. * For nothing is impossible with God. * That is why we live by believing and not by seeing. * I urge you, first of all, to pray for all people. As you make your requests, plead for God's mercy upon them, and give thanks. Pray this way for kings and all others who are in authority, so that we can live in peace and quietness, in godliness and dignity. This is good and pleases God our Savior. * Kind words are like honey—sweet to the soul and healthy for the body. * My dear brothers and sisters, may the grace of our Lord Jesus Christ be with you all. Amen.

Proverbs 19:21 NLT * Proverbs 16:9 NLT * Titus 2:4-5 NLT * Titus 2:7-8 NLT * Proverbs 16:3 NLT * Luke 1:37 NLT * 2 Corinthians 5:7 NLT * 1 Timothy 2:1-3 NLT * Proverbs 16:24 NLT * Galatians 6:18 NLT

JANUARY

11 . . . .

What plans do you need to bring to God?

20 _____ *

_____
_____
_____
_____
_____
_____
_____

20 _____ *

_____
_____
_____
_____
_____
_____
_____

20 _____ *

_____
_____
_____
_____
_____
_____
_____

JANUARY 12

They looked to Him and were radiant, and their faces were not ashamed. * And do not be drunk with wine, in which is dissipation; but be filled with the Spirit, speaking to one another in psalms and hymns and spiritual songs, singing and making melody in your heart to the Lord. * But we all with unveiled face, beholding as in a mirror the glory of the Lord, are being transformed into the same image from glory to glory, just as by the Spirit of the Lord. * Repent therefore and be converted, that your sins may be blotted out, so that times of refreshing may come from the presence of the Lord. * That you may become blameless and harmless, children of God without fault in the midst of a crooked and perverse generation, among whom you shine as lights in the world, holding fast the word of life. * And all who sat in the council, looking steadfastly at him, saw his face as the face of an angel. * He, being full of the Holy Spirit, gazed into heaven and saw the glory of God, and Jesus standing at the right hand of God, and said, "Look! I see the heavens opened and the Son of Man standing at the right hand of God!" * Those who are wise shall shine like the brightness of the firmament, and those who turn many to righteousness like the stars forever and ever. * Husbands, love your wives, just as Christ also loved the church and gave Himself for her, that He might sanctify and cleanse her with the washing of the water by the word, that He might present her to Himself a glorious church, not having spot or wrinkle or any such thing, but that she should be holy and without blemish. * Oh, magnify the LORD with me, and let us exalt His name together. I sought the LORD and He heard me, and delivered me from all my fears. * Greet one another with a kiss of love. Peace to you all who are in Christ Jesus. Amen.

Psalm 34:5 NKJV * Ephesians 5:18-19 NKJV * 2 Corinthians 3:18 NKJV * Acts 3:19 NKJV * Philippians 2:15-16a NKJV * Acts 6:15 NKJV * Acts 7:55-56 NKJV * Daniel 12:3 NKJV * Ephesians 5:25-27 NKJV * Psalm 34:3-4 NKJV * 1 Peter 5:14 NKJV

JANUARY

12 . . . .

Today, you need to be filled with the Holy Spirit to . . .

20 ____ *

_____
_____
_____
_____
_____
_____
_____

20 ____ *

_____
_____
_____
_____
_____
_____
_____

20 ____ *

_____
_____
_____
_____
_____
_____
_____

JANUARY 13

Remember this—a farmer who plants only a few seeds will get a small crop. But the one who plants generously will get a generous crop. You must each make up your own mind as to how much you should give. Don't give reluctantly or in response to pressure. For God loves the person who gives cheerfully. And God will generously provide all you need. Then you will always have everything you need and plenty left over to share with others. As the Scriptures say, "Godly people give generously to the poor. Their good deeds will never be forgotten." For God is the one who gives seed to the farmer and then bread to eat. In the same way, he will give you many opportunities to do good, and he will produce a great harvest of generosity in you. Yes, you will be enriched so that you can give even more generously. And when we take your gifts to those who need them, they will break out in thanksgiving to God. So two good things will happen— the needs of the Christians in Jerusalem will be met, and they will joyfully express their thanksgiving to God. You will be glorifying God through your generous gifts. For your generosity to them will prove that you are obedient to the Good News of Christ. And they will pray for you with deep affection because of the wonderful grace of God shown through you. * We also pray that you will be strengthened with his glorious power so that you will have all the patience and endurance you need. May you be filled with joy, always thanking the Father, who has enabled you to share the inheritance that belongs to God's holy people, who live in the light. * Blessed be the LORD forever! Amen and amen!

2 Corinthians 9:6-14 NLT * Colossians 1:11-12 NLT * Psalm 89:52 NLT

JANUARY

13 . . . .

What good thing is God calling you to do?

20 _____ *

_____
_____
_____
_____
_____
_____
_____

20 _____ *

_____
_____
_____
_____
_____
_____
_____

20 _____ *

_____
_____
_____
_____
_____
_____
_____

JANUARY 14

What is man that You take thought of him, and the son of man that You care for him? * As the deer pants for the water brooks, so my soul pants for You, O God. My soul thirsts for God, for the living God; when shall I come and appear before God? * Draw near to God and He will draw near to you. * The effective prayer of a righteous man can accomplish much. * Then you will call upon Me and come and pray to Me, and I will listen to you. You will seek Me and find Me when you search for Me with all your heart. * They will see His face, and His name will be on their foreheads. * The Spirit and the bride say, "Come." And let the one who hears say, "Come." And let the one who is thirsty come; let the one who wishes take the water of life without cost. * He who testifies to these things says, "Yes, I am coming quickly." Amen. Come, Lord Jesus.

Psalm 8:4 NASB * Psalm 42:1-2 NASB * James 4:8a NASB * James 5:16b NASB * Jeremiah 29:12-13 NASB * Revelation 22:4 NASB * Revelation 22:17 NASB * Revelation 22:20 NASB

JANUARY

14 . . . .

As you draw near to God, what is your heart's prayer?

20 _____ *

_____

_____

_____

_____

_____

_____

20 _____ *

_____

_____

_____

_____

_____

_____

20 _____ *

_____

_____

_____

_____

_____

_____

JANUARY 15

Oh LORD, you have examined my heart and know everything about me. You know when I sit down or stand up. You know my every thought when far away. * You have tested my thoughts and examined my heart in the night. You have scrutinized me and found nothing amiss, for I am determined not to sin in what I say. * Above all else guard your heart for it affects everything you do. * He knows where I am going. And when he has tested me like gold in a fire, he will pronounce me innocent. * The righteous keep moving forward, and those with clean hands become stronger and stronger. * God blesses the people who patiently endure testing. Afterward they will receive the crown of life that God has promised to those who love him. * And now, may the God of peace, who brought again from the dead our Lord Jesus, equip you with all you need for doing his will. May he produce in you, through the power of Jesus Christ, all that is pleasing to him. Jesus is the great Shepherd of the sheep by an everlasting covenant, signed with his blood. To him be glory forever and ever. Amen.

Psalm 139:1-2 NLT * Psalm 17:3 NLT * Proverbs 4:23 NLT * Job 23:10 NLT * Job 17:9 NLT * James 1:12 NLT * Hebrews 13:20-21 NLT

JANUARY

15 . . . .

How has God upheld you?

20 _____ *

_____

_____

_____

_____

_____

_____

_____

20 _____ *

_____

_____

_____

_____

_____

_____

_____

20 _____ *

_____

_____

_____

_____

_____

_____

_____

JANURAY 16

Search me, O God, and know my heart; test me and know my thoughts. Point out anything in me that offends you, and lead me along the path of everlasting life. * My child, don't ignore it when the LORD disciplines you, and don't be discouraged when he corrects you. For the LORD corrects those he loves, just as a father corrects a child in whom he delights. * So you should realize that just as a parent disciplines a child, the LORD your God disciplines you to help you. * But consider the joy of those corrected by God! Do not despise the chastening of the Almighty when you sin. For though he wounds, he also bandages. He strikes, but his hands also heal. * Amen and amen!

Psalm 139:23-24 NLT * Proverbs 3:11-12 NLT * Deuteronomy 8:5 NLT * Job 5:17-18 NLT * Psalm 41:13b NLT

JANUARY

16 . . . .

What area in your life is God correcting?

20 _____ *

_____
_____
_____
_____
_____
_____
_____

20 _____ *

_____
_____
_____
_____
_____
_____
_____

20 _____ *

_____
_____
_____
_____
_____
_____
_____

JANUARY 17

Wait patiently for the LORD. Be brave and courageous. Yes, wait patiently for the LORD. * Those who wait on the LORD will find new strength. They will fly high on wings like eagles. They will run and not grow weary. They will walk and not faint. * You, dear friends, must continue to build your lives on the foundation of your holy faith. And continue to pray as you are directed by the Holy Spirit. Live in such a way that God's love can bless you as you wait for the eternal life that our Lord Jesus Christ in his mercy is going to give you. * And we can be confident that he will listen to us whenever we ask him for anything in line with his will. And if we know he is listening when we make our requests, we can be sure that he will give us what we ask for. * Amen and amen!

Psalm 27:14 NLT * Isaiah 40:31 NLT * Jude 20-21 NLT * 1 John 5:14-15 NLT * Psalm 41:13b NLT

January

17 . . . .

God is calling you to patiently persevere in prayer for whom?

20 _____ *

_____
_____
_____
_____
_____
_____
_____

20 _____ *

_____
_____
_____
_____
_____
_____
_____

20 _____ *

_____
_____
_____
_____
_____
_____
_____

JANUARY 18

If we are thrown into the blazing furnace, the God we serve is able to deliver us from it, and he will deliver us from Your Majesty's hand. * And do not think you can say to yourselves, 'We have Abraham as our father.' I tell you that out of these stones God can raise up children for Abraham. * Yet he did not waver through unbelief regarding the promise of God, but was strengthened in his faith and gave glory to God, being fully persuaded that God had power to do what he had promised. * God loves a cheerful giver. * Now to him who is able to do immeasurably more than all we ask or imagine, according to his power that is at work within us. * That is why I am suffering as I am. Yet this is no cause for shame, because I know whom I have believed, and am convinced that he is able to guard what I have entrusted to him until that day. * Because he himself suffered when he was tempted, he is able to help those who are being tempted. * Therefore he is able to save completely those who come to God through him, because he always lives to intercede for them. * Praise be to his glorious name forever; may the whole earth be filled with his glory. Amen and Amen.

Daniel 3:17 NIV * Matthew 3:9 NIV * Romans 4:20-21 NIV * 2 Corinthians 9:7b NIV * Ephesians 3:20 NIV * 2 Timothy 1:12 NIV * Hebrews 2:18 NIV * Hebrews 7:25 NIV * Psalm 72:19 NIV

JANUARY

18 . . . .

How has God strengthened your faith?

20 _____ *

_____
_____
_____
_____
_____
_____
_____

20 _____ *

_____
_____
_____
_____
_____
_____
_____

20 _____ *

_____
_____
_____
_____
_____
_____
_____

JANUARY 19

I have been crucified with Christ; it is no longer I who live, but Christ lives in me; and the life which I now live in the flesh, I live by faith in the Son of God, who loved me and gave Himself for me. * He chose us in Him before the foundation of the world, that we should be holy and without blame before Him in love, having predestined us to adoption as sons by Jesus Christ to Himself, according to the good pleasure of His will, to the praise of the glory of His grace, by which He made us accepted in the Beloved. * Most assuredly, I say to you, he who hears My word and believes in Him who sent Me has everlasting life, and shall not come into judgment, but has passed from death to life. * Therefore, if anyone is in Christ, he is a new creation; old things have passed away; behold all things have become new. * The grace of the Lord Jesus Christ, and the love of God, and the communion of the Holy Spirit be with you all. Amen.

Galatians 2:20 NKJV * Ephesians 1:4-6 NKJV * John 5:24 NKJV *
2 Corinthians 5:17 NKJV * 2 Corinthians 1314 NKJV

JANUARY

19 . . . .

Every Christian is accepted in the Beloved. No outcasts.

20 _____ *

_____
_____
_____
_____
_____
_____
_____

20 _____ *

_____
_____
_____
_____
_____
_____
_____

20 _____ *

_____
_____
_____
_____
_____
_____
_____

JANUARY 20

When I thought how to understand this, it was too painful for me—until I went into the sanctuary of God; then I understood their end. * I will lift up my eyes to the hills—From whence comes my help? My help comes from the LORD, who made heaven and earth. * I was glad when they said to me, "Let us go into the house of the LORD." * God sets the solitary in families. * God is in the midst of her, she shall not be moved. * But none of these things move me; nor do I count my life dear to myself, so that I may finish my race with joy, and the ministry which I received from the Lord Jesus, to testify to the gospel of the grace of God. * We will not hide these truths from our children but will tell the next generation about the glorious deeds of the LORD. We will tell of his power and the mighty miracles he did. * For we walk by faith and not by sight. * To Him be glory in the church by Christ Jesus to all generations, forever and ever. Amen.

Psalm 73:16-17 NKJV * Psalm 121:1-2 NKJV * Psalm 122:1 NKJV * Psalm 68:6a NKJV * Psalm 46:5a NKJV * Acts 20:24 NKJV * Psalm 78:4 NLT * 2 Corinthians 5:7 NKJV * Ephesians 3:21 NKJV

JANUARY

20 . . . .

God gives understanding in His house.

20 _____ *

_____

_____

_____

_____

_____

_____

_____

20 _____ *

_____

_____

_____

_____

_____

_____

_____

20 _____ *

_____

_____

_____

_____

_____

_____

_____

JANUARY 21

Strengthen the weak hands, and make firm the feeble knees. Say to those who are fearful hearted, "Be strong, do not fear! Behold, your God will come with vengeance, with the recompense of God; He will come to save you." * Bless those who persecute you; bless and do not curse. * Do not be overcome by evil, but overcome evil with good. * For everyone practicing evil hates the light and does not come to the light, lest his deeds should be exposed. He who does the truth comes to the light, that his deeds may be clearly seen, that they have been done in God. * Your obedience has become known to all. * For a tree is known by its fruit. * Be filled with the Spirit. * The fruit of the Spirit is love, joy, peace, longsuffering, kindness, goodness, faithfulness, gentleness, self-control. * Then He said to the woman, "Your faith has saved you. Go in peace." * To God, alone wise, be glory through Jesus Christ forever. Amen.

Isaiah 35:3-4 NKJV * Romans 12:14 NKJV * Romans 12:21 NKJV * John 3:20-21 NKJV * Romans 15:19a NKJV * Matthew 12:33b NKJV * Ephesians 5:18b NKJV * Galatians 5:22-23 NKJV * Luke 7:50 NKJV * Romans 15:27 NKJV

JANUARY

21 . . . .

Obedience to God stabilizes life.

20 _____ *

_____
_____
_____
_____
_____
_____
_____

20 _____ *

_____
_____
_____
_____
_____
_____
_____

20 _____ *

_____
_____
_____
_____
_____
_____
_____

JANUARY 22

Beloved, do not imitate what is evil, but what is good. The one who does good is of God; the one who does evil has not seen God. * Do not love the world nor the things in the world. If anyone loves the world, the love of the Father is not in him. For all that is in the world, the lust of the flesh and the lust of the eyes and the boastful pride of life, is not from the Father, but is from the world. * But put on the Lord Jesus Christ, and make no provision for the flesh in regard to its lusts. * Therefore I urge you, brethren, by the mercies of God, to present your bodies a living and holy sacrifice, acceptable to God, which is your spiritual service of worship. And do not be conformed to this world, but be transformed by the renewing of your mind, so that you may prove what the will of God is, that which is good and acceptable and perfect. * Because it is written, "You shall be holy, for I am holy." * My love be with you all in Christ Jesus. Amen.

3 John 11 NASB * 1 John 2:15-16 NASB * Romans 13:14 NASB * Romans 12:1-2 NASB * 1 Peter 1:16 NASB * 1 Corinthians 16:24 NASB

JANUARY

22 . . . .

Stand strong in your God-given convictions.

20 _____ *

_____
_____
_____
_____
_____
_____
_____
_____

20 _____ *

_____
_____
_____
_____
_____
_____
_____
_____

20 _____ *

_____
_____
_____
_____
_____
_____
_____
_____

JANUARY 23

Therefore let him who thinks he stands take heed lest he fall. * No temptation has overtaken you except such as is common to man; but God is faithful, who will not allow you to be tempted beyond what you are able, but with the temptation will also make the way of escape, that you may be able to bear it. * Therefore I run thus: not with uncertainty. Thus I fight: not as one who beats the air. But I discipline my body and bring it into subjection, lest, when I have preached to others, I myself should become disqualified. * Not that I have already attained, or am already perfected; but I press on, that I may lay hold of that for which Christ Jesus has also laid hold of me. Brethren, I do not count myself to have apprehended; but one thing I do, forgetting those things which are behind and reaching forward to those things which are ahead, I press toward the goal for the prize of the upward call of God in Christ Jesus. * I can do all things through Christ who strengthens me. * The grace of our Lord Jesus Christ be with you all. Amen.

1 Corinthians 10:12 NKJV * 1 Corinthians 10:13 NKJV * 1 Corinthians 9:26-27 NKJV * Philippians 3:12-14 NKJV * Philippians 4:13 NKJV * Philippians 4:23 NKJV

JANUARY

23 . . . .

**Self-discipline recognizes one's own weakness,
and seeks God to strengthen it.**

20 _____ *

_____

_____

_____

_____

_____

_____

_____

20 _____ *

_____

_____

_____

_____

_____

_____

20 _____ *

_____

_____

_____

_____

_____

_____

_____

JANUARY 24

Blessed is he who reads and those who hear the words of this prophecy, and keep those things which are written in it; for the time is near. * For the grace of God that brings salvation has appeared to all men, teaching us that, denying ungodliness and worldly lusts, we should live soberly, righteously, and godly in the present age, looking for the blessed hope and glorious appearing of our great God and Savior Jesus Christ. * And do this, knowing the time, that now it is high time to awake out of sleep; for now our salvation is nearer than when we first believed. * The Lord is not slack concerning His promise, as some count slackness, but is longsuffering toward us, not willing that any should perish but that all should come to repentance. * See then that you walk circumspectly, not as fools but as wise, redeeming the time, because the days are evil. * I must work the works of Him who sent Me while it is day; the night is coming when no one can work. * Therefore you also be ready, for the Son of Man is coming at an hour you do not expect. * For Yours is the kingdom and the power and the glory forever. Amen.

Revelation 1:3 NKJV * Titus 2:11-13 NKJV * Romans 13:11 NKJV * 2 Peter 3:9 NKJV * Ephesians 5:15-16 NKJV * John 9:4 NKJV * Matthew 24:44 NKJV * Matthew 6:13b NKJV

JANUARY

24 . . . .

The time is near for Christ's return.

20 _____ *

_____
_____
_____
_____
_____
_____
_____

20 _____ *

_____
_____
_____
_____
_____
_____
_____

20 _____ *

_____
_____
_____
_____
_____
_____
_____

JANUARY 25

Bless the LORD, O my soul; and all that is within me, bless His holy name! * Praise the LORD! Praise, O servants of the LORD, praise the name of the LORD. * Oh, clap your hands, all you peoples! Shout to God with the voice of triumph! * Sing praises to God, sing praises! Sing praises to our King, sing praises! * Make a joyful shout to the LORD, all you lands! Serve the LORD with gladness; come before His presence with singing. * Oh, give thanks to the LORD, for He is good! For His mercy endures forever. * Be glad in the LORD and rejoice, you righteous; and shout for joy, all you upright in heart. * Oh, send out Your light and Your truth! Let them lead me; let them bring me to Your holy hill and to Your tabernacle. Then will I go to the altar of God, to God my exceeding joy; and on the harp I will praise You, O God, my God. * To the end that my glory may sing praise to You and not be silent. O LORD my God, I will give thanks to You forever. * Let the words of my mouth and the meditation of my heart be acceptable in Your sight, O LORD, my strength and my Redeemer. * Praise the LORD! For it is good to sing praises to our God; for it is pleasant, and praise is beautiful. * Praise the LORD! Praise God in His sanctuary; praise Him in His mighty firmament! * Blessed be the LORD God, the God of Israel, who only does wondrous things! And blessed be His glorious name forever! And let the whole earth be filled with His glory. Amen and Amen.

Psalm 103:1 NKJV * Psalm 113:1 NKJV * Psalm 47:1 NKJV * Psalm 47:6 NKJV * Psalm 100:1-2 NKJV * Psalm 118:1 NKJV * Psalm 32:11 NKJV * Psalm 43:3-4 NKJV * Psalm 30:12 NKJV * Psalm 19:14 NKJV * Psalm 147:1 NKJV * Psalm 150:1 NKJV * Psalm 72:18-19 NKJV

January

25 . . . .

Praise is beautiful!

20 _____ *

_____
_____
_____
_____
_____
_____
_____

20 _____ *

_____
_____
_____
_____
_____
_____
_____

20 _____ *

_____
_____
_____
_____
_____
_____
_____

JANUARY 26

In the year King Uzziah died, I saw the Lord. He was sitting on a lofty throne, and the train of his robe filled the Temple. Hovering around him were mighty seraphim, each with six wings. With two wings they covered their faces, with two they covered their feet, and with the remaining two they flew. In a great chorus they sang, "Holy, holy, holy is the LORD Almighty! The whole earth is filled with his glory!" The glorious singing shook the Temple to its foundations, and the entire sanctuary was filled with smoke. * Then I heard the Lord, asking, "Whom should I send as a messenger to my people? Who will go for us?" And I said, "Lord, I'll go! Send me." And he said, "Yes, go." * God is so rich in mercy, and he loved us so very much, that even while we were dead because of all our sins, he gave us life when he raised Christ from the dead. (It is only by God's special favor that you have been saved!) * Because of Christ and our faith in him, we can now come fearlessly into God's presence, assured of his glad welcome. * When I think of the wisdom and scope of God's plan, I fall to my knees and pray to the Father, the Creator of everything in heaven and on earth. I pray that from his glorious, unlimited resources he will give you mighty inner strength through his Holy Spirit. And I pray that Christ will be more and more at home in your hearts as you trust in him. May your roots go down deep into the soil of God's marvelous love. And may you have the power to understand, as all God's people should, how wide, how long, how high, and how deep his love really is. May you experience the love of Christ, though it is so great you will never fully understand it. Then you will be filled with the fullness of life and power that comes from God. Now glory be to God! By his mighty power at work within us, he is able to accomplish infinitely more than we would ever dare to ask or hope. May he be given glory in the church and in Christ Jesus forever and ever through endless ages. Amen.

Isaiah 6:1-4 NLT * Isaiah 6:8-9a NLT * Ephesians 2:4-5 NLT * Ephesians 3:12 NLT * Ephesians 3:14-21 NLT

JANUARY

26 ....

Will you say, "Lord, I'll go! Send me"?

20 _____ *

_____
_____
_____
_____
_____
_____
_____

20 _____ *

_____
_____
_____
_____
_____
_____
_____

20 _____ *

_____
_____
_____
_____
_____
_____
_____

JANUARY 27

The fear of the LORD is the beginning of wisdom, and the knowledge of the Holy One is understanding. * Therefore we make it our aim, whether present or absent, to be well pleasing to Him. For we must all appear before the judgment seat of Christ, that each one may receive the things done in the body, according to what he has done, whether good or bad. * Obey those who rule over you, and be submissive, for they watch out for your souls, as those who must give an account. Let them do so with joy and not with grief, for that would be unprofitable for you. * In the year that King Uzziah died, I saw the Lord sitting on a throne, high and lifted up, and the train of His robe filled the temple. * So I said: "Woe is me, for I am undone! Because I am a man of unclean lips, and I dwell in the midst of a people of unclean lips; for my eyes have seen the King, the LORD of hosts." * Remember therefore from where you have fallen; repent and do the first works, or else I will come to you quickly and remove your lampstand from its place—unless you repent. * And when I saw Him, I fell at His feet as dead. But He laid His right hand on me, saying to me, "Do not be afraid; I am the First and the Last. I am He who lives, and was dead, and behold, I am alive forevermore. Amen."

Proverbs 9:10 NKJV * 2 Corinthians 5:9-10 NKJV * Hebrews 13:17 NKJV * Isaiah 6:1 NKJV * Isaiah 6:5 NKJV * Revelation 2:5 NKJV * Revelation 1:17-18 NKJV

JANUARY

27 . . . .

Walking in the fear of the Lord brings blessing.

20 _____ *

20 _____ *

20 _____ *

JANUARY 28

Because you are sons, God has sent forth the Spirit of His Son into our hearts, crying, "Abba! Father!" Therefore you are no longer a slave, but a son; and if a son, then an heir through God. * To the praise of the glory of His grace, which He freely bestowed on us in the Beloved. * Also we have obtained an inheritance, having been predestined according to His purpose who works all things after the counsel of His will, to the end that we who were the first to hope in Christ would be to the praise of His glory. * I will give thanks to You, for I am fearfully and wonderfully made; wonderful are Your works, and my soul knows it very well. * Your eyes have seen my unformed substance; and in Your book were all written the days that were ordained for me, when as yet there was not one of them. How precious also are Your thoughts to me, O God! How vast is the sum of them! * And from Jesus Christ, the faithful witness, the firstborn of the dead, and the ruler of the kings of the earth. To Him who loves us and released us from our sins by His blood—and He has made us to be a kingdom, priests to His God and Father—to Him be the glory and the dominion forever and ever. Amen.

Galatians 4:6-7 NASB * Ephesians 1:6 NASB * Ephesians 1:11-12 NASB * Psalm 139:14 NASB * Psalm 139:16-17 NASB * Revelation 1:5-6 NASB

JANUARY

28 . . . .

"Abba, Father . . ."

20 _____ *

_____

20 _____ *

_____

20 _____ *

_____

JANUARY 29

Therefore, as we have opportunity, let us do good to all, especially to those who are of the household of faith. * Not with eyeservice, as men-pleasers, but as bondservants of Christ, doing the will of God from the heart, with goodwill doing service, as to the Lord, and not to men, knowing that whatever good anyone does, he will receive the same from the Lord, whether he is a slave or free. * What does it profit, my brethren, if someone says he has faith but does not have works? Can faith save him? If a brother or sister is naked and destitute of daily food, and one of you says to them, "Depart in peace, be warmed and filled," but you do not give them the things which are needed for the body, what does it profit? Thus also faith by itself, if it does not have works, is dead. * Therefore, to him who knows to do good and does not do it, to him it is sin. * For as the body with the spirit is dead, so faith without works is dead also. * Therefore by Him let us continually offer the sacrifice of praise to God, that is, the fruit of our lips, giving thanks to His name. But do not forget to do good and to share, for with such sacrifices God is well pleased. * Let our people also learn to maintain good works, to meet urgent needs, that they may not be unfruitful. * But as for you, brethren, do not grow weary in doing good. * Likewise, the good works of some are clearly evident, and those that are otherwise cannot be hidden. * So don't get tired of doing what is good. Don't get discouraged and give up, for we will reap a harvest of blessing at the appropriate time. * Now may the God of peace who brought up our Lord Jesus from the dead, that great Shepherd of the sheep, through the blood of the everlasting covenant, make you complete in every good work to do His will, working in you what is well pleasing in His sight, through Jesus Christ, to whom be glory forever and ever. Amen.

Galatians 6:10 NKJV * Ephesians 6:6-8 NKJV * James 2:14-17 NKJV * James 4:17 NKJV * James 2:26 NKJV * Hebrews 13:15-16 NKJV * Titus 3:14 NKJV * 2 Thessalonians 3:13 NKJV * 1 Timothy 5:25 NKJV * Galatians 6:9 NLT * Hebrews 13:20-21 NKJV

JANUARY

29 . . . .

Jesus makes you complete in every good work.

20 _____ *

_____
_____
_____
_____
_____
_____
_____

20 _____ *

_____
_____
_____
_____
_____
_____
_____

20 _____ *

_____
_____
_____
_____
_____
_____
_____

JANUARY 30

If we say that we have no sin, we deceive ourselves, and the truth is not in us. * What fruit did you have then in the things which you are now ashamed? For the end of those things is death. * For the wages of sin is death, but the gift of God is eternal life in Christ Jesus our Lord. * For I acknowledge my transgressions, and my sin is always before me. Against You, You only, have I sinned, and done this evil in Your sight—* I don't understand myself at all, for I really want to do what is right, but I don't do it. Instead I do the very thing I hate. I know perfectly well that what I am doing is wrong, and my bad conscience shows that I agree that the law is good. But I can't help myself, because it is sin inside of me that makes me do these evil things. * When I want to do good, I don't. And when I try not to do wrong, I do it anyway. * If we confess our sins, He is faithful and just to forgive us our sins and to cleanse us from all unrighteousness. * For He made Him who knew no sin to be sin for us, that we might become the righteousness of God in Him. * Create in me a clean heart, O God and renew a steadfast spirit within me. Do not cast me away from Your presence, and do not take Your Holy Spirit from me. Restore to me the joy of Your salvation, and uphold me by Your generous Spirit. * Amen and Amen.

1 John 1:8 NKJV * Romans 6:21 NKJV * Romans 6:23 NKJV * Psalm 51:3-4a NKJV * Romans 7:15-17 NLT * Romans 7:19 NLT * 1 John 1:9 NKJV * 2 Corinthians 5:21 NKJV * Psalm 51:10-12 NKJV * Psalm 72:19b NKJV

JANUARY

30 . . . .

Against God, you have sinned.

20 _____ *

20 _____ *

20 _____ *

JANUARY 31

He who dwells in the secret place of the Most High shall abide under the shadow of the Almighty. I will say of the LORD, "He is my refuge and my fortress; my God, in Him I will trust." * In God (I will praise His word), in God I have put my trust; I will not fear. What can flesh do to me? * He shall send from heaven and save me; He reproaches the one who would swallow me up. God shall send forth His mercy and His truth. * When I am afraid, I will trust in You. * For my soul trusts in You; and in the shadow of Your wings I will make my refuge, until these calamities have passed by. * She broke the flask and poured it on His head. But there were some who were indignant among themselves, and said, "Why was this fragrant oil wasted?" * And they criticized her sharply. * But when Jesus was aware of it, He said to them, "Why do you trouble this woman? For she has done a good work for Me." * "Assuredly, I say to you, wherever this gospel is preached in the whole world, what this woman has done will also be told as a memorial to her." * Amen and Amen.

Psalm 91:1-2 NKJV * Psalm 56:4 NKJV * Psalm 57:3 NKJV * Psalm 56:3 NKJV * Psalm 57:1b NKJV * Mark 14:3b-4 NKJV * Mark 14:5b NKJV * Matthew 26:10 NKJV * Matthew 26:13 NKJV * Psalm 72:19b NKJV

JANUARY

31 . . . .

Jesus defends His own.

20 _____ *

_____
_____
_____
_____
_____
_____
_____

20 _____ *

_____
_____
_____
_____
_____
_____
_____

20 _____ *

_____
_____
_____
_____
_____
_____
_____

FEBRUARY

FEBRUARY 1

Then if my people who are called by my name will humble themselves and pray and seek my face and turn from their wicked ways, I will hear from heaven and will forgive their sins and heal their land. * My prayer is not for the world, but for those you have given me, because they belong to you. * During my time here, I have kept them safe. I guarded them so that not one was lost. * I have given them your word. And the world hates them because they do not belong to the world, just as I do not. I'm not asking you to take them out of the world, but to keep them safe from the evil one. * I am praying not only for these disciples but also for all who will ever believe in me because of their testimony. My prayer for all of them is that they will be one, just as you and I are one, Father—that just as you are in me and I am in you, so they will be in us, and the world will believe you sent me. * And this is the way to have eternal life—to know you, the only true God, and Jesus Christ, the one you sent to the earth. * Amen and amen!

2 Chronicles 7:14 NLT * John 17:9 NLT * John 17:12a NLT * John 17:14-15 NLT * John 17:3 NLT * Psalm 72:19b NLT

FEBRUARY

1 . . . .

How do you need to humble yourself before God?

20 ____ *

20 ____ *

20 ____ *

FEBRUARY 2

God, we meditate on your unfailing love as we worship in your Temple. * I bow before your holy Temple as I worship. I will give thanks to your name for your unfailing love and faithfulness, because your promises are backed by all the honor of your name. * I love your sanctuary, LORD, the place where your glory shines. * For a day in Your courts is better than a thousand. I would rather be a doorkeeper in the house of my God than dwell in the tents of wickedness. * Those who are planted in the house of the LORD shall flourish in the courts of our God. * Lift up your hands in the sanctuary, and bless the LORD. * How happy are those who can live in your house, always singing your praises. * One thing I have desired of the LORD, that will I seek: that I may dwell in the house of the LORD all the days of my life, to behold the beauty of the LORD, and to inquire in His temple. * They looked to Him and were radiant, and their faces were not ashamed. * May he send you help from his sanctuary. * May he grant your heart's desire and fulfill all your plans. * What joy for those you choose to bring near, those who live in your holy courts. What joy awaits us inside your holy Temple. * Amen and amen!

Psalm 48:9 NLT * Psalm 138:2 NLT * Psalm 26:8 NLT * Psalm 84:10 NKJV * Psalm 92:13 NKJV * Psalm 134:2 NKJV * Psalm 84:4 NLT * Psalm 27:4 NKJV * Psalm 34:5 NKJV * Psalm 20:2a NLT * Psalm 20:4 NLT * Psalm 65:4 NLT * Psalm 72:19b NLT

FEBRUARY

2 . . . .

Meditate on God's unfailing love as you worship.

20_____ *

20_____ *

20_____ *

FEBRUARY 3

For we are His workmanship, created in Christ Jesus for good works, which God prepared beforehand that we should walk in them. * Every good gift and every perfect gift is from above, and comes down from the Father of lights, with whom is no variation or shadow of turning. * If any of you lacks wisdom, let him ask of God, who gives to all liberally and without reproach, and it will be given to him. * Then the word of the LORD came to me, saying: "Before I formed you in the womb I knew you; before you were born I sanctified you; I ordained you a prophet to the nations." Then said I: "Ah, Lord GOD! Behold, I cannot speak, for I am a youth." But the LORD said to me: "Do not say, 'I am a youth,' for you shall go to all to whom I send you, and whatever I command you, you shall speak. Do not be afraid of their faces, for I am with you to deliver you," says the LORD. * Amen and Amen.

Ephesians 2:10 NKJV * James 1:17 NKJV * James 1:5 NKJV * Jeremiah 1:4-8 NKJV * Psalm 72:19b NKJV

FEBRUARY

3 . . . .

You are God's workmanship, created with a calling.

20 _____ *

_____

_____

_____

_____

_____

_____

20 _____ *

_____

_____

_____

_____

_____

_____

20 _____ *

_____

_____

_____

_____

_____

_____

FEBRUARY 4

But the LORD said to Samuel, "Do not look at his appearance or at his physical stature, because I have refused him. For the LORD does not see as man sees; for a man looks at the outward appearance, but the LORD looks at the heart." * For the eyes of the LORD run to and fro throughout the whole earth, to show Himself strong on behalf of those whose heart is loyal to Him. * And Samuel said to Jesse, "Are all the young men here?" Then he said, "There remains yet the youngest, and there he is, keeping the sheep." * Now he was ruddy, with bright eyes, and good looking. And the LORD said, "Arise, anoint him; for this is the one!" Then Samuel took the horn of oil and anointed him in the midst of his brothers; and the Spirit of the LORD came upon David from that day forward. * Who is skillful in playing, a mighty man of valor, a man of war, prudent in speech, and a handsome person; and the LORD is with him. * Amen and Amen.

1 Samuel 16:7 NKJV * 2 Chronicles 16:9 NKJV * 1 Samuel 16:11a NKJV * 1 Samuel 16:12b-13a NKJV * 1 Samuel 16:18b NKJV * Psalm 72:19b NKJV

FEBRUARY

4 . . . .

The Lord is searching for loyal hearts.

20 _____ *

_____
_____
_____
_____
_____
_____
_____

20 _____ *

_____
_____
_____
_____
_____
_____
_____

20 _____ *

_____
_____
_____
_____
_____
_____
_____

FEBRUARY 5

Let your wife be a fountain of blessing for you. Rejoice in the wife of your youth. * Delight yourself in the Lord and he will give you the desires of your heart. * Behold, you are fair, my love! Behold, you are fair! You have dove's eyes. * You who dwell in the gardens, the companions listen for your voice—Let me hear it! * The man who finds a wife finds a treasure and receives favor from the LORD. * Only the Lord can give an understanding wife. * Loyalty makes a person attractive. * Ears to hear and eyes to see—both are gifts from the LORD. * The heartfelt counsel of a friend is as sweet as perfume and incense. * As a face is reflected in water, so the heart reflects the person. * As iron sharpens iron, a friend sharpens a friend. * Who can find a virtuous and capable wife? She is worth more than precious rubies. Her husband can trust her, and she will greatly enrich his life. She will not hinder him but help him all her life. * Two people can accomplish more than twice as much as one; they get a better return for their labor. If one person falls, the other can reach out and help. But people who are alone when they fall are in real trouble. And on a cold night, two under the same blanket can gain warmth from each other. But how can one be warm alone? A person standing alone can be attacked and defeated, but two can stand back to back and conquer. Three are even better, for a triple braided cord is not easily broken. * Amen and Amen.

Proverbs 5:18 NLT * Psalm 37:4 NKJV * Song of Solomon 1:15 NKJV * Song of Solomon 8:13 NKJV * Proverbs 18:22 NLT * Proverbs 19:14b NLT * Proverbs 19:22a NLT * Proverbs 20:12 NLT * Proverbs 27:9 NLT * Proverbs 27:19 NLT * Proverbs 27:17 NLT * Proverbs 31:10-12 NLT * Ecclesiastes 4:9-12 NLT * Psalm 72:19b NLT

FEBRUARY

5 . . . .

Why is the role of the wife so important?

20_____ *

_____

_____

_____

_____

_____

_____

20_____ *

_____

_____

_____

_____

_____

_____

20_____ *

_____

_____

_____

_____

_____

_____

FEBRUARY 6

Bondservants, obey in all things your masters according to the flesh, not with eye-service, as men pleasers, but in sincerity of heart, fearing God. And whatever you do, do it heartily, as to the Lord and not to men. * So, my dear brothers and sisters, be strong and steady, always enthusiastic about the Lord's work, for you know that nothing you do for the Lord is ever useless. * If you listen to constructive criticism, you will be at home with the wise. If you reject criticism, you only harm yourself; but if you listen to correction, you grow in understanding. * The LORD hates those who don't keep their word, but he delights in those who do. * A king rejoices in servants who know what they are doing; he is angry with those who cause trouble. * Commit your work to the Lord, and then your plans will succeed. * The king is pleased with righteous lips; he loves those who speak honestly. * Commit yourself to instruction; attune your ears to hear words of knowledge. * Faithful messengers are as refreshing as snow in the heat of summer. They revive the spirit of their employer. * Amen and Amen.

Colossians 3:22-23 NKJV * 1 Corinthians 15:58 NLT * Proverbs 15:31-32 NLT * Proverbs 12:22 NLT * Proverbs 14:35 NLT * Proverbs 16:3 NLT * Proverbs 16:13 NLT * Proverbs 23:12 NLT * Proverbs 25:13 NLT * Psalm 72:19b NLT

FEBRUARY

6 . . . .

**Work unto the Lord in all things.
He sees with perfect clarity.**

20 _____ *

_____

_____

_____

_____

_____

_____

20 _____ *

_____

_____

_____

_____

_____

_____

20 _____ *

_____

_____

_____

_____

_____

_____

FEBRUARY 7

A man who has friends must himself be friendly, but there is a friend who sticks closer than a brother. * A friend loves at all times, and a brother is born for adversity. * Now Jonathan again caused David to vow, because he loved him; for he loved him as he loved his own soul. * As iron sharpens iron, so a man sharpens the countenance of his friend. * And the Scripture was fulfilled which says, "Abraham believed God, and it was accounted to him for righteousness." And he was called the friend of God. * Faithful are the wounds of a friend. * Do not be unequally yoked together with unbelievers. For what fellowship has righteousness with lawlessness? And what communion has light with darkness? * Amen and Amen.

Proverbs 18:24 NKJV * Proverbs 17:17NKJV * 1 Samuel 20:17 NKJV * Proverbs 27:17 NKJV * James 2:23 NKJV * Proverbs 27:6a NKJV * 2 Corinthians 6:14 NKJV * Psalm 41:13b NKJV

FEBRUARY

7 . . . .

What does true friendship entail?

20 _____ *

_____
_____
_____
_____
_____
_____

20 _____ *

_____
_____
_____
_____
_____
_____

20 _____ *

_____
_____
_____
_____
_____
_____

FEBRUARY 8

He was wounded and crushed for our sins. He was beaten that we might have peace. He was whipped, and we were healed! * And because of what he has experienced, my righteous servant will make it possible for many to be counted righteous, for he will bear all their sins. * When he discovered a pearl of great value, he sold everything he owned and bought it! * For a husband is the head of his wife as Christ is head of his body, the church; he gave his life to be her Savior. * The LORD witnessed the vows you and your wife made to each other on your wedding day when you were young. * Didn't the LORD make you one with your wife? In body and spirit you are his. And what does he want? Godly children from your union. So guard yourself; remain loyal to the wife of your youth. * Husbands must love your wives with the same love Christ showed the church. He gave up his life for her to make her holy and clean, washed by baptism and God's word. * The whole earth will acknowledge the LORD and return to him. People from every nation will bow down before him. For the LORD is king! * Future generations will also serve him. Our children will hear about the wonders of the Lord. His righteous acts will be told to those yet unborn. They will hear about everything he has done. * "Hallelujah! For the Lord our God, the Almighty reigns! Let us be glad and rejoice and honor him. For the time has come for the wedding feast of the Lamb, and his bride has prepared herself. She is permitted to wear the finest white linen." (Fine linen represents the good deeds done by the people of God.) * Bless his glorious name forever! Let the whole earth be filled with his glory. Amen and Amen!

Isaiah 53:5 NLT * Isaiah 53:11b NLT * Matthew 13:46 NLT * Ephesians 5:23 NLT * Malachi 2:14b NLT * Malachi 2:15 NLT * Ephesians 5:25-26 NLT * Psalm 22:27-28a NLT * Psalm 22:30-31 NLT * Revelation 19:6b-8 NLT * Psalm 72:19 NLT

FEBRUARY

8 . . . .

How have you experienced Christ's healing in your life?

20 _____ *

_____
_____
_____
_____
_____
_____
_____

20 _____ *

_____
_____
_____
_____
_____
_____
_____

20 _____ *

_____
_____
_____
_____
_____
_____
_____

FEBRUARY 9

Now as they observed the confidence of Peter and John and understood that they were uneducated and untrained men, they were amazed, and began to recognize them as having been with Jesus. And seeing the man who had been healed standing with them, they had nothing to say in reply. * And the hand of the Lord was with them, and a large number who believed turned to the Lord. * But an angel of the Lord spoke to Philip saying, "Get up and go south to the road that descends from Jerusalem to Gaza." (This is a desert road.) So he got up and went; and there was an Ethiopian eunuch, a court official of Candace, queen of the Ethiopians, who was in charge of all her treasure; and he had come to Jerusalem to worship, and he was returning and sitting in his chariot, and was reading the prophet Isaiah. Then the Spirit said to Philip, "Go up and join this chariot." Philip ran up and heard him reading Isaiah the prophet, and said, "Do you understand what you are reading?" * Now there was a disciple at Damascus named Ananias; and the Lord said to him in a vision, "Ananias." And he said, "Here I am, Lord." And the Lord said to him, "Get up and go to the street called Straight, and inquire at the house of Judas for a man from Tarsus named Saul, for he is praying, and he has seen in a vision a man named Ananias come in and lay his hands on him, so that he might regain his sight." But Ananias answered, "Lord, I have heard from many about this man, how much harm he did to Your saints at Jerusalem; and here he has authority from the chief priests to bind all who call on Your name." But the Lord said to him, "Go, for he is a chosen instrument of Mine, to bear My name before the Gentiles and kings and the sons of Israel; for I will show him how much he must suffer for My name's sake." * The grace of our Lord Jesus Christ be with your spirit, brethren. Amen.

Acts 4:13-14 NASB * Acts 11:21 NASB * Acts 8:26-30 NASB * Acts 9:10-15 NASB * Galatians 6:18 NASB

FEBRUARY

9 . . . .

There are so many that need to hear what God shared with you.

20 _____ *

_____
_____
_____
_____
_____
_____
_____

20 _____ *

_____
_____
_____
_____
_____
_____
_____

20 _____ *

_____
_____
_____
_____
_____
_____
_____

FEBRUARY 10

He also chose David His servant, and took him from the sheepfolds; from following the ewes that had young He brought him, to shepherd Jacob His people, and Israel His inheritance. So he shepherded them according to the integrity of his heart, and guided them by the skillfulness of his hands. * I will give you shepherds according to My heart, who will feed you with knowledge and understanding. * He who enters by the door is the shepherd of the sheep. To him the doorkeeper opens, and the sheep hear his voice; and he calls his own sheep by name and leads them out. And when he brings out his own sheep, he goes before them; and the sheep follow him, for they know his voice. Yet they will by no means follow a stranger, but will flee from him, for they do not know the voice of strangers. * I am the good shepherd. The good shepherd gives His life for the sheep. But a hireling, he who is not the shepherd, one who does not own the sheep, sees the wolf coming and leaves the sheep and flees; and the wolf catches the sheep and scatters them. The hireling flees because he is a hireling and does not care about the sheep. I am the good shepherd; and I know My sheep and am known by My own. * "Take heed to the ministry which you have received in the Lord, that you may fulfill it." * Imitate me, just as I also imitate Christ. * This salutation by my own hand—Paul. Remember my chains. Grace be with you. Amen.

Psalm 78:70-72 NKJV * Jeremiah 3:15 NKJV * John 10:2-5 NKJV * John 10:11-14 NKJV * Colossians 4:17b NKJV * 1 Corinthians 11:1 NKJV * Colossians 4:18 NKJV

FEBRUARY

10 . . . .

What example, given by a shepherd, do you want to imitate?

20 _____ *

_____
_____
_____
_____
_____
_____
_____

20 _____ *

_____
_____
_____
_____
_____
_____
_____

20 _____ *

_____
_____
_____
_____
_____
_____
_____

FEBRUARY 11

No eye has seen, no ear has heard, and no mind has imagined what God has prepared for those who love him. * For with God nothing will be impossible. * Walk in wisdom toward those who are outside, redeeming the time. Let your speech always be with grace, seasoned with salt, that you may know how you ought to answer each one. * Let the word of Christ dwell in you richly in all wisdom, teaching and admonishing one another in psalms and hymns and spiritual songs, singing with grace in your hearts to the Lord. And whatever you do in word or deed, do all in the name of the Lord Jesus, giving thanks to God the Father through Him. * Your obedience has become known to all. * Therefore, whether you eat or drink or whatever you do, do all to the glory of God. * And whatever you do, do it heartily, as to the Lord and not to men, knowing that from the Lord you will receive the reward of the inheritance for you serve the Lord Christ. * For I am not ashamed of the gospel of Christ, for it is the power of God to salvation for everyone who believes, for the Jew first and also for the Greek. * And the God of peace will crush Satan under your feet shortly. The grace of our Lord Jesus Christ be with you. Amen.

1 Corinthians 2:9 NLT * Luke 1:37 NKJV * Colossians 3:16-17 NKJV * Romans 16:19a NKJV * 1 Corinthians 10:31 NKJV * Colossians 4:5-6 NKJV * Colossians 3:23 NKJV * Romans 1:16 NKJV * Romans 16:20 NKJV

FEBRUARY

11 . . . .

God has great plans for you.

20 _____ *

_____

_____

_____

_____

_____

_____

_____

20 _____ *

_____

_____

_____

_____

_____

_____

_____

20 _____ *

_____

_____

_____

_____

_____

_____

_____

FEBRUARY 12

Then He said to them, "The harvest truly is great, but the laborers are few; therefore pray the Lord of the harvest to send out laborers into His harvest." * Whatever I tell you in the dark, speak in the light; and what you hear in the ear, preach on the housetops. * "Go to the Temple and give the people this message of life!" * O God, you are my God; I earnestly search for you. My soul thirsts for you; my whole body longs for you in this parched and weary land where there is no water. I have seen you in your sanctuary and gazed upon your power and glory. * One thing I have desired of the LORD, that will I seek: That I may dwell in the house of the LORD all the days of my life, to behold the beauty of the LORD, and to inquire in His temple. * After breakfast Jesus said to Simon Peter, "Simon son of John, do you love me more than these?" "Yes, Lord," Peter replied, "you know I love you." "Then feed my lambs." Jesus told him. Jesus repeated the question: "Simon son of John, do you love me?" "Yes, Lord," Peter said, "you know I love you." "Then take care of my sheep," Jesus said. Once more he asked him, "Simon son of John, do you love me?" Peter was grieved that Jesus asked the question a third time. He said, "Lord, you know everything. You know I love you." Jesus said, "Then feed my sheep." * "Go therefore and make disciples of all the nations, baptizing them in the name of the Father and the Son and of the Holy Spirit, teaching them to observe all things that I have commanded you; and lo, I am with you always, even to the end of the age." Amen.

Luke 10:2 NKJV * Matthew 10:27 NKJV * Acts 5:20 NLT * Psalm 63:1-2 NLT * Psalm 27:4 NKJV * John 21:15-17 NLT * Matthew 28:19-20 NKJV

FEBRUARY

12 . . . .

People are thirsting for truth. Will you share?

20 _____ *

_____
_____
_____
_____
_____
_____
_____

20 _____ *

_____
_____
_____
_____
_____
_____
_____

20 _____ *

_____
_____
_____
_____
_____
_____
_____

FEBRUARY 13

Sitting down, He called the twelve and said to them, "If anyone wants to be first, he shall be last of all and servant of all." * You call Me Teacher and Lord; and you are right, for so I am. If I then, the Lord and the Teacher, washed your feet, you also ought to wash one another's feet. For I gave you an example that you also should do as I did to you. * Every branch in Me that does not bear fruit, He takes away; and every branch that bears fruit, He prunes it so that it may bear more fruit. * Greater love has no one than this, that one lay down his life for his friends. * The end of all things is near; therefore, be of sound judgment and sober spirit for the purpose of prayer. Above all, keep fervent in your love for one another, because love covers a multitude of sins. Be hospitable to one another without complaint. As each one has received a special gift, employ it in serving one another as good stewards of the manifold grace of God. * Now the God of peace, who brought up from the dead the great Shepherd of the sheep through the blood of the eternal covenant, even Jesus our Lord, equip you in every good thing to do His will, working in us that which is pleasing in His sight, through Jesus Christ, to whom be the glory forever and ever. Amen.

Mark 9:35 NASB * John 13:13-15 NASB * John 15:2 NASB * John 15:13 NASB * 1 Peter 4:7-10 NASB * Hebrews 13:20-21 NASB

FEBRUARY

13 . . . .

How has God called you to serve?

20 ____ *

_____
_____
_____
_____
_____
_____
_____

20 ____ *

_____
_____
_____
_____
_____
_____
_____

20 ____ *

_____
_____
_____
_____
_____
_____
_____

FEBRUARY 14

Wait for the LORD; be strong and let your heart take courage; yes, wait for the LORD. * For a thousand years in Your sight are like yesterday when it passes by, or as a watch in the night. * So teach us to number our days, that we may present to You a heart of wisdom. * Therefore be careful how you walk, not as unwise men but as wise, making the most of your time, because the days are evil. * Do this, knowing the time, that it is already the hour for you to awaken from sleep; for now salvation is nearer to us than when we believed. * The Lord is not slow about His promise, as some count slowness, but is patient toward you, not wishing for any to perish but for all to come to repentance. * Let us not lose heart in doing good, for in due time we will reap if we do not grow weary. * For the vision is yet for the appointed time; it hastens toward the goal and it will not fail. Though it tarries, wait for it; for it will certainly come, it will not delay. * Conduct yourselves with wisdom toward outsiders, making the most of the opportunity. Let your speech always be with grace, as though seasoned with salt, so that you will know how you should respond to each person. * But do not let this one fact escape your notice, beloved, that with the Lord one day is like a thousand years, and a thousand years like one day. * But grow in the grace and knowledge of our Lord and Savior Jesus Christ. To Him be the glory, both now and to the day of eternity. Amen.

Psalm 27:14 NASB * Psalm 90:4 NASB * Psalm 90:12 NASB * Ephesians 5:15-16 NASB * Romans 13:11 NASB * 2 Peter 3:9 NASB * Galatians 6:9 NASB * Habakkuk 2:3 NASB * Colossians 4:5-6 NASB * 2 Peter 3:8 NASB * 2 Peter 3:18 NASB

FEBRUARY

14 . . . .

What is God calling you to do while you wait?

20 _____

_____

_____

_____

_____

_____

_____

20 _____

_____

_____

_____

_____

_____

_____

20 _____

_____

_____

_____

_____

_____

_____

FEBRUARY 15

There is a time for everything, and a season for every activity under the heavens. * A time to be born and a time to die, a time to plant and a time to uproot. * A time to kill and a time to heal, a time to tear down and a time to build. * A time to weep and a time to laugh, a time to mourn and a time to dance. * A time to scatter stones and a time to gather them, a time to embrace and a time to refrain from embracing. * A time to search and a time to give up, a time to keep and a time to throw away. * A time to tear and a time to mend, a time to be silent and a time to speak. * A time to love and a time to hate, a time for war and a time for peace. * He has made everything beautiful in its time. He has also set eternity in the human heart; yet no one can fathom what God has done from beginning to end. * To the only wise God be glory forever through Jesus Christ! Amen.

Ecclesiastes 3:1 NIV * Ecclesiastes 3:2 NIV * Ecclesiastes 3:3 NIV * Ecclesiastes 3:4 NIV * Ecclesiastes 3:5 NIV * Ecclesiastes 3:6 NIV * Ecclesiastes 3:7 NIV * Ecclesiastes 3:8 NIV * Ecclesiastes 3:11 NIV * Romans 16:27 NIV

FEBRUARY

15 . . . .

It is the time to . . .

20 _____ *

_____
_____
_____
_____
_____
_____
_____

20 _____ *

_____
_____
_____
_____
_____
_____
_____

20 _____ *

_____
_____
_____
_____
_____
_____
_____

FEBRUARY 16

Hannah was in deep anguish, crying bitterly as she prayed to the LORD. And she made this vow: "O LORD Almighty, if you will look down upon my sorrow and answer my prayer and give me a son, then I will give him back to you. He will be yours for his entire lifetime, and as a sign that he has been dedicated to the LORD, his hair will never be cut." * The LORD remembered her request, and in due time she gave birth to a son. She named him Samuel, for she said, "I asked the LORD for him." * Zechariah and Elizabeth were righteous in God's eyes, careful to obey all of the Lord's commandments and regulations. They had no children because Elizabeth was barren, and now they were both very old. * But the angel said, "Don't be afraid, Zechariah! For God has heard your prayer, and your wife, Elizabeth, will bear you a son! And you are to name him John." * "He will precede the coming of the Lord, preparing the people for his arrival. He will turn the hearts of the fathers to their children, and he will change disobedient minds to accept godly wisdom." * "How kind the Lord is!" she exclaimed. "He has taken away my disgrace of having no children!" * I love the LORD because he hears and answers my prayers. Because he bends down and listens, I will pray as long as I have breath! * He gives the barren woman a home, so that she becomes a happy mother. Praise the LORD! * Amen and Amen.

1 Samuel 1:10-11 NLT * 1 Samuel 1:19b-20 NLT * Luke 1:6 NLT * Luke 1:13 NLT * Luke 1:17b NLT * Luke 1:25 NLT * Psalm 116:1-2 NLT * Psalm 113:9 NLT * Psalm 41:13b NLT

FEBRUARY

16 ....

How has God heard your prayer?

20 _____ *

_____
_____
_____
_____
_____
_____
_____

20 _____ *

_____
_____
_____
_____
_____
_____
_____

20 _____ *

_____
_____
_____
_____
_____
_____
_____

FEBRUARY 17

Teach your children to choose the right path, and when they are older, they will remain upon it. * Job would purify his children. He would get up each morning and offer a burnt offering for each of them. For Job said to himself, "Perhaps my children have sinned and have cursed God in their hearts." This was Job's regular practice. * Children are a gift from the LORD; they are a reward from him. Children born to a young man are like sharp arrows in a warrior's hands. How happy is the man whose quiver is full of them! * Happy are those who fear the LORD. Yes, happy are those who delight in doing what he commands. Their children will be successful everywhere; an entire generation of godly people will be blessed. * When darkness overtakes the godly, light will come bursting in. They are generous, compassionate, and righteous. * They do not fear bad news; they confidently trust the LORD to care for them. They are confident and fearless and can face their foes triumphantly. They give generously to those in need. Their good deeds will never be forgotten. They will have influence and honor. * Amen and Amen.

Proverbs 22:6 NLT * Job 1:5b NLT * Psalm 127:3-5a NLT * Psalm 112:1-2 NLT * Psalm 112:4 NLT * Psalm 112:7-9 NLT * Psalm 41:13b NLT

FEBRUARY

17 . . . .

What is your prayer for your family?

20_____ *

_____
_____
_____
_____
_____
_____
_____

20_____ *

_____
_____
_____
_____
_____
_____
_____

20_____ *

_____
_____
_____
_____
_____
_____
_____

FEBRUARY 18

I will cause you to become the father of a great nation. I will bless you and make you famous, and I will make you a blessing to others. I will bless those who bless you and curse those who curse you. All the families of the earth will be blessed through you. * "Stay here with the donkey," Abraham told the young men. "The boy and I will travel a little farther. We will worship there, and then we will come right back." * I will go wherever you go and live wherever you live. Your people will be my people, and your God will be my God. * The entire family got up early the next morning and went to worship the LORD once more. * Ezra the priest brought the scroll of the law before the assembly, which included the men and women and all the children old enough to understand. * Then Ezra praised the LORD, the great God, and all the people chanted, "Amen! Amen!" as they lifted their hands toward heaven. Then they bowed down and worshiped the LORD with their faces to the ground. * They took turns confessing their sins and worshiping the LORD their God. * Amen and Amen.

Genesis 12:2-3 NLT * Genesis 22:5 NLT * Ruth 1:16b NLT * 1 Samuel 1:19a NLT * Nehemiah 8:1 NLT * Nehemiah 8:6 NLT * Nehemiah 9:3b NLT * Psalm 41:13b NLT

FEBRUARY

18 . . . .

Faithfulness takes faith.

20 _____ *

_____

_____

_____

_____

_____

_____

20 _____ *

_____

_____

_____

_____

_____

_____

20 _____ *

_____

_____

_____

_____

_____

_____

FEBRUARY 19

But You are the same, and Your years will have no end. * "I am the Alpha and the Omega, the Beginning and the End," says the Lord, "who is and who was and who is to come, the Almighty." * "For I am the LORD, I do not change." * Oh, give thanks to the LORD, for He is good! For His mercy endures forever. * For I am persuaded that neither death nor life, nor angels nor principalities nor powers, nor things present nor things to come, nor height nor depth, nor any other created thing, shall be able to separate us from the love of God which is in Christ Jesus our Lord. * Jesus Christ is the same yesterday, today, and forever. * Amen and Amen.

Psalm 102:27 NKJV * Revelation 1:8 NKJV * Malachi 3:6a NKJV * Psalm 136:1 NKJV * Romans 8:38-39 NKJV * Hebrews 13:8 NKJV * Psalm 41:13b NKJV

FEBRUARY

19 . . . .

The Beginning and the End will never change.

20 _____ *

---

20 _____ *

---

20 _____ *

FEBRUARY 20

Now there was one, Anna, a prophetess. * This woman was a widow of about eighty-four years, who did not depart from the temple, but served God with fastings and prayers night and day. And coming in that instant she gave thanks to the Lord, and spoke of Him to all those who looked for redemption in Jerusalem. * How then shall they call on Him in whom they have not believed? And how shall they believe in Him of whom they have not heard? And how shall they hear without a preacher? And how shall they preach unless they are sent? As it is written: "How beautiful are the feet of those who preach the gospel of peace, who bring glad tidings of good things!" * My love be with you all in Christ Jesus. Amen.

Luke 2:36 NKJV * Luke 2:37-38 NKJV * Romans 10:14-15 NKJV * 1 Corinthians 16:24 NKJV

FEBRUARY

20 . . . .

**Will you thank God for allowing you to share
the Good News?**

20 _____ *

_____
_____
_____
_____
_____
_____
_____

20 _____ *

_____
_____
_____
_____
_____
_____
_____

20 _____ *

_____
_____
_____
_____
_____
_____
_____

FEBRUARY 21

The one thing I ask of the LORD—the thing I seek the most—is to live in the house of the LORD all the days of my life, delighting in the LORD's perfections and meditating in his Temple. * Think of it—the LORD has healed me! I will sing his praises with instruments every day of my life in the Temple of the LORD. * I will sing of the tender mercies of the LORD forever! Young and old will hear of your faithfulness. * Future generations will also serve him. Our children will hear about the wonders of the Lord. * Let the Holy Spirit fill and control you. Then you will sing psalms and hymns and spiritual songs among yourselves, making music to the Lord in your hearts. * And you will always give thanks for everything to God the Father in the name of our Lord Jesus Christ. And further you will submit to one another out of reverence for Christ. * No eye has seen, no ear has heard, and no mind has imagined what God has prepared for those who love him. * Blessed be the LORD forever! Amen and amen!

Psalm 27:4 NLT * Isaiah 38:20 NLT * Psalm 89:1 NLT * Psalm 22:30 NLT * Ephesians 5:18-19 NLT * Ephesians 5:20-21 NLT * 1 Corinthians 2:9b NLT * Psalm 89:52 NLT

FEBRUARY

21 . . . .

Delighting in the LORD's perfections restores a soul.

20 _____ *

_____

_____

_____

_____

_____

_____

_____

20 _____ *

_____

_____

_____

_____

_____

_____

_____

20 _____ *

_____

_____

_____

_____

_____

_____

_____

FEBRUARY 22

I love your sanctuary, LORD, the place where your glory shines. * My heart has heard you say, "Come and talk with me." And my heart responds, "LORD, I am coming." * My life is an example to many, because you have been my strength and protection. That is why I can never stop praising you; I declare your glory all day long. * The LORD is my shepherd; I have everything I need. * Surely your goodness and unfailing love will pursue me all the days of my life, and I will live in the house of the LORD forever. * Bless his glorious name forever! Let the whole earth be filled with his glory. Amen and Amen!

Psalm 26:8 NLT * Psalm 27:8 NLT * Psalm 71:7-8 NLT * Psalm 23:1 NLT * Psalm 23:6 NLT * Psalm 72:19 NLT

FEBRUARY

22 . . . .

Is your life filled with self-efficacy or God dependency?

20 _____ *

_____

_____

_____

_____

_____

_____

_____

20 _____ *

_____

_____

_____

_____

_____

_____

_____

20 _____ *

_____

_____

_____

_____

_____

_____

_____

FEBRUARY 23

Everything that has happened to me here has helped to spread the Good News. * And because of my imprisonment, many of the Christians here have gained confidence and become more bold in telling others about Christ. * For I am not ashamed of this Good News about Christ. It is the power of God at work, saving everyone who believes—Jews first and also Gentiles. * It is not that we think we can do anything of lasting value by ourselves. Our only power and success come from God. * I don't want anyone to think more highly of me than what they can actually see in my life and my message, even though I have received wonderful revelations from God. But to keep me from getting puffed up, I was given a thorn in my flesh, a messenger from Satan to torment me and keep me from getting proud. * Since I know it is all for Christ's good, I am quite content with my weaknesses and with insults, hardships, persecutions, and calamities. For when I am weak, then I am strong. * Pray for me, too. Ask God to give me the right words as I boldly explain God's secret plan that the Good News is for the Gentiles, too. I am in chains now for preaching this message as God's ambassador. But pray that I will keep on speaking boldly for him, as I should. * To Him be glory forever and ever. Amen.

Philippians 1:12b NLT * Philippians 1:14 NLT * Romans 1:16 NLT * 2 Corinthians 3:5 NLT * 2 Corinthians 12:6b-7 NLT * 2 Corinthians 12:10 NLT * Ephesians 6:19-20 NLT * Hebrews 13:22b NLT

FEBRUARY

23 . . . .

Power and success come from God.

20 _____ *

_____

20 _____ *

_____

20 _____ *

_____

FEBRUARY 24

Your unfailing love will last forever. Your faithfulness is as enduring as the heavens. * O LORD God Almighty! Where is there anyone as mighty as you, LORD? Faithfulness is your very character. * If we are unfaithful, he remains faithful, for he cannot deny himself. * Overwhelming victory is ours through Christ, who loved us. * For God has said, "I will never fail you. I will never forsake you." This is why we can say with confidence, "The Lord is my helper, so I will not be afraid. What can mere mortals do to me?" * Blessed be the LORD forever! Amen and amen!

Psalm 89:2 NLT * Psalm 89:8 NLT * 2 Timothy 2:13 NLT * Romans 8:37b NLT * Hebrews 13:5b-6 NLT * Psalm 89:52 NLT

FEBRUARY

24 . . . .

**The Lord is your Helper, and faithfulness
is His very character.**

20 _____ *

_____

_____

_____

_____

_____

_____

20 _____ *

_____

_____

_____

_____

_____

_____

20 _____ *

_____

_____

_____

_____

_____

_____

FEBRUARY 25

Happy are those who hear the joyful call to worship, for they will walk in the light of your presence, LORD. * In Your presence is fullness of joy. * Shout with joy to the LORD, O earth! Worship the LORD with gladness. Come before him, singing with joy. * Happy are people of integrity, who follow the law of the LORD. Happy are those who obey his decrees and search for him with all their hearts. They do not compromise with evil, and they walk only in his paths. * Oh, that my actions would consistently reflect your principles! * Then those who feared the LORD spoke with each other, and the LORD listened to what they said. In his presence, a scroll of remembrance was written to record the names of those who feared him and loved to think about him. "They will be my people," says the LORD Almighty. "On the day when I act, they will be my own special treasure. I will spare them as a father spares an obedient and dutiful child." * To Him be glory forever and ever. Amen.

Psalm 89:15 NLT * Psalm 16:11b NKJV * Psalm 100:1 NLT * Psalm 119:1-3 NLT * Psalm 119:5 NLT * Malachi 3:16-17 NLT * Hebrews 13:22b NLT

FEBRUARY

25 . . . .

Happy are people of integrity.

20 _____ *

_____
_____
_____
_____
_____
_____
_____

20 _____ *

_____
_____
_____
_____
_____
_____
_____

20 _____ *

_____
_____
_____
_____
_____
_____
_____

FEBRUARY 26

Pray for us, for our conscience is clear and we want to live honorably in everything we do. * You yourselves are our witnesses—and so is God—that we were pure and honest and faultless toward all you believers. And you know that we treated each of you as a father treats his own children. We pleaded with you, encouraged you, and urged you to live your lives in a way that God would consider worthy. For he called you into his Kingdom to share his glory. * For I know that as you pray for me and as the Spirit of Jesus Christ helps me, this will all turn out for my deliverance. * For we speak as messengers who have been approved by God to be entrusted with the Good News. Our purpose is to please God, not people. He is the one who examines the motives of our hearts. * Pray at all times and on every occasion in the power of the Holy Spirit. Stay alert and be persistent in your prayers for all Christians everywhere. * Devote yourselves to prayer with an alert mind and a thankful heart. * And pray for me, too. Ask God to give me the right words as I boldly explain God's secret plan that the Good News is for the Gentiles too. * Don't forget to pray for us, too, that God will give us many opportunities to preach about his secret plan—that Christ is also for you Gentiles. That is why I am here in chains. Pray that I will proclaim this message as clearly as I should. * Pray first that the Lord's message will spread rapidly and be honored wherever it goes, just as when it came to you. Pray, too, that we will be saved from wicked and evil people, for not everyone believes in the Lord. But the Lord is faithful. * After all, what gives us hope and joy, and what is our proud reward and crown? It is you! Yes, you will bring us much joy as we stand together before our Lord Jesus when he comes back again. For you are our pride and joy. * To God, who alone is wise, be the glory forever through Jesus Christ. Amen.

Hebrews 13:18 NLT * 1 Thessalonians 2:10-12 NLT * Philippians 1:19 NLT * 1 Thessalonians 2:4 NLT * Ephesians 6:18 NLT * Colossians 4:2 NLT * Ephesians 6:19 NLT * Colossians 4:3-4 NLT * 2 Thessalonians 3:1b-3a NLT *1 Thessalonians 2:19-20 NLT * Romans 16:27 NLT

FEBRUARY

26 . . . .

Our purpose is to please God, not people.

20 _____ *

_____
_____
_____
_____
_____
_____
_____

20 _____ *

_____
_____
_____
_____
_____
_____
_____

20 _____ *

_____
_____
_____
_____
_____
_____
_____

FEBRUARY 27

Your word I have treasured in my heart, that I may not sin against You. * And the devil said to Him, "If You are the Son of God, tell this stone to become bread." And Jesus answered him, "It is written, 'MAN SHALL NOT LIVE ON BREAD ALONE.'" * Therefore, He had to be like His brethren in all things, so that He might become a merciful and faithful high priest in things pertaining to God, to make propitiation for the sins of the people. For since He Himself was tempted in that which He has suffered, He is able to come to the aid of those who are tempted. * For the word of God is living and active and sharper than any two-edged sword, and piercing as far as the division of soul and spirit, of both joints and marrow, and able to judge the thoughts and intentions of the heart. * While it is said, "TODAY IF YOU HEAR HIS VOICE, DO NOT HARDEN YOUR HEARTS, AS WHEN THEY PROVOKED ME." * Arise, go to Nineveh the great city and proclaim to it the proclamation which I am going to tell you. * Grace be with all those who love our Lord Jesus Christ with incorruptible love. * Amen, and Amen.

Psalm 119:11 NASB * Luke 4:3-4 NASB * Hebrews 2:17-18 NASB * Hebrews 4:12 NASB * Hebrews 3:15 NASB * Jonah 3:2 NASB * Ephesians 6:24 NASB * Psalm 72:19 NASB

FEBRUARY

27 . . . .

God's Word is a powerful weapon defeating darkness.

20 ____ *

_____
_____
_____
_____
_____
_____
_____

20 ____ *

_____
_____
_____
_____
_____
_____
_____

20 ____ *

_____
_____
_____
_____
_____
_____
_____

FEBRUARY 28

And you will seek Me and find Me, when you search for Me with all your heart. * Blessed are those who keep His testimonies, who seek Him with the whole heart! * With my whole heart I have sought You; oh, let me not wander from Your commandments! * I delight to do Your will, O my God, and Your law is within my heart. * When You said, "Seek My face," my heart said to You, "Your face, LORD, I will seek." * One thing I have desired of the LORD, that I will seek: that I may dwell in the house of the LORD all the days of my life, to behold the beauty of the LORD, and to inquire in His temple. * But without faith it is impossible to please Him, for he who comes to God must believe that He is, and that He is a rewarder of those who diligently seek Him. * Draw near to God and He will draw near to you. * Brethren, the grace of our Lord Jesus Christ be with your spirit. Amen.

Jeremiah 29:13 NKJV * Psalm 119:2 NKJV * Psalm 119:10 NKJV * Psalm 40:8 NKJV * Psalm 27:8 NKJV * Psalm 27:4 NKJV * Hebrews 11:6 NKJV * James 4:8a NKJV * Galatians 6:18 NKJV

FEBRUARY

28 . . . .

Are you seeking God with your whole heart?

20 _____ *

_____
_____
_____
_____
_____
_____
_____

20 _____ *

_____
_____
_____
_____
_____
_____
_____

20 _____ *

_____
_____
_____
_____
_____
_____
_____

FEBRUARY 29

He who dwells in the secret place of the Most High shall abide under the shadow of the Almighty. I will say of the LORD, "He is my refuge and my fortress; my God, in Him I will trust." * Trust in the LORD forever, for YAH, the LORD, is everlasting strength. For He brings down those who dwell on high, the lofty city; He lays it low, He lays it low to the ground, He brings it down to the dust. The foot shall tread it down—the feet of the poor and the steps of the needy. * Surely He shall deliver you from the snare of the fowler and from the perilous pestilence. He shall cover you with His feathers, and under His wings you shall take refuge; His truth shall be your shield and buckler. You shall not be afraid of the terror by night, nor of the arrow that flies by day. Nor of the pestilence that walks in darkness, nor of the destruction that lays waste at noonday. * Jesus said to him, "I am the way, the truth, and the life. No one comes to the Father except through Me." * Let not your heart be troubled; you believe in God, believe also in Me. * A thousand may fall at your side, and ten thousand at your right hand; but it shall not come near you. Only with your eyes shall you look, and see the reward of the wicked. Because you have made the LORD, who is my refuge, even the Most High, your dwelling place, no evil shall befall you, nor shall any plague come near your dwelling; for He shall give His angels charge over you, to keep you in all your ways. In their hands they shall bear you up, lest you dash your foot against a stone. * Open the gates, that the righteous nation which keeps truth may enter in. You will keep him in perfect peace, whose mind is stayed on You, because he trusts in You. * Because he has set his love upon Me, therefore I will deliver him; I will set him on high, because he has known My name. He shall call upon Me, and I will answer him; I will be with him in trouble; I will deliver him and honor him. With long life I will satisfy him, and show him My salvation. * Now to the King eternal, immortal, invisible, to God who alone is wise, be honor and glory forever and ever. Amen.

Psalm 91:1-2 NKJV * Isaiah 26:3-6 NKJV * Psalm 91:3-6 NKJV * John 14:6 NKJV * John 14:1 NKJV * Psalm 91:7-12 NKJV * Isaiah 26:2-3 NKJV * Psalm 91:14-16 NKJV * 1 Timothy 1:17 NKJV

FEBRUARY

29 . . . .

God's Presence protects.

20 _____ *

_____
_____
_____
_____
_____
_____
_____

20 _____ *

_____
_____
_____
_____
_____
_____
_____
_____

20 _____ *

_____
_____
_____
_____
_____
_____
_____
_____

MARCH

MARCH 1

Here is my final conclusion: Fear God and obey his commands, for this is the duty of every person. God will judge us for everything we do, including every secret thing, whether good or bad. * But even though a person sins a hundred times and still lives a long time, I know that those who fear God will be better off. The wicked will never live long, good lives, for they do not fear God. Their days will never grow long like the evening shadows. * So try to walk a middle course—but those who fear God will succeed either way. * Fear of the LORD is the beginning of wisdom. Knowledge of the Holy One results in understanding. * Fear of the LORD is the beginning of knowledge. Only fools despise wisdom and discipline. * Reverence for the LORD is the foundation of true wisdom. The rewards of wisdom come to all who obey him. Praise his name forever! * Praise the LORD! Happy are those who fear the LORD. Yes, happy are those who delight in doing what he commands. * Bless his glorious name forever! Let the whole earth be filled with his glory. Amen and Amen.

Ecclesiastes 12:13-14 NLT * Ecclesiastes 8:12-13 NLT * Ecclesiastes 7:18 NLT * Proverbs 9:10 NLT * Proverbs 1:7 NLT * Psalm 111:10 NLT * Psalm 112:1 NLT * Psalm 72:19 NLT

MARCH

1 . . . .

Walking in the fear of the Lord is foundational.

20 _____ *

_____
_____
_____
_____
_____
_____

20 _____ *

_____
_____
_____
_____
_____
_____

20 _____ *

_____
_____
_____
_____
_____
_____

MARCH 2

How happy are those who fear the LORD—all who follow his ways! You will enjoy the fruit of your labor. How happy you will be! How rich your life! Your wife will be like a fruitful vine, flourishing within your home. And look at all those children! There they sit around your table as vigorous and healthy as young olive trees. That is the LORD's reward for those who fear him. * Children are a gift from the LORD; they are a reward from him. Children born to a young man are like sharp arrows in a warrior's hands. How happy is the man whose quiver is full of them! * Then the LORD brought Abram outside beneath the night sky and told him, "Look up into the heavens and count the stars if you can. Your descendants will be like that—too many to count!" * For we are God's masterpiece. He has created us anew in Christ Jesus, so that we can do the good things he planned for us long ago. * Bless his glorious name forever! Let the whole earth be filled with his glory. Amen and amen!

Psalm 128:1-4 NLT * Psalm 127:3-5a NLT * Genesis 15:5 NLT * Ephesians 2:10 NLT * Psalm 72:19 NLT

MARCH

2 ·

What is God's promise to your heart?

20 _____ *

_____

_____

_____

_____

_____

_____

_____

20 _____ *

_____

_____

_____

_____

_____

_____

20 _____ *

_____

_____

_____

_____

_____

_____

MARCH 3

But as for me, how good it is to be near God! I have made the Sovereign LORD my shelter, and I will tell everyone about the wonderful things you do. * I can never escape from your spirit! I can never get away from your presence! * O LORD, you have examined my heart and know everything about me. * Though our hearts are filled with sins, you forgive them all. * For he understands how weak we are; he knows we are only dust. * What joy for those you choose to bring near, those who live in your holy courts. What joys await us inside your holy Temple. * I have seen you in your sanctuary and gazed upon your power and glory. Your unfailing love is better to me than life itself; how I praise you! I will honor you as long as I live, lifting up my hands to you in prayer. * You faithfully answer our prayers with awesome deeds, O God our savior. You are the hope of everyone on earth, even those who sail on distant seas. * We thank you, O God! We give thanks because you are near. People everywhere tell of your mighty miracles. * Bless the LORD, the God of Israel, who lives forever from eternal ages past. Amen and amen!

Psalm 73:28 NLT * Psalm 139:7 NLT * Psalm 139:1 NLT * Psalm 65:3 NLT * Psalm 103:14 NLT * Psalm 65:4 NLT * Psalm 63:2-4 NLT * Psalm 65:5 NLT * Psalm 75:1 NLT * Psalm 41:13 NLT

MARCH

3 . . . .

You can never escape God's presence.

20 ____ *

_____
_____
_____
_____
_____
_____

20 ____ *

_____
_____
_____
_____
_____
_____

20 ____ *

_____
_____
_____
_____
_____
_____

MARCH 4

Rejoice in the Lord always. Again I will say, rejoice! * Glory in His holy name; let the hearts of those rejoice who seek the LORD! * Though the fig tree may not blossom, no fruit be on the vines; though the labor of the olive may fail, and the fields yield no food; though the flock may be cut off from the fold, and there be no herd in the stalls—Yet I will rejoice in the LORD, I will joy in the God of my salvation. * The LORD your God in your midst, the Mighty One, will save; He will rejoice over you with gladness, He will quiet you with His love, He will rejoice over you with singing. * Those who are wise shall shine like the brightness of the firmament, and those who turn many to righteousness like the stars forever and ever. * So I will restore to you the years that the swarming locust has eaten. * Amen and amen!

Philippians 4:4 NKJV * Psalm 105:3 NKJV * Habakkuk 3:17-18 NKJV * Zephaniah 3:17 NKJV * Daniel 12:3 NKJV * Joel 2:25a NKJV * Psalm 41:13b NKJV

MARCH

4 . . . .

God rejoices over you with gladness. Rejoice!

20 _____ *

_____
_____
_____
_____
_____
_____
_____
_____

20 _____ *

_____
_____
_____
_____
_____
_____
_____
_____

20 _____ *

_____
_____
_____
_____
_____
_____
_____
_____

MARCH 5

I will sing to the LORD all my life; I will sing praise to my God as long as I live. * Sing to him, sing praise to him; tell of all his wonderful acts. * I will praise you, LORD, among the nations; I will sing of you among the peoples. * Your decrees are the theme of my song wherever I lodge. * He put a new song in my mouth, a hymn of praise to our God. Many will see and fear the LORD and put their trust in him. * Because your love is better than life, my lips will glorify you. I will praise you as long as I live, and in your name I will lift up my hands. * Praise be to his glorious name forever; may the whole earth be filled with his glory. Amen and Amen.

Psalm 104:33 NIV * Psalm 105:2 NIV * Psalm 108:3 NIV * Psalm 119:54 NIV * Psalm 40:3 NIV * Psalm 63:3-4 NIV * Psalm 72:19 NIV

MARCH

5 . . . .

God's love is matchless.

20 _____

_____
_____
_____
_____
_____
_____
_____

20 _____

_____
_____
_____
_____
_____
_____
_____

20 _____

_____
_____
_____
_____
_____
_____
_____

MARCH 6

You are my hiding place and my shield; I hope in Your word. * You are my hiding place; You shall preserve me from trouble; You shall surround me with songs of deliverance. * The angel of the LORD encamps all around those who fear Him, and delivers them. * For the arms of the wicked shall be broken, but the LORD upholds the righteous. * No evil shall befall you, nor shall any plague come near your dwelling; for He shall give His angels charge over you, to keep you in all your ways. In their hands they shall bear you up, lest you dash your foot against a stone. * Truly my soul silently waits for God; from Him comes my salvation. He only is my rock and my salvation; He is my defense; I shall not be greatly moved. * Trust in Him at all times, you people; pour out your heart before Him; God is a refuge for us. * Amen and Amen.

Psalm 119:114 NKJV * Psalm 32:7 NKJV * Psalm 34:7 NKJV * Psalm 37:17 NKJV * Psalm 62:1-2 NKJV * Psalm 91:10-12 NKJV * Psalm 72:19b NKJV

MARCH

6 ·

The Perfect Hiding Place shields His own.

20 _____ *

_____
_____
_____
_____
_____
_____
_____
_____

20 _____ *

_____
_____
_____
_____
_____
_____
_____
_____

20 _____ *

_____
_____
_____
_____
_____
_____
_____
_____

MARCH 7

You have given him his heart's desire, and You have not withheld the request of his lips. * May my meditation be sweet to Him; I will be glad in the LORD. * Delight yourself in the LORD; and He will give you the desires of your heart. * Blessed be God, who has not turned away my prayer nor His lovingkindness from me. * By awesome deeds You answer us in righteousness, O God of our salvation, You who are the trust of all the ends of the earth and of the farthest sea. * The LORD is my shepherd, I shall not want. * And blessed be His glorious name forever; and may the whole earth be filled with His glory. Amen, and Amen.

Psalm 21:2 NASB * Psalm 104:34 NKJV * Psalm 37:4 NASB * Psalm 66:20 NASB * Psalm 65:5 NASB * Psalm 23:1 NASB * Psalm 72:19b NASB

MARCH

7 ·

May my meditation be sweet to Him.

20 _____ *

---

20 _____ *

---

20 _____ *

MARCH 8

Come, bless the LORD, all you servants of the LORD, who stand by night in the house of the LORD! Lift up your hands to the holy place and bless the LORD! * Bless the LORD, O my soul, and all that is within me, bless his holy name! Bless the LORD, O my soul, and forget not all his benefits, who forgives all your iniquity, who heals all your diseases, who redeems your life from the pit, who crowns you with steadfast love and mercy, who satisfies you with good so that your youth is renewed like the eagle's. * I will extol you, my God and King, and bless your name forever and ever. Every day I will bless you and praise your name forever and ever. * All your works shall give thanks to you, O LORD, and all your saints shall bless you! They shall speak of the glory of your kingdom and tell of your power, to make known to the children of man your mighty deeds, and the glorious splendor of your kingdom. * Amen and Amen!

Psalm 134:1-2 ESV * Psalm 103:1-5 ESV * Psalm 145:1-2 ESV * Psalm 145:10-12 ESV * Psalm 72:19b ESV

MARCH

8 . . . .

Bless the LORD, O my soul!

20 _____ *

_____
_____
_____
_____
_____
_____
_____

20 _____ *

_____
_____
_____
_____
_____
_____
_____

20 _____ *

_____
_____
_____
_____
_____
_____
_____

MARCH 9

But as it is written: "Eye has not seen, nor ear heard, nor have entered into the heart of man the things which God has prepared for those who love Him." * I have been crucified with Christ; it is no longer I who live, but Christ lives in me; and the life which I now live in the flesh, I live by faith in the Son of God, who loved me and gave Himself for me. * Be filled with the Spirit, speaking to one another in psalms and hymns and spiritual songs, singing and making melody in your heart to the Lord, giving thanks always for all things to God the Father in the name of our Lord Jesus Christ, submitting to one another in the fear of God. * And let us not grow weary while doing good, for in due season we shall reap if we do not lose heart. Therefore, as we have opportunity, let us do good to all, especially to those who are of the household of faith. * Brethren, the grace of our Lord Jesus Christ be with your spirit. Amen.

1 Corinthians 2:9 NKJV * Galatians 2:20 NKJV * Ephesians 5:18b-21 NKJV * Galatians 6:9-10 NKJV * Galatians 6:18 NKJV

MARCH

9 ·

God's prepared path may differ from your original intent.

20 _____ *

---

20 _____ *

---

20 _____ *

MARCH 10

At midnight I will rise to give thanks to You, because of Your righteous judgments. * Your commands make me wiser than my enemies, for your commands are my constant guide. * Your word is a lamp to my feet and a light to my path. * I am afflicted very much; revive me according to Your word. * I have inclined my heart to perform Your statutes forever, to the very end. * The entrance of Your word gives light; it gives understanding to the simple. * Make Your face shine upon Your servant, and teach me Your statutes. * Your word is very pure; therefore Your servant loves it. * I rejoice at Your word as one who finds great treasure. * My lips shall utter praise, for You teach me Your statutes. * My tongue shall speak of Your word, for all Your commandments are righteousness. * I long for Your salvation, O Lord, and Your law is my delight. * Amen, and Amen.

Psalm 119:62 NKJV * Psalm 119:98 NLT * Psalm 119:105 NKJV * Psalm 119:107 NKJV * Psalm 119:112 NKJV * Psalm 119:130 NKJV * Psalm 119:135 NKJV * Psalm 119:140 NKJV * Psalm 119:162 NKJV * Psalm 119:171 NKJV * Psalm 119:172 NKJV * Psalm 119:174 NKJV * Psalm 72:19b KJV

MARCH

10 . . . .

God teaches His words of truth.

20 _____ *

_____
_____
_____
_____
_____
_____
_____

20 _____ *

_____
_____
_____
_____
_____
_____
_____

20 _____ *

_____
_____
_____
_____
_____
_____
_____

MARCH 11

Serve the LORD with gladness! Come into his presence with singing! * Praise the LORD! For it is good to sing praises to our God; for it is pleasant, and a song of praise is fitting. * Seek the LORD and his strength; seek his presence continually! * Enter his gates with thanksgiving, and his courts with praise! Give thanks to him; bless his name! * The eyes of the LORD are toward the righteous and his ears toward their cry. * I cry aloud to God, aloud to God, and he will hear me. * He heals the brokenhearted and binds up their wounds. * The LORD redeems the life of his servants; none of those who take refuge in him will be condemned. * You open your hand; you satisfy the desire of every living thing. * You make known to me the path of life; in your presence there is fullness of joy; at your right hand are pleasures forevermore. * I said, "Let me remember my song in the night; let me meditate in my heart." Then my spirit made a diligent search. * By day the LORD commands his steadfast love, and at night his song is with me, a prayer to the God of my life. * Blessed be his glorious name forever; may the whole earth be filled with his glory! Amen and Amen!

Psalm 100:2 ESV * Psalm 147:1 ESV * Psalm 105:4 ESV * Psalm 100:4 ESV * Psalm 34:15 ESV * Psalm 77:1 ESV * Psalm 147:3 ESV * Psalm 34:22 ESV * Psalm 145:16 ESV * Psalm 16:11 ESV * Psalm 77:6 ESV * Psalm 42:8 ESV * Psalm 72:19 ESV

MARCH

11 . . . .

God hears your voice.

20 _____ *

_____
_____
_____
_____
_____
_____
_____

20 _____ *

_____
_____
_____
_____
_____
_____
_____

20 _____ *

_____
_____
_____
_____
_____
_____
_____

MARCH 12

Then this Daniel began distinguishing himself among the commissioners and satraps because he possessed an extraordinary spirit, and the king planned to appoint him over the entire kingdom. Then the commissioners and satraps began trying to find a ground of accusation against Daniel in regard to government affairs; but they could find no ground of accusation or evidence of corruption, inasmuch as he was faithful, and no negligence or corruption was to be found in him. Then these men said, "We will not find any ground of accusation against this Daniel unless we find it against him with regard to the law of his God." * Now when Daniel knew that the document was signed, he entered his house (now in his roof chamber he had windows open toward Jerusalem); and he continued kneeling on his knees three times a day, praying and giving thanks before his God, as he had been doing previously. * Then the king gave orders, and Daniel was brought in and cast into the lions' den. The king spoke and said to Daniel, "Your God whom you constantly serve will Himself deliver you." * Then the king went off to his palace and spent the night fasting, and no entertainment was brought before him; and his sleep fled from him. Then the king arose at dawn, at the break of day, and went in haste to the lions' den. * Then Daniel spoke to the king, "O king, live forever! My God has sent His angel and shut the lions' mouths and they have not harmed me, inasmuch as I was found innocent before Him; and also toward you, O king, I have committed no crime." * The king then gave orders, and they brought those men who had maliciously accused Daniel, and they cast them, their children and their wives into the lions' den; and they had not reached the bottom of the den before the lions overpowered them and crushed all their bones. Then Darius the king wrote to all the peoples, nations and men of every language who were living in all the land: "May your peace abound! I make a decree that in all the dominion of my kingdom men are to fear and tremble before the God of Daniel; for He is the living God and enduring forever, and His kingdom is one which will not be destroyed, and His dominion will be forever. * He grants a treasure of good sense to the godly. He is their shield, protecting those who walk with integrity. * Amen, and Amen.

Daniel 6:3-5 NASB * Daniel 6:10 NASB * Daniel 6:16 NASB * Daniel 6:18-19 NASB * Daniel 6:21-22 NASB * Daniel 6:24-26 NASB * Proverbs 2:7 NLT * Psalm 72:19b NASB

MARCH

12 . . . .

If God is for you, who can be against you?

20 _____ *

_____

_____
_____
_____
_____
_____
_____

20 _____ *

_____

_____
_____
_____
_____
_____
_____

20 _____ *

_____

_____
_____
_____
_____
_____
_____

MARCH 13

Now when Sanballat, Tobiah, the Arabs, the Ammonites and the Ashdodites heard that the repair of the walls of Jerusalem went on, and that the breaches began to be closed, they were very angry. All of them conspired together to come and fight against Jerusalem and to cause a disturbance in it. But we prayed to our God, and because of them we set up a guard against them day and night. * Our enemies said, "They will not know or see until we come among them, kill them and put a stop to the work." * When I saw their fear, I rose and spoke to the nobles, the officials and the rest of the people: "Do not be afraid of them; remember the Lord who is great and awesome, and fight for your brothers, your sons, your daughters, your wives and your houses." When our enemies heard that it was known to us, and that God had frustrated their plan, then all of us returned to the wall, each one to his work. * So we carried on the work with half of them holding spears from dawn until the stars appeared. At that time I also said to the people, "Let each man with his servant spend the night within Jerusalem so that they may be a guard for us by night and a laborer by day." So neither I, my brothers, my servants, nor the men of the guard who followed me, none of us removed our clothes, each took his weapon even to the water. * Without wise leadership, a nation falls. * Amen, and Amen.

Nehemiah 4:7-9 NASB * Nehemiah 4:11 NASB * Nehemiah 4:14-15 NASB * Nehemiah 4:21-23 NASB * Proverbs 11:14a NLT * Psalm 72:19b NASB

MARCH

13 . . . .

A nation rests under wise leadership.

20 _____ *

_____
_____
_____
_____
_____
_____
_____

20 _____ *

_____
_____
_____
_____
_____
_____
_____

20 _____ *

_____
_____
_____
_____
_____
_____
_____

MARCH 14

Then I said, "I will not make mention of Him, nor speak anymore in His name." But His word was in my heart like a burning fire shut up in my bones; I was weary of holding it back, and I could not. * Shadrach, Meshach, and Abed-Nego answered and said to the king, "O Nebuchadnezzar, we have no need to answer you in this matter. If that is the case, our God whom we serve is able to deliver us from the burning fiery furnace, and He will deliver us from your hand, O king. But if not, let it be known to you, O king, that we do not serve your gods, nor will we worship the gold image which you have set up." * "You stiff-necked and uncircumcised in heart and ears! You always resist the Holy Spirit; as your fathers did, so do you. Which of the prophets did your fathers not persecute? And they killed those who foretold the coming of the Just One, of whom you now have become the betrayers and murderers, who have received the law by the direct of angels and have not kept it." When they heard these things they were cut to the heart, and they gnashed at him with their teeth. But he, being full of the Holy Spirit, gazed into heaven and saw the glory of God, and Jesus standing at the right hand of God, and said, "Look! I see the heavens opened and the Son of Man standing at the right hand of God!" Then they cried out with a loud voice, stopped their ears, and ran at him with one accord. * And they stoned Stephen as he was calling on God and saying, "Lord Jesus, receive my spirit." Then he knelt down and cried out with a loud voice, "Lord, do not charge them with this sin." And when he had said this, he fell asleep. * Fire tests the purity of silver and gold, but the Lord tests the heart. * Amen, and Amen

Jeremiah 20:9 NKJV * Daniel 3:16-17 NKJV * Acts 7:51-57 NKJV * Acts 7:59-60 NKJV * Proverbs 17:4 NLT * Psalm 72:19b NASB

MARCH

14 . . . .

Where was your heart while you were in the fire of adversity?

20_____ *

_____
_____
_____
_____
_____
_____
_____

20_____ *

_____
_____
_____
_____
_____
_____
_____

20_____ *

_____
_____
_____
_____
_____
_____
_____

MARCH 15

I will give thanks to You, for I am fearfully and wonderfully made; wonderful are Your works, and my soul knows it very well. * Your eyes have seen my unformed substance; and in Your book were all written the days that were ordained for me, when as yet there was not one of them. * For we are His workmanship, created in Christ Jesus for good works, which God prepared beforehand so that we would walk in them. * That is what the Scriptures mean when they say, "No eye has seen, no ear has heard, and no mind has imagined what God has prepared for those who love him." * For I know the thoughts that I think toward you, says the Lord, thoughts of peace and not of evil, to give you a future and a hope. * Now the God of peace, who brought up from the dead the great Shepherd of the sheep through the blood of the eternal covenant, even Jesus our Lord, equip you in every good thing to do His will, working in us that which is pleasing in His sight, through Jesus Christ, to whom be the glory forever and ever. Amen.

Psalm 139:14 NASB * Psalm 139:16 NASB * Ephesians 2:10 NASB * 1 Corinthians 2:9 NLT * Jeremiah 29:11 NKJV * Hebrews 13:20-21 NASB

MARCH

15 . . . .

God's thoughts about you are full of peace.

20 _____ *

_____

_____

_____

_____

_____

_____

_____

20 _____ *

_____

_____

_____

_____

_____

_____

_____

20 _____ *

_____

_____

_____

_____

_____

_____

_____

MARCH 16

So also you, since you are zealous of spiritual gifts, seek to abound for the edification of the church. * But earnestly desire the greater gifts. And I show you a still more excellent way. * Love is patient, love is kind and is not jealous; love does not brag and is not arrogant, does not act unbecomingly; it does not seek its own, is not provoked, does not take into account a wrong suffered, does not rejoice in unrighteousness, but rejoices with the truth; bears all things, believes all things, hopes all things, endures all things. Love never fails; but if there are gifts of prophecy, they will be done away; if there are tongues they will cease; if there is knowledge, it will be done away. For we know in part and we prophesy in part; but when the perfect comes, the partial will be done away. * For now we see in a mirror dimly, but then face to face; now I know in part, but then I will know fully just as I also have been fully known. * Therefore be careful how you walk, not as unwise men but as wise, making the most of your time, because the days are evil. * To Him be the glory in the church and in Christ Jesus to all generations forever and ever. Amen.

1 Corinthians 14:12 NASB * 1 Corinthians 12:31 NASB * 1 Corinthians 13:4-10 NASB * 1 Corinthians 13:12 NASB * Ephesians 5:15-16 NASB * Ephesians 3:21 NASB

MARCH

16 ....

How are you edifying one another?

20 _____ *

---

20 _____ *

---

20 _____ *

MARCH 17

And whoever does not bear his cross and come after Me cannot be My disciple. * If I then, your Lord and Teacher, have washed your feet, you also ought to wash one another's feet. * Peter, seeing him, said to Jesus, "But Lord, what about this man?" Jesus said to him, "If I will that he remain till I come, what is that to you? You follow Me." * My life is worth nothing unless I use it for doing the work assigned to me by the Lord Jesus—the work of telling others the Good News about God's wonderful kindness and love. * Being confident of this very thing, that He who has begun a good work in you will complete it until the day of Jesus Christ. * For I am not ashamed of the gospel of Christ, for it is the power of God to salvation for everyone who believes, for the Jew first and also for the Greek. For in it the righteousness of God is revealed from faith to faith: as it is written, "The just shall live by faith." * To God, alone wise, be glory through Jesus Christ forever. Amen.

Luke 14:27 NKJV * John 13:14 NKJV * John 21:21-22 NKJV * Acts 20:24 NLT * Philippians 1:6 NKJV * Romans 1:16-17 NKJV * Romans 16:27 NKJV

MARCH

17 . . . .

Focus on what God has called you to do.

20____ *

_____
_____
_____
_____
_____
_____
_____

20____ *

_____
_____
_____
_____
_____
_____
_____

20____ *

_____
_____
_____
_____
_____
_____
_____

MARCH 18

"Thus has the LORD of hosts said, 'Dispense true justice and practice kindness and compassion each to his brother.'" * He has told you, O man, what is good; and what does the LORD require of you but to do justice, to love kindness, and to walk humbly with your God? * Righteousness and justice are the foundation of Your throne; lovingkindness and truth go before You. * Prepare to meet your God, O Israel. * And He said, "Truly I say to you, this poor widow put in more than all of them; for they all out of their surplus put into the offering; but she out of her poverty put in all that she had to live on." * While He was in Bethany at the home of Simon the leper, and reclining at the table, there came a woman with an alabaster vial of very costly perfume of pure nard; and she broke the vial and poured it over His head. But some were indignantly remarking to one another, "Why has this perfume been wasted? For this perfume might have been sold for over three hundred denarii, and the money given to the poor." And they were scolding her. But Jesus said, "Let her alone; why do you bother her? She has done a good deed to Me. For you will always have the poor with you, and whenever you wish you can do good to them; but you do not always have Me. She has done what she could; she has anointed My body beforehand for the burial. Truly I say to you, wherever the gospel is preached in the whole world, what this woman has done will also be spoken of in memory of her." * Then I will make up to you for the years that the swarming locust has eaten. * And it will come about that whoever calls on the name of the LORD will be delivered. * Now to our God and Father be the glory forever and ever. Amen.

Zechariah 7:9 NASB * Micah 6:8 NASB * Psalm 89:14 NASB * Amos 4:12b NASB * Luke 21:3-4 NASB * Mark 14:3-9 NASB * Joel 2:25a NASB * Joel 2:32a NASB * Philippians 4:20 NASB

MARCH

18 . . . .

What happens when you walk humbly before God?

20 _____ *

_____

_____

_____

_____

_____

_____

20 _____ *

_____

_____

_____

_____

_____

_____

20 _____ *

_____

_____

_____

_____

_____

_____

MARCH 19

Every word of God is pure; He is a shield to those who put their trust in Him. * Your word is very pure; therefore Your servant loves it. * For You, O LORD, will bless the righteous; with favor You will surround him as with a shield. * As for God, His way is perfect; the word of the LORD is proven; He is a shield to all who trust in Him. * You also have given me the shield of your salvation; Your right hand has held me up, Your gentleness has made me great. * You, O LORD, are a shield for me, my glory and the One who lifts up my head. * Truly my soul silently waits for God; from Him comes my salvation. He only is my rock and my salvation; He is my defense; I shall not be greatly moved. * As for me, You uphold me in my integrity, and set me before Your face forever. Blessed be the LORD God of Israel from everlasting to everlasting! Amen and Amen.

Proverbs 30:5 NKJV * Psalm 119:140 NKJV * Psalm 5:12 NKJV * Psalm 18:30 NKJV * Psalm 18:35 NKJV * Psalm 3:3 NKJV * Psalm 62:1-2 NKJV * Psalm 41:12-13 NKJV

MARCH

19 . . . .

The Word of God is your purest defense.

20 _____ *

_____
_____
_____
_____
_____
_____
_____

20 _____ *

_____
_____
_____
_____
_____
_____
_____

20 _____ *

_____
_____
_____
_____
_____
_____
_____

MARCH 20

Therefore be patient, brethren, until the coming of the Lord. See how the farmer waits for the precious fruit of the earth, wait patiently for it until it receives the early or latter rain. You also be patient. Establish your hearts, for the coming of the Lord is at hand. * The Lord isn't really being slow about his promise to return, as some people think. No, he is being patient for your sake. He does not want anyone to perish, so he is giving more time for everyone to repent. * And so, dear friends, while you are waiting for these things to happen, make every effort to live a pure and blameless life. And be at peace with God. * In this you greatly rejoice, though now for a little while, if need be, you have been grieved by various trials, that the genuineness of your faith, being more precious than gold that perishes, though it is tested by fire, may be found to praise, honor, and glory at the revelation of Jesus Christ, whom having not seen you love. Though now you do not see Him, yet believing, you rejoice with joy inexpressible and full of glory, receiving the end of your faith—the salvation of your souls. * So think clearly and exercise self-control. Look forward to the special blessings that will come to you at the return of Jesus Christ. * We are bound to give thanks to God always for you, brethren beloved by the Lord, because God from the beginning chose you for salvation through sanctification by the Spirit and belief in the truth, to which He called you by our gospel, for the obtaining of the glory of our Lord Jesus Christ. * He who is the faithful witness to all these things says, "Yes, I am coming soon!" Amen! Come, Lord Jesus!

James 5:7-8 NKJV * 2 Peter 3:9 NLT * 2 Peter 3:14 NLT * 1 Peter 1:6-9 NKJV * 1 Peter 1:13 NLT * 2 Thessalonians 2:13-14 NKJV * Revelation 22:20 NLT

MARCH

20 ....

Fruit is born as you patiently wait.

*20*_____ *

_____
_____
_____
_____
_____
_____
_____

*20*_____ *

_____
_____
_____
_____
_____
_____
_____

*20*_____ *

_____
_____
_____
_____
_____
_____
_____

MARCH 21

Fear not, for I have redeemed you; I have called you by your name; you are Mine. * Do not remember the former things, nor consider the things of old. Behold, I will do a new thing, now it shall spring forth; shall you not know it? I will even make a road in the wilderness and rivers in the desert. * He has made everything beautiful in its time. * A time to laugh * A time to dance. * A time to be born. * And a time to heal. * A time to weep. * And a time to mourn. * A time to embrace, and a time to refrain from embracing. * A time to keep silence, and a time to speak. * And a time to hate; a time of war. * A time to love. * And a time of peace. * Also He has put eternity in their hearts, except that no one can find out the work that God does from beginning to end. * For I know the thoughts that I think toward you, says the LORD, thoughts of peace and not of evil, to give you a future and a hope. * Grace be with you all. Amen.

Isaiah 43:1b NKJV * Isaiah 43:18-19 NKJV * Ecclesiastes 3:11a NKJV * Ecclesiastes 3:4b NKJV * Ecclesiastes 3:4d NKJV * Ecclesiastes 3:2a NKJV * Ecclesiastes 3:3a NKJV * Ecclesiastes 3:4a NKJV * Ecclesiastes 4c NKJV * Ecclesiastes 5b NKJV * Ecclesiastes 3:7b NKJV * Ecclesiastes 3:8b NKJV * Ecclesiastes 3:8a NKJV * Ecclesiastes 3:8d NKJV * Ecclesiastes 3:11b NKJV * Jeremiah 29:11 NKJV * Hebrews 13:25 NKJV

MARCH

21 . . . .

God loves you in every season of life.

20 _____ *

_____
_____
_____
_____
_____
_____
_____

20 _____ *

_____
_____
_____
_____
_____
_____
_____

20 _____ *

_____
_____
_____
_____
_____
_____
_____

MARCH 22

Give unto the LORD the glory due to His name; worship the LORD in the beauty of holiness. * And when he had consulted with the people, he appointed those who should sing to the LORD, and who should praise the beauty of holiness, as they went out before the army and were saying: "Praise the LORD, for His mercy endures forever." Now when they began to sing and to praise, the LORD set ambushes against the people of Ammon, Moab, and Mount Seir, who had come against Judah; and they were defeated. * Give to the LORD the glory due His name; bring an offering, and come before Him. Oh, worship the LORD in the beauty of holiness! * Therefore by Him let us continually offer the sacrifice of praise to God, that is, the fruit of our lips, giving thanks to His name. * You are worthy, O Lord, to receive glory and honor and power; for You created all things, and by Your will they exist and were created. * The grace of our Lord Jesus Christ be with you all. Amen

Psalm 29:2 NKJV * 2 Chronicles 20:21 NKJV * 1 Chronicles 16:29 NKJV * Hebrews 13:15 NKJV * Revelation 4:11 NKJV * Revelation 22:21 NKJV

MARCH

22 . . . .

Will you worship the Lord in the beauty of holiness?

20 _____ *

_____

_____
_____
_____
_____
_____
_____

20 _____ *

_____

_____
_____
_____
_____
_____
_____

20 _____ *

_____

_____
_____
_____
_____
_____
_____

MARCH 23

Thus says the LORD, the King of Israel, and his Redeemer, the LORD of hosts: I am the First and I am the Last; besides Me there is no God. * Most assuredly, I say to you, before Abraham was, I AM. * Fear not, for I am with you; be not dismayed, for I am your God; I will strengthen you, I will help you, I will uphold you with my righteous right hand. * For I am the LORD, I do not change. * I am the light of the world. He who follows Me shall not walk in darkness, but have the light of life. * In Him was life, and the life was the light of men. * I am the bread of life. He who comes to Me shall never hunger, and he who believes in Me shall never thirst. * I am from above. * I am not of this world. * I am the door. If anyone enters by Me, he will be saved, and will go in and out and find pasture. * I am the good shepherd. The good shepherd gives His life for the sheep. * I am the resurrection and the life. He who believes in Me, though he may die, he shall live. * I am the way, the truth and the life. No one comes to the Father except through Me. * "I am the Alpha and the Omega, the Beginning and the End," says the Lord, "who is and who was and who is to come, the Almighty." * Do not be afraid; I am the First and the Last. I am He who lives, and was dead, and behold, I am alive forevermore. Amen.

Isaiah 44:6 NKJV * John 8:58 NKJV * Isaiah 41:10 NKJV * Malachi 3:6 NKJV * John 8:12b NKJV * John 1:4 NKJV * John 6:35 NKJV * John 8:23a NKJV * John 8:23b NKJV * John 10:9 NKJV * John 10:11 NKJV * John 11:25 NKJV * John 14:6 NKJV * Revelation 1:8 NKJV * Revelation 1:17b NKJV

MARCH

23 . . . .

The Great I AM provides for you in every way.

20 _____ *

_____
_____
_____
_____
_____
_____
_____

20 _____ *

_____
_____
_____
_____
_____
_____
_____

20 _____ *

_____
_____
_____
_____
_____
_____
_____

MARCH 24

But earnestly desire the best gifts. And yet I show you a more excellent way. * The greatest of these is love. * Greater love has no one than this, than to lay down one's life for his friends. * Beloved, let us love one another, for love is of God; and everyone who loves is born of God and knows God. He who does not love does not know God, for God is love. In this the love of God was manifested toward us, that God has sent His only begotten Son into the world, that we might live through Him. * We love Him because He first loved us. * Therefore, be imitators of God as dear children. And walk in love, as Christ also has loved us and given Himself for us, an offering and a sacrifice to God for a sweet-smelling aroma. * We know how much God loves us, and we have put our trust in Him. God is love, and all who live in love live in God, and God lives in them. And as we live in God, our love grows more perfect. So we will not be afraid on the day of judgment, but can face him with confidence because we are like Christ here in this world. * Love is patient and kind. Love is not jealous or boastful or proud or rude. Love does not demand its own way. Love is not irritable, and it keeps no record of when it has been wronged. It is never glad about injustice but rejoices whenever the truth wins out. Love never gives up, never loses faith, is always hopeful, and endures through every circumstance. Love will last forever. * My little children, let us not love in word or in tongue, but in deed and truth. * There is no fear in love; but perfect love casts out fear, because fear involves torment. But he who fears has not been made perfect in love. * Little children, keep yourselves from idols. Amen.

1 Corinthians 12:31 NKJV * 1 Corinthians 13:13 NKJV * John 15:13 NKJV * 1 John 4:7-9 NKJV * 1 John 4:19 NKJV * Ephesians 5:1-2 NKJV * 1 John 4:16-17 NLT * 1 Corinthians 13:4-8a NLT * 1 John 3:18 NKJV * 1 John 4:18 NKJV * 1 John 4:21 NKJV

MARCH

24 . . . .

You are made perfect in love.

20 _____ *

---

20 _____ *

---

20 _____ *

MARCH 25

For whatever is born of God overcomes the world. And this is the victory that has overcome the world—our faith. * Now faith is the substance of things hoped for, the evidence of things not seen. * But without faith it is impossible to please Him, for he who comes to God must believe that He is, and that He is a rewarder of those who diligently seek Him. By faith Noah, being divinely warned of things not yet seen, moved with godly fear, prepared an ark for the saving of his household, by which he condemned the world and became heir of the righteousness which is according to faith. By faith Abraham obeyed when he was called to go out to the place which he would receive as an inheritance. And he went out, not knowing where he was going. * By faith Abraham, when he was tested, offered up Isaac, and he who had received the promises offered up his only begotten son. * By faith they passed through the Red Sea as by dry land, whereas the Egyptians, attempting to do so, were drowned. By faith the walls of Jericho fell down after they were encircled for seven days. * Women received their dead back to life again. Others were tortured, not accepting deliverance, that they might obtain a better resurrection. Still others had trial of mockings and scourgings, yes, and of chains and imprisonment. * For we walk by faith and not by sight. * My love be with you all in Christ Jesus. Amen.

1 John 5:4 NKJV * Hebrews 11:1 NKJV * Hebrews 11:6-8 NKJV * Hebrews 11:17 NKJV * Hebrews 11:29-30 NKJV * Hebrews 11:35-36 NKJV * 2 Corinthians 5:7 NKJV * 1 Corinthians 16:24 NKJV

MARCH

25 . . . .

Every obedient step strengthens your faith.

20 _____ *

_____

_____

_____

_____

_____

_____

_____

20 _____ *

_____

_____

_____

_____

_____

_____

_____

20 _____ *

_____

_____

_____

_____

_____

_____

_____

MARCH 26

And I will give you shepherds according to My heart, who will feed you with knowledge and understanding. * A hireling, he who is not the shepherd, one who does not own the sheep, sees the wolf coming and leaves the sheep and flees; and the wolf catches the sheep and scatters them. The hireling flees because he is a hireling and does not care about the sheep. * But we were gentle among you, just as a nursing mother cherishes her own children. So affectionately longing for you, we were well pleased to impart to you not only the gospel of God, but also our own lives, because you had become dear to us. * You are witnesses, and God also, how devoutly and justly and blamelessly we behaved ourselves among you who believe; as you know how we exhorted, and comforted and charged every one of you, as a father does his own children, that you would walk worthy of God who calls you into His own kingdom and glory. * Therefore we also pray always for you that our God would count you worthy of this calling, and fulfill all the good pleasure of His goodness and the work of faith with power, that the name of our Lord Jesus Christ may be glorified in you, and you in Him, according to the grace of our God and the Lord Jesus Christ. * Grace be with you all. Amen.

Jeremiah 3:15 NKJV * John 10:12-13 NKJV * 1 Thessalonians 2:7-8 NKJV * 1 Thessalonians 2:10-12 NKJV * 2 Thessalonians 1:11-12 NKJV * Hebrews 13:25 NKJV

MARCH

26 . . . .

Who has God called you to disciple? Who is discipling you?

20 _____ *

_____

_____

_____

_____

_____

_____

20 _____ *

_____

_____

_____

_____

_____

_____

20 _____ *

_____

_____

_____

_____

_____

_____

_____

MARCH 27

Let nothing be done through selfish ambition or conceit, but in lowliness of mind let each esteem others better than himself. Let each of you look out not only for his own interests, but also for the interests of others. * Do all things without complaining and disputing, that you may become blameless and harmless, children of God without fault in the midst of a crooked and perverse generation, among whom you shine as lights in the world, holding fast the word of life, so that I may rejoice in the day of Christ that I have not run in vain or labored in vain. * You are the light of the world. A city that is set on a hill that cannot be hidden. Nor do they light a lamp and put it under a basket, but on a lampstand, and it gives light to all who are in the house. Let your light so shine before men, that they may see your good works and glorify your Father in heaven. * To God, alone wise, be glory through Jesus Christ forever. Amen.

Philippians 2:3-4 NKJV * Philippians 2:14-16 NKJV * Matthew 5:13-16 NKJV * Romans 16:27 NKJV

MARCH

27 . . . .

You shine as lights in a dark world.

20 _____ *

_____
_____
_____
_____
_____
_____
_____

20 _____ *

_____
_____
_____
_____
_____
_____
_____

20 _____ *

_____
_____
_____
_____
_____
_____
_____

MARCH 28

Anyone who loves a pure heart and gracious speech is the king's friend. * Never let loyalty and kindness get away from you! Wear them like a necklace, write them deep within your heart. Then you will find favor with both God and people, and you will gain a good reputation. * Above all else guard your heart for it effects everything you do. * People with integrity have firm footing. * The godliness of good people rescues them. * The whole city celebrates when the godly succeed. * Your own soul is nourished when you are kind. * The name of the Lord is a strong fortress; the godly run to him and are safe. * A friend is always loyal, and a brother is born to help in time of need. * A person's words can be life-giving water; words of true wisdom are as refreshing as a bubbling brook. * The heartfelt counsel of a friend is as sweet as perfume and incense. * We can make our plans, but the Lord determines our steps. * As a face is reflected in water, so the heart reflects a person. * You have preserved my life because I am innocent; you have brought me into your presence forever. * Amen and Amen.

Proverbs 22:11 NLT * Proverbs 3:3-4 NLT * Proverbs 4:23 NLT * Proverbs 10:9a NLT * Proverbs 11:6a NLT * Proverbs 11:6a NLT * Proverbs 11:17a NLT * Proverbs 18:10 NLT * Proverbs 17:17 NLT * Proverbs 18:4 NLT * Proverbs 27:9 NLT * Proverbs 16:9 NLT * Proverbs 27:19 NLT * Psalm 41:12 NLT * Psalm 41:13b NLT

MARCH

28 . . . .

Cherished wisdom.

20 _____ *

_____

_____

_____

_____

_____

_____

20 _____ *

_____

_____

_____

_____

_____

_____

20 _____ *

_____

_____

_____

_____

_____

_____

MARCH 29

"Before I formed you in the womb I knew you; before you were born I sanctified you; I ordained you a prophet to the nations." Then said I: "Ah, Lord God! Behold I cannot speak, for I am a youth." But the LORD said to me: "Do not say, 'I am a youth,' For you shall go to all to whom I send you, and whatever I command you, you shall speak. Do not be afraid of their faces, for I am with you to deliver you," says the LORD. * Let no one despise your youth, but be an example to the believers in word, in conduct, in love, in spirit, in faith, in purity. * Do not neglect the gift that is in you, which was given to you by prophecy with the laying on of hands of the eldership. * Therefore I remind you to stir up the gift of God which is in you through the laying on of my hands. For God has not given us a spirit of fear, but of power and of love and of sound mind. * "Go therefore and make disciples of all nations, baptizing them in the name of the Father and of the Son and of the Holy Spirit, teaching them to observe all things that I have commanded you; and lo, I am with you always, even to the end of the age." Amen.

Jeremiah 1:5-8 NKJV * 1 Timothy 4:12 NKJV * 1 Timothy 4:14 NKJV * 2 Timothy 1:6-7 NKJV * Matthew 28:19-20 NKJV

MARCH

29 . . . .

Stir up the gift of God which is in you!

20 _____ *

_____
_____
_____
_____
_____
_____
_____

20 _____ *

_____
_____
_____
_____
_____
_____
_____

20 _____ *

_____
_____
_____
_____
_____
_____
_____

MARCH 30

So we fasted and entreated our God for this, and He answered our prayer. * Sing to Him, sing praises to Him; speak of all His wonders. Glory in His holy name; let the heart of those who seek the LORD be glad. Seek the LORD and His strength; seek His face continually. * Give to the LORD the glory due His name; bring an offering, and come before Him. Oh, worship the LORD in the beauty of holiness. * May my prayer be counted as incense before You; the lifting up of my hands as the evening offering. * I will praise You, for I am fearfully and wonderfully made; marvelous are Your works, and that my soul knows very well. * I will extol You, my God, O King, and I will bless Your name forever and ever. Every day I will bless You, and I will praise Your name forever and ever. Great is the LORD, and highly to be praised, and His greatness is unsearchable. * The eyes of all look to You, and You give them their food in due time. You open Your hand and satisfy the desire of every living thing. The LORD is righteous in all His ways and kind in all His deeds. The LORD is near to all who call upon Him, to all who call upon Him in truth. * And blessed be His glorious name forever; and may the whole earth be filled with His glory. Amen, and Amen.

Ezra 8:23 NKJV * 1 Chronicles 16:9-11 NASB * 1 Chronicles 16:29 NKJV * Psalm 141:2 NASB * Psalm 139:14 NKJV * Psalm 145:1-3 NASB * Psalm 145:15-18 NASB * Psalm 72:19 NASB

MARCH

30 ....

Blessed be His glorious name forever!

20 _____ *

_____

_____

_____

_____

_____

_____

_____

20 _____ *

_____

_____

_____

_____

_____

_____

_____

20 _____ *

_____

_____

_____

_____

_____

_____

_____

MARCH 31

O God, You are my God; early will I seek You; my soul thirsts for You; my flesh longs for You in a dry and thirsty land where there is no water. So I have looked for You in the sanctuary, to see Your power and Your glory. Because Your lovingkindness is better than life, my lips shall praise You. Thus, I will bless You while I live; I will lift up my hands in Your name. * My lips shall greatly rejoice when I sing to You, and my soul, which You have redeemed. My tongue also shall talk of Your righteousness all the day long; for they are confounded, for they are brought to shame who seek my hurt. * He has redeemed my soul in peace from the battle that was against me, for there were many against me. * When I thought how to understand this, it was too painful for me—until I went into the sanctuary of God; then I understood their end. * Truly my soul silently waits for God; from Him comes my salvation. He only is my rock and my salvation; He is my defense; I shall not be greatly moved. * Amen and Amen.

Psalm 63:1-4 NKJV * Psalm 71:23-24 NKJV * Psalm 55:18 NKJV * Psalm 73:16-17 NKJV * Psalm 62:1-2 NKJV * Psalm 41:13b NKJV

MARCH

31 . . . .

He has redeemed my soul in peace.

20 _____ *

_____

_____
_____
_____
_____
_____
_____

20 _____ *

_____
_____
_____
_____
_____
_____

20 _____ *

_____
_____
_____
_____
_____
_____

APRIL

APRIL 1

Fear not, for I am with you; be not dismayed, for I am your God. I will strengthen you, yes, I will help you, I will uphold you with My righteous right hand. * A bruised reed He will not break. And smoking flax He will not quench; He will bring forth justice for truth. * For I, the LORD your God, will hold your right hand, saying to you, "Fear not, I will help you." * I will never leave you nor forsake you. * There is no fear in love; but perfect love casts out fear, because fear involves torment. But he who fears has not been made perfect in love. * It is love that really builds up the church. * The LORD is my helper; I will not fear. What can man do to me? * This is why I remind you to fan into flames the spiritual gift God gave you when I laid my hands on you. For God has not given us a spirit of fear and timidity, but of power, love, and self-discipline. * Then those who feared the LORD spoke with each other, and the LORD listened to what they said. In his presence, a scroll of remembrance was written to record the names of those who feared him and loved to think about him. "They will be my people." Says the LORD Almighty. "On the day when I act, they will be my special treasure. I will spare them as a father spares an obedient and dutiful child. Then you will again see the difference between the righteous and the wicked, between those who serve God and those who do not." * Little children, keep yourselves from idols. Amen.

Isaiah 41:10 NKJV * Isaiah 42:3 NKJV * Isaiah 41:13 NKJV * Hebrews 13:5b NKJV * 1 John 4:18 NKJV * 1 Corinthians 8:1b NLT * Hebrews 13:6 NKJV * 2 Timothy 1:6-7 NLT * Malachi 3:16-18 NLT * 1 John 5:21 NKJV

APRIL

1 . . . .

Fear God—the One who is Perfect Love!

20 _____ *

_____

_____

_____

_____

_____

_____

_____

20 _____ *

_____

_____

_____

_____

_____

_____

_____

20 _____ *

_____

_____

_____

_____

_____

_____

_____

APRIL 2

And he, having received such a command, threw them into the inner prison and fastened their feet in the stocks. But about midnight Paul and Silas were praying and singing hymns of praise to God, and the prisoners were listening to them; and suddenly there came a great earthquake, so that the foundations of the prison house were shaken; and immediately all the doors were opened and everyone's chains were unfastened. When the jailer awoke and saw the prison doors opened, he drew his sword and was about to kill himself, supposing that the prisoners had escaped. But Paul cried out with a loud voice, saying, "Do not harm yourself, for we are all here!" * And after he brought them out, he said, "Sirs, what must I do to be saved?" They said, "Believe in the Lord Jesus, and you will be saved, you and your household." * If anyone comes to Me, and does not hate his own father and mother and wife and children and brothers and sisters, yes, and even his own life, he cannot be My disciple. Whoever does not carry his own cross and come after Me cannot be My disciple. * The grace of our Lord Jesus Christ be with your spirit, brethren. Amen.

Acts 16:24-28 NASB * Acts 16:30-31 NASB * Luke 14:26-27 NASB * Galatians 6:18 NASB

APRIL

2 . . . .

People are watching your example.

20 _____ *

_____
_____
_____
_____
_____
_____
_____

20 _____ *

_____
_____
_____
_____
_____
_____
_____

20 _____ *

_____
_____
_____
_____
_____
_____
_____

APRIL 3

Brethren, if a man is overtaken in any trespass, you who are spiritual restore such a one in a spirit of gentleness, considering yourself lest you also be tempted. Bear one another's burdens, and so fulfill the law of Christ. * For you, brethren have been called to liberty; only do not use liberty as an opportunity for the flesh, but through love serve one another. For all the law is fulfilled in one word, even in this: "You shall love your neighbor as yourself." * Therefore, as we have opportunity, let us do good to all, especially to those who are of the household of faith. * For by grace you have been saved through faith, and that not of yourselves; it is the gift of God, not of works, lest anyone should boast. For we are His workmanship, created in Christ Jesus for good works, which God prepared beforehand that we should walk in them. * I, therefore, the prisoner of the Lord, beseech you to walk worthy of the calling with which you were called, with all lowliness and gentleness, with longsuffering, bearing with one another in love, endeavoring to keep the unity of the Spirit in the bond of peace. * Having then gifts differing according to the grace that is given to us, let us use them: if prophecy, let us prophesy in proportion to our faith; or ministry, let us use it in our ministering; he who teaches, in teaching; he who exhorts, in exhortation; he who gives, with liberality; he who leads, with diligence; he who shows mercy, with cheerfulness. * Amen and Amen.

Galatians 6:1-2 NKJV * Galatians 5:13-14 NKJV * Galatians 5:10 NKJV * Ephesians 2:8-10 NKJV * Ephesians 4:1-3 NKJV * Romans 12:6-8 NKJV * Psalm 41:13b NKJV

APRIL

3 . . . .

How is God calling you to serve one another?

20 _____ *

_____
_____
_____
_____
_____
_____
_____

20 _____ *

_____
_____
_____
_____
_____
_____
_____

20 _____ *

_____
_____
_____
_____
_____
_____
_____

APRIL 4

The LORD will command His lovingkindness in the daytime, and in the night His song shall be with me—A prayer to the God of my life. * O LORD, You have searched me and known me. * My lips shall greatly rejoice when I sing to You, and my soul, which You have redeemed. * Oh come, let us worship and bow down; let us kneel before the LORD our Maker. For He is our God, and we are the people of His pasture, and the sheep of His hand. * Serve the LORD with gladness; come before His presence with singing. * God be merciful to us and bless us, and cause His face to shine upon us, that Your way may be known on earth, Your salvation among all nations. * And blessed be His glorious name forever! And let the whole earth be filled with His glory. Amen and Amen.

Psalm 42:8 NKJV * Psalm 139:1 NKJV * Psalm 69:23 NKJV * Psalm 95:6-7 NKJV * Psalm 100:2 NKJV * Psalm 67:1-2 NKJV * Psalm 72:19 NKJV

APRIL

4 . . . .

Is there a song that mirrors your prayer?

20 _____ *

_____

_____
_____
_____
_____
_____
_____

20 _____ *

_____
_____
_____
_____
_____
_____
_____

20 _____ *

_____
_____
_____
_____
_____
_____

APRIL 5

The effective fervent prayer of a righteous man avails much. * The righteous keep moving forward and those with clean hands become stronger and stronger. * Indeed we count them blessed who endure. You have heard of the perseverance of Job and seen the end intended by the Lord—that the Lord is very compassionate and merciful. * Therefore we also, since we are surrounded by so great a cloud of witnesses, let us lay aside every weight, and the sin which so easily ensnares us, and let us run with endurance the race that is set before us, looking unto Jesus, the author and finisher of our faith, who for the joy that was set before Him endured the cross, despising the shame, and has sat down at the right hand of the throne of God. * Now to Him who is able to keep you from stumbling, and to present you faultless before the presence of His glory with exceeding joy, to God our Savior, who alone is wise, be glory and majesty, dominion and power, both now and forever. Amen.

James 5:16b NKJV * Job 17:9 NLT * James 5:11 NKJV * Hebrews 12:1-2 NKJV * Jude 24-25 NKJV

APRIL

5 . . . .

Focus on Jesus!

20 _____ *

_____

_____
_____
_____
_____
_____
_____

20 _____ *

_____
_____
_____
_____
_____
_____
_____

20 _____ *

_____
_____
_____
_____
_____
_____
_____

APRIL 6

Then the people cried out to Moses, and when Moses prayed to the LORD, the fire was quenched. * Elijah was a man with a nature like ours, and he prayed earnestly that it would not rain; and it did not rain on the land for three years and six months. And he prayed again, and the heaven gave rain, and the earth produced fruit. * Then another angel, having a golden censer, came and stood at the altar. He was given much incense, that he should offer it with the prayers of all the saints upon the golden altar which was before the throne. And the smoke of the incense, with the prayers of the saints, ascended before God from the angel's hand. * Now this is the confidence that we have in Him, that if we ask anything according to His will, He hears us. And if we know that He hears us, whatever we ask, we know that we have the petitions that we have asked of Him. * Amen and Amen.

Numbers 11:2 NKJV * James 5:17-18 NKJV * Revelation 8:3-4 NKJV * 1 John 5:14-15 NKJV * Psalm 72:19b NKJV

APRIL

6 . . . .

A heart of prayer seeks God's will to pray His heart.

20 _____ *

20 _____ *

20 _____ *

APRIL 7

My brethren, if any among you strays from the truth and one turns him back, let him know that he who turns a sinner from the error of his way will save his soul from death and will cover a multitude of sins. * For through the grace give to me I say to everyone among you not to think more highly of himself than he ought to think; but to think so as to have sound judgment, as God has allotted to each a measure of faith. * Brethren, even if anyone is caught in any trespass, you who are spiritual, restore such a one in a spirit of gentleness; each one looking to yourself, so that you too will not be tempted. Bear one another's burdens, and thereby fulfill the law of Christ. For if anyone thinks he is something when he is nothing, he deceives himself. * Therefore, strengthen the hands that are weak and the knees that are feeble, and make straight paths for your feet, so that the limb which is lame may not be put out of joint, but rather be healed. * Grace be with you all. * Blessed be the LORD, the God of Israel, from everlasting to everlasting. Amen and Amen.

James 5:19-20 NASB * Romans 12:3 NASB * Galatians 6:1-3 NASB * Hebrews 12:12-13 NASB * Hebrews 13:25 NASB * Psalm 41:13 NASB

APRIL

7 . . . .

Will you help carry a friend's burden to the foot of the cross?

20 _____ *

_____
_____
_____
_____
_____
_____
_____

20 _____ *

_____
_____
_____
_____
_____
_____
_____

20 _____ *

_____
_____
_____
_____
_____
_____
_____

APRIL 8

But you have an anointing from the Holy One, and you know all things. * But the anointing which you have received from Him abides in you, and you do not need that anyone teach you; but as the same anointing teaches you concerning all things, and is true, and is not a lie, and just as it has taught you, you will abide in Him. * I am the true vine, and My Father is the vinedresser. Every branch in Me that does not bear fruit He takes away; and every branch that bears fruit He prunes, that it may bear more fruit. You are already clean because of the word which I have spoken to you. Abide in Me, and I in you. As the branch cannot bear fruit of itself, unless it abides in the vine, neither can you, unless you abide in Me. I am the vine, you are the branches. He who abides in Me, and I in him, bears much fruit; for without Me you can do nothing. * If you abide in Me, and My words abide in you, you will ask what you desire, and it shall be done for you. * Let us therefore come boldly to the throne of grace, that we may obtain mercy and find grace to help in time of need. * Grace be with you all. Amen.

1 John 2:20 NKJV * 1 John 2:27 NKJV * John 15:1-5 NKJV * John 15:7 NKJV * Hebrews 4:16 NKJV * Hebrews 13:25 NKJV

APRIL

8 . . . .

Anointing comes from abiding in Christ.

20 _____ *

_____
_____
_____
_____
_____
_____

20 _____ *

_____
_____
_____
_____
_____
_____
_____

20 _____ *

_____
_____
_____
_____
_____
_____
_____

APRIL 9

For this reason I remind you to kindle afresh the gift of God which is in you through the laying on of my hands. * For the word of God is living and powerful, and sharper than any two-edged sword, piercing even to the division of soul and spirit, and of joints and marrow, and is a discerner of the thoughts and intents of the heart. * You therefore must endure hardship as a good soldier of Jesus Christ. * Therefore take heed to yourselves and to all the flock, among which the Holy Spirit has made you overseers, to shepherd the church of God which He purchased with His own blood. * Shepherd the flock of God which is among you, serving as overseers, not by compulsion but willingly, not for dishonest gain but eagerly; nor as being Lords over those entrusted to you, but being examples to the flock; and when the Chief Shepherd appears you will receive the crown of glory that does not fade away. * But the end of all things is at hand; therefore be serious and watchful in your prayers. * Greet one another with a kiss of love. Peace to you all who are in Christ Jesus. Amen.

2 Timothy 1:6 NASB * Hebrews 4:12 NKJV * 2 Timothy 2:3 NKJV * Acts 20:28 NKJV * 1 Peter 5:2-4 NKJV * 1 Peter 4:7 NKJV * 1 Peter 5:14 NKJV

APRIL

9 ·

**Too many people want authority without responsibility.
What's your responsibility?**

20 _____ *

_____

_____
_____
_____
_____
_____
_____

20 _____ *

_____

_____
_____
_____
_____
_____
_____

20 _____ *

_____

_____
_____
_____
_____
_____
_____

APRIL 10

For you did not receive the spirit of bondage again to fear, but you received the Spirit of adoption by whom we cry out, "Abba, Father." * Just as He chose us in Him before the foundation of the world, that we should be holy and without blame before Him in love, having pre-destined us to adoption as sons by Jesus Christ to Himself, according to the good pleasure of His will, to the praise of the glory of His grace, by which He made us accepted in the Beloved. * And because you are sons, God has sent forth the Spirit of His Son into your hearts, crying out "Abba, Father!" Therefore you are no longer a slave but a son, and if a son, then an heir of God through Christ. * Behold what manner of love the Father has bestowed on us, that we should be called children of God! Therefore the world does not know us, because it did not know Him. * Amen and Amen.

Romans 8:15 NKJV * Ephesians 1:4-6 NKJV * Galatians 4:6-7 NKJV * 1 John 3:1 NKJV * Psalm 72:19b NKJV

APRIL

10 . . . .

You are an adopted heir with an eternal inheritance.

20 _____ *

_____
_____
_____
_____
_____
_____
_____

20 _____ *

_____
_____
_____
_____
_____
_____
_____

20 _____ *

_____
_____
_____
_____
_____
_____
_____

APRIL 11

The glory of the LORD shall be revealed, and all flesh shall see it together; for the mouth of the LORD has spoken. * And the Word became flesh and dwelt among us, and we beheld His glory, the glory as of the only begotten of the Father, full of grace and truth. * Therefore, having been justified by faith, we have peace with God through our Lord Jesus Christ, through whom also we have access by faith into this grace in which we stand, and rejoice in hope of the glory of God. * Now then, we are ambassadors for Christ, as though God were pleading through us: we implore you on Christ's behalf, be reconciled to God. For He made Him who knew no sin to be sin for us, that we might become the righteousness of God in Him. * The grace of our Lord Jesus Christ be with you all. Amen.

Isaiah 40:5 NKJV * John 1:14 NKJV * Romans 5:1-2 NKJV * 2 Corinthians 5:20-21 NKJV * 2 Thessalonians 3:18 NKJV

APRIL

11 •

You are an ambassador for Christ.

20 _____ *

_____

_____

_____

_____

_____

_____

_____

20 _____ *

_____

_____

_____

_____

_____

_____

_____

20 _____ *

_____

_____

_____

_____

_____

_____

_____

APRIL 12

Thus says the LORD: "Let not the wise man glory in his wisdom, let not the mighty man glory in his might, nor let the rich man glory in his riches; but let him who glories glory in this, that he understands and knows Me, that I am the LORD, exercising lovingkindness, judgment, and righteousness in the earth. For in these I delight," says the LORD. * No king is saved by the multitude of an army; a mighty man is not delivered by great strength. A horse is a vain hope for safety; neither shall it deliver any by its great strength. Behold, the eye of the LORD is on those who fear Him, on those who hope in His mercy. * For you see your calling, brethren, that not many wise according to the flesh, not many mighty, not many noble, are called. But God has chosen the foolish things of the world to put to shame the wise, and God has chosen the weak things of the world to put to shame the things which are mighty; and the base things of the world and the things which are despised God has chosen, and the things which are not, to bring to nothing the things that are, that no flesh should glory in His presence. But of Him you are in Christ Jesus, who became for us wisdom from God—and righteousness and sanctification and redemption—that, as it is written, "He who glories, let him glory in the LORD." * Amen and Amen.

Jeremiah 9:23-24 NKJV * Psalm 33:16-18 NKJV * 1 Corinthians 1:26-31 NKJV * Psalm 72:19b NKJV

APRIL

12 . . . .

Glory in the LORD.

20 _____ *

_____
_____
_____
_____
_____
_____
_____

20 _____ *

_____
_____
_____
_____
_____
_____
_____

20 _____ *

_____
_____
_____
_____
_____
_____
_____

APRIL 13

Pursue peace with all people, and holiness, without which no one will see the Lord: looking carefully lest anyone fall short of the grace of God; lest any root of bitterness springing up cause trouble, and by this many become defiled. * He who says he is in the light, and hates his brother, is in darkness until now. He who loves his brother abides in the light, and there is no cause for stumbling in him. * Prove by the way that you live that you have really turned from your sins and turned to God. * You are a chosen generation, a royal priesthood, a holy nation, His own special people, that you may proclaim the praises of Him who called you out of darkness into His marvelous light, who once were not a people but are now the people of God, who had not obtained mercy but now have obtained mercy. * Love suffers long and is kind. * Does not rejoice in iniquity, but rejoices in the truth. * Love builds up. * The grace of our Lord Jesus Christ be with you all. Amen.

Hebrews 12:14-15 NKJV * 1 John 2:9-10 NKJV * Matthew 3:8 NLT * 1 Peter 2:9-10 NKJV * 1 Corinthians 13:4a NKJV * 1 Corinthians 13:6 NKJV * 1 Corinthians 8:1b ESV * Romans 16:24 NKJV

APRIL

13 ....

How have you proven that you have turned from your sins?

20 _____ *

_____
_____
_____
_____
_____
_____

20 _____ *

_____
_____
_____
_____
_____
_____

20 _____ *

_____
_____
_____
_____
_____
_____

APRIL 14

Rejoice in the Lord always. Again I will say, rejoice! * Give to the LORD the glory due His name; bring an offering, and come before Him. Oh, worship the LORD in the beauty of holiness. * Make a joyful shout to the LORD, all you lands! Serve the LORD with gladness; come before His presence with singing. Know that the LORD, He is God; it is He who has made us, and not we ourselves; we are His people and the sheep of His pasture. Enter into His gates with thanksgiving, and into His courts with praise. Be thankful to Him, and bless His name. * Oh, give thanks to the LORD! Call upon His name; make known His deeds among the peoples! Sing to Him, sing psalms to Him; talk of all His wondrous works! Glory in His holy name; let the hearts of those rejoice who seek the Lord! Seek the LORD and His strength; seek His face evermore! * And blessed be His glorious name forever! And let the whole earth be filled with His glory. Amen and Amen.

Philippians 4:4 NKJV * 1 Chronicles 16:29 NKJV * Psalm 100:1-4 NKJV * 1 Chronicles 16:8-11 NKJV * Psalm 72:19 NKJV

APRIL

14 . . . .

You are the sheep of His pasture.

20 _____ *

---

20 _____ *

---

20 _____ *

APRIL 15

Let your gentleness be known to all men. The Lord is at hand. * So then, my beloved brethren, let every man be swift to hear, slow to speak, slow to wrath; for the wrath of man does not produce the righteousness of God. * Repent therefore and be converted, that your sins may be blotted out, so that times of refreshing may come from the presence of the Lord, and that He may send Jesus Christ, who was preached to you before, whom heaven must receive until the times of restoration of all things, which God has spoken by the mouth of all His holy prophets since the world began. * You also be patient. Establish your hearts, for the coming of the Lord is at hand. * Now may the Lord direct your hearts into the love of God and into the patience of Christ. * Watch therefore, for you do not know what hour your Lord is coming. * But he who endures to the end shall be saved. * Now may the God of peace Himself sanctify you completely; and may your whole spirit, soul, and body be preserved blameless at the coming of our Lord Jesus Christ. He who calls you is faithful, who also will do it. * The grace of our Lord Jesus Christ be with you. Amen.

Philippians 4:5 NKJV * James 1:19-20 NKJV * Acts 3:19-21 NKJV * James 5:8 NKJV * 2 Thessalonians 3:5 NKJV * Matthew 24:42 NKJV * Mark 13:13b NKJV * 1 Thessalonians 5:23-24 NKJV * 1 Thessalonians 5:28 NKJV

APRIL

15 . . . .

How are you going to endure to the end?

20 _____ *

_____
_____
_____
_____
_____
_____
_____

20 _____ *

_____
_____
_____
_____
_____
_____
_____

20 _____ *

_____
_____
_____
_____
_____
_____
_____

APRIL 16

Through the LORD's mercies we are not consumed, because His compassions fail not. They are new every morning; great is Your faithfulness. * Rejoice always, pray without ceasing, in everything give thanks; for this is the will of God in Christ Jesus for you. * If we are faithless, He remains faithful; He cannot deny Himself. * For I am the LORD, I do not change; therefore you are not consumed, O sons of Jacob. * O LORD, be gracious to us; we have waited for You. Be their arm every morning, our salvation also in time of trouble. * "The LORD is my portion," says my soul, "Therefore I hope in Him." * Therefore I will look to the LORD; I will wait for the God of my salvation; My God will hear me. * And blessed be His glorious name forever! And let the whole earth be filled with His glory. Amen and Amen.

Lamentations 3:22-23 NKJV * 1 Thessalonians 5:16-18 NKJV * 2 Timothy 2:13 NKJV * Malachi 3:6 NKJV * Isaiah 33:2 NKJV * Lamentations 3:24 NKJV * Micah 7:7 NKJV * Psalm 72:19 NKJV

APRIL

16 ....

The Lord's mercies are new every morning. Rejoice!

20 _____ *

_____

_____

_____

_____

_____

_____

_____

20 _____ *

_____

_____

_____

_____

_____

_____

_____

20 _____ *

_____

_____

_____

_____

_____

_____

_____

APRIL 17

Do not gloat over me, my enemy! Though I have fallen, I will rise. Though I sit in darkness, the LORD will be my light. * For though the righteous fall seven times, they rise again, but the wicked stumble when calamity strikes. * Your word is a lamp to my feet, a light to my path. * Redeem me from human oppression, that I may obey your precepts. Make your face shine on your servant and teach me your decrees. Streams of tears flow from my eyes, for your law is not obeyed. * Many people say, "Who will show us better times?" Let the smile of your face shine on us, LORD. You have given me greater joy than those who have abundant harvests of grain and wine. I will lie down in peace and sleep, for you alone, O LORD, will keep me safe. * Peace to the brothers and sisters, and love with faith from God the Father and the Lord Jesus Christ. Grace to all who love our Lord Jesus Christ with an undying love. * Amen and Amen.

Micah 7:8 NIV * Proverbs 24:16 NIV * Psalm 119:105 NIV * Psalm 119:134-136 NIV * Psalm 4:6-8 NLT * Ephesians 6:23-24 NIV * Psalm 41:13b NIV

APRIL

17 . . . .

Let the smile on Your face shine on us, Lord!

20 _____ *

_____
_____
_____
_____
_____
_____
_____

20 _____ *

_____
_____
_____
_____
_____
_____

20 _____ *

_____
_____
_____
_____
_____
_____

APRIL 18

Direct my footsteps according to your word; let no sin rule over me. *
Turn my eyes away from worthless things; preserve my life according
to your word. Fulfill your promise to your servant, so that you may be
feared. * Therefore do not let sin reign in your mortal body so that you
obey its evil desires. Do not offer any part of yourself to sin as an instrument of wickedness, but rather offer yourselves to God as those who have
been brought from death to life; and offer every part of yourself to him
as an instrument of righteousness. For sin shall no longer be your master,
because you are not under the law, but under grace. * For it is by grace
you have been saved, through faith—and this is not from yourselves, it
is the gift of God—not by works, so that no one can boast. * If you keep
yourself pure, you will be a special utensil for honorable use. Your life will
be clean, and you will be ready for the Master to use you for every good
work. Run from anything that stimulates youthful lusts. Instead, pursue
righteous living, faithfulness, love, and peace. Enjoy the companionship
of those who call on the Lord with pure hearts. * The grace of our Lord
Jesus Christ be with your spirit, brothers and sisters. Amen.

Psalm 119:133 NIV * Psalm 119:37-38 NIV * Romans 6:12-14 NIV *
Ephesians 2:8-9 NIV * 2 Timothy 2:21-22 NLT * Galatians 6:18 NIV

APRIL

18 . . . .

Call on the Lord with a pure heart.

20 _____ *

_____
_____
_____
_____
_____
_____
_____

20 _____ *

_____
_____
_____
_____
_____
_____
_____

20 _____ *

_____
_____
_____
_____
_____
_____
_____

APRIL 19

You, however, smear me with lies; you are worthless physicians, all of you! If only you would be altogether silent! For you, that would be wisdom. * Though the arrogant have smeared me with lies, I keep your precepts with all my heart. * Those who walk righteously and speak what is right, who reject gain from extortion and keep their hands from accepting bribes, who stop their ears against plots of murder and shut their eyes against contemplating evil—they are the ones who will dwell on the heights, whose refuge will be the mountain fortress. Their bread will be supplied, and water will not fail them. * Who may ascend the mountain of the LORD? Who may stand in his holy place? The one who has clean hands and a pure heart, who does not trust in an idol or swear by a false god. * LORD, who may dwell in your sacred tent? Who may live on your holy mountain? The one whose walk is blameless, who does what is righteous, who speaks the truth from their heart; whose tongue utters no slander, who does no wrong to a neighbor, and casts no slur on others; who despises a vile person but honors those who fear the LORD; who keeps an oath even when it hurts, and does not change their mind; who lends money to the poor without interest; who does not accept a bribe against the innocent. Whoever does these things will never be shaken. * Amen and Amen.

Job 13:4-5 NIV * Psalm 119:69 NIV * Isaiah 33:15-16 NIV * Psalm 24:3-4 NIV * Psalm 15:1-5 NIV * Psalm 72:19b NIV

APRIL

19 . . . .

Do you speak the truth from a sincere heart?

20 _____ *

_____

_____

_____

_____

_____

_____

20 _____ *

_____

_____

_____

_____

_____

_____

20 _____ *

_____

_____

_____

_____

_____

_____

APRIL 20

The Lord's bond-servant must not be quarrelsome, but be kind to all, able to teach, patient when wronged, with gentleness correcting those who are in opposition, if perhaps God may grant them repentance leading to the knowledge of the truth, and they may come to their senses and escape from the snare of the devil, having been held captive by him to do his will. * But as for you, speak the things which are fitting for sound doctrine. Older men are to be temperate, dignified, sensible, sound in faith, in love, in perseverance. Older women likewise are to be reverent in their behavior, not malicious gossips nor enslaved to much wine, teaching what is good. * For whatever things were written before were written for our learning, that we through the patience and comfort of the Scriptures might have hope. * So we have the prophetic word made more sure, to which you do well to pay attention as to a lamp shining in a dark place, until the day dawns and the morning star arises in your hearts. But know this first of all, that no prophecy of Scripture is a matter of one's own interpretation, for no prophecy was ever made by an act of human will, but men moved by the Holy Spirit spoke from God. * But grow in the grace and knowledge of our Lord and Savior Jesus Christ. To Him be the glory, both now and to the day of eternity. Amen.

2 Timothy 2:24-26 NASB * Titus 2:1-3 NASB * 2 Timothy 3:16-17 NASB * Romans 15:4 NKJV * 2 Peter 1:19-21 NASB * 2 Peter 3:18 NASB

APRIL

20 . . . .

**Through the patience and comfort of Scripture,
we have hope.**

20 _____ *

_____

_____

_____

_____

_____

_____

_____

20 _____ *

_____

_____

_____

_____

_____

_____

_____

20 _____ *

_____

_____

_____

_____

_____

_____

_____

APRIL 21

Give ear to my words, O LORD, consider my meditation. Give heed to the voice of my cry, my King and my God, for to You I will pray. * I pray, LORD God of heaven, O great and awesome God, You who keep Your covenant and mercy with those who love You and observe Your commandments, please let Your ear be attentive and Your eyes open, that You may hear the prayer of Your servant which I pray before You now, day and night, for the children of Israel Your servants, and confess the sins of the children of Israel which we have sinned against You. Both my father's house and I have sinned. We have acted very corruptly against You, and have not kept the commandments, the statutes, nor the ordinances which You commanded Your servant Moses. Remember, I pray, the word You commanded Your servant Moses, saying, "If you are unfaithful, I will scatter you among the nations; but if you return to Me, and keep My commandments and do them, though some of you were cast out to the farthest part of the heavens, yet I will gather them from there, and bring them to the place which I have chosen as a dwelling for My name." Now these are Your servants and Your people, whom You have redeemed by Your great power, and by Your strong hand. O Lord, I pray, please let Your ear be attentive to the prayer of Your servants who desire to fear Your name; and let Your servant prosper this day, I pray, and grant him mercy in the sight of this man. * Amen and Amen.

Psalm 5:1-2 NKJV * Nehemiah 1:5-11 NKJV * Psalm 72:19b NKJV

APRIL

21 ....

O LORD, consider my meditation.

20 _____ *

_____
_____
_____
_____
_____
_____
_____

20 _____ *

_____
_____
_____
_____
_____
_____
_____

20 _____ *

_____
_____
_____
_____
_____
_____
_____

APRIL 22

But beware lest somehow this liberty of yours become a stumbling block to those who are weak. * And so, by sinning against the brethren and wounding their conscience when it is weak, you sin against Christ. * Therefore bear fruits worthy of repentance. * For if you are living according to the flesh, you must die; but if by the Spirit you are putting to death the deeds of the body, you will live. * And having been freed from sin, you became slaves of righteousness. * Therefore I run in such a way, as not without aim; I box in such a way, as not beating the air; but I discipline my body and make it my slave, so that, after I have preached to others, I myself will not be disqualified. * The grace of the Lord Jesus be with you. My love be with you all in Christ Jesus. Amen.

1 Corinthians 8:9 NKJV * 1 Corinthians 8:12 NASB * Matthew 3:8 NKJV * Romans 8:13 NASB * Romans 6:18 NASB * 1 Corinthians 9:26-27 NASB * 1 Corinthians 16:23-24 NASB

APRIL

22 . . . .

How is God calling you to grow in self-discipline?

20 _____ *

_____

_____

_____

_____

_____

_____

20 _____ *

_____

_____

_____

_____

_____

_____

20 _____ *

_____

_____

_____

_____

_____

_____

APRIL 23

My voice You shall hear in the morning, O LORD; in the morning I will direct it to You, and I will look up. * Evening and morning and at noon I will pray, and cry aloud, and He shall hear my voice. He has redeemed my soul in peace from the battle that was against me, for there were many against me. * Sing, O daughter of Zion! Shout, O Israel! Be glad and rejoice with all your heart, O daughter of Jerusalem! The LORD has taken away your judgments, He has cast out your enemy. The King of Israel, the LORD, is in your midst; you shall see disaster no more. * Behold, at that time I will deal with all who afflict you; I will save the lame, and gather those who were driven out; I will appoint them for praise and fame in every land where they were put to shame. * "No weapon formed against you shall prosper, and every tongue which rises against you in judgment you shall condemn. This is the heritage of the servants of the LORD, and their righteousness is from Me," says the LORD. * Amen and Amen.

Psalm 5:3 NKJV * Psalm 55:17-18 NKJV * Zephaniah 3:14-15 NKJV * Zephaniah 3:19 NKJV * Isaiah 54:17 NKJV * Psalm 72:19b NKJV

APRIL

23 . . . .

No weapon formed against you shall prosper. Amen!

20 _____ *

_____
_____
_____
_____
_____
_____
_____

20 _____ *

_____
_____
_____
_____
_____
_____
_____

20 _____ *

_____
_____
_____
_____
_____
_____
_____

APRIL 24

So I will save you, and you shall be a blessing. Do not fear, let your hands be strong. * In that day it shall be said to Jerusalem: "Do not fear; Zion, let not your hands be weak. The LORD your God in your midst, the Mighty One, will save; He will rejoice over you with gladness, He will quiet you with His love, He will rejoice over you with singing." * So take a new grip with your tired hands and stand firm on your shaky legs. Mark out a straight path for your feet. Then those who follow you, though they are weak and lame, will not stumble and fall but will become strong. * And the God of peace will crush Satan under your feet shortly. The grace of our Lord Jesus Christ be with you. Amen.

Zechariah 8:13 NKJV * Zephaniah 3:16-17 NKJV * Hebrews 12:12-13 NLT * Romans 16:20 NKJV

APRIL

24 . . . .

Will those following you become strong?

*20*_____ *

_____
_____
_____
_____
_____
_____
_____

*20*_____ *

_____
_____
_____
_____
_____
_____
_____

*20*_____ *

_____
_____
_____
_____
_____
_____
_____

APRIL 25

Though the fig tree should not blossom and there be no fruit on the vines, though the yield of the olive should fail and the fields produce no food, though the flock should be cut off from the fold and there be no cattle in the stalls, yet I will exult in the LORD, I will rejoice in the God of my salvation. The Lord GOD is my strength, and He has made my feet like hinds' feet, and makes me walk on my high places. * Surely my soul remembers and is bowed down within me. This I recall to my mind, therefore I have hope. The LORD's lovingkindnesses indeed never cease, for His compassions never fail. They are new every morning; great is Your faithfulness. * I call on Your name, O LORD, out of the lowest pit. You have heard my voice, "Do not hide Your ear from my prayer for relief, from my cry for help." You drew near when I called on You; You said, "Do not fear!" O Lord, You have pleaded my soul's cause; You have redeemed my life. * Bless the LORD, O my soul, and all that is within me, bless His holy name. Bless the LORD, O my soul, and forget none of His benefits; who pardons all your iniquities, who heals all your diseases; who redeems your life from the pit, who crowns you with lovingkindness and compassion; who satisfies your years with good things, so that your youth is renewed like the eagles. * Bless the LORD, O my soul. Praise the LORD! * To the only wise God, through Jesus Christ, be the glory forever. Amen.

Habakkuk 3:17-19 NASB * Lamentations 3:20-23 NASB * Lamentations 3:55-58 NASB * Psalm 103:1-5 NASB * Psalm 104:35b NASB * Romans 16:27 NASB

APRIL

25 . . . .

The LORD God is my strength.

20 _____ *

---

20 _____ *

---

20 _____ *

APRIL 26

"For from the rising of the sun, even to it's going down, My name shall be great among the Gentiles; in every place incense shall be offered to My name, and a pure offering; for My name shall be great among the nations," says the LORD of hosts. * So shall they fear the name of the LORD from the west, and His glory from the rising of the sun; when the enemy comes in like a flood, the Spirit of the LORD will lift up a standard against him. * "As for Me," says the LORD, "this is My covenant with them: My Spirit who is upon you, and My words which I have put in your mouth, shall not depart from your mouth, nor from the mouth of your descendants, nor from the mouth of your descendants' descendants," says the LORD, "from this time and forevermore." * Lift up your eyes all around, and see: they all gather together, they come to you; your sons shall come from afar, and your daughters shall be nursed at your side. Then you shall see and become radiant, and your heart shall swell with joy; because the abundance of the sea shall be turned to you, the wealth of the Gentiles shall come to you. * I desire therefore that the men pray everywhere, lifting up holy hands, without wrath and doubting. * The grace of our Lord Jesus Christ be with you all. Amen.

Malachi 1:11 NKJV * Isaiah 59:19 NKJV * Isaiah 59:21 NKJV * Isaiah 60:4-5 NKJV * 1 Timothy 2:8 NKJV * Revelation 22:21 NKJV

APRIL

26 . . . .

Will you ask the Lord to fill you with His Holy Spirit?

20 _____ *

_____
_____
_____
_____
_____
_____

20 _____ *

_____
_____
_____
_____
_____
_____

20 _____ *

_____
_____
_____
_____
_____
_____

APRIL 27

Jesus answered and said to her, "If you knew the gift of God, and who it is who says to you, 'Give Me a drink,' you would have asked Him, and He would have given you living water." * "Whoever drinks of this water will thirst again, but whoever drinks of the water I shall give him will never thirst. But the water I shall give him will become in him a fountain of water springing up into everlasting life." * Therefore with joy you will draw water from the wells of salvation. * For I will pour water on him who is thirsty, and floods on the dry ground; I will pour My Spirit on your descendants, and My blessing on your offspring; they will spring up among the grass like willows by the watercourses. * And Jesus said to them, "I am the bread of life. He who comes to Me shall never hunger, and he who believes in Me shall never thirst." * And the Spirit and the bride say, "Come!" And let him who hears say, "Come!" And let him who thirsts come. Whoever desires, let him take the water of life freely. * Amen. Even so, come, Lord Jesus!

John 4:10 NKJV * John 4:13-14 NKJV * Isaiah 12:3 NKJV * Isaiah 44:3-4 NKJV * John 6:35 NKJV * Revelation 22:17 NKJV * Revelation 22:20b NKJV

APRIL

27 ....

Are you thirsty?

20 _____

_____

_____

_____

_____

_____

_____

20 _____

_____

_____

_____

_____

_____

_____

20 _____

_____

_____

_____

_____

_____

_____

APRIL 28

Worship God. * Holy, holy, holy, Lord God Almighty, Who was and is and is to come! * You are worthy, O Lord, to receive glory and honor and power; for You created all things, and by Your will they exist and were created. * You are worthy to take the scroll, and to open its seals; for You were slain, and have redeemed us to God by Your blood. Out of every tribe and tongue and people and nation, and have made us kings and priests to our God; and we shall reign on the earth. * Worthy is the Lamb who was slain to receive power and riches and wisdom, and strength and honor and glory and blessing! * Blessing and honor and glory and power be to Him who sits on the throne, and to the Lamb, forever and ever! * We give You thanks, O Lord God Almighty, the One who is and who was and who is to come, because You have taken Your great power and reigned. The nations were angry, and Your wrath has come, and the time of the dead, that they should be judged, and that You should reward Your servants the prophets and the saints, and those who fear Your name, small and great, and should destroy those who destroy the earth. * The grace of our Lord Jesus Christ be with you all. Amen.

Revelation 22:9b NKJV * Revelation 4:8b NKJV * Revelation 4:11 NKJV * Revelation 5:9-10 NKJV * Revelation 5:12 NKJV * Revelation 5:13b * Revelation 11:17-18 NKJV * Revelation 22:21 NKJV

APRIL

28 . . . .

Worship God.

20 _____ *

_____
_____
_____
_____
_____
_____
_____

20 _____ *

_____
_____
_____
_____
_____
_____
_____

20 _____ *

_____
_____
_____
_____
_____
_____
_____

APRIL 29

Then Jesus said, "Come to me all of you who are weary and carry heavy burdens, and I will give you rest. Take my yoke upon you. Let me teach you, because I am humble and gentle, and you will find rest for your souls. For my yoke fits perfectly, and the burden I give you is light." * All of us must quickly carry out the tasks assigned us by the one who sent me, because there is little time left before the night falls and all work comes to an end. * For God's gifts and his call can never be withdrawn. * God has given each of us the ability to do certain things well. So if God has given you the ability to prophesy, speak out when you have faith that God is speaking through you. If your gift is that of serving others, serve them well. If you are a teacher, do a good job of teaching. If your gift is to encourage others, do it! If you have money, share it generously. If God has given you leadership ability, take the responsibility seriously. And if you have a gift for showing kindness to others, do it gladly. Don't just pretend that you love others. Really love them. Hate what is wrong. Stand on the side of the good. Love each other with genuine affection, and take delight in honoring each other. Never be lazy in your work, but serve the Lord enthusiastically. Be glad for all God is planning for you. Be patient in trouble, and always be prayerful. * To God, who alone is wise, be the glory forever through Jesus Christ. Amen.

Matthew 11:28-30 NLT * John 9:4 NLT * Romans 11:29 NLT * Romans 12:6-12 NLT * Romans 16:27 NLT

APRIL

29 . . . .

The Lord's yoke fits you perfectly.

20 _____ *

_____
_____
_____
_____
_____
_____
_____

20 _____ *

_____
_____
_____
_____
_____
_____
_____

20 _____ *

_____
_____
_____
_____
_____
_____
_____

APRIL 30

Fear not, for I am with you; be not dismayed, for I am your God. I will strengthen you, yes, I will help you, I will uphold you with My righteous right hand. * I am the LORD, that is My name; and My glory I will not give to another, nor My praise to carved images. * But now, thus says the LORD, who created you, O Jacob, and He who formed you, O Israel: "Fear not, for I have redeemed you; I have called you by your name; You are Mine." * Since you were precious in My sight, You have been honored, and I have loved you; therefore I will give men for you, and people for your life. * "You are My witnesses," says the LORD, "And My servant whom I have chosen, that you may know and believe Me, and understand that I am He. Before Me there was no God formed, nor shall there be after Me. I, even I, am the LORD, and besides Me there is no savior. I have declared and saved, I have proclaimed, and there was no foreign god among you; therefore you are My witnesses," says the LORD, "that I am God." * Amen and Amen.

Isaiah 41:10 NKJV * Isaiah 42:8 NKJV * Isaiah 43:1 NKJV * Isaiah 43:4 NKJV * Isaiah 43:10-12 NKJV * Psalm 72:19b NKJV

APRIL

30 ....

God loves you.

20 _____ *

_____

_____
_____
_____
_____
_____
_____

20 _____ *

_____

_____
_____
_____
_____
_____
_____

20 _____ *

_____

_____
_____
_____
_____
_____
_____

MAY

253

MAY 1

A bruised reed He will not break, and smoking flax He will not quench; He will bring forth justice for truth. * When you pass through waters, I will be with you; and through rivers, they shall not overflow you. When you walk through the fire, you shall not be burned, nor shall the flame scorch you. * "Even them I will bring to My holy mountain, and make them joyful in My house of prayer. Their burnt offerings and their sacrifices *will be* accepted on My altar; for My house shall be called a house of prayer for all nations." The Lord God, who gathers the outcasts of Israel, says, "Yet I will gather to him *Others* besides those who are gathered to him." * "Instead of your shame you shall have double honor , and instead of confusion they shall rejoice in their portion. Therefore in their land they shall possess double; everlasting joy shall be theirs. For I, the Lord, love justice; I hate robbery for burnt offering; I will direct their work in truth, and will make with them an everlasting covenant. Their descendants shall be known among the Gentiles, and their offspring among the people. All who see them shall acknowledge them, that they are the posterity whom the Lord has blessed." I will greatly rejoice in the Lord, my soul shall be joyful in my God; for He has clothed me with the garments of salvation, He has covered me with the robe of righteousness, as a bridegroom decks himself with ornaments, and as a bride adorns herself with her jewels. * Amen and Amen.

Isaiah 42:3 NKJV * Isaiah 43:2 NKJV * Isaiah 56:7-8 NKJV * Isaiah 61:7-10 NKJV * Psalm 72:19b NKJV

MAY

1 . . . .

God gathers the outcasts.

20 _____ *

_____
_____
_____
_____
_____
_____
_____

20 _____ *

_____
_____
_____
_____
_____
_____
_____

20 _____ *

_____
_____
_____
_____
_____
_____
_____

MAY 2

The high and lofty one who inhabits eternity, the Holy One, says this: "I live in that high and holy place with those whose spirits are contrite and humble. I refresh the humble and give new courage to those with repentant hearts. For I will not fight against you forever; I will not always show my anger. If I did, all people would pass away—all the souls I have made. I was angry and punished these greedy people. I withdrew myself from them, but they went right on sinning. I have seen what they do, but I will heal them anyway! I will lead them and comfort those who mourn. Then words of praise will be on their lips. May they have peace, both near and far, for I will heal them all," says the LORD. * God blesses those who mourn, for they will be comforted. * May the grace of our Lord Jesus Christ, the love of God, and the fellowship of the Holy Spirit be with you all. Amen.

Isaiah 57:15-19 NLT * Matthew 5:4 NLT * 2 Corinthians 13:13 NLT

MAY

2 ·

What do you need to repent of?

20 _____ *

_____
_____
_____
_____
_____
_____
_____

20 _____ *

_____
_____
_____
_____
_____
_____
_____

20 _____ *

_____
_____
_____
_____
_____
_____
_____

MAY 3

The Spirit of the Lord God is upon Me, because the LORD has anointed Me to preach good tidings to the poor; He has sent Me to heal the brokenhearted, to proclaim liberty to the captives, and the opening of the prison to those who are bound. * "Your light shall break forth like the morning, Your healing shall spring forth speedily, and your righteousness shall go before you; the glory of the LORD shall be your rear guard . Then you shall call, and the LORD will answer; you shall cry, and He will say, 'Here I am.' If you take away the yoke from your midst, the pointing of the finger, and speaking wickedness, if you extend your soul to the hungry and satisfy the afflicted soul, then your light shall dawn in the darkness, and your darkness shall be as the noonday. The LORD will guide you continually and satisfy your soul in drought, and strengthen your bones; you shall be like a watered garden, and like a spring of water, whose waters do not fail." * Blessed are those who hunger and thirst for righteousness, for they shall be filled. * Grace be with all those who love our Lord Jesus Christ in sincerity. Amen.

Isaiah 61:1 NKJV * Isaiah 58:8-11 NKJV * Matthew 5:6 NKJV * Ephesians 6:24 NKJV

MAY

3 . . . .

When you cry out to God, He says, "Here I am."

20 _____ *

_____
_____
_____
_____
_____
_____
_____

20 _____ *

_____
_____
_____
_____
_____
_____
_____

20 _____ *

_____
_____
_____
_____
_____
_____
_____

MAY 4

And many of the Samaritans of that city believed in Him because of the word of the woman who testified, "He told me all that I ever did." So when the Samaritans had come to Him, they urged Him to stay with them; and He stayed there two days. And many more believed because of His own word. * Now the first day of the week Mary Magdalene went to the tomb early, while it was still dark, and saw that the stone had been taken away from the tomb. Then she ran and came to Simon Peter, and to the other disciple, whom Jesus loved, and said to them, "They have taken away the Lord out of the tomb, and we do not know where they have laid Him." * But Mary stood outside by the tomb weeping. * Jesus said to her, "Woman, why are you weeping? Whom are you seeking?" She, supposing Him to be the gardener, said to Him, "Sir, if You have carried Him away, tell me where You have laid Him, and I will take Him away." Jesus said to her, "Mary!" She turned and said to Him, "Rabboni!" (which is to say, Teacher). Jesus said to her, "Do not cling to Me, for I have not yet ascended to My Father; but go to My brethren and say to them, 'I am ascending to My Father and your Father, and to My God and your God.'" Mary Magdalene came and told the disciples that she had seen the Lord, and that He had spoken these things to her. * And He said to them, "Go into all the world and preach the gospel to every creature. He who believes and is baptized will be saved; but he who does not believe will be condemned." * And they went out and preached everywhere, the Lord working with them and confirming the word through the accompanying signs. Amen.

John 4:39-41 NKJV * John 20:1-2 NKJV * John 20:11a NKJV * John 20:15-18 NKJV * Mark 16:15-16 NKJV * Mark 16:20 NKJV

MAY

4 ·

Share what you know.

20 _____ *

_____
_____
_____
_____
_____
_____
_____

20 _____ *

_____
_____
_____
_____
_____
_____
_____

20 _____ *

_____
_____
_____
_____
_____
_____
_____

MAY 5

Now faith is the substance of things hoped for, the evidence of things not seen. * So Jesus came again to Cana of Galilee where He had made the water wine. And there was a certain nobleman whose son was sick at Capernaum. When he heard that Jesus had come out of Judea into Galilee, he went to Him and implored Him to come down and heal his son, for he was at the point of death. Then Jesus said to him, "Unless you people see signs and wonders, you will by no means believe." The nobleman said to Him, "Sir, come down before my child dies!" Jesus said to him, "Go your way; your son lives." So the man believed the word that Jesus spoke to him, and he went his way. And as he was now going down, his servants met him and told him, saying, "Your son lives!" * But as they sailed He fell asleep. And a windstorm came down on the lake, and they were filling with water, and were in jeopardy. And they came to Him and awoke Him, saying, "Master, Master, we are perishing!" Then He arose and rebuked the wind and the raging of the water. And they ceased, and there was a calm. But He said to them, "Where is your faith?" And they were afraid, and marveled, saying to one another, "Who can this be? For He commands even the winds and water, and they obey Him!" * And when they heard that He was alive and had been seen by her, they did not believe. After that, He appeared in another form to two of them as they walked and went into the country. And they went and told it to the rest, but they did not believe them either. Later He appeared to the eleven as they sat at the table; and he rebuked their unbelief and hardness of heart, because they did not believe those who had seen Him after He had risen. * Jesus said to him, "Thomas, because you have seen Me, you have believed. Blessed are those who have not seen and yet have believed." * But without faith it is impossible to please Him, for he who comes to God must believe that He is, and that He is a rewarder of those who diligently seek Him. * Grace be with you all. Amen.

Hebrews 11:1 NKJV * John 4:46-51 NKJV * Luke 8:23-25 NKJV * Mark 16:11-14 NKJV * John 20:29 NKJV * Hebrews 11:6 NKJV * Hebrews 13:25 NKJV

MAY

5 . . . .

Through the eyes of faith, you see what others are blind to.

20_____ *

_____
_____
_____
_____
_____
_____
_____

20_____ *

_____
_____
_____
_____
_____
_____
_____

20_____ *

_____
_____
_____
_____
_____
_____
_____

MAY 6

Now this is the testimony of John, when the Jews sent priests and Levites from Jerusalem to ask him, "Who are you?" He confessed, and did not deny, but confessed, "I am not the Christ." * He said: "I am the voice of one crying in the wilderness: 'Make straight the way of the LORD,' as the prophet Isaiah said." * John answered and said, "A man can receive nothing unless it has been given to him from heaven. You yourselves bear me witness, that I said, 'I am not the Christ,' but, 'I have been sent before Him.' He who has the bride is the bridegroom; but the friend of the bridegroom, who stands and hears him, rejoices greatly because of the bridegroom's voice. Therefore this joy of mine is fulfilled. He must increase, but I must decrease." * Jesus answered and said to them, "Go and tell John the things you have seen and heard: that the blind see, the lame walk, the lepers are cleansed, the deaf hear, the dead are raised, the poor have the gospel preached to them. And blessed is he who is not offended because of Me." When the messengers of John had departed, He began to speak to the multitudes concerning John: "What did you go out into the wilderness to see? A reed shaken by the wind? But what did you go out to see? A man clothed in soft garments? Indeed those who are gorgeously appareled and live in luxury are in kings' courts. But what did you go out to see? A prophet? Yes, I say to you, and more than a prophet. This is *he* of whom it is written: 'Behold, I send My messenger before Your face, who will prepare Your way before You.' For I say to you, among those born of women there is not a greater prophet than John the Baptist; but he who is least in the kingdom of God is greater than he." * Amen and Amen.

John 1:19-20 NKJV * John 1:23 NKJV * John 3:27-30 NKJV * Luke 7:22-28 NKJV * Psalm 72:19b NKJV

MAY

6 ·

Jesus affirms His faithful servants.

20 _____ *

---

20 _____ *

---

20 _____ *

MAY 7

The fear of the Lord is the beginning of wisdom, and the knowledge of the Holy One is understanding. * Remind everyone of these things, and command them in God's name to stop fighting over words. Such arguments are useless, and they can ruin those who hear them. Work hard so God can approve you. Be a good worker, one who does not need to be ashamed and who correctly explains the word of truth. * It is God's will that your good lives should silence those who make foolish accusations against you. * Wisdom is justified by all her children. * Thus also faith by itself, if it does not have works is dead. * Reverence for the LORD is the foundation of true wisdom. The rewards of wisdom come to all who obey him. Praise his name forever! * Amen and amen!

Proverbs 9:10 NKJV * 2 Timothy 2:14-15 NLT * 1 Peter 2:15 NLT * Luke 7:35 NKJV * James 2:17 NKJV * Psalm 111:10 NLT * Psalm 72:19b NLT

MAY

7 . . . .

Knowledge of God's truth needs active obedience.

20 _____ *

_____
_____
_____
_____
_____
_____
_____

20 _____ *

_____
_____
_____
_____
_____
_____
_____

20 _____ *

_____
_____
_____
_____
_____
_____
_____

MAY 8

For see, today I have made you immune to their attacks. You are strong like a fortified city that cannot be captured, like an iron pillar or a bronze wall. None of the kings, officials, priests, or people of Judah will be able to stand against you. They will try, but they will fail. For I am with you, and I will take care of you. I, the LORD, have spoken! * Teach these new disciples to obey all the commands I have given you. And be sure of this: I am with you always, even to the end of the age. * Who dares accuse us whom God has chosen for his own? Will God? No! He is the one who has given us right standing with himself. Who then will condemn us? Will Christ Jesus? No, for he is the one who died for us and was raised to life for us and is sitting at the place of highest honor next to God, pleading for us. Can anything separate us from Christ's love? Does it mean he no longer loves us if we have trouble or calamity, or are persecuted, or are hungry or cold or in danger or threatened with death? Even the Scriptures say, "For your sake we are killed every day; we are being slaughtered like sheep." No, despite all these things, overwhelming victory is ours through Christ, who loved us. * To God, who alone is wise, be the glory forever through Jesus Christ. Amen.

Jeremiah 1:18-19 NLT * Matthew 28:20 NLT * Romans 8:33-37 NLT * Romans 16:27 NLT

MAY

8 . . . .

Overwhelming victory is ours through Christ, who loves us.

20 _____ *

_____
_____
_____
_____
_____
_____
_____

20 _____ *

_____
_____
_____
_____
_____
_____
_____

20 _____ *

_____
_____
_____
_____
_____
_____
_____

MAY 9

Now, dear brothers and sisters, I appeal to you by the authority of the Lord Jesus Christ to stop arguing among yourselves. Let there be real harmony so there won't be divisions in the church. I plead with you to be of one mind, united in thought and purpose. * Be humble and gentle. Be patient with each other, making allowance for each other's faults because of your love. Always keep yourselves united in the Holy Spirit, and bind yourselves together with peace. We are all one body, we have the same Spirit, and we have all been called to the same glorious future. * Is there any encouragement from belonging to Christ? Any comfort from his love? Any fellowship in the Spirit? Are your hearts tender and sympathetic? Then make me truly happy by agreeing wholeheartedly with each other, loving one another, and working together with one heart and purpose. Don't be selfish; don't live to make a good impression on others. Be humble, thinking of others as better than yourself. Don't think only about your own affairs, but be interested in others, too, and what they are doing. Your attitude should be the same that Christ Jesus had. * Now glory be to God our Father forever and ever. Amen.

1 Corinthians 1:10 NLT * Ephesians 4:2-4 NLT * Philippians 2:1-5 NLT * Philippians 4:20 NLT

MAY

9 . . . .

Is there any encouragement from belonging to Christ?

20 _____ *

_____

_____
_____
_____
_____
_____
_____

20 _____ *

_____
_____
_____
_____
_____
_____

20 _____ *

_____
_____
_____
_____
_____
_____

MAY 10

It is God who saved us and chose us to live a holy life. He did this not because we deserved it, but because that was his plan long before the world began—to show love and kindness to us through Christ Jesus. * For no one can ever be made right in God's sight by doing what his law commands. For the more we know God's law, the clearer it becomes that we aren't obeying it. * For when I tried to keep the law, I realized I could never earn God's approval. So I died to the law so that I might live for God. I have been crucified with Christ. I myself no longer live but Christ lives in me. So I live my life in this earthly body by trusting in the Son of God, who loved me and gave himself for me. I am not one of those who treats the grace of God as meaningless. For if we could be saved by keeping the law then there was no need for Christ to die. * We are made right in God's sight when we trust in Jesus Christ to take away our sins. And we all can be saved in this same way, no matter who we are or what we have done. For all have sinned; all fall short of God's glorious standard. Yet now God in his gracious kindness declares us not guilty. He has done this through Christ Jesus, who has freed us by taking away our sins. * For God made Christ, who never sinned, to be the offering for our sin, so that we could be made right with God through Christ. * May the grace of our Lord Jesus Christ, the love of God, and the fellowship of the Holy Spirit be with you all. Amen.

2 Timothy 1:9 NLT * Romans 3:20 NLT * Galatians 2:19-21 NLT * Romans 3:22-24 NLT * 2 Corinthians 5:21 NLT * 2 Corinthians 13:13 NLT

MAY

10 . . . .

How expensive is grace?

20 _____ *

_____
_____
_____
_____
_____
_____
_____

20 _____ *

_____
_____
_____
_____
_____
_____
_____

20 _____ *

_____
_____
_____
_____
_____
_____
_____

MAY 11

The first time I was brought before the judge, no one was with me. Everyone had abandoned me. I hope it will not be counted against them. But the Lord stood with me and gave me strength, that I might preach the Good News in all its fullness for all the Gentiles to hear. And he saved me from certain death. * I pray that from his glorious unlimited resources he will give you mighty inner strength through his Holy Spirit. * And may you have the power to understand, as all God's people should, how wide, how long, how high, and how deep his love really is. May you experience the love of Christ, though it is so great you will never fully understand it. Then you will be filled with the fullness of life and power that comes from God. * We also pray that you will be strengthened with his glorious power so that you will have all the patience and endurance you need. May you be filled with joy, always thanking the Father, who has enabled you to share the inheritance that belongs to God's holy people, who live in the light. For he has rescued us from the one who rules in the kingdom of darkness, and he has brought us into the Kingdom of his dear Son. * Yes, and the Lord will deliver me from every evil attack and will bring me safely to his heavenly Kingdom. To God be the glory forever and ever. Amen.

2 Timothy 2:16-17 NLT * Ephesians 3:16 NLT * Ephesians 3:18-19 NLT * Colossians 1:11-13 NLT * 2 Timothy 2:18 NLT

MAY

11 . . . .

The Lord will stand with you and give you strength.

20 _____ *

_____
_____
_____
_____
_____
_____
_____

20 _____ *

_____
_____
_____
_____
_____
_____
_____

20 _____ *

_____
_____
_____
_____
_____
_____
_____

MAY 12

God has purchased our freedom with his blood and has forgiven all our sins. * So if the Son sets you free, you will indeed be free. * And you will know the truth, and the truth will set you free. * This truth gives them the confidence of eternal life, which God promised them before the world began—and he cannot lie. * But people who aren't Christians can't understand these truths of God's Spirit. It all sounds foolish to them because only those who have the Spirit can understand what the Spirit means. * So now there is no condemnation for those who belong to Christ. For the power of the life-giving Spirit has freed you through Christ Jesus from the power of sin that leads to death. * So Christ has really set us free. Now make sure that you stay free, and don't get tied up again in slavery to the law. * My dear brothers and sisters, may the grace of our Lord Jesus Christ be with you all. Amen.

Colossians 1:14 NLT * John 8: 36 NLT * John 8:32 NLT * Titus 1:2 NLT * 1 Corinthians 2:14 NLT * Romans 8:1-2 NLT * Galatians 5:1 NLT * Galatians 6:18 NLT

MAY

12 . . . .

The truth sets you free.

20 _____ *

_____
_____
_____
_____
_____
_____
_____

20 _____ *

_____
_____
_____
_____
_____
_____
_____

20 _____ *

_____
_____
_____
_____
_____
_____
_____

MAY 13

And suddenly a voice came from heaven, saying, "This is My beloved Son, in whom I am well pleased." * For the Father loves the Son, and shows Him all things that He Himself does; and He will show Him greater works than these, that you may marvel. For as the Father raises the dead and gives life to them, even so the Son gives life to whom He will. For the Father judges no one, but has committed all judgment to the Son, that all should honor the Son just as they honor the Father. He who does not honor the Son does not honor the Father who sent Him. * Jesus said to her, "I am the resurrection and the life. He who believes in Me, though he may die, he shall live." * If anyone serves Me, let him follow Me; and where I am, there My servant will be also. If anyone serves Me, him My Father will honor. * Jesus spoke these words, lifted up His eyes to heaven, and said: "Father, the hour has come. Glorify Your Son, that Your Son also may glorify You, as You have given Him authority over all flesh, that He should give eternal life to as many as You have given Him. And this is eternal life, that they may know You, the only true God, and Jesus Christ whom You have sent. I have glorified You on the earth. I have finished the work which You have given Me to do. * Amen and Amen.

Matthew 3:17 NKJV * John 5:20-23 NKJV * John 11:25 NKJV * John 12:26 NKJV * John 17:1-4 NKJV * Psalm 72:19b NKJV

MAY

13 . . . .

He who honors the Son, honors the Father.

20 _____ *

_____
_____
_____
_____
_____
_____
_____

20 _____ *

_____
_____
_____
_____
_____
_____
_____

20 _____ *

_____
_____
_____
_____
_____
_____
_____

MAY 14

Let not your hearts be troubled. Believe in God; believe also in me. *
Peace I leave with you; my peace I give to you. Not as the world gives do
I give to you. Let not your hearts be troubled, neither let them be afraid.
* Therefore I tell you, do not be anxious about your life, what you will eat
or what you will drink, nor about your body, what you will put on. Is not
life more than food, and the body more than clothing? * I tell you, my
friends, do not fear those who kill the body, and after that have nothing
more that they can do. But I will warn you whom to fear: fear him who,
after he has killed, has authority to cast into hell. Yes, I tell you, fear him!
Are not five sparrows sold for two pennies? And not one of them is forgotten before God. Why, even the hairs of your head are all numbered.
Fear not; you are of more value than many sparrows. * And when they
bring you before the synagogues and the rulers and the authorities, do
not be anxious about how you should defend yourself or what you should
say, for the Holy Spirit will teach you in that very hour what you ought to
say. * Fear not, for I am with you; be not dismayed, for I am your God; I
will strengthen you, I will help you, I will uphold you with my righteous
right hand. * Amen and Amen!

John 14:1 ESV * John 14:27 ESV * Matthew 6:25 ESV * Luke 12:4-7
ESV * Luke 12:11-12 ESV * Isaiah 41:10 ESV * Psalm 72:19b ESV

MAY

14 ....

How have you experienced Christ's peace amidst turmoil?

20 _____ *

---

20 _____ *

---

20 _____ *

MAY 15

Surely God is good to Israel, to those who are pure in heart! But as for me, my feet came close to stumbling, my steps had almost slipped. * Establish my footsteps in Your word, and do not let any iniquity have dominion over me. * If we say that we have no sin, we are deceiving ourselves and the truth is not in us. If we confess our sins, He is faithful and righteous to forgive us our sins and to cleanse us from all unrighteousness. If we say that we have not sinned, we make Him a liar and His word is not in us. * Therefore, laying aside falsehood, speak truth each one of you with his neighbor, for we are members of one another. Be angry, and yet do not sin; do not let the sun go down on your anger, and do not give the devil an opportunity. * Therefore if you are presenting your offering at the altar, and there remember that your brother has something against you, leave your offering there before the altar and go; first be reconciled to your brother, and then come and present your offering. * Blessed are the pure in heart, for they shall see God. * Blessed are the peacemakers, for they shall be called sons of God. * And lo, I am with you always, even to the end of the age. Amen.

Psalm 73:1-2 NASB * Psalm 119:133 NASB * 1 John 1:8-10 NASB * Ephesians 4:25-27 NASB * Matthew 5:23-24 NASB * Matthew 5:8 NASB * Matthew 5:9 NASB * Matthew 28:20b NKJV

MAY

15 . . . .

God is good to those who are pure in heart.

20 ____ *

_____
_____
_____
_____
_____
_____
_____

20 ____ *

_____
_____
_____
_____
_____
_____
_____

20 ____ *

_____
_____
_____
_____
_____
_____
_____

MAY 16

When I thought how to understand this, it was too painful for me—until I went into the sanctuary of God; then I understood their end. * O house of Jacob, come and let us walk in the light of the LORD. * For you were once in darkness, but now you are light in the Lord. Walk as children of light (for the fruit of the Spirit is in all goodness, righteousness, and truth), finding out what is acceptable to the Lord. * Therefore be imitators of God as dear children. And walk in love, as Christ also has loved us and given Himself for us, an offering and a sacrifice to God for a sweet-smelling aroma. * As you therefore have received Christ Jesus the Lord, so walk in Him, rooted and built up in Him and established in the faith as you have been taught, abounding in it with thanksgiving. * And though the Lord gives you the bread of adversity and the water of affliction, yet your teachers will not be moved into a corner anymore, but your eyes shall see your teachers. Your ears shall hear a word behind you, saying, "This is the way, walk in it," whenever you turn to the right hand or whenever you turn to the left. * To God, alone wise, be glory through Jesus Christ forever. Amen.

Psalm 73:16-17 NKJV * Isaiah 2:5 NKJV * Ephesians 5:8-10 NKJV * Ephesians 5:1-2 NKJV * Colossians 2:6 NKJV * Isaiah 30:20-21 NKJV * Romans 16:27 NKJV

MAY

16 . . . .

Bring every issue into the light of the Lord.

20 _____ *

_____
_____
_____
_____
_____
_____
_____

20 _____ *

_____
_____
_____
_____
_____
_____
_____

20 _____ *

_____
_____
_____
_____
_____
_____
_____

MAY 17

Redeem me from man's oppression, that I may keep your precepts. * I hate and abhor lying, but I love Your law. * Moreover the light of the moon will be as the light of the sun, and the light of the sun will be sevenfold, as the light of seven days, in the day that the LORD binds up the bruise of His people and heals the stroke of their wound. * The sun shall no longer be your light by day, nor for brightness shall the moon give light to you; but the LORD will be to you an everlasting light, and your God your glory. Your sun shall no longer go down, nor shall your moon withdraw itself; for the LORD will be your everlasting light, and the days of your mourning shall be ended. * Instead of your shame you shall have double honor, and instead of confusion they shall rejoice in their portion. Therefore in their land they shall possess double; everlasting joy shall be theirs. For I, the LORD love justice; I hate robbery for burnt offering; I will direct their work in truth, and will make with them an everlasting covenant. * And I will give you shepherds according to My heart, who will feed you with knowledge and understanding. * Amen and Amen.

Psalm 119:134 ESV * Psalm 119:163 NKJV * Isaiah 30:26 NKJV * Isaiah 60:19-20 NKJV * Isaiah 61:7-8 NKJV * Jeremiah 3:15 NKJV * Psalm 72:19b NKJV

MAY

17 . . . .

What is God's promise to you?

20 _____ *

_____
_____
_____
_____
_____
_____
_____

20 _____ *

_____
_____
_____
_____
_____
_____
_____

20 _____ *

_____
_____
_____
_____
_____
_____
_____

MAY 18

If you have run with footmen, and they have wearied you, then how can you contend with horses? And if in the land of peace, in which you trusted, they wearied you, then how will you do in the floodplain of the Jordan? * Then Joshua told the people, "Purify yourselves, for tomorrow the LORD will do great wonders among you." * "And it shall come to pass, as soon as the soles of the feet of the priests who bear the ark of the LORD, the Lord of all the earth, shall rest in the waters of the Jordan, that the waters of the Jordan shall be cut off, the waters that come down from upstream, and they shall stand as a heap." So it was, when the people set out from their camp to cross over the Jordan, with the priests bearing the ark of the covenant before the people, and as those who bore the ark came to the Jordan, and the feet of the priests who bore the ark dipped in the edge of the water (for the Jordan overflows all its banks during the whole time of harvest), that the waters which came down from upstream stood still. * Then the priests who bore the ark of the covenant of the LORD stood firm on dry ground in the midst of the Jordan; and all Israel crossed over on dry ground, until all the people had crossed completely over the Jordan. * For with God nothing will be impossible. * Now may the God of peace who brought up our Lord Jesus from the dead, that great Shepherd of the sheep, through the blood of the everlasting covenant, make you complete in every good work to do His will, working in you what is well pleasing in His sight, through Jesus Christ, to whom be glory forever and ever. Amen.

Jeremiah 12:5 NKJV * Joshua 3:5 NLT * Joshua 3:13-16a NKJV * Joshua 3:17 NKJV * Luke 1:37 NKJV * Hebrews 13:20-21 NKJV

MAY

18 . . . .

Do you hear God saying to you today, "Purify yourselves"?

20 _____ *

_____
_____
_____
_____
_____
_____
_____

20 _____ *

_____
_____
_____
_____
_____
_____
_____

20 _____ *

_____
_____
_____
_____
_____
_____
_____

MAY 19

Therefore, since we are receiving a kingdom which cannot be shaken, let us have grace, by which we may serve God acceptably with reverence and godly fear. * By faith Noah, being divinely warned of things not yet seen, moved with godly fear, prepared an ark for the saving of his household, by which he condemned the world and became heir of the righteousness which is according to faith. * So also Christ did not glorify Himself to become High Priest, but it was He who said to Him: "You are My Son, today I have begotten You." * Who, in the days of His flesh, when He had offered up prayers and supplications, with vehement cries and tears to Him who was able to save Him from death, and was heard because of His godly fear, though He was a Son, yet He learned obedience by the things which He suffered. And having been perfected, He became the author of eternal salvation to all who obey Him. * For we do not have a High Priest who cannot sympathize with our weaknesses, but was in all points tempted as we are, yet without sin. Let us therefore come boldly to the throne of grace, that we may obtain mercy and find grace to help in time of need. * Grace be with you all. Amen.

Hebrews 12:28 NKJV * Hebrews 11:7 NKJV * Hebrews 5:5 NKJV * Hebrews 5:7-9 NKJV * Hebrews 4:15-16 NKJV * Hebrews 13:25 NKJV

MAY

19 . . . .

Jesus is your best sympathizer. Go to Him.

20 _____ *

_____
_____
_____
_____
_____
_____
_____

20 _____ *

_____
_____
_____
_____
_____
_____
_____

20 _____ *

_____
_____
_____
_____
_____
_____
_____

MAY 20

Therefore by Him let us continually offer the sacrifice of praise to God, that is, the fruit of our lips, giving thanks to His name. But do not forget to do good and to share, for with such sacrifices God is well pleased. * Take words with you, and return to the LORD. Say to Him, "Take away all iniquity; receive us graciously, for we will offer the sacrifices of our lips." * Giving thanks always for all things to God the Father in the name of our Lord Jesus Christ. * I will bless the LORD at all times; His praise shall continually be in my mouth. My soul shall make its boast in the LORD; the humble shall hear of it and be glad. Oh, magnify the LORD with me, and let us exalt His name together. * Trust in the LORD, and do good; dwell in the land, and feed on His faithfulness. * But as for you, brethren, do not grow weary in doing good. * For God is not unjust to forget your work and labor of love which you have shown toward His name, in that you have ministered to the saints, and do minister. * The grace of our Lord Jesus Christ be with you all. Amen.

Hebrews 13:15-16 NKJV * Hosea 14:2 NKJV * Ephesians 5:20 NKJV * Psalm 34:1-3 NKJV * Psalm 37:3 NKJV * 2 Thessalonians 3:13 NKJV * Hebrews 6:10 NKJV * Philippians 4:23 NKJV

MAY

20 ....

Feed on God's faithfulness.

20 _____ *

_____
_____
_____
_____
_____
_____
_____

20 _____ *

_____
_____
_____
_____
_____
_____
_____

20 _____ *

_____
_____
_____
_____
_____
_____
_____

MAY 21

That night the LORD appeared to Solomon in a dream, and God said, "What do you want? Ask, and I will give it to you!" * "Give me an understanding mind so that I can govern your people well and know the difference between right and wrong. For who by himself is able to govern this great nation of yours?" The Lord was pleased with Solomon's reply and was glad that he had asked for wisdom. So God replied, "Because you have asked for wisdom in governing my people and have not asked for a long life or riches for yourself or the death of your enemies—I will give you what you asked for! I will give you a wise and understanding mind such as no one else has ever had or ever will have! And I will also give you what you did not ask for—riches and honor! No other king in all the world will be compared to you for the rest of your life! * As they approached Jericho, a blind beggar was sitting beside the road. * So he began shouting, "Jesus, Son of David, have mercy on me!" The crowds ahead of Jesus tried to hush the man, but he only shouted louder, "Son of David, have mercy on me!" When Jesus heard him, he stopped and ordered that the man be brought to him. Then Jesus asked the man, "What do you want me to do for you?" "Lord," he pleaded, "I want to see!" And Jesus said, "All right, you can see! Your faith has healed you." * Amen and Amen.

1 Kings 3:5 NLT * 1 Kings 3:9-13 NLT * Luke 18:35 NLT * Luke 18:38-42 NLT * Psalm 72:19b NLT

MAY

21 . . . .

What do you want?

20 _____ *

_____
_____
_____
_____
_____
_____
_____

20 _____ *

_____
_____
_____
_____
_____
_____
_____

20 _____ *

_____
_____
_____
_____
_____
_____
_____

MAY 22

From there Isaac moved to Beersheba, where the LORD appeared to him on the night of his arrival. "I am the God of your father, Abraham," he said. "Do not be afraid, for I am with you and will bless you. I will give you many descendants, and they will become a great nation. I will do this because of my promise to Abraham, my servant." Then Isaac built an altar there and worshiped the LORD. He set up his camp at that place, and his servants dug a well. * At sundown he arrived at a good place to set up camp and stopped there for the night. Jacob found a stone for a pillow and lay down to sleep. As he slept, he dreamed of a stairway that reached from earth to heaven. And he saw the angels of God going up and down on it. At the top of the stairway stood the LORD, and he said, "I am the LORD, the God of your grandfather Abraham and the God of your father, Isaac. The ground you are lying on belongs to you. I will give it to you and your descendants." * "What's more, I will be with you, and I will protect you wherever you go. I will someday bring you safely back to this land. I will be with you constantly until I have finished giving you everything I have promised." Then Jacob woke up and said, "Surely the LORD is in this place, and I wasn't even aware of it." * The next morning he got up very early. He took the stone he had used as a pillow and set it upright as a memorial pillar. Then he poured olive oil over it. He named the place Bethel—"house of God"—though the name of the nearby village was Luz. * "This memorial pillar will become a place for worshipping God, and I will give God a tenth of everything he gives me." * Amen and Amen.

Genesis 26:23-25 NLT * Genesis 28:11-14 NLT * Genesis 28:15-16 NLT * Genesis 28:18-19 NLT * Genesis 28:22 NLT * Psalm 72:19b NLT

MAY

22 . . . .

What memorial do you need as a reminder of God's promise?

20 _____ *

_____

_____

_____

_____

_____

_____

_____

20 _____ *

_____

_____

_____

_____

_____

_____

_____

20 _____ *

_____

_____

_____

_____

_____

_____

_____

MAY 23

He felt great pity for the crowds that came, because their problems were so great and they didn't know where to go for help. They were like sheep without a shepherd. * For a shepherd enters through the gate. The gate-keeper opens the gate for him, and the sheep hear his voice and come to him. He calls his own sheep by name and leads them out. After he has gathered his own flock, he walks ahead of them, and they follow him because they recognize his voice. They won't follow a stranger; they will run from him because they don't recognize his voice. * However, those the Father has given me will come to me, and I will never reject them. * He said to his disciples, "The harvest is so great, but the workers are so few. So pray to the Lord who is in charge of the harvest; ask him to send out more workers for his fields." * Amen and Amen.

Matthew 9:36 NLT * John 10:2-5 NLT * John 6:37 NLT * Matthew 9:37-38 NLT * Psalm 72:19b NLT

MAY

23 . . . .

Sheep know their shepherd's voice.

20 _____ *

---

20 _____ *

---

20 _____ *

MAY 24

God is not a man, that he should lie. He is not a human, that he should change his mind. Has he ever spoken and failed to act? Has he ever promised and not carried it through? * God is faithful, by whom you were called into the fellowship of His Son, Jesus Christ our Lord. * If we are faithless, He remains faithful; He cannot deny Himself. * Let us hold fast the confession of our hope without wavering, for He who promised is faithful. * No temptation has overtaken you except such as is common to man; but God is faithful, who will not allow you to be tempted beyond what you are able, but with the temptation will also make the way of escape, that you may be able to bear it. * To God, alone wise, be glory through Jesus Christ forever. Amen.

Numbers 23:19 NLT * 1 Corinthians 1:9 NKJV * 2 Timothy 2:13 NKJV * Hebrews 10:23 NKJV * 1 Corinthians 10:13 NKJV * Romans 16:27 NKJV

MAY

24 . . . .

He who promised is faithful.

20 ____ *

_____

_____

_____

_____

_____

_____

_____

20 ____ *

_____

_____

_____

_____

_____

_____

_____

20 ____ *

_____

_____

_____

_____

_____

_____

_____

MAY 25

Love never gives up, never loses faith, is always hopeful, and endures through every circumstance. * Many waters cannot quench love; neither can rivers drown it. * Love is patient and kind. Love is not jealous or boastful or proud or rude. * I want you to promise, O women of Jerusalem, not to awaken love until the time is right. * For love is as strong as death, and its jealousy is as enduring as the grave. Love flashes like fire, the brightest kind of flame. * Love does not demand its own way. Love is not irritable, and it keeps no record of when it has been wronged. It is never glad about injustice but rejoices whenever the truth wins out. * One night as I was sleeping my heart awakened in a dream. I heard the voice of my lover. He was knocking at my bedroom door. "Open to me, my darling, my treasure, my lovely dove," he said, "for I have been out in the night. My head is soaked with dew, my hair with the wetness of the night." But I said, "I have taken off my robe. Should I get dressed again? I have washed my feet. Should I get them soiled?" * My lover tried to unlatch the door, and my heart thrilled within me. I jumped up to open it. * I opened to my lover, but he was gone. I yearned for even his voice! I searched for him, but I couldn't find him anywhere. I called to him, but there was no reply. * Make this promise to me, O women of Jerusalem! If you find my beloved one, tell him I am sick with love. * You must make allowance for each other's faults and forgive the person who offends you. Remember, the Lord forgave you, so you must forgive others. * Let us continue to love one another, for love comes from God. Anyone who loves is born of God and knows God. * Love is what binds us all together in perfect harmony. * Amen and Amen.

1 Corinthians 13:7 NLT * Song of Solomon 8:7 NLT * 1 Corinthians 13:4-5a NLT * Song of Solomon 8:4 NLT * Song of Solomon 8:6b NLT * 1 Corinthians 13:5-6 NLT * Song of Solomon 5:2-3 NLT * Song of Solomon 5:4-5a NLT * Song of Solomon 5:6 NLT * Song of Solomon 5:8 NLT * Colossians 3:13 NLT * 1 John 4:7 NLT * Colossians 3:14b NLT * Psalm 72:19b NLT

MAY

25 ·

Love never gives up.

20 ____ *

_____
_____
_____
_____
_____
_____

20 ____ *

_____
_____
_____
_____
_____
_____

20 ____ *

_____
_____
_____
_____
_____
_____

MAY 26

"Therefore, behold, I will allure her, will bring her into the wilderness, and speak comfort to her. I will give her her vineyards from there, and the Valley of Achor as a door of hope; she shall sing there, as in the days of her youth, as in the day when she came up from the land of Egypt. And it shall be, in that day," says the LORD, "That you will call me 'My Husband,' And no longer call Me 'My Master.'" * "I will betroth you to Me forever; yes, I will betroth you to Me in righteousness and justice, in lovingkindness and mercy; I will betroth you to Me in faithfulness, and you shall know the LORD." * Sow for yourselves righteousness; reap in mercy; break up your fallow ground, for it is time to seek the LORD, till He comes and rains righteousness on you. * Yet I am the LORD your God ever since the land of Egypt, and you shall know no God but Me; for there is no savior besides Me. I knew you in the wilderness, in the land of great drought. When they had pasture, they were filled; they were filled and their heart was exalted; therefore they forgot Me. * O Israel, return to the LORD your God, for you have stumbled because of your iniquity; take words with you, and return to the LORD. Say to Him, "Take away all iniquity; receive us graciously, for we will offer the sacrifices of our lips." * Who is wise? Let him understand these things. Who is prudent? Let him know them. For the ways of the LORD are right; the righteous walk in them, but transgressors stumble in them. * Amen and Amen.

Hosea 2:14-16 NKJV * Hosea 2:19-20 NKJV * Hosea 10:12 NKJV * Hosea 13:4-6 NKJV * Hosea 14:1-2 NKJV * Hosea 14:9 NKJV * Psalm 72:19b NKJV

MAY

26 . . . .

God's heart is to heal you with righteousness.

20 _____ *

20 _____ *

20 _____ *

MAY 27

Seek the LORD while he may be found; call on him while he is near. Let the wicked forsake their ways and the unrighteous their thoughts. Let them turn to the LORD, and he will have mercy on them, and to our God, for he will freely pardon. * Finally, brothers and sisters, whatever is true, whatever is noble, whatever is right, whatever is pure, whatever is lovely, whatever is admirable—if anything is excellent or praiseworthy—think about such things. * Keep this Book of the Law always on your lips; meditate on it day and night, so that you may be careful to do everything written in it. Then you will be prosperous and successful. * I have hidden your word in my heart that I might not sin against you. * My love to all of you in Christ Jesus. Amen.

Isaiah 55:6-7 NIV * Philippians 4:8 NIV * Joshua 1:8 NIV * Psalm 119:11 NIV * 1 Corinthians 16:24 NIV

MAY

27 . . . .

Right thinking leads to right actions.

20 _____ *

_____
_____
_____
_____
_____
_____
_____

20 _____ *

_____
_____
_____
_____
_____
_____
_____

20 _____ *

_____
_____
_____
_____
_____
_____
_____

MAY 28

It shall come to pass that before they call, I will answer; and while they are still speaking, I will hear. * For I know the thoughts that I think toward you, says the LORD, thoughts of peace and not of evil, to give you a future and a hope. * I will go before you and make the crooked paths straight; I will break in pieces the gates of bronze and cut the bars of iron. I will give you the treasures of darkness and hidden riches of secret places, that you may know that I, the LORD, who call you by your name, am the God of Israel. * Can a woman forget her nursing child, and not have compassion on the son of her womb? Surely they may forget, yet I will not forget you. See, I have inscribed you on the palms of My hands. * So shall My word be that goes forth from My mouth; it shall not return to Me void, but it shall accomplish what I please, and it shall prosper in the thing for which I sent it. * Call to Me, and I will answer you, and show you great and mighty things, which you do not know. * Amen and Amen.

Isaiah 65:24 NKJV * Jeremiah 29:11 NKJV * Isaiah 45:2-3 NKJV * Isaiah 49:15-16a NKJV * Isaiah 55:11 NKJV * Jeremiah 33:3 NKJV * Psalm 72:19 b NKJV

MAY

28 . . . .

You can walk the path made straight by Christ.

20 _____ *

_____
_____
_____
_____
_____
_____
_____

20 _____ *

_____
_____
_____
_____
_____
_____
_____

20 _____ *

_____
_____
_____
_____
_____
_____
_____

MAY 29

For it seems to me unreasonable to send a prisoner and not specify the charges against him. * For you brethren, have been called to liberty; only do not use liberty as an opportunity for the flesh, but through love serve one another. * Now the Lord is the Spirit; and where the Spirit of the Lord is, there is liberty. But we all, with unveiled face, beholding as in a mirror the glory of the Lord, are being transformed into the same image from glory to glory, just as by the Spirit of the Lord. * See then that you walk circumspectly not as fools but as wise, redeeming the time, because the days are evil. Therefore do not be unwise, but understand what the will of the Lord is. And do not be drunk with wine, in which is dissipation; but be filled with the Spirit, speaking to one another in psalms and hymns and spiritual songs, singing and making melody in your heart to the Lord, giving thanks always for all things to God the Father in the name of our Lord Jesus Christ, submitting to one another in the fear of God. * Grace be with all those who love our Lord Jesus Christ in sincerity. Amen.

Acts 25:27 NKJV * Galatians 5:13 NKJV * 2 Corinthians 3:17-18 NKJV * Ephesians 5:15-21 NKJV * Ephesians 6:24 NKJV

MAY

29 . . . .

Are you serving others with the love of Jesus Christ?

20_____ *

20_____ *

20_____ *

MAY 30

Yet give attention to your servant's prayer and his plea for mercy, LORD my God. Hear the cry and the prayer that your servant is praying in your presence this day. May your eyes be open toward this temple night and day, this place of which you said, "My Name shall be there," so that you will hear the prayer your servant prays toward this place. Hear the supplication of your servant and of your people Israel when they pray toward this place. Hear from heaven, your dwelling place, and when you hear, forgive. * Those who sow with tears will reap with songs of joy. Those who go out weeping, carrying seed to sow, will return with songs of joy, carrying sheaves with them. * For the sake of my family and friends, I will say, "Peace be within you." For the sake of the house of the LORD our God, I will seek your prosperity. * Amen and Amen.

1 Kings 8:28-30 NIV * Psalm 126:5-6 NIV * Psalm 122:8-9 NIV * Psalm 72:19b NIV

MAY

30 ....

Hear in heaven; and when You hear, Lord, please forgive!

20 _____ *

_____

_____
_____
_____
_____
_____
_____

20 _____ *

_____
_____
_____
_____
_____
_____

20 _____ *

_____
_____
_____
_____
_____
_____

MAY 31

But a generous man devises generous things, and by generosity he shall stand. * There are many plans in a man's heart, nevertheless the LORD's counsel—that will stand. * When a man's ways please the LORD, he makes even his enemies to be at peace with him. * When the righteous rejoice, there is great glory; but when the wicked arise, men hide themselves. * Do you indeed speak righteousness, you silent ones? Do you judge uprightly, you sons of men? * Blessed is the nation whose God is the LORD, the people He has chosen as His own inheritance. * Now may the God of peace who brought up our Lord Jesus from the dead, that great Shepherd of the sheep, through the blood of the everlasting covenant, make you complete in every good work to do His will, working in you what is well pleasing in His sight, through Jesus Christ, to whom be glory forever and ever. Amen

Isaiah 32:8 NKJV * Proverbs 19:21 NKJV * Proverbs 16:7 NKJV * Proverbs 28:12 NKJV * Psalm 58:1 NKJV * Psalm 33:12 NKJV * Hebrews 13:20-21 NKJV

MAY

31 . . . .

Blessed is the nation whose God is the LORD.

20 _____ *

_____
_____
_____
_____
_____
_____
_____

20 _____ *

_____
_____
_____
_____
_____
_____
_____

20 _____ *

_____
_____
_____
_____
_____
_____
_____

JUNE

JUNE 1

A man's heart plans his way, but the LORD directs his steps. * A ruler who lacks understanding is a great oppressor, but he who hates covetousness will prolong his days. * I know that the LORD will maintain the cause of the afflicted, and justice for the poor. Surely the righteous shall give thanks to Your name; the upright shall dwell in Your presence. * I desire therefore that the men pray everywhere, lifting up holy hands, without wrath and doubting; in like manner also, that the women adorn themselves in modest apparel, with propriety and moderation, not with braided hair or gold or pearls or costly clothing, but, which is proper for women professing godliness, with good works. * And without controversy great is the mystery of godliness: God was manifested in the flesh, justified in the Spirit, seen by angels, preached among the Gentiles, believed on in the world, received up in glory. * Grace be with you all. Amen.

Proverbs 16:9 NKJV * Proverbs 18:16 NKJV * Psalm 140:12-13 NKJV * 1 Timothy 2:8-10 NKJV * 1 Timothy 3:16 NKJV * Hebrews 13:25 NKJV

JUNE

1

· ·

The Lord always directs our steps to righteousness.

20 _____ *

_____
_____
_____
_____
_____
_____
_____

20 _____ *

_____
_____
_____
_____
_____
_____
_____

20 _____ *

_____
_____
_____
_____
_____
_____
_____

JUNE 2

He who is of a proud heart stirs up strife, but he who trusts in the LORD will be prospered. * Trust in the Lord with all your heart and lean not on your own understanding; in all your ways acknowledge Him and He will direct your paths. * Thus says the LORD: "Let not the wise man glory in his wisdom, let not the mighty man glory in his might, nor let the rich man glory in his riches; but let him who glories glory in this, that he understands and knows Me, that I am the LORD, exercising lovingkindness, judgment, and righteousness in the earth. For in these I delight," says the LORD. * For everyone will be seasoned with fire, and every sacrifice will be seasoned with salt. Salt is good, but if the salt loses its flavor, how will you season it? Have salt in yourselves, and have peace with one another. * Amen and Amen.

Proverbs 28:25 NKJV * Proverbs 3:5-6 NKJV * Jeremiah 9:23-24 NKJV * Mark 9:49-50 NKJV

JUNE

2 . . . .

Does your knowledge of God determine your trust in Him?

20 _____ *

_____

_____

_____

_____

_____

_____

_____

20 _____ *

_____

_____

_____

_____

_____

_____

_____

20 _____ *

_____

_____

_____

_____

_____

_____

_____

JUNE 3

I said, "I beseech You, O LORD God of heaven, the great and awesome God, who preserves the covenant and lovingkindness for those who love Him and keep His commandments, let Your ear now be attentive and Your eyes open to hear the prayer of Your servant which I am praying before You now, day and night, on behalf of the sons of Israel Your servants, confessing the sins of the sons of Israel which we have sinned against You; I and my father's house have sinned. We have acted very corruptly against You and have not kept the commandments, nor the statutes, nor the ordinances which You commanded Your servant Moses. Remember the word which You commanded Your servant Moses, saying, 'If you are unfaithful I will scatter you among the peoples; but *if* you return to Me and keep My commandments and do them, though those of you who have been scattered were in the most remote part of the heavens, I will gather them from there and will bring them to the place where I have chosen to cause My name to dwell.' They are Your servants and Your people whom You redeemed by Your great power and by Your strong hand. * Pray for the peace of Jerusalem: "May they prosper who love you. May peace be within your walls, and prosperity within your palaces." * Brethren, my heart's desire and my prayer to God for them is for *their* salvation. * Amen, and Amen.

Nehemiah 1:5-10 NASB * Psalm 122:6-7 NASB * Romans 10:1 NASB * Psalm 72:19b NASB

JUNE

3 ....

Pray for the peace of Jerusalem.

20_____ *

_____

_____

_____

_____

_____

_____

20_____ *

_____

_____

_____

_____

_____

_____

20_____ *

_____

_____

_____

_____

_____

_____

JUNE 4

"For all those things My hand has made, and all those things exist," says the Lord, "But on this one will I look: on him who is poor and of a contrite spirit, and who trembles at My word." * The eyes of all look expectantly to You, and You give them their food in due season. You open Your hand and satisfy the desire of every living thing. * The LORD is near to all who call upon Him, to all who call upon Him in truth. * You are my hiding place and my shield; I hope in Your word. * Uphold me according to Your word, that I may live; and do not let me be ashamed of my hope. * Plead my cause and redeem me; revive me according to Your word. * Let my supplication come before You; deliver me according to Your word. My lips shall utter praise, for You teach me Your statutes. My tongue shall speak of Your word, for all Your commandments are righteousness. Let Your hand become my help, for I have chosen Your precepts. I long for Your salvation, O LORD, And Your law is my delight. * Amen and Amen.

Isaiah 66:2 NKJV * Psalm 145:15-16 NKJV * Psalm 145:18 NKJV * Psalm 119:114 NKJV * Psalm 119:116 NKJV * Psalm 119:154 NKJV * Psalm 119:170-174 NKJV * Psalm 72:19b NKJV

JUNE

4 . . . .

Do you tremble at God's word?

20 _____ *

_____
_____
_____
_____
_____
_____
_____

20 _____ *

_____
_____
_____
_____
_____
_____
_____

20 _____ *

_____
_____
_____
_____
_____
_____
_____

JUNE 5

Your word I have hidden in my heart, that I might not sin against You. * Your word is a lamp to my feet and a light to my path. * The entrance of Your word gives light; it gives understanding to the simple. * Direct my steps by Your word, and let no iniquity have dominion over me. * Your word is very pure; therefore Your servant loves it. * I rise before the dawning of the morning, and cry for help; I hope in Your word. * Plead my cause and redeem me; revive me according to Your word. * I see the treacherous, and am disgusted, because they do not keep Your word. * Princes persecute me without a cause, but my heart stands in awe of Your word. * I rejoice at Your word as one who finds great treasure. * Let my supplication come before You; deliver me according to Your word. * Sanctify them by Your truth. Your word is truth. * For I am not ashamed of the gospel of Christ, for it is the power of God to salvation for everyone who believes. * And how shall they preach unless they are sent? As it is written: "How beautiful are the feet of those who preach the gospel of peace, who bring glad tidings of good things!" * And He said to them, "Go into all the world and preach the gospel to every creature." * And they went out and preached everywhere, the Lord working with them and confirming the word through the accompanying signs. Amen.

Psalm 119:11 NKJV * Psalm 119:105 NKJV * Psalm 119:130 NKJV * Psalm 119:133 NKJV * Psalm 119:140 NKJV * Psalm 119:147 NKJV * Psalm 119:154 NKJV * Psalm 119:158 NKJV * Psalm 119:161 NKJV * Psalm 119:162 NKJV * Psalm 119:170 NKJV * John 17:17 NKJV * Romans 1:16 NKJV * Romans 10:15 NKJV * Mark 16:15 NKJV * Mark 16:20 NKJV

JUNE

5 . . . .

God's word is all-sufficient.

20 _____ *

_____

_____

_____

_____

_____

_____

20 _____ *

_____

_____

_____

_____

_____

_____

20 _____ *

_____

_____

_____

_____

_____

_____

JUNE 6

All the Father gives Me will come to Me, and the one who comes to Me I will by no means cast out. * My sheep hear My voice, and I know them, and they follow Me. And I give them eternal life, and they shall never perish; neither shall anyone snatch them out of My hand. * Let us draw near with a true heart in full assurance of faith, having our hearts sprinkled from an evil conscience and our bodies washed with pure water. Let us hold fast the confession of our hope without wavering, for He who promised is faithful. * For "whoever calls on the name of the LORD shall be saved." * Being confident of this very thing, that He who has begun a good work in you will complete it until the day of Jesus Christ. * And this is the testimony: that God has given us eternal life, and this life is in His Son. He who has the Son has life; he who does not have the Son of God does not have life. These things I have written to you who believe in the name of the Son of God, that you may know that you have eternal life, and that you may continue to believe in the name of the Son of God. * If we confess our sins, He is faithful and just to forgive us our sins and to cleanse us from all unrighteousness. * Little children, keep yourselves from idols. Amen.

John 6:37 NKJV * John 10:27-28 NKJV * Hebrews 10:22-23 NKJV * Romans 10:13 NKJV * Philippians 1:6 NKJV * 1 John 5:11-13 NKJV * 1 John 1:9 NKJV * 1 John 5:21 NKJV

JUNE

6 . . . .

True life is experienced in Jesus Christ.

20 _____ *

_____
_____
_____
_____
_____
_____

20 _____ *

_____
_____
_____
_____
_____
_____
_____

20 _____ *

_____
_____
_____
_____
_____
_____
_____

JUNE 7

And so, dear brothers and sisters, I plead with you to give your bodies to God. Let them be a living and holy sacrifice—the kind he will accept. When you think of what he has done for you, is this too much to ask? * And do not be conformed to this world, but be transformed by the renewing of your mind, that you may prove what is that good and acceptable and perfect will of God. * I command you to love each other in the same way that I love you. * It is love that really builds up the church. * For the body does not consist of one member but of many. * Your love for one another will prove to the world that you are my disciples. * Repent therefore and be converted, that your sins may be blotted out, so that times of refreshing may come from the presence of the Lord. * If we say that we have no sin, we deceive ourselves, and the truth is not in us. If we confess our sins, He is faithful and just to forgive us our sins and to cleanse us from all unrighteousness. * Because you have obeyed my command to persevere, I will protect you from the great time of testing that will come upon the whole world to test those who belong to this world. Look, I am coming quickly. Hold on to what you have, so that no one will take away your crown. All who are victorious will become pillars in the Temple of my God, and they will never have to leave it. And I will write my God's name on them, and they will be citizens in the city of my God— * "Surely I am coming quickly." Amen.

Romans 12:1 NLT * Romans 12:2 NKJV * John 15:12 NLT * 1 Corinthians 8:1b NLT * 1 Corinthians 12:14 ESV * John 13:35 NLT * Acts 3:19 NKJV * 1 John 1:8-9 NKJV * Revelation 3:10-12a NLT * Revelation 22:20b NKJV

JUNE

7 . . . .

**Do you need to renew your mind in how you
think of others?**

20 ____ *

---

20 ____ *

---

20 ____ *

JUNE 8

Therefore, knowing the fear of the Lord, we persuade others. But what we are is known to God, and I hope it is known also to your conscience. We are not commending ourselves to you again but giving you cause to boast about us, so that you may be able to answer those who boast about outward appearance and not about what is in the heart. * For our boast is this, the testimony of our conscience, that we behaved in the world with simplicity and godly sincerity, not by earthly wisdom but by the grace of God, and supremely so toward you. * Behold, now is the favorable time; behold, now is the day of salvation. We put no obstacle in anyone's way, so that no fault may be found with our ministry, but as servants of God we commend ourselves in every way: by great endurance, in afflictions, hardships, calamities, beatings, imprisonments, riots, labors, sleepless nights, hunger; by purity, knowledge, patience, kindness, the Holy Spirit, genuine love; by truthful speech, and the power of God; with the weapons of righteousness for the right hand and for the left; through honor and dishonor, through slander and praise. We are treated as imposters, and yet are true; as unknown, and yet well known; as dying, and behold, we live; as punished, and yet not killed; as sorrowful, yet always rejoicing; as poor, yet making many rich; as having nothing, yet possessing everything. * So the church throughout all Judea and Galilee and Samaria had peace and was being built up. And walking in the fear of the Lord and in the comfort of the Holy Spirit, it multiplied. * Amen and Amen!

2 Corinthians 5:11-12 ESV * 2 Corinthians 1:12 ESV * 2 Corinthians 6:2b-10 ESV * Acts 9:31 ESV * Psalm 72:19b ESV

JUNE

8 . . . .

Is your conscience clear?

20 _____ *

_____

_____
_____
_____
_____
_____
_____

20 _____ *

_____

_____
_____
_____
_____
_____
_____

20 _____ *

_____

_____
_____
_____
_____
_____
_____

JUNE 9

It is right for me to feel this way about you all, because I hold you in my heart, for you are all partakers with me of grace, both in my imprisonment and in the defense and confirmation of the gospel. * You yourselves are our letters of recommendation, written on our hearts, to be known and read by all. * I will most gladly spend and be spent for your souls. If I love you more, am I to be loved less? * We have spoken freely to you, Corinthians; our heart is wide open. * In return (I speak as to children) widen your hearts also. * Since you seek proof that Christ is speaking in me. He is not weak in dealing with you, but is powerful among you. For he was crucified in weakness, but lives by the power of God. For we also are weak in him, but in dealing with you we will live with him by the power of God. * For we are glad when we are weak and you are strong. Your restoration is what we pray for. * My love be with you all in Christ Jesus. Amen.

Philippians 1:7 ESV * 2 Corinthians 3:2 ESV * 2 Corinthians 12:15 ESV * 2 Corinthians 6:11 ESV * 2 Corinthians 6:13 ESV * 2 Corinthians 13:3-4 ESV * 2 Corinthians 13:9 ESV * 1 Corinthians 16:24 ESV

JUNE

9 . . . .

Will you pray for the restoration of believers?

20_____ *

_____

_____

_____

_____

_____

_____

20_____ *

_____

_____

_____

_____

_____

_____

20_____ *

_____

_____

_____

_____

_____

_____

JUNE 10

They shall be mine, says the LORD of hosts, in the day when I make up my treasured possession, and I will spare them as a man spares his son who serves him. * As a father shows compassion to his children, so the LORD shows compassion to those who fear him. * For as high as the heavens are above the earth, so great is his steadfast love toward those who fear him. * But the steadfast love of the LORD is from everlasting to everlasting on those who fear him, and his righteousness to children's children, to those who keep his covenant and remember to do his commandments. * Then once more you shall see the distinction between the righteous and the wicked, between one who serves God and one who does not serve him. * For behold, the day is coming, burning like an oven, when all the arrogant and all evildoers will be stubble. The day that is coming shall set them ablaze, says the LORD of hosts, so that it will leave them neither root nor branch. But for you who fear my name, the sun of righteousness shall rise with healing in its wings. You shall go out leaping like calves from the stall. And you shall tread down the wicked, for they will be ashes under the soles of your feet, on the day when I act, says the LORD of hosts. * Amen and Amen!

Malachi 3:17 ESV * Psalm 103:13 ESV * Psalm 103:11 ESV * Psalm 103:17-18 ESV * Malachi 3:18 ESV * Malachi 4:1-3 ESV * Psalm 72:19b ESV

JUNE

10 . . . .

You are God's treasured possession.

20 _____ *

_____

_____

_____

_____

_____

_____

_____

20 _____ *

_____

_____

_____

_____

_____

_____

_____

20 _____ *

_____

_____

_____

_____

_____

_____

_____

_____

JUNE 11

Then they cried out to the LORD in their trouble, and He saved them out of their distresses. He sent His word and healed them, and delivered them from their destructions. * The LORD is good, a stronghold in the day of trouble; and He knows those who trust in Him. * The voice of joy and the voice of gladness, the voice of the bridegroom and the voice of the bride, the voice of those who will say: "Praise the LORD of hosts, for the LORD is good, for His mercy endures forever." * Oh, give thanks to the LORD, for He is good! For His mercy endures forever. Let the redeemed of the LORD say so, whom He has redeemed from the hand of the enemy. * For He satisfies the longing soul, and fills the hungry soul with goodness. * Amen and Amen.

Psalm 107:19-20 NKJV * Nahum 1:7 NKJV * Jeremiah 33:11 NKJV * Psalm 107:1-2 NKJV * Psalm 107:9 NKJV * Psalm 72:19b NKJV

JUNE

11 . . . .

Let the redeemed, rejoice!

20 _____ *

_____
_____
_____
_____
_____
_____
_____

20 _____ *

_____
_____
_____
_____
_____
_____
_____

20 _____ *

_____
_____
_____
_____
_____
_____
_____

JUNE 12

Yea, though I walk through the valley of the shadow of death, I will fear no evil; for You are with me; Your rod and Your staff, they comfort me. * And the LORD, He is the One who goes before you. He will be with you, He will not leave you nor forsake you; do not fear nor be dismayed. * Then Job arose, tore his robe, and shaved his head; and fell to the ground and worshiped. And he said: "Naked I came from my mother's womb, and naked shall I return there. The LORD gave, and the LORD has taken away; blessed be the name of the LORD." In all this Job did not sin nor charge God with wrong. * Moreover Job continued his discourse, and said: "As God lives, who has taken away my justice, and the Almighty, who has made my soul bitter, as long as my breath is in me, and the breath of God in my nostrils, my lips will not speak wickedness, nor my tongue utter deceit. Far be it from me that I should say you are right; till I die I will not put away my integrity from me. My righteousness I hold fast, and will not let it go; my heart shall not reproach me as long as I live." * Yet the righteous will hold to his way, and he who has clean hands will be stronger and stronger. * Then Job answered the LORD and said: "I know that You can do everything, and that no purpose of Yours can be withheld from You." * "Listen, please, and let me speak; You said, 'I will question you, and you shall answer Me.' I have heard of You by the hearing of the ear, but now my eyes see You. Therefore I abhor myself, and repent in dust and ashes." And so it was, after the LORD had spoken these words to Job, that the LORD said to Eliphaz the Temanite, "My wrath is aroused against you and your two friends, for you have not spoken of Me what is right, as My servant Job has." * And the LORD restored Job's losses when he prayed for his friends. Indeed the LORD gave Job twice as much as he had before. * Grace be with you all. Amen.

Psalm 23:4 NKJV * Deuteronomy 31:8 NKJV * Job 1:20-22 NKJV * Job 27:1-6 NKJV * Job 17:9 NKJV * Job 42:1-2 NKJV * Job 42:4-7 NKJV * Job 42:10 NKJV * Hebrews 13:25 NKJV

JUNE

12 . . . .

When you look back on your steps in history, what do you see?

20_____ *

_____
_____
_____
_____
_____
_____
_____

20_____ *

_____
_____
_____
_____
_____
_____
_____

20_____ *

_____
_____
_____
_____
_____
_____
_____

JUNE 13

You prepare a table before me in the presence of my enemies; You anoint my head with oil; my cup runs over. * He brought me to the banqueting house, and his banner over me was love. * Because you have made the LORD, who is my refuge, even the Most High, your dwelling place, no evil shall befall you, nor shall any plague come near your dwelling; for He shall give His angels charge over you to keep you in all your ways. In their hands they shall bear you up, lest you dash your foot against a stone. * Let your garments always be white, and let your head lack no oil. * Behold, how good and how pleasant it is for brethren to dwell together in unity! It is like the precious oil upon the head, running down on the beard, the beard of Aaron, running down on the edge of his garments. * Amen and Amen.

Psalm 23:5 NKJV * Song of Solomon 2:4 NKJV * Psalm 91:9-12 NKJV * Ecclesiastes 9:8 NKJV * Psalm 133:1-2 NKJV * Psalm 72:19b NKJV

JUNE

13 . . . .

**Unity: when you look at a group of people,
you see one anointing.**

20 _____ *

_____
_____
_____
_____
_____
_____

20 _____ *

_____
_____
_____
_____
_____
_____

20 _____ *

_____
_____
_____
_____
_____
_____

JUNE 14

Surely goodness and mercy shall follow me all the days of my life; and I will dwell in the house of the LORD forever. * Blessed be the God and Father of our Lord Jesus Christ, who has blessed us with every spiritual blessing in the heavenly places in Christ, just as He chose us in Him before the foundation of the world, that we should be holy and without blame before Him in love, having predestined us to adoption as sons by Jesus Christ to Himself, according to the good pleasure of His will, to the praise of the glory of His grace, by which He made us accepted in the Beloved. In Him we have redemption through His blood, the forgiveness of sins, according to the riches of His grace which He made to abound toward us in all wisdom and prudence, having made known to us the mystery of His will, according to His good pleasure which He purposed in Himself. * Those who are planted in the house of the LORD shall flourish in the courts of our God. They shall still bear fruit in old age; they shall be fresh and flourishing, to declare that the LORD is upright; He is my rock, and there is no unrighteousness in Him. * Now to Him who is able to do exceedingly abundantly above all that we ask or think, according to the power that works in us, to Him be glory in the church by Christ Jesus to all generations, forever and ever. Amen.

Psalm 23:6 NKJV * Ephesians 1:3-9 NKJV * Psalm 92:13-15 NKJV * Ephesians 3:20-21 NKJV

JUNE

14 . . . .

One who flourishes has a close continual walk with God.

20 _____ *

_____
_____
_____
_____
_____
_____
_____

20 _____ *

_____
_____
_____
_____
_____
_____
_____

20 _____ *

_____
_____
_____
_____
_____
_____
_____

JUNE 15

The LORD is my shepherd, I lack nothing. * He tends his flock like a shepherd: he gathers the lambs in his arms and carries them close to his heart; he gently leads those that have young. * Therefore Jesus said again, "Very truly I tell you, I am the gate for the sheep." * I am the good shepherd. The good shepherd lays down his life for the sheep. The hired hand is not the shepherd and does not own the sheep. So when he sees the wolf coming, he abandons the sheep and runs away. Then the wolf attacks the flock and scatters it. The man runs away because he is a hired hand and cares nothing for the sheep. I am the good shepherd; I know my sheep and my sheep know me— * Then I will give you shepherds after my own heart, who will lead you with knowledge and understanding. * Be shepherds of God's flock that is under your care, watching over them—not because you must, but because you are willing, as God wants you to be; not pursuing dishonest gain, but eager to serve; not lording it over those entrusted to you, but being examples to the flock. And when the Chief Shepherd appears, you will receive the crown of glory that will never fade away. * Grace be with you all. * Amen and Amen.

Psalm 23:1 NIV * Isaiah 40:11 NIV * John 10:7 NIV * John 10:11-14 NIV * Jeremiah 3:15 NIV * 1 Peter 5:2-4 NIV * Hebrews 13:25 NIV * Psalm 41:13b NIV

JUNE

15 . . . .

**A hireling is there for the money;
a shepherd is there for the sheep.**

20 _____ *

_____
_____
_____
_____
_____
_____
_____

20 _____ *

_____
_____
_____
_____
_____
_____
_____

20 _____ *

_____
_____
_____
_____
_____
_____
_____

JUNE 16

He makes me to lie down in green pastures; He leads me beside the still waters. * Son of man, prophesy against the shepherds of Israel, prophesy and say to them, "Thus says the Lord God to the shepherds: 'Woe to the shepherds of Israel who feed themselves! Should not the shepherds feed the flocks? You eat the fat and clothe yourselves with the wool; you slaughter the fatlings, but you do not feed the flock. The weak you have not strengthened, nor have you healed those who were sick, nor bound up the broken, nor brought back what was driven away, nor sought what was lost; but with force and cruelty you have ruled them. So they were scattered because there was no shepherd; and they became food for all the beasts of the field when they were scattered. My sheep wandered through all the mountains, and on every high hill; yes, My flock was scattered over the whole face of the earth, and no one was seeking or searching for them.'" * Indeed I Myself will search for My sheep and seek them out. * "I will feed My flock, and I will make them lie down," says the Lord God. "I will seek what was lost and bring back what was driven away, bind up the broken and strengthen what was sick." * Come to Me, all you who labor and are heavy laden, and I will give you rest. Take My yoke upon you and learn from Me, for I am gentle and lowly in heart, and you will find rest for your souls. For My yoke is easy and My burden is light. * Amen and Amen.

Psalm 23:2 NKJV * Ezekiel 34:2-6 NKJV * Ezekiel 34:11b NKJV * Ezekiel 34:15-16a NKJV * Matthew 11:28-30 NKJV * Psalm 72:19b NKJV

JUNE

16 . . . .

Jehovah-Raah, your Shepherd, will make you rest.

20 _____ *

20 _____ *

20 _____ *

JUNE 17

He restores my soul. He leads me in paths of righteousness for his name's sake. * And those who go astray in spirit will come to understanding, and those who murmur will accept instruction. * I will sprinkle clean water on you, and you shall be clean from all your uncleannesses, and from all your idols I will cleanse you. And I will give you a new heart, and a new spirit I will put within you. And I will remove the heart of stone from your flesh and give you a heart of flesh. And I will put my Spirit within you, and cause you to walk in my statutes and be careful to obey my rules. * And though the Lord give you the bread of adversity and the water of affliction, yet your Teacher will not hide himself anymore, but your eyes shall see your Teacher. And your ears shall hear a word behind you, saying, "This is the way, walk in it," when you turn to the right or when you turn to the left. * I will restore to you the years that the swarming locust has eaten. * Bless the LORD, O my soul, and all that is within me, bless his holy name! Bless the LORD, O my soul, and forget not all his benefits, who forgives all your iniquity, who heals all your diseases, who redeems your life from the pit, who crowns you with steadfast love and mercy, who satisfies you with good so that your youth is renewed like the eagles. * For you are my rock and my fortress; and for your name's sake you lead me and guide me; you take me out of the net they have hidden for me, for you are my refuge. Into your hand I commit my spirit; you have redeemed me, O LORD, faithful God. * Amen and Amen!

Psalm 23:3 ESV * Isaiah 29:24 ESV * Ezekiel 36:25-27 ESV * Isaiah 30:20-21 ESV * Joel 2:25a ESV * Psalm 103:1-5 ESV * Psalm 31:3-5 ESV * Psalm 72:19b ESV

JUNE

17 . . . .

He restores my soul.

20 ____ *

_____

20 ____ *

_____

20 ____ *

_____

JUNE 18

What man of you, having a hundred sheep, if he loses one of them, does not leave the ninety-nine in the wilderness, and go after the one which is lost until he finds it? And when he has found it, he lays it on his shoulders, rejoicing. And when he comes home, he calls together his friends and neighbors, saying to them, "Rejoice with me, for I have found my sheep which was lost!" I say to you that likewise there will be more joy in heaven over one sinner who repents than over ninety-nine just persons who need no repentance. * Or what woman, having ten silver coins, if she loses one coin, does not light a lamp, sweep the house, and search carefully until she finds it? And when she has found it, she calls her friends and neighbors together, saying, "Rejoice with me, for I have found the piece which I lost!" Likewise, I say to you, there is joy in the presence of the angels of God over one sinner who repents. * Amen and Amen.

Luke 15:4-7 NKJV * Luke 15:8-10 NKJV * Psalm 72:19b NKJV

JUNE

18 ....

Do you chase the wandering?

20 _____ *

_____
_____
_____
_____
_____
_____
_____

20 _____ *

_____
_____
_____
_____
_____
_____
_____

20 _____ *

_____
_____
_____
_____
_____
_____
_____

JUNE 19

And the apostles said to the Lord, "Increase our faith." So the Lord said, "If you have faith as a mustard seed, you can say to this mulberry tree, 'Be pulled up by the roots and be planted in the sea,' and it would obey you." * Let no one despise your youth, but be an example to the believers in word, in conduct, in love, in spirit, in faith, in purity. * Walk in wisdom toward those who are outside, redeeming the time. Let your speech always be with grace, seasoned with salt, that you may know how you ought to answer each one. * And walk in love as Christ also has loved us and given Himself for us, an offering and a sacrifice to God for a sweet smelling aroma. * Love is patient and is kind. * It is never glad about injustice but rejoices whenever the truth wins out. * So you see, the Lord knows how to rescue godly people from their trials, even while punishing the wicked right up until the day of judgment. * The Lord isn't really being slow about his promise to return, as some people think. No, he is being patient for your sake. He does not want anyone to perish, so he is giving more time for everyone to repent. * And so, dear friends, while you are waiting for these things to happen, make every effort to live a pure and blameless life. And be at peace with God. * To Him be the glory both now and forever. Amen.

Luke 17:5-6 NKJV * 1 Timothy 4:12 NKJV * Colossians 4:5-6 NKJV * Ephesians 5:2 NKJV * 1 Corinthians 13:4a NLT * 1 Corinthians 13:6 NLT * 2 Peter 2:9 NLT * 2 Peter 3:9 NLT * 2 Peter 3:14 NLT * 2 Peter 3:18b NKJV

JUNE

19 . . . .

Are you at peace with God?

20 _____ *

_____

20 _____ *

_____

20 _____ *

_____

JUNE 20

Now godliness with contentment is great gain. * It is not that we think we can do anything of lasting value by ourselves. Our only power and success come from God. * Every good gift and every perfect gift is from above, and comes down from the Father of lights, with whom there is no variation or shadow of turning. * And God is able to make all grace abound toward you, that you, always having all sufficiency in all things, may have an abundance for every good work. * For God loves a cheerful giver. * As His divine power has given us all things that pertain to life and godliness, through the knowledge of Him who called us by glory and virtue by which we have been given to us exceedingly great and precious promises, that through these you may be partakers of the divine nature, having escaped the corruption that is in the world through lust. * But reject profane and old wives' fables, and exercise yourself toward godliness. For bodily exercise profits a little, but godliness is profitable for all things, having promise of the life that now is and of that which is to come. * The grace of our Lord Jesus Christ be with you all. Amen.

1 Timothy 6:6 NKJV * 2 Corinthians 3:5 NLT * James 1:17 NKJV * 2 Corinthians 9:8 NKJV * 2 Corinthians 9:7b NKJV * 2 Peter 1:3-4 NKJV * 1 Timothy 4:7-8 NKJV * Revelation 22:21 NKJV

JUNE

20 . . . .

May grace abound and your contentment grow.

20 _____ *

_____
_____
_____
_____
_____
_____
_____

20 _____ *

_____
_____
_____
_____
_____
_____
_____

20 _____ *

_____
_____
_____
_____
_____
_____
_____

JUNE 21

But you, O man of God, flee these things and pursue righteousness, godliness, faith, love, patience, gentleness. * Therefore I exhort first of all that supplications, prayers, intercessions, and giving of thanks be made for all men, for kings and all who are in authority, that we may lead a quiet and peaceable life in all godliness and reverence. For this is good and acceptable in the sight of God our Savior, who desires all men to be saved and to come to the knowledge of the truth. * Therefore, having been justified by faith, we have peace with God through our Lord Jesus Christ, through whom also we have access by faith into this grace in which we stand, and rejoice in hope of the glory of God. * Now hope does not disappoint, because the love of God has been poured out in our hearts by the Holy Spirit who was given to us. * My brethren, count it all joy when you fall into various trials, knowing that the testing of your faith produces patience. But let patience have its perfect work, that you may be perfect and complete, lacking nothing. * Rejoice in the Lord always. Again I will say, rejoice! Let your gentleness be known to all men. The Lord is at hand. * The grace of our Lord Jesus Christ be with you all. Amen.

1 Timothy 6:11 NKJV * 1 Timothy 2:1-4 NKJV * Romans 5:1-2 NKJV * Romans 5:5 NKJV * James 1:2-4 NKJV * Philippians 4:4-5 NKJV * Philippians 4:23 NKJV

JUNE

21 . . . .

Let your gentleness be known to all.

20 _____ *

_____
_____
_____
_____
_____
_____
_____

20 _____ *

_____
_____
_____
_____
_____
_____
_____

20 _____ *

_____
_____
_____
_____
_____
_____
_____

JUNE 22

And not only that, but we also glory in tribulations, knowing that tribulation produces perseverance; and perseverance character; and character, hope. * Knowing God leads to self-control. Self-control leads to patient endurance, and patient endurance leads to godliness. Godliness leads to love for other Christians, and finally you will grow to have genuine love for everyone. The more you grow like this, the more you will become productive and useful in your knowledge of our Lord Jesus Christ. * For our present troubles are quite small and won't last very long. Yet they produce in us an immeasurably great glory that will last forever! * We are pressed on every side by troubles, but we are not crushed and broken. We are perplexed, but we don't give up and quit. We are hunted down but God never abandons us. We get knocked down, but we get up again and keep going. * So we don't look at the troubles we can see right now; rather, we look forward to what we have not yet seen. For the troubles we see will soon be over, but the joys to come will last forever. * This hope we have as an anchor of the soul, both sure and steadfast, and which enters the Presence behind the veil. * Grace be with you all. Amen.

Romans 5:3-4 NKJV * 2 Peter 1:6-8 NLT * 2 Corinthians 4:17 NLT * 2 Corinthians 4:8-9 NLT * 2 Corinthians 4:18 NLT * Hebrews 6:19 NKJV * Hebrews 13:25 NKJV

JUNE

22 . . . .

Why does knowing God lead to self-control?

20 _____ *

_____

_____

_____

_____

_____

_____

_____

20 _____ *

_____

_____

_____

_____

_____

_____

_____

20 _____ *

_____

_____

_____

_____

_____

_____

_____

JUNE 23

May God bless you with his special favor and wonderful peace as you come to know Jesus, our God and Lord, better and better. As we know Jesus better, his divine power gives us everything we need for living a godly life. He has called us to receive his own glory and goodness! * When Jesus had finished saying all these things, he looked up to heaven and said, "Father, the time has come. Glorify your Son so he can give glory back to you. For you have given him authority over everyone in all the earth. He gives eternal life to each one you have given him. And this is the way to have eternal life—to know you, the only true God, and Jesus Christ, the one you sent to earth." * "My prayer is not for the world, but for those you have given me, because they belong to you. And all of them, since they are mine, belong to you; and you have given them back to me, so they are my glory! Now I am departing the world; I am leaving them behind and coming to you. Holy Father, keep them and care for them—all those you have given me—so that they will be united just as we are." * "I'm not asking you to take them out of the world, but to keep them safe from the evil one. They are not part of this world any more than I am. Make them pure and holy by teaching them your words of truth." * "I am praying not only for these disciples but also for all who will ever believe in me because of their testimony. My prayer for all of them is that they will be one, just as you and I are one, Father—that just as you are in me and I am in you, so they will be in us, and the world will believe you sent me. I have given them the glory you gave me, so that they may be one, as we are—I in them and you in me, all being perfected into one. Then the world will know that you sent me and will understand that you love them as much as you love me." * LORD, there is no one like you! For you are great, and your name is full of power. * All power is his forever and ever. Amen.

2 Peter 1:2-3 NLT * John 17:1-3 NLT * John 17:9-11 NLT * John 17:15-17 NLT * John 17:20-23 NLT * Jeremiah 10:6 NLT * 1 Peter 5:11 NLT

JUNE

23 . . . .

God loves you like He loves His Son.

20 _____ *

_____
_____
_____
_____
_____
_____
_____

20 _____ *

_____
_____
_____
_____
_____
_____
_____

20 _____ *

_____
_____
_____
_____
_____
_____
_____

JUNE 24

My lips shall greatly rejoice when I sing to You, and my soul, which You have redeemed. My tongue also shall talk of Your righteousness all the day long; for they are confounded, for they are brought to shame who seek my hurt. * The people said to Saul, "Shall Jonathan die, who has accomplished this great deliverance in Israel? Certainly not! As the LORD lives, not one hair of his head shall fall to the ground, for he has worked with God this day." So the people rescued Jonathan and he did not die. * Hear the word of the LORD, O nations, and declare it in the isles afar off, and say, 'He who scattered Israel will gather him, and keep him as a shepherd does his flock.' For the LORD has redeemed Jacob, and ransomed him from the hand of one stronger than he. Therefore they shall come and sing in the height of Zion, streaming to the goodness of the LORD—for wheat and new wine and oil, for the young of the flock and the herd; their souls shall be like a well-watered garden, and they shall sorrow no more at all. * Redeem Israel, O God, out of all their troubles! * Therefore thus says the LORD, who redeemed Abraham, concerning the house of Jacob: "Jacob shall not now be ashamed, nor shall his face now grow pale; but when he sees his children, the work of My hands, in his midst, they will hallow My name, and hallow the Holy One of Jacob, and fear the God of Israel." * Grace be with all those who love our Lord Jesus Christ in sincerity. Amen.

Psalm 71:23-24 NKJV * 1 Samuel 14:45 NKJV * Jeremiah 31:10-12 NKJV * Psalm 25:22 NKJV * Isaiah 29:22-23 NKJV * Ephesians 6:24 NKJV

JUNE

24 ....

Redemption graces the soul of all who believe.

20 _____ *

_____
_____
_____
_____
_____
_____
_____

20 _____ *

_____
_____
_____
_____
_____
_____
_____

20 _____ *

_____
_____
_____
_____
_____
_____
_____

JUNE 25

Don't say, "I will get even for this wrong." Wait for the LORD to handle the matter. * The LORD's searchlight penetrates the human spirit, exposing every hidden motive. * Justice is a joy to the godly, but it causes dismay among evildoers. * Those who shut their ears to the cries of the poor will be ignored in their own time of need. * The prudent person foresees danger ahead and takes precautions; the simpleton goes blindly on and suffers the consequences. * A person who gets ahead by oppressing the poor or by showering gifts on the rich will end in poverty. * Dear friends, never avenge yourselves. Leave that to God. For it is written, "I will take vengeance; I will repay those who deserve it," says the Lord. Instead, do what the Scriptures say: "If your enemies are hungry, feed them. If they are thirsty, give them something to drink, and they will be ashamed of what they have done to you." Don't let evil get the best of you, but conquer evil by doing good. * To God, who alone is wise, be the glory forever through Jesus Christ. Amen.

Proverbs 20:22 NLT * Proverbs 20:27 NLT * Proverbs 21:15 NLT * Proverbs 21:13 NLT * Proverbs 22:3 NLT * Proverbs 22:16 NLT * Romans 12:19-21 NLT * Romans 16:27 NLT

JUNE

25 . . . .

Conquer evil by doing good.

20 _____ *

_____

_____
_____
_____
_____
_____
_____

20 _____ *

_____

_____
_____
_____
_____
_____
_____

20 _____ *

_____

_____
_____
_____
_____
_____
_____

JUNE 26

True humility and fear of the LORD lead to riches, honor, and a long life. * The humble also shall increase their joy in the LORD, and the poor among men shall rejoice in the Holy One of Israel. * For whoever exalts himself will be humbled, and he who humbles himself will be exalted. * Let nothing be done through selfish ambition or conceit, but in lowliness of mind let each esteem others better than himself. Let each of you look out not only for his own interests, but also for the interests of others. * Therefore, as the elect of God, holy and beloved, put on tender mercies, kindness, humility, meekness, long-suffering. * For thus says the High and Lofty One Who inhabits eternity, whose name is Holy: "I dwell in the high and holy place, with him who has a contrite and humble spirit, to revive the spirit of the humble, and to revive the heart of the contrite ones. For I will not contend forever, nor will I always be angry; for the spirit would fail before Me, and the souls which I have made. For the iniquity of his covetousness I was angry and struck him; I hid and was angry, and he went on backsliding in the way of his heart. I have seen his ways, and will heal him; I will also lead him, and restore comforts to him and to his mourners. I create the fruit of the lips: peace, peace to him who is far off and to him who is near," says the LORD, "And I will heal him." * If My people who are called by My name will humble themselves, and pray and seek My face, and turn from their wicked ways, then I will hear from heaven, and will forgive their sin and heal their land. * Now to the King eternal, immortal, invisible, to God who alone is wise, be honor and glory forever and ever. Amen.

Proverbs 22:4 NLT * Isaiah 29:19 NKJV * Luke 14:11 NKJV * Philippians 2:3-4 NKJV * Colossians 3:12 NKJV * Isaiah 57:15-19 NKJV * 2 Chronicles 7:14 NKJV * 1 Timothy 1:17 NKJV

JUNE

26 . . . .

God, in His holiness, dwells with the humble.

20 _____ *

_____

_____

_____

_____

_____

_____

20 _____ *

_____

_____

_____

_____

_____

_____

20 _____ *

_____

_____

_____

_____

_____

_____

JUNE 27

No, the kind of fasting I want calls you to free those who are wrongly imprisoned and to stop oppressing those who work for you. Treat them fairly and give them what they earn. I want you to share your food with the hungry and to welcome poor wanderers into your homes. Give clothes to those who need them, and do not hide from relatives who need your help. If you do these things, your salvation will come like the dawn. Yes, your healing will come quickly. Your godliness will lead you forward, and the glory of the LORD will protect you from behind. Then when you call, the LORD will answer. "Yes, I am here," he will quickly reply. Stop oppressing the helpless and stop making false accusations and spreading vicious rumors! Feed the hungry and help those in trouble. Then your light will shine out from the darkness, and the darkness around you will be as bright as day. * Blessed are those who are generous, because they feed the poor. * My dear brothers and sisters, may the grace of our Lord Jesus Christ be with you all. Amen.

Isaiah 58:6-10 NLT * Proverbs 22:9 NLT * Galatians 6:18 NLT

JUNE

27 ....

Who can you reach out to today?

20 _____ *

---

20 _____ *

---

20 _____ *

JUNE 28

Faithful messengers are as refreshing as snow in the heat of summer. They revive the spirit of their employer. * There is no wisdom or understanding or counsel against the LORD. * Yes, each of us will have to give a personal account to God. So don't condemn each other anymore. Decide instead to live in such a way that you will not put an obstacle in another Christian's path. * Don't steal the land of defenseless orphans by moving the ancient boundary markers, for their Redeemer is strong. He himself will bring their charges against you. * As a face is reflected in water, so the heart reflects a person. * The wicked run away when no one is chasing them, but the godly are as bold as lions. * Greed causes fighting; trusting the LORD leads to prosperity. * Know the state of your flocks, and put your heart into caring for your herds. * Care for the flock of God entrusted to you. Watch over it willingly, not grudgingly—not for what you will get out of it, but because you are eager to serve God. Don't Lord it over the people assigned to your care, but lead them by your good example. And when the head Shepherd comes, your reward will be a never ending share in his glory and honor. * But grow in the special favor and knowledge of our Lord and Savior Jesus Christ. To him be glory and honor, both now and forevermore. Amen.

Proverbs 25:13 NLT * Proverbs 21:30 NKJV * Romans 14:12-13 NLT * Proverbs 23:10-11 NLT * Proverbs 27:19 NLT * Proverbs 28:1 NLT * Proverbs 28:25 NLT * Proverbs 27:23 NLT * 1 Peter 5:2-4 NLT * 2 Peter 3:18 NLT

JUNE

28 . . . .

God's wisdom supersedes all.

20 _____ *

_____
_____
_____
_____
_____
_____
_____
_____

20 _____ *

_____
_____
_____
_____
_____
_____
_____
_____

20 _____ *

_____
_____
_____
_____
_____
_____
_____
_____

JUNE 29

No lion shall be there, nor shall any ravenous beast go up on it; it shall not be found there. But the redeemed shall walk there, and the ransomed of the LORD shall return, and come to Zion with singing, with everlasting joy on their heads. They shall obtain joy and gladness, and sorrow and sighing shall flee away. * For the LORD will comfort Zion, He will comfort all her waste places; He will make her wilderness like Eden, and her desert like her garden of the LORD; joy and gladness will be found in it, thanksgiving and the voice of melody. * Thus says your Lord, the LORD and your God, Who pleads the cause of His people: "See, I have taken out of your hand the cup of trembling, the dregs of the cup of My fury; you shall no longer drink it. But I will put it into the hand of those who afflict you, who said to you, 'Lie down, that we may walk over you.' And you have laid your body like the ground, and as the street, for those who walk over." * Your watchman shall lift up their voices, with their voices they shall sing together; for they shall see eye to eye when the LORD brings back Zion. Break forth into joy, sing together, you waste places of Jerusalem! For the LORD has comforted His people, He has redeemed Jerusalem. * And blessed be His glorious name forever! And let the whole earth be filled with His glory. Amen and Amen.

Isaiah 35:9-10 NKJV * Isaiah 51:3 NKJV * Isaiah 51:22-23 NKJV * Isaiah 52:8-9 NKJV * Psalm 72:19 NKJV

JUNE

29 . . . .

The redeemed walk together, not over each other.

20 _____ *

_____

_____

_____

_____

_____

_____

_____

20 _____ *

_____

_____

_____

_____

_____

_____

_____

20 _____ *

_____

_____

_____

_____

_____

_____

_____

JUNE 30

But the day of the Lord will come like a thief. The heavens will disappear with a roar; the elements will be destroyed by fire, and the earth and everything done in it will be laid bare. Since everything will be destroyed in this way, what kind of people ought you to be? You ought to live holy and godly lives as you look forward to the day of God and speed its coming. That day will bring about the destruction of the heavens by fire, and the elements will melt in the heat. But in keeping with his promise we are looking forward to a new heaven and a new earth, where righteousness dwells. So then, dear friends, since you are looking forward to this, make every effort to be found spotless, blameless and at peace with him. * Therefore, since we have been justified through faith, we have peace with God through our Lord Jesus Christ, through whom we have gained access by faith into this grace in which we now stand. And we boast in the hope of the glory of God. * For he himself is our peace, who has made the two groups one and has destroyed the barrier, the dividing wall of hostility, by setting aside in his flesh the law with its commands and regulations. His purpose was to create in himself one new humanity out of the two, thus making peace, and in one body to reconcile both of them to God through the cross, by which he put to death their hostility. * The fruit of that righteousness will be peace; its effect will be quietness and confidence forever. * Grace to all who love our Lord Jesus Christ with an undying love. * Amen and Amen.

2 Peter 3:10-14 NIV * Romans 5:1-2 NIV * Ephesians 2:14-16 NIV * Isaiah 32:17 NIV * Ephesians 6:24 NIV * Psalm 72:19b NIV

JUNE

30 . . . .

Jesus Christ laid down His life so you could experience peace.

20 _____ *

_____

_____

_____

_____

_____

_____

_____

20 _____ *

_____

_____

_____

_____

_____

_____

_____

20 _____ *

_____

_____

_____

_____

_____

_____

_____

JULY

JULY 1

Then He went into the temple and began to drive out those who bought and sold in it, saying to them, "It is written, 'My house is a house of prayer,' but you have made it a 'den of thieves.'" * Deceit is in the heart of those who devise evil, but counselors of peace have joy. * A righteous man hates lying, but a wicked man is loathsome and comes to shame. * Truth stands the test of time; lies are soon exposed. * Lying lips are an abomination to the LORD, but those who deal truthfully are His delight. * But Peter said, "Ananias, why has Satan filled your heart to lie to the Holy Spirit and keep back part of the price of the land for yourself? While it remained, was it not your own? And after it was sold, was it not in your own control? Why have you conceived this thing in your heart? You have not lied to men but to God." * Who is a liar but he who denies that Jesus is the Christ? He is antichrist who denies the Father and the Son. * We know that we are of God, and the whole world lies under the sway of the wicked one. And we know that the Son of God has come and has given us an understanding, that we may know Him who is true; and we are in Him who is true, in His Son Jesus Christ. This is the true God and eternal life. Little children, keep yourselves from idols. Amen.

Luke 19:45-46 NKJV * Proverbs 12:20 NKJV * Proverbs 13:5 NKJV * Proverbs 12:19 NLT * Proverbs 12:22 NKJV * Acts 5:3-4 NKJV * 1 John 2:22 NKJV * 1 John 5:19-21 NKJV

JULY

1 . . . .

Lying is not loving.

20 _____ *

_____
_____
_____
_____
_____
_____
_____

20 _____ *

_____
_____
_____
_____
_____
_____
_____

20 _____ *

_____
_____
_____
_____
_____
_____
_____

JULY 2

Righteousness guards him whose way is blameless, but wickedness overthrows the sinner. * For whatever is born of God overcomes the world. And this is the victory that has overcome the world—our faith. Who is he who overcomes the world, but he who believes that Jesus is the Son of God? * You are of God, little children, and have overcome them, because He who is in you is greater than he who is in the world. * These things I have spoken to you, that in Me you may have peace. In the world you will have tribulations; but be of good cheer, I have overcome the world. * Peace I leave with you, My peace I give to you; not as the world gives do I give to you. Let not your heart be troubled, neither let it be afraid. * But thanks be to God, who gives us victory through our Lord Jesus Christ. * To God our Savior, who alone is wise, be glory and majesty, dominion and power, both now and forever. Amen.

Proverbs 13:6 NKJV * 1 John 5:4-5 NKJV * 1 John 4:4 NKJV * John 16:33 NKJV * John 14:27 NKJV * 1 Corinthians 15:57 NKJV * Jude 1:25 NKJV

JULY

2

· ·

With Jesus Christ as your Savior, you will overcome.

20_____ *

_____
_____
_____
_____
_____
_____
_____

20_____ *

_____
_____
_____
_____
_____
_____
_____

20_____ *

_____
_____
_____
_____
_____
_____
_____

JULY 3

But I say to you that for every idle word men may speak, they will give an account of it in the day of judgment. For by your words you will be justified, and by your words you will be condemned. * A good man out of the treasure of his heart brings forth good; and an evil man out of the evil treasure of his heart brings forth evil. For out of the abundance of the heart the mouth speaks. * We all make many mistakes, but those who control their tongues can also control themselves in every other way. * The tongue is a small thing, but what enormous damage it can do. A tiny spark can set a great forest on fire. And the tongue is a flame of fire. It is full of wickedness that can ruin your whole life. It can turn the entire course of your life into a blazing flame of destruction, for it is set on fire by hell itself. People can tame all kinds of animals and birds and reptiles and fish, but no one can tame the tongue. It is an uncontrollable evil, full of deadly poison. Sometimes it praises our Lord and Father, and sometimes it breaks out into curses against those who have been made in the image of God. And so blessing and cursing come pouring out of the same mouth. Surely my brothers and sisters, this is not right! * Amen and amen!

Matthew 12:36-37 NKJV * Luke 6:45 NKJV * James 3:2-10 NLT * Psalm 72:19b NLT

JULY

3 . . . .

**The tongue is a flame of fire.
Do you have yours under control?**

20 _____ *

_____

_____
_____
_____
_____
_____
_____

20 _____ *

_____
_____
_____
_____
_____
_____
_____

20 _____ *

_____
_____
_____
_____
_____
_____
_____

JULY 4

Blessed is the nation whose God is the LORD, the people He has chosen as His own inheritance. The LORD looks from heaven; He sees all the sons of men. From the place of His dwelling He looks on all the inhabitants of the earth; He fashions their hearts individually; He considers all their works. No king is saved by the multitude of an army; a mighty man is not delivered by great strength. * Behold, the eye of the LORD is on those who fear Him, on those who hope in His mercy, to deliver their soul from death, and to keep them alive in famine. * He does not preserve the life of the wicked, but gives justice to the oppressed. He does not withdraw His eyes from the righteous; but they are on the throne with kings, for He has seated them forever, and they are exalted. * Pray for the peace of Jerusalem: "May they prosper who love you. Peace be within your walls, prosperity within your palaces." For the sake of my brethren and companions, I will now say, "Peace be within you." Because of the house of the LORD our God I will seek your good. * Hear a just cause, O LORD, attend to my cry; give ear to my prayer which is not from deceitful lips. Let my vindication come from Your presence; let Your eyes look on the things that are upright. * Keep me as the apple of Your eye; hide me under the shadow of Your wings, from the wicked who oppress me, from my deadly enemies who surround me. They have closed up their fat hearts; with their mouths they speak proudly. * As for me, I will see Your face in righteousness; I shall be satisfied when I awake in Your likeness. * God is able to make you strong, just as the Good News says. It is the message about Jesus Christ and his plan for you Gentiles, a plan kept secret from the beginning of time. But now as the prophets foretold and as the eternal God has commanded, this message is made known to all Gentiles everywhere, so that they might believe and obey Christ. To God, who alone is wise, be glory forever through Jesus Christ. Amen.

Psalm 33:12-16 NKJV * Psalm 33:18-19 NKJV * Job 36:6-7 NKJV * Psalm 122:6-9 NKJV * Psalm 17:1-2 NKJV * Psalm 17:8-10 NKJV * Psalm 17:15 NKJV * Romans 16:25-27 NLT

July

4 . . . .

Blessed is the nation that supports Israel.

20 _____ *

_____
_____
_____
_____
_____
_____
_____

20 _____ *

_____
_____
_____
_____
_____
_____
_____

20 _____ *

_____
_____
_____
_____
_____
_____
_____

JULY 5

God is in the midst of her, she shall not be moved; God shall help her, just at the break of dawn. * "No weapon formed against you shall prosper, and every tongue which rises against you in judgment You shall condemn. This is the heritage of the servants of the LORD, and their righteousness is from Me," says the LORD. * You are of God, little children, and have overcome them, because He who is in you is greater than he who is in the world. * Do not marvel my brethren, if the world hates you. * If the world hates you, you know that it hated Me before it hated you. * He who hates Me hates My Father also. * If we receive the witness of men, the witness of God is greater; for this is the witness of God which He has testified of His Son. He who believes in the Son of God has the witness in himself; he who does not believe God has made Him a liar, because he has not believed the testimony that God has given of His Son. And this is the testimony: that God has given us eternal life, and this life is in His Son. He who has the Son has life; he who does not have the Son of God does not have life. * And Jesus said to them, "I am the bread of life. He who comes to Me shall never hunger, and he who believes in Me shall never thirst. * Most assuredly, I say to you, he who believes in Me has everlasting life. I am the bread of life. * Now to Him who is able to keep you from stumbling, and to present you faultless before the presence of His glory with exceeding joy, to God our Savior, who alone is wise, be glory and majesty, dominion and power, both now and forever. Amen.

Psalm 46:5 NKJV * Isaiah 54:17 NKJV * 1 John 4:4 NKJV * 1 John 3:13 NKJV * John 15:18 NKJV * John 15:23 NKJV * 1 John 5:9-12 NKJV * John 6:35 NKJV * John 6:47-48 NKJV * Jude 1:24-25 NKJV

JULY

5   . . . .

The world's hatred is weak in comparison to God's love.

20 _____ *

_____
_____
_____
_____
_____
_____
_____

20 _____ *

_____
_____
_____
_____
_____
_____
_____

20 _____ *

_____
_____
_____
_____
_____
_____
_____

JULY 6

But you, dear friends, must continue to build your lives on the foundation of your holy faith. And continue to pray as you are directed by the Holy Spirit. Live in such a way that God's love can bless you as you wait for the eternal life that our Lord Jesus Christ in his mercy is going to give you. Show mercy to those whose faith is wavering. Rescue others by snatching them from the flames of judgment. There are still others to whom you need to show mercy, but be careful that you aren't contaminated by their sins. * Be sure to do what you should, for then you will enjoy the personal satisfaction of having done your work well, and you won't need to compare yourself to anyone else. * While knowledge may make us feel important, it is love that really builds up the church. * So encourage each other and build each other up, just as you are already doing. * God blesses those who realize their need for him, for the Kingdom of Heaven is given to them. God blesses those who mourn, for they will be comforted. God blesses those who are gentle and lowly, for the whole earth will belong to them. God blesses those who are hungry and thirsty for justice, for they will receive it in full. God blesses those who are merciful, for they will be shown mercy. God blesses those whose hearts are pure, for they will see God. God blesses those who work for peace, for they will be called the children of God. God blesses those who are persecuted because they live for God, for the Kingdom of Heaven is theirs. God blesses you when you are mocked and persecuted and lied about because you are my followers. Be happy about it! Be very glad! For a great reward awaits you in heaven. And remember, the ancient prophets were persecuted, too. * You are the light of the world—like a city on a mountain, glowing in the night for all to see. Don't hide your light under a basket! Instead, put it on a stand and let it shine for all. In the same way, let your good deeds shine out for all to see, so that everyone will praise your heavenly Father. * May our Lord Jesus Christ and God our Father, who loved us and in his special favor gave us everlasting comfort and good hope, comfort your hearts and give you strength in every good thing you do and say. * Bless His glorious name forever! Let the whole earth be filled with his glory. Amen and Amen.

Jude 1:20-23 NLT * Galatians 6:4 NLT * 1 Corinthians 8:1b NLT * 1 Thessalonians 5:11 NLT * Matthew 5:3-12 NLT * Matthew 5:14-16 NLT * 2 Thessalonians 2:16-17 NLT * Psalm 72:19 NLT

JULY

6 . . . .

Live in such a way that God's love can bless you as you wait.

20 _____ *

20 _____ *

20 _____ *

JULY 7

Trust in the Lord with all your heart; do not depend on your own understanding. Seek his will in all you do, and he will direct your paths. * Give generously for your gifts will return to you later. * If you wait for perfect conditions, you will never get anything done. * Be sure to stay busy and plant a variety of crops, for you never know which will grow—perhaps they all will. * Finishing is better than starting. Patience is better than pride. * There is a time for everything, a season for every activity under heaven. * A time to be quiet and a time to speak up. * A time to cry and a time to laugh. * Never let loyalty and kindness get away from you! Wear them like a necklace; write them deep within your heart. * God has made everything beautiful for its own time. He has planted eternity in the human heart, but even so, people cannot see the whole scope of God's work from beginning to end. * A person standing alone can be attacked and defeated, but two can stand back to back and conquer. Three are even better, for a triple-braided cord is not easily broken. * There is not a single person in all the earth who is always good and never sins. Don't eavesdrop on others—you may hear your servant laughing at you. For you know how often you yourself have laughed at others. All along I have tried my best to let wisdom guide my thoughts and actions. I said to myself, "I am determined to be wise." But it didn't really work. * Amen and Amen.

Proverbs 3:5-6 NLT * Ecclesiastes 11:1 NLT * Ecclesiastes 11:4 NLT * Ecclesiastes 11:6 NLT * Ecclesiastes 7:8 NLT * Ecclesiastes 3:1 NLT * Ecclesiastes 3:7b NLT * Ecclesiastes 3:4a NLT * Proverbs 3:3 NLT * Ecclesiastes 3:11 NLT * Ecclesiastes 4:12 NLT * Ecclesiastes 7:20-23 NLT * Psalm 72:19b NLT

JULY

7 . . . .

Do people grow when they are around you?

20 _____ *

_____
_____
_____
_____
_____
_____
_____

20 _____ *

_____
_____
_____
_____
_____
_____
_____

20 _____ *

_____
_____
_____
_____
_____
_____
_____

JULY 8

But the Lord is faithful who will establish you and guard you from the evil one. * The LORD is your keeper; the LORD is your shade at your right hand. The sun shall not strike you by day, nor the moon by night. The LORD shall preserve you from all evil; He shall preserve your soul. The LORD shall preserve your going out and your coming in from this time forth, and even forevermore. * Now may the God of peace Himself sanctify you completely; and may your whole spirit, soul, and body be preserved blameless at the coming of our Lord Jesus Christ. He who calls you is faithful, who also will do it. * Therefore let him who thinks he stands take heed lest he fall. No temptation has overtaken you except such as is common to man; but God is faithful, who will not allow you to be tempted beyond what you are able, but with the temptation will also make the way of escape, that you may be able to bear it. * Awake, you who sleep, arise from the dead, and Christ will give you light. * Grace be with all those who love our Lord Jesus Christ in sincerity. Amen.

2 Thessalonians 3:3 NKJV * Psalm 121:5-8 NKJV * 1 Thessalonians 5:23-24 NKJV * 1 Corinthians 10:12-13 NKJV * Ephesians 5:14 NKJV * Ephesians 6:24 NKJV

JULY

8 . . . .

The Lord will establish you.

20 _____ *

_____

_____
_____
_____
_____
_____
_____

20 _____ *

_____

_____
_____
_____
_____
_____
_____

20 _____ *

_____

_____
_____
_____
_____
_____
_____
_____

JULY 9

You younger men, accept authority of the elders. And all of you, serve each other in humility, for "God sets himself against the proud, but he shows favor to the humble. So humble yourselves under the mighty power of God, and in his good time he will honor you." * Fire tests the purity of silver and gold, but the LORD tests the heart. * Human plans, no matter how wise or well advised, cannot stand against the LORD. * If you listen to constructive criticism, you will be at home among the wise. If you reject criticism, you only harm yourself; but if you listen to correction, you grow in understanding. Fear of the LORD teaches a person to be wise; humility precedes honor. * The LORD despises those who acquit the guilty and condemn the innocent. * Avoiding a fight is a mark of honor; only fools insist on quarreling. * People may think they are doing what is right, but the LORD examines the heart. * Pride goes before destruction, and haughtiness before a fall. * Telling lies about others is as harmful as hitting them with an ax, wounding them with a sword, or shooting them with a sharp arrow. * Prove by the way that you live that you have really turned from your sins and turned to God. * For the Scriptures say, "If you want a happy life and good days, keep your tongue from speaking evil, and keep your lips from telling lies. Turn away from evil and do good. Work hard at living in peace with others. The eyes of the Lord watch over those who do right, and his ears are open to their prayers. But the Lord turns his face against those who do evil." * The godly walk with integrity; blessed are their children after them. * Now glory be to God! By his mighty power at work within us, he is able to accomplish infinitely more than we would ever dare to ask or hope. May he be given glory in the church and in Christ Jesus forever and ever through endless ages. Amen.

1 Peter 5:5-6 NLT * Proverbs 17:3 NLT * Proverbs 21:30 NLT * Proverbs 15:33 NLT * Proverbs 17:15 NLT * Proverbs 20:3 NLT * Proverbs 21:2 NLT * Proverbs 16:18 NLT * Proverbs 25:18 NLT * Matthew 3:8 NLT * 1 Peter 3: 10-12 NLT * Proverbs 20:7 NLT * Ephesians 3:20-21 NLT

JULY

9

Humble yourselves under the mighty power of God.

20 _____ *

20 _____ *

20 _____ *

JULY 10

When I think of the wisdom and scope of God's plan, I fall to my knees and pray to the Father, the Creator of everything in heaven and on earth. I pray that from his glorious, unlimited resources he will give you mighty inner strength through His Holy Spirit. And I pray that Christ will be more and more at home in your hearts as you trust in him. May your roots go down deep into the soil of God's marvelous love. And may you have the power to understand, as all God's people should, how wide, how long, how high, and how deep his love really is. * We know how much God loves us, and we have put our trust in him. God is love and all who live in love live in God, and God lives in them. And as we live in God, our love grows more perfect. So we will not be afraid on the day of judgment, but we can face him with confidence because we are like Christ here in this world. Such love has no fear because perfect love expels all fear. If we are afraid, it is for fear of judgment, and this shows that his love has not been perfected in us. We love each other as a result of his loving us first. * May God's grace be upon all who love our Lord Jesus Christ with an undying love. * Amen and Amen.

Ephesians 3:14-19 NLT * 1 John 4:16-19 NLT * Ephesians 6:24 NLT * Psalm 72:19b NLT

JULY

10 ·

Do you grasp how deep God's love is for you?

20 ____ *

_____

_____

_____

_____

_____

_____

_____

20 ____ *

_____

_____

_____

_____

_____

_____

_____

20 ____ *

_____

_____

_____

_____

_____

_____

_____

JULY 11

Victory comes from you, O LORD, may your blessings rest on your people. * Listen to my cry for help, my King and my God, for I will never pray to anyone but you. Listen to my voice in the morning, LORD, each morning I bring my requests to you and wait expectantly. * I cried out to the LORD, and he answered me from his holy mountain. I lay down and slept. I woke up in safety, for the LORD was watching over me. I am not afraid of ten thousand enemies who surround me on every side. Arise, O LORD! Rescue me, my God! Slap all my enemies in the face! Shatter the teeth of the wicked! * O God, you take no pleasure in wickedness; you cannot tolerate the slightest sin. Therefore, the proud will not be allowed to stand in your presence, for you hate all who do evil. You will destroy those who tell lies. The LORD detests murderers and deceivers. Because of your unfailing love, I can enter your house; with deepest awe I will worship at your Temple. Lead me in the right path, O LORD, or my enemies will conquer me. Tell me clearly what to do, and show me which way to turn. * Amen and Amen.

Psalm 3:8 NLT * Psalm 5:2-3 NLT * Psalm 3:4-7 NLT * Psalm 5:5-8 NLT * Psalm 72:19b NLT

JULY

11 . . . .

Pray expectantly.

20_____ *

20_____ *

20_____ *

JULY 12

Would not God search this out? For He knows the secrets of the heart. * Yet for Your sake we are killed all day long; we are accounted as sheep for the slaughter. * And David said to Gad, "I am in great distress. Please let us fall into the hands of the LORD, for His mercies are great; but do not let me fall into the hands of man." * And when the angel stretched out His hand over Jerusalem to destroy it, the LORD relented from the destruction, and said to the angel who was destroying the people, "It is enough; now restrain your hand." And the angel of the LORD was by the threshing floor of Araunah the Jebusite. * Then David spoke to the LORD when he saw the angel who was striking the people, and said, "Surely I have sinned, and I have done wickedly; but these sheep, what have they done? Let Your hand, I pray, be against me and against my father's house." * And Gad came that day to David and said to him, "Go up, erect an altar to the LORD on the threshing floor of Araunah the Jebusite." * Then the king said to Araunah, "No, but I will surely buy it from you for a price; nor will I offer burnt offerings to the LORD my God with that which costs me nothing." So David bought the threshing floor and the oxen for fifty shekels of silver. And David built there an altar to the LORD, and offered burnt offerings and peace offerings. So the LORD heeded the prayers for the land, and the plague was withdrawn from Israel. * Now to the King eternal, immortal, invisible, to God who alone is wise, be honor and glory forever and ever. Amen.

Psalm 44:21 NKJV * Psalm 44:22 NKJV * 2 Samuel 24:14 NKJV * 2 Samuel 24:16 NKJV * 2 Samuel 24:17 NKJV * 2 Samuel 24:18 NKJV * 2 Samuel 24:24-25 NKJV * 1 Timothy 1:17 NKJV

JULY

12 . . . .

God knows the secrets of the heart.

20 _____ *

_____
_____
_____
_____
_____
_____
_____
_____

20 _____ *

_____
_____
_____
_____
_____
_____
_____
_____

20 _____ *

_____
_____
_____
_____
_____
_____
_____
_____

JULY 13

The LORD Almighty says to the priests: "A son honors his father, and a servant respects his master. I am your father and master, but where are the honor and respect I deserve? You have despised my name! But you ask, 'How have we ever despised your name?' You have despised my name by offering defiled sacrifices on my altar. Then you ask, 'How have we defiled the sacrifices?' You defile them by saying the altar of the LORD deserves no respect. When you give blind animals as sacrifices, isn't that wrong? And isn't it wrong to offer animals that are crippled and diseased? Try giving gifts like that to your governor, and see how pleased he is!" says the LORD Almighty. "Go ahead, beg God to be merciful to you! But when you bring that kind of offering, why should he show you any favor at all?" asks the LORD Almighty. "I wish that someone among you would shut the Temple doors so that these worthless sacrifices could not be offered! I am not at all pleased with you," says the LORD Almighty, "and I will not accept your offerings. But my name is honored by people of other nations from morning till night. All around the world they offer sweet incense and pure offerings in honor of my name. For my name is great among the nations," says the LORD Almighty. "But you dishonor my name with your actions. By bringing contemptible food, you are saying it's all right to defile the LORD's table. You say, 'It's too hard to serve the LORD,' and you turn up your noses at his commands," says the LORD Almighty. "Think of it! Animals that are stolen and mutilated, crippled and sick—presented as offerings! Should I accept from you such offerings as these?" asks the LORD. "Cursed is the cheat who promises to give a fine ram from his flock but then sacrifices a defective one to the Lord. For I am a great king," says the LORD Almighty, "and my name is feared among the nations!" * Jesus replied, "Your problem is that you don't know the Scriptures, and you don't know the power of God." * Jesus replied, "'You must love the Lord your God with all your heart, all your soul, and all your mind.' This is the first and greatest commandment. A second is equally important: 'Love your neighbor as yourself.' All the other commandments and all the demands of the prophets are based on these two commandments." * To Him be the glory and the dominion forever and ever. Amen.

Malachi 1:6-14 NLT * Matthew 23:29 NLT * Matthew 22:37-40 NLT * 1 Peter 5:11 NKJV

JULY

13 . . . .

How are you honoring and respecting God's name?

20 _____ *

_____
_____
_____
_____
_____
_____
_____

20 _____ *

_____
_____
_____
_____
_____
_____
_____

20 _____ *

_____
_____
_____
_____
_____
_____
_____

JULY 14

But his servant said, "What? Shall I set this before one hundred men?" He said again, "Give it to the people, that they may eat; for thus says the LORD: 'They shall eat and have some left over.'" So he set it before them; and they ate and had some left over, according to the word of the LORD. * And He said to them, "Come aside by yourselves to a deserted place and rest a while." For there were many coming and going, and they did not even have time to eat. So they departed to a deserted place in the boat by themselves. But the multitudes saw them departing, and many knew Him and ran there on foot from all the cities. They arrived before them and came together to Him. And Jesus, when He came out, saw a great multitude and was moved with compassion for them, because they were like sheep not having a shepherd. So He began to teach them many things. When the day was now far spent, His disciples came to Him and said, "This is a deserted place, and already the hour is late. Send them away, that they may go into the surrounding country and villages and buy themselves bread; for they have nothing to eat." But He answered and said to them, "You give them something to eat." And they said to Him, "Shall we go and buy two hundred denarii worth of bread and give them something to eat?" But He said to them, "How many loaves do you have? Go and see." And when they found out they said, "Five, and two fish." Then He commanded them to make them all sit down in groups on the green grass. So they sat down in ranks, in hundreds and fifties. And when He had taken the five loaves and the two fish, He looked up to heaven, blessed and broke the loaves, and gave them to His disciples to set before them, and the two fish He divided among them all. So they all ate and were filled. And they took up twelve baskets full of fragments and of the fish. Now those who had eaten the loaves were about five thousand men. * And my God shall supply all your need according to His riches in glory by Christ Jesus. Now to our God and Father be glory forever and ever. Amen.

2 Kings 4:43-44 NKJV * Mark 6:31-43 NKJV * Philippians 4:19-20 NKJV

July

14 . . . .

God feeds the hungry.

20 _____ *

_____

_____
_____
_____
_____
_____
_____

20 _____ *

_____

_____
_____
_____
_____
_____
_____

20 _____ *

_____

_____
_____
_____
_____
_____
_____
_____

JULY 15

So I sought for a man among them who would make a wall, and stand in the gap before Me on behalf of the land, that I should not destroy it; but I found no one. * Therefore, to him who knows to do good and does not do it, to him it is sin. * Moreover, as for me, far be it from me that I should sin against the LORD in ceasing to pray for you. * Bear one another's burdens, and so fulfill the law of Christ. * Therefore I exhort first of all that supplications, prayers, intercessions, and giving of thanks be made for all men. * I desire therefore that the men pray everywhere, lifting up holy hands, without wrath and doubting. * Is anyone among you suffering? Let him pray. Is anyone cheerful? Let him sing psalms. Is anyone among you sick? Let him call for the elders of the church, and let them pray over him, anointing him with oil in the name of the Lord. And the prayer of faith will save the sick, and the Lord will raise him up. And if he has committed sins, he will be forgiven. * For if our heart condemns us, God is greater than our heart, and knows all things. * The grace of our Lord Jesus Christ be with you. Amen.

Ezekiel 22:30 NKJV * James 4:17 NKJV * 1 Samuel 12:23a NKJV * Galatians 6:2 NKJV * 1 Timothy 2:1 NKJV * 1 Timothy 2:8 NKJV * James 5:13-15 NKJV * 1 John 3:20 NKJV * 1 Thessalonians 5:28 NKJV

JULY

15 . . . .

Will you stand in the gap?

20 _____ *

_____
_____
_____
_____
_____
_____
_____

20 _____ *

_____
_____
_____
_____
_____
_____
_____

20 _____ *

_____
_____
_____
_____
_____
_____
_____

JULY 16

But did He not make them one, having a remnant of the Spirit? And why one? He seeks godly offspring. Therefore take heed to your spirit, and let none deal treacherously with the wife of his youth. * Can two walk together, unless they are agreed? * Two are better than one, because they have a good reward for their labor. For if they fall, one will lift up his companion. But woe to him who is alone when he falls, for he has no one to help him up. Again, if two lie down together, they will keep warm; but how can one be warm alone? Though one may be overpowered by another, two can withstand him. And a threefold cord is not quickly broken. * Let your fountain be blessed, and rejoice with the wife of your youth. * An excellent wife is the crown of her husband, but she who causes shame is like rottenness in his bones. * He who finds a wife finds a good thing, and obtains favor from the LORD. * A man who has friends must himself be friendly, but there is a friend who sticks closer than a brother. * You can make many plans, but the Lord's purpose will prevail. * The righteous man walks in his integrity; his children are blessed after him. * Blessed is every one who fears the Lord, who walks in His ways. * Your wife shall be like a fruitful vine in the very heart of your house, your children like olive plants all around your table. Behold, thus shall the man be blessed who fears the Lord. * Unless the Lord builds the house, they labor in vain who build it; unless the Lord guards the city, the watchman stays awake in vain. * Behold, children are a heritage from the LORD, the fruit of the womb is a reward. Like arrows in the hand of a warrior, so are the children of one's youth. Happy is the man who has his quiver full of them; they shall not be ashamed, but shall speak with their enemies in the gate. * Amen and Amen.

Malachi 2:15 NKJV * Amos 3:3 NKJV * Ecclesiastes 4:9-12 NKJV * Proverbs 5:18 NKJV * Proverbs 12:4 NKJV * Proverbs 18:22 NKJV * Proverbs 18:24 NKJV * Proverbs 19:21 NLT * Proverbs 20:7 NKJV * Psalm 128:1 NKJV * Psalm 128:3-4 NKJV * Psalm 127:1 NKJV * Psalm 127:3-5 NKJV * Psalm 72:19b NKJV

JULY

16 . . . .

What family are you praying for?

20 _____ *

_____

_____

_____

_____

_____

_____

_____

20 _____ *

_____

_____

_____

_____

_____

_____

_____

20 _____ *

_____

_____

_____

_____

_____

_____

_____

JULY 17

Every word of God is tested; He is a shield to those who take refuge in Him. * As for God, His way is blameless; the word of the LORD is tried; He is a shield to all who take refuge in Him. * Not to us, O LORD, not to us, but to Your name give glory because of Your lovingkindness, because of Your truth. * O Israel, trust in the LORD; He is their help and their shield. O house of Aaron, trust in the LORD; He is their help and their shield. You who fear the LORD, trust in the LORD; He is their help and their shield. * He will bless those who fear the LORD, the small together with the great. * For the LORD God is a sun and shield; the LORD gives grace and glory; no good thing does He withhold from those who walk uprightly. * The God of peace will soon crush Satan under your feet. The grace of our Lord Jesus be with you. * Blessed be the LORD, the God of Israel, from everlasting to everlasting. Amen and Amen.

Proverbs 30:5 NASB * Psalm 18:30 NASB * Psalm 115:1 NASB * Psalm 115:9-11 NASB * Psalm 115:13 NASB * Psalm 84:11 NASB * Romans 16:20 NASB * Psalm 41:13 NASB

JULY

17 . . . .

God does not withhold good from those who walk uprightly.

20 _____ *

_____

_____

_____

_____

_____

_____

_____

20 _____ *

_____

_____

_____

_____

_____

_____

_____

20 _____ *

_____

_____

_____

_____

_____

_____

_____

JULY 18

Why have You broken down its hedges, so that all who pass that way pick its fruit? A boar from the forest eats it away and whatever moves in the field feeds on it. * Do not deliver the soul of Your turtledove to the wild beast; do not forget the life of Your afflicted forever. Consider the covenant; for the dark places of the land are full of the habitations of violence. Let not the oppressed return dishonored; let the afflicted and needy praise Your name. * O God, restore us and cause Your face to shine upon us, and we will be saved. * So we Your people and the sheep of Your pasture will give thanks to You forever; to all generations we will tell of Your praise. * For He is our God, and we are the people of His pasture and the sheep of His hand. Today, if you would hear His voice. * Let Your hand be upon the man of Your right hand, upon the son of man whom You made strong for Yourself. Then we shall not turn back from You; revive us, and we will call upon Your name. * To the only wise God, through Jesus Christ, be the glory forever. Amen.

Psalm 80:12-13 NASB * Psalm 74:19-21 NASB * Psalm 80:3 NASB * Psalm 79:13 NASB * Psalm 95:7 NASB * Psalm 80:17-18 NASB * Romans 16:27 NASB

JULY

18 ·

God has not forgotten you.

20 _____ *

_____
_____
_____
_____
_____
_____
_____

20 _____ *

_____
_____
_____
_____
_____
_____
_____

20 _____ *

_____
_____
_____
_____
_____
_____
_____

JULY 19

When I thought how to understand this, it was too painful for me—until I went into the sanctuary of God; then I understood their end. * I will sing of mercy and justice; to You, O LORD, I will sing praises. I will behave wisely in a perfect way. Oh, when will You come to me? I will walk within my house with a perfect heart. * The grass withers, the flower fades, but the word of our God stands forever. * Cease from anger, and forsake wrath; do not fret—it only causes harm. For evildoers shall be cut off; but those who wait on the LORD, they shall inherit the earth. * All the horns of the wicked I will cut off, but the horns of the righteous shall be exalted. * God is the Judge: He puts down one, and exalts another. * Every valley shall be exalted and every mountain brought low; the crooked places shall be made straight and the rough places smooth; the glory of the LORD shall be revealed, and all flesh shall see it together; for the mouth of the LORD has spoken. * Finally, brethren, farewell. Become complete. Be of good comfort, be of one mind, live in peace; and the God of love and peace will be with you. Greet one another with a holy kiss. All the saints greet you. The grace of the Lord Jesus Christ, and the love of God, and the communion of the Holy Spirit be with you all. Amen.

Psalm 73:16-17 NKJV * Psalm 101:1-2 NKJV * Isaiah 40:8 NKJV * Psalm 37:8-9 NKJV * Psalm 75:10 NKJV * Psalm 75:7 NKJV * Isaiah 40:4-5 NKJV * 2 Corinthians 13:11-14 NKJV

July

19 . . . .

The glory of the Lord will be revealed.

20 _____ *

_____

_____

_____

_____

_____

_____

_____

20 _____ *

_____

_____

_____

_____

_____

_____

_____

20 _____ *

_____

_____

_____

_____

_____

_____

_____

JULY 20

How precious is Your lovingkindness, O God! Therefore the children of men put their trust under the shadow of Your wings. They are abundantly satisfied with the fullness of Your house, and You give them drink from the river of Your pleasures. For with You is the fountain of life; in Your light we see light. * He who dwells in the secret place of the Most High shall abide under the shadow of the Almighty. I will say of the LORD, "He is my refuge and my fortress; My God, in Him I will trust." * Trust in the LORD with all your heart, and lean not on your own understanding; in all your ways acknowledge Him, and He shall direct your paths. * Your testimonies are very sure; holiness adorns Your house, O LORD, forever. * For thus says the High and Lofty One who inhabits eternity, whose name is Holy: "I dwell in the high and holy place, with him who has a contrite and humble spirit, to revive the spirit of the humble, and to revive the heart of the contrite ones." * And lo, I am with you always, even to the end of the age. Amen.

Psalm 36:7-9 NKJV * Psalm 91:1-2 NKJV * Proverbs 3:5-6 NKJV * Psalm 93:5 NKJV * Isaiah 57:15 NKJV * Matthew 28:20b NKJV

JULY

20 ....

God's name is Holy.

20 _____ *

---

20 _____ *

---

20 _____ *

JULY 21

An oracle within my heart concerning the transgression of the wicked: There is no fear of God before his eyes. * My flesh trembles for fear of You, and I am afraid of Your judgments. * Let not the foot of pride come against me, and let not the hand of the wicked drive me away. There the workers of iniquity have fallen; they have been cast down and are not able to rise. * Let me be reconciled with all who fear you and know your decrees, may I be blameless in keeping your principles; then I will never be ashamed. * The lofty looks of man shall be humbled, the haughtiness of men shall be bowed down, and the LORD alone shall be exalted in that day. For the day of the LORD of hosts shall come upon everything proud and lofty, upon everything lifted up—and it shall be brought low. * For the great day of His wrath has come, and who is able to stand? * Repent therefore and be converted, that your sins may be blotted out, so that times of refreshing may come from the presence of the Lord. * Amen and Amen.

Psalm 36:1 NKJV * Psalm 119:120 NKJV * Psalm 36:11-12 NKJV * Psalm 119:79-80 NLT * Isaiah 2:11-12 NKJV * Revelation 6:17 NKJV * Acts 3:19 NKJV * Psalm 72:19b NKJV

JULY

21 . . . .

Lord, forgive me of my pride.

20 ____ *

_____

_____
_____
_____
_____
_____
_____

20 ____ *

_____

_____
_____
_____
_____
_____
_____

20 ____ *

_____

_____
_____
_____
_____
_____
_____

JULY 22

For every house is built by someone, but the builder of all things is God. Now Moses was faithful in all His house as a servant, for a testimony of those things which were to be spoken later; but Christ was faithful as a Son over His house—whose house we are, if we hold fast our confidence and the boast of our hope firm until the end. * So then you are no longer strangers and aliens, but you are fellow citizens with the saints, and are of God's household, having been built on the foundation of the apostles and prophets, Christ Jesus Himself being the corner stone, in whom the whole building, being fitted together, is growing into a holy temple in the Lord, in whom you also are being built together into a dwelling of God in the Spirit. * Behold, how good and how pleasant it is for brothers to dwell together in unity! It is like the precious oil upon the head, coming down upon the beard, even Aaron's beard, coming down upon the edges of his robes. * Let brotherly love continue. * The grace of our Lord Jesus Christ be with you all. Amen.

Hebrews 3:4-6 NASB * Ephesians 2:19-22 NASB * Psalm 133:1-2 NASB * Hebrews 13:1 NKJV * Romans 16:24 NASB

JULY

22 . . . .

You won't have a strong structure of people walking in unity if Jesus Christ is not the cornerstone.

20 _____ *

_____
_____
_____
_____
_____
_____
_____

20 _____ *

_____
_____
_____
_____
_____
_____
_____

20 _____ *

_____
_____
_____
_____
_____
_____
_____

JULY 23

I speak the truth in Christ—I am not lying, my conscience confirms it through the Holy Spirit. * I care very little if I am judged by you or by any human court; indeed, I do not even judge myself. My conscience is clear, but that does not make me innocent. It is the Lord who judges me. Therefore judge nothing before the appointed time; wait until the Lord comes. He will bring to light what is hidden in darkness and will expose the motives of the heart. At that time each will receive their praise from God. * Now this is our boast: Our conscience testifies that we have conducted ourselves in the world, and especially in our relations with you, with integrity and godly sincerity. We have done so, relying not on worldly wisdom but on God's grace. * So we make it our goal to please him, whether we are at home in the body or away from it. For we must all appear before the judgment seat of Christ, so that each of us may receive what is due us for the things done while in the body, whether good or bad. Since, then, we know what it is to fear the Lord, we try to persuade others. What we are is plain to God, and I hope it is also plain to your conscience. * Pray for us. We are sure that we have a clear conscience and desire to live honorably in every way. * Grace be with you all. * Amen and Amen.

Romans 9:1 NIV * 1 Corinthians 4:3-5 NIV * 2 Corinthians 1:12 NIV * 2 Corinthians 5:9-11 NIV * Hebrews 13:18 NIV * Hebrews 13:25 NIV * Psalm 41:13b NIV

JULY

23 . . . .

Keep Jesus at the center of logistics.

20 _____ *

_____

_____

_____

_____

_____

_____

_____

20 _____ *

_____

_____

_____

_____

_____

_____

_____

20 _____ *

_____

_____

_____

_____

_____

_____

_____

JULY 24

Bring my soul out of prison, that I may praise Your name; the righteous shall surround me, for You shall deal bountifully with me. * Revive me, O LORD, for Your name's sake! For Your righteousness' sake bring my soul out of trouble. In Your mercy cut off my enemies, and destroy those who afflict my soul; for I am Your servant. * I am Yours, save me, for I have sought your precepts. * If your law had not been my delight, I would have perished in my affliction. I will never forget your precepts, for by them you have given me life. * Oh how I love Your law! It is my meditation all the day. Your commandments make me wiser than my enemies, for it is ever with me. I have more understanding than all my teachers, for your testimonies are my meditation. I understand more than the aged, for I keep Your precepts. I hold back my feet from every evil way, in order to keep Your word. I do not turn aside from Your rules, for You have taught me. How sweet are Your words to my taste, sweeter than honey to my mouth! * For You are my rock and my fortress; therefore, for Your name's sake, lead me and guide me. Pull me out of the net which they have secretly laid for me, for You are my strength. In Your hand I commit my spirit; You have redeemed me, O LORD God of truth. * Amen and Amen!

Psalm 142:7 NKJV * Psalm 143:11-12 NKJV * Psalm 119:94 ESV * Psalm 119:92-93 ESV * Psalm 119:97-103 ESV * Psalm 31:3-5 NKJV * Psalm 72:19b ESV

JULY

24 . . . .

**God knows what is afflicting your soul;
He will take care of it.**

20 _____ *

_____
_____
_____
_____
_____
_____
_____

20 _____ *

_____
_____
_____
_____
_____
_____
_____

20 _____ *

_____
_____
_____
_____
_____
_____
_____

JULY 25

A fool gives full vent to his anger, but a wise person quietly holds it back. * "Don't sin by letting anger gain control over you." Don't let the sun go down while you are still angry, for anger gives a mighty foothold to the Devil. * A king who is fair to the poor will have a long reign. * The godly know the rights of the poor; the wicked don't care to know. * Your gold and silver have become worthless. The very wealth you were counting on will eat away your flesh in hell. This treasure you have accumulated will stand as evidence against you on the day of judgment. For listen! Hear the cries of the field workers whom you have cheated of their pay. The wages you held back cry out against you. The cries of the reapers have reached the ears of the Lord Almighty. You have spent your years on earth in luxury, satisfying your every whim. Now your hearts are nice and fat, ready for the slaughter. You have condemned and killed good people who had no power to defend themselves against you. * Whoever stubbornly refuses to accept criticism will suddenly be broken beyond repair. * Evil people are trapped by sin, but the righteous escape, shouting for joy. * The bloodthirsty hate the honest, but the upright seek out the honest. * So put away all falsehood and "tell your neighbor the truth" because we belong to each other. * If a ruler honors liars, all his advisors will be wicked. * When the wicked are in authority, sin increases. But the godly will live to see the tyrant's downfall. * Many seek the ruler's favor, but justice comes from the Lord. The godly despise the wicked; the wicked despise the godly. * Fearing people is a dangerous trap, but to trust the Lord means safety. * When the people cry to the LORD for help against those who oppress them, he will send them a savior who will rescue them. * Blessed be the LORD forever! Amen and amen!

Proverbs 29:11 NLT * Ephesians 4:26-27 NLT * Proverbs 19:14 NLT * Proverbs 29:7 NLT * James 5:3-6 NLT * Proverbs 29:1 NLT * Proverbs 29:6 NLT * Proverbs 29:10 NLT * Ephesians 4:25 NLT * Proverbs 29:12 NLT * Proverbs 29:16 NLT * Proverbs 29:26-27 NLT * Proverbs 29:25 NLT * Isaiah 19:20b NLT * Psalm 89:52 NLT

July

25 . . . .

Are you quick to vent your anger?

20 _____ *

_____
_____
_____
_____
_____
_____
_____

20 _____ *

_____
_____
_____
_____
_____
_____
_____

20 _____ *

_____
_____
_____
_____
_____
_____
_____

JULY 26

"Nevertheless My lovingkindness I will not utterly take from him, nor allow My faithfulness to fail. My covenant I will not break, nor alter the word that has gone out of My lips. Once I have sworn by My holiness; I will not lie to David: his seed shall endure forever, and his throne as the sun before Me; it will be established forever like the moon, even like the faithful witness in the sky." * "Behold, the days are coming," says the LORD, "that I will perform that good thing which I have promised to the house of Israel and to the house of Judah: In those days and at that time I will cause to grow up to David a Branch of righteousness; He shall execute judgment and righteousness in the earth. In those days Judah will be saved, and Jerusalem will dwell safely. And this is the name by which she will be called: THE LORD OUR RIGHTEOUSNESS. For thus says the LORD: 'David shall never lack a man to sit on the throne of the house of Israel; nor shall the priests, the Levites, lack a man to offer burnt offerings before Me, to kindle grain offerings, and to sacrifice continually.'" * For God so loved the world that He gave His only begotten Son, that whoever believes in Him should not perish but have everlasting life. * Blessed be the LORD for evermore! Amen, and Amen.

Psalm 89:33-37 NKJV * Jeremiah 33:14-18 NKJV * John 3:16 NKJV * Psalm 89:52 KJV

JULY

26 . . . .

**God laid the foundation in His promises,
backed by the power of His name.**

20 _____ *

_____

_____

_____

_____

_____

_____

_____

20 _____ *

_____

_____

_____

_____

_____

_____

_____

20 _____ *

_____

_____

_____

_____

_____

_____

_____

JULY 27

For a thousand years in Your sight are like yesterday when it passes by, or as a watch in the night. * So teach us to number our days, that we may present to You a heart of wisdom. * There is an appointed time for everything. And there is a time for every event under heaven—a time to give birth and a time to die; a time to plant and a time to uproot what is planted. A time to kill and a time to heal; a time to tear down and a time to build up. A time to weep and a time to laugh; a time to mourn and a time to dance. A time to throw stones and a time to gather stones; a time to embrace and a time to shun embracing. A time to search and a time to give up as lost; a time to keep and a time to throw away. A time to tear apart and a time to sew together; a time to be silent and a time to speak. A time to love and a time to hate; a time for war and a time for peace. * He has made everything appropriate in its time. He has also set eternity in their heart, yet so that man will not find out the work which God has done from the beginning even to the end. * But do not let this one fact escape your notice, beloved, that with the Lord one day is like a thousand years, and a thousand years like one day. The Lord is not slow about His promise, as some count slowness, but is patient toward you, not wishing for any to perish but for all to come to repentance. * And so, dear friends, while you are waiting for these things to happen, make every effort to live a pure and blameless life. And be at peace with God. * But grow in the special favor and knowledge of our Lord and Savior Jesus Christ. To him be all glory and honor, both now and forevermore. Amen.

Psalm 90:4 NASB * Psalm 90:12 NASB * Ecclesiastes 3:1-8 NASB * Ecclesiastes 3:11 NASB * 2 Peter 3:8-9 NASB * 2 Peter 3:14 NLT * 2 Peter 3:18 NLT

July

27 . . . .

Do you long for heaven more today than yesterday?

20 _____ *

_____
_____
_____
_____
_____
_____
_____

20 _____ *

_____
_____
_____
_____
_____
_____
_____

20 _____ *

_____
_____
_____
_____
_____
_____
_____

JULY 28

And let the beauty of the LORD our God be upon us, and establish the work of our hands for us; yes, establish the work of our hands. * I must work the works of Him who sent Me while it is day; the night is coming when no one can work. * Therefore, my beloved brethren, be steadfast, immoveable, always abounding in the work of the Lord, knowing that your labor is not in vain in the Lord. * Walk in wisdom toward those who are outside, redeeming the time. Let your speech always be with grace, seasoned with salt, that you may know how you ought to answer each one. * See then that you walk circumspectly, not as fools but as wise, redeeming the time, because the days are evil. Therefore, do not be unwise, but understand what the will of the Lord is. * You are the light of the world. A city that is set on a hill cannot be hidden. Nor do they light a lamp and put it under a basket, but on a lamp stand, and it gives light to all who are in the house. Let your light so shine before men, that they may see your good works and glorify your Father in heaven. * My love be with you all in Christ Jesus. Amen

Psalm 90:17 NKJV * John 9:4 NKJV * 1 Corinthians 15:58 NKJV * Colossians 4:5-6 NKJV * Matthew 5:14-16 NKJV * 1 Corinthians 15:24 NKJV

JULY

28 . . . .

God will place you where you will be most effective for Him.

20 _____ *

---

20 _____ *

---

20 _____ *

JULY 29

You are good, and do good; teach me your statutes. * Good and upright is the LORD; therefore He teaches sinners in the way. * Do good, O LORD, to those who are good, and to those who are upright in their hearts. * For the LORD God is a sun and shield; the LORD will give grace and glory; no good thing will He withhold from those who walk uprightly. * Praise the LORD! Oh, give thanks to the LORD, for He is good! For His mercy endures forever. Who can utter the mighty acts of the LORD? Who can declare all His praise? * Oh, taste and see that the LORD is good; blessed is the man who trusts in Him! * The LORD is good, a stronghold in the day of trouble; and He knows those who trust in Him. * For the LORD is good; His mercy is everlasting, and His truth endures to all generations. * Indeed it came to pass, when the trumpeters and singers were as one, to make one sound to be heard in praising and thanking the LORD, and when they lifted up their voice with the trumpets and cymbals and instruments of music, and praised the LORD, saying: "For He is good, for His mercy endures forever," that the house, the house of the LORD, was filled with a cloud, so that the priests could not continue ministering because of the cloud; for the glory of the LORD filled the house of God. * Grace with all those who love our Lord Jesus Christ in sincerity. Amen.

Psalm 119:68 NKJV * Psalm 25:8 NKJV * Psalm 125:4 NKJV * Psalm 84:11 NKJV * Psalm 106:1-2 NKJV * Psalm 34:8 NKJV * Nahum 1:7 NKJV * Psalm 100:5 NKJV * 2 Chronicles 5:13-14 NKJV * Ephesians 6:24 NKJV

JULY

29 . . . .

**Thank you, Lord, for You are good and
Your mercy everlasting.**

20 _____ *

_____
_____
_____
_____
_____
_____
_____

20 _____ *

_____
_____
_____
_____
_____
_____
_____

20 _____ *

_____
_____
_____
_____
_____
_____
_____

JULY 30

And the glory of the LORD came into the temple by way of the gate which faces toward the east. The Spirit lifted me up and brought me into the inner court; and behold the glory of the LORD filled the temple. * "For I," says the LORD, "will be a wall of fire all around her, and I will be the glory in her midst." * God is in the midst of her, she shall not be moved; God shall help her, just at the break of dawn. * The sun shall no longer be your light by day, nor for brightness shall the moon give light to you; but the LORD will be to you an everlasting light, and your God your glory. * The city had no need of the sun or of the moon to shine in it, for the glory of God illuminated it. The Lamb is its light. * And there shall be no more curse, but the throne of God and of the Lamb shall be in it, and His servants shall serve Him. They shall see His face, and His name shall be on their foreheads. There shall be no night there: They need no lamp nor light of the sun, for the Lord God gives them light. And they shall reign forever and ever. * He who testifies to these things says, "Surely I am coming quickly." Amen. Even so, come, Lord Jesus!

Ezekiel 43:4-5 NKJV * Zechariah 2:5 NKJV * Psalm 46:5 NKJV * Isaiah 60:19 NKJV * Revelation 21:23 NKJV * Revelation 22:3-5 NKJV * Revelation 22:20 NKJV

JULY

30 . . . .

The Lord is in the midst of His people.

20 _____ *

_____
_____
_____
_____
_____
_____
_____
_____

20 _____ *

_____
_____
_____
_____
_____
_____
_____
_____

20 _____ *

_____
_____
_____
_____
_____
_____
_____
_____

JULY 31

Then I will give you shepherds after My own heart, who will feed you on knowledge and understanding. * Remember those who led you, who spoke the word of God to you; and considering the result of their conduct, imitate their faith. * Obey your leaders and submit to them, for they keep watch over your souls as those who will give an account. Let them do this with joy and not with grief, for this would be unprofitable for you. * But we request of you, brethren, that you appreciate those who diligently labor among you, and have charge over you in the Lord and give you instruction, and that you esteem them very highly in love because of your work. Live in peace with one another. * May the Lord direct your hearts into the love of God and into the steadfastness of Christ. * Now the God of peace, who brought up from the dead the great Shepherd of the sheep through the blood of the eternal covenant, even Jesus our Lord, equip you in every good thing to do His will, working in us that which is pleasing in His sight, through Jesus Christ, to whom be the glory forever and ever. Amen.

Jeremiah 3:15 NASB * Hebrews 13:7 NASB * Hebrews 13:17 NASB * 1 Thessalonians 5:12-13 NASB * 2 Thessalonians 3:5 NASB * Hebrews 13:20-21 NASB

July

31 ....

Will you pray for your leaders?

20 _____ *

_____
_____
_____
_____
_____
_____
_____
_____

20 _____ *

_____
_____
_____
_____
_____
_____
_____
_____

20 _____ *

_____
_____
_____
_____
_____
_____
_____
_____

AUGUST

AUGUST 1

But this I say: He who sows sparingly will also reap sparingly, and he who sows bountifully will also reap bountifully. So let each one give as he purposes in his heart, not grudgingly or of necessity; for God loves a cheerful giver. And God is able to make all grace abound toward you, that you, always having all sufficiency in all things, may have an abundance for every good work. * If there is among you a poor man of your brethren, within any of the gates in your land which the LORD your God is giving you, you shall not harden your heart nor shut your hand from your poor brother, but you shall open your hand wide to him and willingly lend sufficient for his need, whatever he needs. * You shall surely give to him, and your heart should not be grieved when you give to him, because for this thing the LORD your God will bless you in all your works and in all to which you put your hand. * Now may He who supplies seed to the sower, and bread for food, supply and multiply the seed you have sown and increase the fruits of your righteousness, while you are enriched in everything for all liberality, which causes thanksgiving through us to God. * And by their prayers for you, who long for you because of the exceeding grace of God in you. Thanks be to God for His indescribable gift! * My love be with you all in Christ Jesus. Amen.

2 Corinthians 9:6-8 NKJV * Deuteronomy 15:7-8 NKJV * Deuteronomy 15:10 NKJV * 2 Corinthians 9:10-11 NKJV * 2 Corinthians 9:14-15 NKJV * 1 Corinthians 16:24 NKJV

AUGUST

1 . . . .

May the Lord multiply the seed you have sown.

20 _____ *

_____

_____

_____

_____

_____

_____

_____

20 _____ *

_____

_____

_____

_____

_____

_____

_____

20 _____ *

_____

_____

_____

_____

_____

_____

_____

AUGUST 2

The heart of her husband safely trusts her; so he will have no lack of gain. She does him good and not evil all the days of her life. * She considers a field and buys it; from her profits she plants a vineyard. She girds herself with strength, and strengthens her arms. She perceives that her merchandise is good, and her lamp does not go out by night. * She extends her hand to the poor, yes, she reaches out her hands to the needy. * Her husband is known in the gates, when he sits among the elders of the land. * Strength and honor are her clothing; she shall rejoice in time to come. She opens her mouth with wisdom, and on her tongue is the law of kindness. She watches over the ways of her household, and does not eat the bread of idleness. Her children rise up and call her blessed; her husband also, and he praises her: "Many daughters have done well, but you excel them all." Charm is deceitful and beauty is passing, but a woman who fears the LORD, she shall be praised. Give her of the fruit of her hands, and let her own works praise her in the gates. * Therefore, my beloved brethren, be steadfast, immoveable, always abounding in the work of the Lord, knowing that your labor is not in vain in the Lord. * To God, alone wise, be glory through Jesus Christ forever. Amen

Proverbs 31:11-12 NKJV * Proverbs 31:16-17 NKJV * Proverbs 31:20 NKJV * Proverbs 31:23 NKJV * Proverbs 31:25-31 NKJV * 1 Corinthians 15:58 NKJV * Romans 16:27 NKJV

AUGUST

2 ·

Remain steadfast; your work is not in vain.

20 _____ *

_____

_____

_____

_____

_____

_____

_____

20 _____ *

_____

_____

_____

_____

_____

_____

_____

20 _____ *

_____

_____

_____

_____

_____

_____

_____

AUGUST 3

Then the LORD replied to me, "If racing against mere men makes you tired, how will you race against the horses? If you stumble and fall on open ground, what will you do in the thickets near the Jordan?" * Two are better than one, because they have a good reward for their labor. For if they fall, one will lift up his companion. But woe to him who is alone when he falls, for he has no one to help him up. * And He called the twelve to Himself, and began to send them out two by two, and gave them power over unclean spirits. * He sent them to preach the kingdom of God and to heal the sick. * Therefore do not fear them. For there is nothing covered that will not be revealed, and hidden that will not be known. Whatever I tell you in the dark, speak in the light; and what you hear in the ear, preach on the housetops. And do not fear those who kill the body but cannot kill the soul. But rather fear Him who is able to destroy both soul and body in hell. Are not two sparrows sold for a copper coin? And not one of them falls to the ground apart from our Father's will. But the very hairs of your head are all numbered. Do not fear therefore; you are of more value than many sparrows. Therefore whoever confesses Me before men, him I will confess before My Father who is in heaven. * The grace of the Lord Jesus Christ, and the love of God, and the communion of the Holy Spirit be with you all. Amen.

Jeremiah 12:5 NLT * Ecclesiastes 4:9-10 NKJV * Mark 6:7 NKJV * Luke 9:2 NKJV * Matthew 10:26-32 NKJV * 2 Corinthians 13:14 NKJV

AUGUST

3 . . . .

**If what you are facing today makes you tired,
find a friend you can train with.**

*20*_____ *

_____
_____
_____
_____
_____
_____
_____

*20*_____ *

_____
_____
_____
_____
_____
_____
_____

*20*_____ *

_____
_____
_____
_____
_____
_____
_____

449

AUGUST 4

The LORD is my light and my salvation; whom shall I fear? The LORD is the strength of my life; of whom shall I be afraid? * I would have lost heart, unless I had believed that I would see the goodness of the LORD in the land of the living. Wait on the LORD; be of good courage, and He shall strengthen your heart; wait, I say, on the LORD! * The LORD will give strength to His people; the LORD will bless His people with peace. * Blessed be the LORD, because He has heard the voice of my supplications! The LORD is my strength and my shield; my heart trusted in Him, and I am helped; therefore my heart greatly rejoices, and with my song I will praise Him. The Lord is their strength, And He is the saving refuge of His anointed. Save Your people, and bless Your inheritance; shepherd them also, and bear them up forever. * Blessed be the LORD forevermore! Amen and Amen.

Psalm 27:1 NKJV * Psalm 27:13-14 NKJV * Psalm 29:11 NKJV * Psalm 28:6-9 NKJV * Psalm 89:52 NKJV

AUGUST

4 . . . .

I would have lost heart, unless I had believed that I would see the goodness of the LORD in the land of the living.

20 _____ *

20 _____ *

20 _____ *

AUGUST 5

After these things I heard a loud voice of a great multitude in heaven, saying, "Alleluia! Salvation and glory and honor and power belong to the Lord our God!" * God has spoken once, twice I have heard this: that power belongs to God. * You are worthy, O Lord, to receive glory and honor and power; for You created all things, and by Your will they exist and were created. * Worthy is the Lamb who was slain to receive power and riches and wisdom, and strength and honor and glory and blessing! * Let all the earth fear the LORD; let all the inhabitants of the world stand in awe of Him. For He spoke, and it was done; He commanded, and it stood fast. The LORD brings the counsel of nations to nothing; He makes the plans of the peoples of no effect. The counsel of the LORD stands forever, the plans of His heart to all generations. Blessed is the nation whose God is the LORD, the people He has chosen as His own inheritance. * To God, alone wise, be glory through Jesus Christ forever. Amen.

Revelation 19:1 NKJV * Psalm 62:11 NKJV * Revelation 4:11 NKJV * Revelation 5:12 NKJV * Psalm 33:8-12 NKJV * Romans 16:27 NKJV

AUGUST

5 •

Alleluia!

20 _____ *

_____
_____
_____
_____
_____
_____
_____

20 _____ *

_____
_____
_____
_____
_____
_____
_____

20 _____ *

_____
_____
_____
_____
_____
_____
_____

AUGUST 6

The LORD looks from heaven; He sees all the sons of men. From the place of His dwelling He looks on all the inhabitants of the earth; He fashions their hearts individually; He considers all their works. * Behold the eye of the LORD is on those who fear Him, on those who hope in His mercy. * The LORD is in His holy temple, the LORD's throne is in heaven; His eyes behold, His eyelids test the sons of men. The LORD tests the righteous, but the wicked and the one who loves violence His soul hates. Upon the wicked He will rain coals; fire and brimstone and a burning wind shall be the portion of their cup. For the LORD is righteous, He loves righteousness; His countenance beholds the upright. * He gives them security, and they rely on it; yet His eyes are on their ways. * The eyes of the LORD are in every place, keeping watch on the evil and the good. * You are great in counsel and mighty in work, for Your eyes are open to all the ways of the sons of men, to give everyone according to his ways and according to the fruit of his doings. * Let Your mercy, O LORD, be upon us, just as we hope in You. * And blessed be His glorious name forever! And let the whole earth be filled with His glory. Amen and Amen.

Psalm 33:13-15 NKJV * Psalm 33:18 NKJV * Psalm 11:4-7 NKJV * Job 24:23 NKJV * Proverbs 15:3 NKJV * Jeremiah 32:19 NKJV * Psalm 33:22 NKJV * Psalm 72:19 NKJV

AUGUST

6 . . . .

God made your heart.

*20*_____ *

_____
_____
_____
_____
_____
_____
_____

*20*_____ *

_____
_____
_____
_____
_____
_____
_____

*20*_____ *

_____
_____
_____
_____
_____
_____
_____

AUGUST 7

Therefore, my dear brothers and sisters, stand firm. Let nothing move you. Always give yourselves fully to the work of the Lord, because you know that your labor in the Lord is not in vain. * Whatever you do, work at it with all your heart, as working for the Lord, not for human masters, since you know that you will receive an inheritance from the Lord as a reward. It is the Lord Christ you are serving. * Be wise in the way you act toward outsiders; make the most of every opportunity. Let your conversation be always full of grace, seasoned with salt, so that you may know how to answer everyone. * Many are the plans in a person's heart, but it is the LORD's purpose that prevails. * The fruit of the righteous is a tree of life, and the one who is wise saves lives. * But the day of the Lord will come like a thief. The heavens will disappear with a roar; the elements will be destroyed by fire, and the earth and everything done in it will be laid bare. Since everything will be destroyed in this way, what kind of people ought you to be? You ought to live holy and godly lives as you look forward to the day of God and speed its coming. That day will bring about the destruction of the heavens by fire, and the elements will melt in the heat. But in keeping with his promise we are looking forward to a new heaven and a new earth, where righteousness dwells. So then, dear friends, since you are looking forward to this, make every effort to be found spotless, blameless and at peace with him. Bear in mind that our Lord's patience means salvation. * To him be glory both now and forever! Amen.

1 Corinthians 15:58 NIV * Colossians 3:23-24 NIV * Colossians 4:5-6 NIV * Proverbs 19:21 NIV * Proverbs 11:30 NIV * 2 Peter 3:10-15a NIV * 2 Peter 3:18b NIV

AUGUST

7 . . . .

Will you reach the lost the Lord is waiting for?

20 _____ *

_____

_____

_____

_____

_____

_____

20 _____ *

_____

_____

_____

_____

_____

_____

20 _____ *

_____

_____

_____

_____

_____

_____

AUGUST 8

Looking for the blessed hope and glorious appearing of our great God and Savior Jesus Christ, who gave Himself for us, that He might redeem us from every lawless deed and purify for Himself His own special people, zealous for good works. * For by grace you have been saved through faith, and that not of yourselves; it is the gift of God, not of works, lest anyone should boast. For we are His workmanship, created in Christ Jesus for good works, which God prepared beforehand that we should walk in them. * But now in Christ Jesus you who once were far off have been brought near by the blood of Christ. For He Himself is our peace, who has made both one, and has broken down the middle wall of separation, having abolished in His flesh the enmity, that is, the law of commandments contained in ordinances, so as to create in Himself one new man from the two, thus making peace, and that He might reconcile them both to God in one body through the cross, thereby putting to death the enmity. * I have been crucified with Christ, it is no longer I who live, but Christ who lives in me; and the life which I now live in the flesh, I live by faith in the Son of God, who loved me, and gave Himself for me. I do not set aside the grace of God; for if righteousness comes through the law, then Christ died in vain. * Now you have every spiritual gift you need as you eagerly wait for the return of our Lord Jesus Christ. He will keep you strong right up to the end, and he will keep you free from all blame on the great day when our Lord Jesus Christ returns. God will surely do this for you, for he always does just what he says, and he is the one who invited you into this wonderful friendship with his Son, Jesus Christ our Lord. * Set your mind on things above, not on things on the earth. For you died, and your life is hidden with Christ in God. When Christ who is our life appears, then you also will appear with Him in glory. * Grace to you and peace from God the Father and our Lord Jesus Christ, who gave Himself for our sins, that He might deliver us from this present evil age, according to the will of our God and Father, to whom be glory forever and ever. Amen.

Titus 2:13-14 NKJV * Ephesians 2:8-10 NKJV * Ephesians 2:13-16 NKJV * Galatians 2:20-21 NKJV * 1 Corinthians 1:7-9 NLT * Colossians 3:2-4 NKJV * Galatians 1:3-5 NKJV

AUGUST

8 . . . .

What are you zealous for?

20 _____ *

_____
_____
_____
_____
_____
_____
_____

20 _____ *

_____
_____
_____
_____
_____
_____
_____

20 _____ *

_____
_____
_____
_____
_____
_____
_____

AUGUST 9

Love must be sincere. Hate what is evil; cling to what is good. Be devoted to one another in love. Honor one another above yourselves. Never be lacking in zeal, but keep your spiritual fervor, serving the Lord. Be joyful in hope, patient in affliction, faithful in prayer. Share with the Lord's people who are in need. Practice hospitality. * Greet all God's people in Christ Jesus. The brothers and sisters who are with me send greetings. * Epaphras, who is one of you and a servant of Christ Jesus, sends greetings. He is always wrestling in prayer for you, that you may stand firm in all the will of God, mature and fully assured. I vouch for him that he is working hard for you and for those at Laodicea and Hierapolis. Our dear friend Luke, the doctor, and Demas send greetings. * Greet Priscilla and Aquila, my co-workers in Christ Jesus. They risked their lives for me. Not only I but all the churches of the Gentiles are grateful to them. * My fellow prisoner Aristarchus sends you his greetings, as does Mark, the cousin of Barnabas. (You have received instructions about him; if he comes to you, welcome him.) Jesus, who is called Justus, also sends greetings. These are the only Jews among my co-workers for the kingdom of God, and they have proved a comfort to me. * I commend to you our sister Phoebe, a deacon of the church in Cenchrea. I ask you to receive her in the Lord in a way worthy of his people and to give her any help she may need from you, for she has been the benefactor to many people, including me. * Timothy, my co-worker, sends his greetings to you, as do Lucius, Jason and Sosipater, my fellow Jews. I, Tertius, who wrote down this letter, greet you in the Lord. Gaius, whose hospitality I and the whole church here enjoy, sends you his greetings. Erastus, who is the city's director of public works, and our brother Quartus send you their greetings. * Greet Mary, who worked very hard for you. * All the brothers and sisters here send you greetings. Greet one another with a holy kiss. * Follow my example, as I follow the example of Christ. * The grace of our Lord Jesus Christ be with you all. Amen.

Romans 12:9-13 NIV * Philippians 4:21 NIV * Colossians 4:12-14 NIV * Romans 16:3-4 NIV * Colossians 4:10-11 NIV * Romans 16:1-2 NIV * Romans 16:21-23 NIV * Romans 16:6 NIV * 1 Corinthians 16:20 NIV * 1 Corinthians 11:1 NIV * Romans 16:24 KJV

AUGUST

9 . . . .

Who do you need to greet today?

20_____ *

_____

_____

_____

_____

_____

_____

_____

20_____ *

_____

_____

_____

_____

_____

_____

_____

20_____ *

_____

_____

_____

_____

_____

_____

_____

AUGUST 10

How blessed are your men, how blessed are these your servants who stand before you continually and hear your wisdom. Blessed be the LORD your God who delighted in you, setting you on His throne as king for the LORD your God; because your God loved Israel establishing forever, therefore He made you king over them, to do justice and righteousness. * As for you, if you walk before Me as your father David walked, even to do according to all that I have commanded you, and will keep My statutes and My ordinances, then I will establish your royal throne as I covenanted with your father David, saying, "You shall not lack a man to be ruler in Israel." But if you turn away and forsake My statutes and My commandments which I have set before you, and go and serve other gods and worship them, then I will uproot you from My land which I have given you, and this house which I have consecrated for My name I will cast out of My sight and I will make it a proverb and a byword among all peoples. * For you are a holy people to the LORD your God; the LORD your God has chosen you to be a people for His own possession out of all the peoples who are on the face of the earth. The LORD did not set His love on you nor choose you because you were more in number than any of the peoples, for you were the fewest of all peoples, but because the LORD loved you and kept the oath which He swore to your forefathers, the LORD brought you out by a mighty hand and redeemed you from the house of slavery, from the hand of Pharaoh king of Egypt. Know therefore that the LORD your God, He is God, the faithful God, who keeps His covenant and His lovingkindness to a thousandth generation with those who love Him and keep His commandments; but repays those who hate Him to their faces, to destroy them; He will not delay with him who hates Him, He will repay him to his face. * The grace of the Lord Jesus Christ be with your spirit. * Amen and Amen.

2 Chronicles 9:7-8 NASB * 2 Chronicles 7:17-20 NASB * Deuteronomy 7:6-10 NASB * Philippians 4:23 NASB * Psalm 41:13b NASB

AUGUST

10 ·

Every nation needs justice and righteousness.

20 _____ *

_____
_____
_____
_____
_____
_____
_____

20 _____ *

_____
_____
_____
_____
_____
_____
_____

20 _____ *

_____
_____
_____
_____
_____
_____
_____

AUGUST 11

I waited patiently for the LORD to help me, and he turned to me and heard my cry. * Save me, O God, for the floodwaters are up to my neck. Deeper and deeper I sink into the mire; I can't find a foothold to stand on. I am in deep water, and the floods overwhelm me. I am exhausted from crying for help; my throat is parched and dry. My eyes are swollen with weeping, waiting for my God to help me. * Be patient in the presence of the LORD, and wait patiently for him to act. * The LORD is wonderfully good to those who wait for him and seek him. So it is good to wait quietly for salvation from the LORD. * For the LORD does not abandon anyone forever. * He lifted me out of the pit of despair, out of the mud and the mire. He set my feet on solid ground and steadied me as I walked along. * The steps of the godly are directed by the LORD, He delights in every detail of their lives. Though they stumble they will not fall, for the LORD holds them by the hand. * We are pressed on every side by troubles, but we are not crushed and broken. We are perplexed, but we don't give up and quit. We are hunted down, but God never abandons us. We get knocked down, but we get up again and keep going. Through suffering, these bodies of ours constantly share in the death of Jesus so that the life of Jesus may also be seen in our bodies. Yes, we live under constant danger of death because we serve Jesus, so that the life of Jesus will be obvious in our dying bodies. So we live in the face of death, but it has resulted in eternal life for you. * That is why we never give up. Though our bodies are dying, our spirits are being renewed every day. For our present troubles are quite small and wont last very long. Yet they produce for us an immeasurably great glory that will last forever! So we don't look at the troubles we can see right now, rather, we look forward to what we have not yet seen. For the troubles we see will soon be over, but the joys to come will last forever. * My dear brothers and sisters, may the grace of our Lord Jesus Christ be with you all. Amen.

Psalm 40:1 NLT * Psalm 69:1-3 NLT * Psalm 37:7 NLT * Lamentations 3:25-26 NLT * Lamentations 3:31 NLT * Psalm 40:2 NLT * Psalm 37:23-24 NLT * 2 Corinthians 4:8-12 NLT * 2 Corinthians 4:16-18 NLT * Galatians 6:18 NLT

AUGUST

11 ....

Will you come alongside those who are suffering in silence?

20 _____ *

20 _____ *

20 _____ *

AUGUST 12

He has given me a new song to sing, a hymn of praise to our God. Many will see what he has done and be astounded. They will put their trust in the LORD. Oh, the joys of those who trust in the LORD who have no confidence in the proud or in those who worship idols. * Hear, O Israel! The LORD is our God, the LORD alone. And you must love the LORD your God with all your heart, all your soul, and all your strength. And you must commit yourselves wholeheartedly to these commands I am giving you today. Repeat them again and again to your children. Talk about them when you are at home and when you are away on a journey, when you are lying down and when you are getting up. Tie them to your hands as a reminder, and wear them on your forehead. Write them on the doorposts of your house and on your gates. * Come to Christ, who is the living cornerstone of God's temple. He was rejected by the people, but he is precious to God who chose him. And now God is building you, as living stones, into his spiritual temple. What's more, you are God's holy priests, who offer spiritual sacrifices that please him because of Jesus Christ. As the Scriptures express it, "I am placing a stone in Jerusalem, a chosen cornerstone, and anyone who believes in him will never be disappointed." Yes, he is very precious to you who believe. But for those who reject him, "The stone that was rejected by the builders has now become the cornerstone." And the Scriptures also say, "He is the stone that makes people stumble, the rock that will make them fall." They stumble because they do not listen to God's word or obey it, and so they meet the fate that has been planned for them. But you are not like that, for you are a chosen people. You are a kingdom of priests, God's holy nation, his very own possession. This is so you can show others the goodness of God, for he called you out of darkness into his wonderful light. Once you were not a people; now you are the people of God. Once you received none of God's mercy; now you have received his mercy. * Amen and Amen.

Psalm 40:3-4 NLT * Deuteronomy 6:4-9 NLT * 1 Peter 2:4-10 NLT * Psalm 72:19b NLT

AUGUST

12 . . . .

How are you committing yourself wholeheartedly to these commands: to love the Lord your God with all your heart, all your soul, and all your strength?

20 _____ *

_____
_____
_____
_____
_____
_____
_____

20 _____ *

_____
_____
_____
_____
_____
_____
_____

20 _____ *

_____
_____
_____
_____
_____
_____
_____

AUGUST 13

O LORD my God, you have done many miracles for us. Your plans for us are too numerous to list. If I tried to recite all your wonderful deeds, I would never come to the end of them. * Who else among the gods is like you, O LORD? Who is glorious in holiness like you—so awesome in splendor, performing such wonders? You raised up your hand, and the earth swallowed our enemies. With unfailing love you will lead this people whom you have ransomed. You will guide them in your strength to the place where your holiness dwells. * "My thoughts are completely different from yours," says the LORD. "And my ways are far beyond anything you could imagine. For just as the heavens are higher than the earth, so are my ways higher than your ways and my thoughts higher than your thoughts. * "Be just and fair to all," says the LORD. "Do what is right and good, for I am coming soon to rescue you. Blessed are those who are careful to do this. Blessed are those who honor my Sabbath days of rest by refusing to work. And blessed are those who keep themselves from doing wrong." * I will bring them also to my holy mountain of Jerusalem and will fill them with joy in my house of prayer. I will accept their burnt offerings and sacrifices, because my Temple will be called a house of prayer for all nations. For the Sovereign LORD, who brings back the outcasts of Israel, says: I will bring others, too, besides my people Israel. * I will praise your mighty deeds, O Sovereign LORD. I will tell everyone that you alone are just and good. * We will not hide these truths from our children, but will tell the next generation about the glorious deeds of the LORD. We will tell of his power and the mighty miracles he did. * So the next generation might know them—even the children not yet born—so they in turn might teach their children. So each generation can set its hope anew on God, remembering his glorious miracles and obeying his commands. * Now to Him who is able to do exceedingly abundantly above all that we ask or think, according to the power that works in us, to Him be glory in the church by Christ Jesus to all generations, forever and ever. Amen.

Psalm 40:5 NLT * Exodus 15:11-13 NLT * Isaiah 55:8-9 NLT * Isaiah 56:1-2 NLT * Isaiah 56:7-8 NLT * Psalm 71:16 NLT * Psalm 78:4 NLT * Psalm 78:6-7 NLT * Ephesians 3:20-21 NKJV

AUGUST

13 ....

**God is able to do exceedingly abundantly above all you
ask or think, and He wants to.**

20 _____ *

20 _____ *

20 _____ *

AUGUST 14

You take no delight in sacrifices or offerings. Now that you have made me listen, I finally understand—you don't require burnt offerings or sin offerings. * But Samuel replied, "What is more pleasing to the LORD: your burnt offerings and sacrifices or your obedience to his voice? Obedience is far better than sacrifice. Listening to him is much better than offering the fat of rams. * Christ said, "You did not want animal sacrifices or grain offerings or animals burned on the alter or other offerings for sin, nor were you pleased with them" (though they are required by the law of Moses). Then he added, "Look, I have come to do your will." He cancels the first covenant in order to establish the second. And what God wants is for us to be made holy by the sacrifice of the body of Jesus Christ once for all time. Under the old covenant, the priest stands before the altar day after day, offering sacrifices that can never take away sins. But our High Priest offered himself to God as one sacrifice for sins, good for all time. Then he sat down at the place of highest honor at God's right hand. There he waits until his enemies are humbled as a footstool under his feet. For by that one offering he perfected forever all those whom he is making holy. The Holy Spirit also testifies that this is so. First he says, "This is the new covenant I will make with my people on that day, says the Lord: I will put my laws in their hearts so they will understand them, and I will write them on their minds so they will obey them." Then he adds, "I will never again remember their sins and lawless deeds." Now when sins have been forgiven, there is no need to offer any more sacrifices. And so, dear brothers and sisters, we can boldly enter heaven's Most Holy Place because of the blood of Jesus. * Because of Christ and our faith in him, we can now come fearlessly into God's presence assured of his glad welcome. * To him be glory forever and ever. Amen.

Psalm 40:6 NLT * 1 Samuel 15:22 NLT * Hebrews 10:8-19 NLT * Ephesians 3:12 NLT * Hebrews 13:21b NLT

AUGUST

14 . . . .

Do you listen to God?

20 _____ *

_____

_____

_____

_____

_____

_____

20 _____ *

_____

_____

_____

_____

_____

_____

20 _____ *

_____

_____

_____

_____

_____

_____

AUGUST 15

Then I said, "Look, I have come. And this has been written about me in your scroll: I take joy in doing your will, my God, for your law is written on my heart." * My heart has heard you say, "Come and talk with me." And my heart responds, "LORD, I am coming." * My life is an example to many, because you have been my strength and protection. That is why I can never stop praising you; I declare your glory all day long. * Sing to him; yes, sing his praises. Tell everyone about his miracles. Exult his holy name; O worshipers of the LORD, rejoice! Search for the LORD and for his strength, and keep on searching. * Forever, O LORD, your word stands firm in heaven. Your faithfulness extends to every generation, as enduring as the earth you created. Your laws remain true today, for everything serves your plans. If your law hadn't sustained me with joy, I would have died in my misery. I will never forget your commandments for you have used them to restore my joy and health. * In Your presence is fullness of joy. * And I can't stop! If I say I'll never mention the LORD or speak in his name, his word burns in my heart like a fire. It's like a fire in my bones! I am weary of holding it in! * I love the LORD because he hears and answers my prayers. Because he bends down and listens, I will pray as long as I have breath! * Praise the LORD, I tell myself; with my whole heart, I will praise his holy name. Praise the LORD, I tell myself, and never forget the good things he does for me. * Blessed be the LORD forever! Amen and Amen!

Psalm 40:7-8 NLT * Psalm 27:8 NLT * Psalm 70:7-8 NLT * Psalm 105:2-4 NLT * Psalm 119:89-93 NLT * Psalm 16:11b NKJV * Jeremiah 20:9 NLT * Psalm 116:1-2 NLT * Psalm 103:1-2 NLT * Psalm 89:52 NLT

AUGUST

15 . . . .

**My life is an example to many because
God is my strength and protection.**

20 _____ *

_____

_____

_____

_____

_____

_____

_____

20 _____ *

_____

_____

_____

_____

_____

_____

_____

20 _____ *

_____

_____

_____

_____

_____

_____

_____

AUGUST 16

I have told all your people about your justice, I have not been afraid to speak out, as you, O LORD, well know. I have not kept this good news hidden in my heart, I have talked about your faithfulness and saving power. I have told everyone in the great assembly of your unfailing love and faithfulness. * I have done the Lord's work humbly—yes, and with tears. I have endured the trials that came to me from the plots of the Jews. Yet I never shrank from telling you the truth, either publicly or in your homes. I have had one message for Jews and Gentiles alike—the necessity of turning from sin and turning to God, and of faith in our Lord Jesus. * But my life is worth nothing unless I use it for doing the work assigned me by the Lord Jesus—the work of telling others the Good News about God's wonderful kindness and love. * And now beware! Be sure that you feed and shepherd God's flock—his church, purchased with his blood— over whom the Holy Spirit has appointed you as elders. * And I am sure that God, who began the good work within you, will continue his work until it is finally finished on that day when Christ Jesus comes back again. * For I live in eager expectation and hope that I will never do anything that causes me shame, but that I will always be bold for Christ, as I have been in the past, and that my life will always honor Christ, whether I live or I die. For to me, living is for Christ, and dying is even better. Yet if I live, that means fruitful service for Christ. I really don't know which is better. I'm torn between two desires: Sometimes I want to live, and sometimes I long to go and be with Christ. That would be far better for me, but it is better for you that I live. I am convinced of this, so I will continue with you so that you will grow and experience the joy of your faith. * Amen and Amen.

Psalm 40:9-10 NLT * Acts 20:19-20 NLT * Acts 20:24 NLT * Acts 20:28 NLT * Philippians 1:6 NLT * Philippians 1:20-25 NLT * Psalm 72:19b NLT

AUGUST

16 ....

**The joy of your faith will overflow as you share
the Good News.**

20 _____ *

_____
_____
_____
_____
_____
_____

20 _____ *

_____
_____
_____
_____
_____
_____

20 _____ *

_____
_____
_____
_____
_____
_____

AUGUST 17

LORD, don't hold back your tender mercies from me. My only hope is in your unfailing love and faithfulness. For troubles surround me—too many to count! They pile up so high I can't see my way out. They are more numerous than the hairs on my head. I have lost all my courage. Please, LORD rescue me! Come quickly, LORD, and help me. May those who try to destroy me be humiliated and put to shame. May those who take delight in my trouble be turned back in disgrace. Let them be horrified by their shame, for they said, "Aha! We've got him now!" * I am the favorite topic of town gossip, and all the drunkards sing about me. * For I am mocked and shamed for your sake; humiliation is written all over my face. * Those who hate me without cause are more numerous than the hairs on my head. These enemies who seek to destroy me are doing so without cause. They attack me with lies, demanding that I give back what I didn't steal. * You know the insults I endure—the humiliation and disgrace. You have seen all my enemies and know what they have said. Their insults have broken my heart, and I am in despair. If only one person would show some pity; if only one would turn and comfort me. * When I weep and fast before the LORD, they scoff at me. * But I keep right on praying to you, LORD, hoping this is the time you will show me favor. * Come and rescue me; from all my enemies. * I am suffering and in pain. Rescue me, O God, by your saving power. Then I will praise God's name with singing, and I will honor him with thanksgiving. For this will please the LORD more than sacrificing an ox or presenting a bull with its horns and hooves. The humble will see their God at work and be glad. Let all who seek God's help live in joy. For the LORD hears the cries of his needy ones; he does not despise his people who are oppressed. * For we are not fighting against people made of flesh and blood, but against the evil rulers and authorities of the unseen world, against those mighty powers of darkness who rule this world, and against wicked spirits in the heavenly realms. * Glory and honor to God forever and ever. He is the eternal King, the unseen one who never dies; he alone is God. Amen.

Psalm 40:11-15 NLT * Psalm 69:12 NLT * Psalm 69:7 NLT * Psalm 69:4 NLT * Psalm 69:19-20 NLT * Psalm 69:10 NLT * Psalm 69:13 NLT * Psalm 69:18 NLT * Psalm 69:29-33 NLT * Ephesians 6:12 NLT * 1 Timothy 1:17 NLT

AUGUST

17 . . . .

**The battle is unseen by men, but seen by God.
He rescues.**

20 ____ *

---

20 ____ *

---

20 ____ *

AUGUST 18

But may all who search for you be filled with joy and gladness. May those who love your salvation repeatedly shout, "The LORD is great!" As for me, I am poor and needy, but the Lord is thinking about me right now. You are my helper and my savior. Do not delay, O my God. * Teach me how to live, O LORD, lead me along the path of honesty, for my enemies are waiting for me to fall. Do not let me fall into their hands, for they accuse me of things I've never done, and breathe out violence against me. Yet I am confident that I will see the LORD's goodness while I am here in the land of the living. Wait patiently for the LORD. Be brave and courageous. Yes, wait patiently for the LORD. * It is God's will that your good lives should silence those who make foolish accusations against you. * For God is pleased with you when, for the sake of your conscience, you patiently endure unfair treatment. Of course, you get no credit for being patient if you are beaten for doing wrong. But if you suffer for doing right and are patient beneath the blows, God is pleased with you. This suffering is all part of what God has called you to. Christ, who suffered for you is your example. Follow in his steps. He never sinned, and he never deceived anyone. He did not retaliate when he was insulted. When he suffered, he did not threaten to get even. He left his case in the hands of God, who always judges fairly. He personally carried away our sins in his own body on the cross so we can be dead to sin and live for what is right. You have been healed by his wounds. Once you were wandering like lost sheep. But now you have turned to your Shepherd, the Guardian of your souls. * To him be all glory and honor, both now and forevermore. Amen.

Psalm 40:16-17 NLT * Psalm 27:11-14 NLT * 1 Peter 2:15 NLT * 1 Peter 2:19-25 NLT * 2 Peter 3:18b NLT

AUGUST

18 . . . .

The path of honesty is traversed by few. Why?

20 _____ *

20 _____ *

20 _____ *

AUGUST 19

If my people who are called by My name will humble themselves and pray and seek My face, and turn from their wicked ways, then I will hear from heaven, and will forgive their sin and heal their land. * After this, Joseph of Arimathea, being a disciple of Jesus, but secretly, for fear of the Jews, asked Pilate that he might take away the body of Jesus; and Pilate gave him permission. So he came and took the body of Jesus. And Nicodemus, who at first came to Jesus by night, also came, bringing a mixture of myrrh and aloes, about a hundred pounds. Then they took the body of Jesus, and bound it in strips of linen with spices, as the custom of the Jews is to bury. Now in the place where He was crucified there was a garden, and in the garden a new tomb in which no one had yet been laid. So there they laid Jesus, because of the Jews' Preparation Day, for the tomb was nearby. Now the first day of the week Mary Magdalene went to the tomb early, while it was still dark, and saw that the stone had been taken away from the tomb. Then she ran and came to Simon Peter, and to the other disciple, whom Jesus loved, and said to them, "They have taken away the Lord out of the tomb, and we do not know where they have laid Him." * And their words seemed to them like idle tales, and they did not believe them. But Peter arose and ran to the tomb; and stooping down, he saw the linen cloths lying by themselves; and he departed, marveling to himself at what had happened. * But Mary stood outside the tomb weeping, and as she wept she stooped down and looked into the tomb. And she saw two angels in white sitting, one at the head and the other at the feet, where the body of Jesus had lain. Then they said to her, "Woman, why are you weeping?" She said to them, "Because they have taken away my Lord, and I do not know where they have laid Him." Now when she had said this, she turned around and saw Jesus standing there, and did not know that it was Jesus. Jesus said to her, "Woman, why are you weeping? Whom are you seeking?" She, supposing Him to be the gardener, said to Him, "Sir, if You have carried Him away, tell me where You have laid Him, and I will take Him away." Jesus said to her, "Mary!" She turned and said to Him, "Rabboni!" (which is to say, Teacher). Jesus said to her, "Do not cling to Me, for I have not yet ascended to My Father; but go to My brethren and say to them, 'I am ascending to My Father and your Father, and to My God and your God.'" * Amen and Amen.

2 Chronicles 7:14 NKJV * John 19:38- 20:2 NKJV * Luke 24:11-12 NKJV * John 20:11-17 NKJV * Psalm 72:19b NKJV

AUGUST

19 . . . .

How is God calling you to be bold today?

20 _____ *

20 _____ *

20 _____ *

AUGUST 20

When he saw the crowds, he had compassion on them, because they were harassed and helpless, like a sheep without a shepherd. Then he said to his disciples, "The harvest is plentiful but the workers are few. Ask the Lord of the harvest, therefore, to send out workers into his harvest field." * I am the good shepherd. The good shepherd lays down his life for the sheep. The hired hand is not the shepherd and does not own the sheep. So when he sees the wolf coming, he abandons the sheep and runs away. Then the wolf attacks the flock and scatters it. The man runs away because he is a hired hand and cares nothing for the sheep. I am the good shepherd; I know my sheep and my sheep know me—just as the Father knows me and I know the Father—and I lay down my life for the sheep. I have other sheep that are not of this sheep pen. I must bring them also. They too will listen to my voice, and there shall be one flock and one shepherd. * My sheep listen to my voice; I know them, and they follow me. * You know, brothers and sisters, that our visit to you was not without results. We had previously suffered and been treated outrageously in Philippi, as you know, but with the help of our God we dared to tell you his gospel in the face of strong opposition. For the appeal we make does not spring from error or impure motives, nor are we trying to trick you. On the contrary, we speak as those approved by God to be entrusted with the gospel. We are not trying to please people but God, who tests our hearts. You know we never used flattery, nor did we put on a mask to cover up greed—God is our witness. We were not looking for praise from people, not from you or anyone else, even though as apostles of Christ we could have asserted our authority. Instead, we were like young children among you. Just as a nursing mother cares for her children, so we cared for you. Because we loved you so much, we were delighted to share with you not only the gospel of God but our lives as well. Surely you remember, brothers and sisters, our toil and hardship; we worked night and day in order not to be a burden to anyone while we preached the gospel of God to you. You are witnesses, and so is God, of how holy, righteous and blameless we were among you who believed. For you know that we dealt with each of you as a father deals with his own children, encouraging, comforting and urging you to live lives worthy of God, who calls you into his kingdom and glory. * To him be glory in the church and in Christ Jesus throughout all generations, for ever and ever! Amen.

Matthew 9:36-38 NIV * John 10:11-16 NIV * John 10:27 NIV * 1 Thessalonians 2:4-12 NIV * Ephesians 3:21 NIV

AUGUST

20 . . . .

Do you know where to go to for help?

20 _____ *

_____

_____

_____

_____

_____

_____

_____

20 _____ *

_____

_____

_____

_____

_____

_____

_____

20 _____ *

_____

_____

_____

_____

_____

_____

_____

AUGUST 21

As the deer pants for streams of water, so I long for you, O God. I thirst for God, the living God. When can I come and stand before him? * Who may worship in your sanctuary, LORD? Who may enter your presence on your holy hill? Those who lead blameless lives and do what is right, speaking the truth from sincere hearts. Those who refuse to slander others or harm their neighbors or speak evil of their friends. Those who despise persistent sinners, and honor the faithful followers of the LORD and keep their promises even when it hurts. Those who do not charge interest on the money they lend, and who refuse to accept bribes to testify against the innocent. Such people will stand firm forever. * Who may climb the mountain of the LORD? Who may stand in his holy place? Only those whose hands and hearts are pure, who do not worship idols and never tell lies. They will receive the LORD's blessing and have right standing with God their savior. They alone may enter God's presence and worship the God of Israel. * Truly God is good to Israel, to those whose hearts are pure. * If we say we have no sin, we are only fooling ourselves and refusing to accept the truth. But if we confess our sins to him, he is faithful and just to forgive us and to cleanse us from every wrong. * What this means is that those who become Christians become new persons. They are not the same anymore, for the old life is gone. A new life has begun! * For God made Christ, who never sinned, to be the offering for our sin, so that we could be made right with God through Christ. * Because of Christ and our faith in him, we can now come fearlessly into God's presence assured of his glad welcome. * Bless the LORD, the God of Israel, who lives forever from eternal ages past. Amen and Amen.

Psalm 42:1-2 NLT * Psalm 15:1-5 NLT * Psalm 24:2-6 NLT * Psalm 73:1 NLT * 1 John 1:8-9 NLT * 2 Corinthians 5:17 NLT * 2 Corinthians 5:21 NLT * Ephesians 3:12 NLT * Psalm 41:13 NLT

AUGUST

21 ....

The best Q & A with God asks what question?

20_____ *

_____
_____
_____
_____
_____
_____
_____

20_____ *

_____
_____
_____
_____
_____
_____
_____

20_____ *

_____
_____
_____
_____
_____
_____
_____

AUGUST 22

The LORD will command His lovingkindness in the daytime, and in the night His songs shall be with me—a prayer to the God of my life. * Be my strong refuge, to which I may resort continually; You have given the commandment to save me, for You are my rock and my fortress. * I call to remembrance my song in the night; I meditate within my heart, and my spirit makes diligent search. * I remember Your name in the night, O LORD, and I keep Your law. * At midnight I will rise to give thanks to You, because of Your righteous judgments. * My eyes are awake through the night watches, that I may meditate on Your word. Hear my voice according to Your lovingkindness; O LORD, revive me according to Your justice. * But at midnight Paul and Silas were praying and singing hymns to God, and the prisoners were listening to them. Suddenly there was a great earthquake, so that the foundations of the prison were shaken; and immediately all the doors were opened and everyone's chains were loosed. And the keeper of the prison, awaking from sleep and seeing the prison doors open, supposing the prisoners had fled, drew his sword and was about to kill himself. But Paul called with a loud voice, saying, "Do yourself no harm, for we are all here." Then he called for a light, ran in, and fell down trembling before Paul and Silas. And he brought them out and said, "Sirs, what must I do to be saved?" So they said, "Believe on the Lord Jesus Christ, and you will be saved, you and your household." Then they spoke the word of the Lord to him and to all who were in his house. And he took them the same hour of the night and washed their stripes. And immediately he and his family were baptized. Now when he had brought them into his house, he set food before them; and he rejoiced, having believed in God with all his household. * Amen and Amen.

Psalm 42:8 NKJV * Psalm 71:3 NKJV * Psalm 77:6 NKJV * Psalm 119:55 NKJV * Psalm 119:62 NKJV * Psalm 119:148-149 NKJV * Acts 16:25-34 NKJV * Psalm 72:19b NKJV

AUGUST

22 . . . .

Remember your song in the night and the healing that came.

20 _____ *

20 _____ *

20 _____ *

AUGUST 23

God blesses those who realize their need for him, for the Kingdom of Heaven is given to them. * Someone came to Jesus with this question: "Teacher, what good things must I do to have eternal life?" "Why ask me about what is good?" Jesus replied. "Only God is good. But to answer your question, you can receive eternal life if you keep the commandments." "Which ones?" the man asked. And Jesus replied: "'Do not murder. Do not commit adultery. Do not steal. Do not testify falsely. Honor your father and mother. Love your neighbor as yourself.'" "I've obeyed all these commandments," the young man replied. "What else must I do?" Jesus told him, "If you want to be perfect, go and sell all you have and give the money to the poor, and you will have treasure in heaven. Then come, follow me." But when the young man heard this, he went sadly away because he had many possessions. Then Jesus said to his disciples, "I tell you the truth, it is very hard for a rich person to get into the Kingdom of Heaven. I say it again—it is easier for a camel to go through the eye of a needle than for a rich person to enter the Kingdom of God!" The disciples were astounded. "Then who in the world can be saved?" they asked. Jesus looked at them intently and said, "Humanly speaking, it is impossible. But with God everything is possible." Then Peter said to him, "We've given up everything to follow you. What will we get out of it?" And Jesus replied, "I assure you that when I, the Son of Man, sit upon my glorious throne in the Kingdom, you who have been my followers will also sit on twelve thrones, judging the twelve tribes of Israel. And everyone who has given up houses or brothers or sisters or father or mother or children or property, for my sake, will receive a hundred times as much in return and will have eternal life. But many who seem to be important now will be the least important then, and those who are considered least here will be the greatest then. * Amen and amen!

Matthew 5:3 NLT * Matthew 19:16-30 NLT * Psalm 72:19b NLT

AUGUST

23 . . . .

How have you realized your need for Jesus Christ?

20 _____ *

_____
_____
_____
_____
_____
_____
_____

20 _____ *

_____
_____
_____
_____
_____
_____
_____

20 _____ *

_____
_____
_____
_____
_____
_____
_____

AUGUST 24

Blessed are those who mourn, for they shall be comforted. * Also He spoke this parable to some who trusted in themselves that they were righteous, and despised others: "Two men went up to the temple to pray, one a Pharisee and the other a tax collector. The Pharisee stood and prayed thus with himself, 'God, I thank You that I am not like other men—extortioners, unjust, adulterers, or even as this tax collector. I fast twice a week; I give tithes of all that I possess.' And the tax collector, standing afar off, would not so much as raise his eyes to heaven, but beat his breast, saying, 'God, be merciful to me a sinner!' I tell you, this man went down to his house justified rather than the other; for everyone who exalts himself will be humbled, and he who humbles himself will be exalted." * For all have sinned; all fall short of God's glorious standard. Yet now God in his gracious kindness declares us not guilty. He has done this through Christ Jesus, who has freed us by taking away our sins. For God sent Jesus to take the punishment for our sins and to satisfy God's anger against us. We are made right with God when we believe that Jesus shed his blood, sacrificing his life for us. God was being entirely fair and just when he did not punish those who sinned in former times. And he is entirely fair and just in this present time when he declares sinners to be right in his sight because they believe in Jesus. Can we boast, then, that we have done anything to be accepted by God? No, because our acquittal is not based on our good deeds. It is based on our faith. So we are made right with God through faith and not by obeying the law. * To God, alone wise, be glory through Jesus Christ forever. Amen.

Matthew 5:4 NKJV * Luke 18:9-14 NKJV * Romans 3:23-28 NLT * Romans 16:27 NKJV

AUGUST

24 . . . .

Are you quick to ask God to forgive you of your sin?

20____ *

_____
_____
_____
_____
_____
_____
_____

20____ *

_____
_____
_____
_____
_____
_____
_____

20____ *

_____
_____
_____
_____
_____
_____
_____

AUGUST 25

Blessed are the meek, for they shall inherit the earth. * And while He was being accused by the chief priests and elders, He answered nothing. Then Pilate said to Him, "Do You not hear how many things they testify against You?" But He answered him not one word, so that the governor marveled greatly. * Then the soldiers of the governor took Jesus into the Praetorium and gathered the whole garrison around Him. And they stripped Him and put a scarlet robe on Him. When they had twisted a crown of thorns, they put it on His head, and a reed in His right hand. And they bowed the knee before Him and mocked Him, saying, "Hail, King of the Jews!" Then they spat on Him, and took the reed and struck Him on the head. And when they had mocked Him, they took the robe off Him, put His own clothes on Him and led Him away to be crucified. * The soldiers also mocked Him, coming and offering Him sour wine, and saying, "If You are the King of the Jews, save Yourself." And an inscription also was written over Him in letters of Greek, Latin, and Hebrew: THIS IS THE KING OF THE JEWS. Then one of the criminals who were hanged blasphemed Him, saying, "If You are the Christ, save Yourself and us." But the other, answering, rebuked him, saying, "Do you not even fear God, seeing you are under the same condemnation? And we indeed justly, for we receive the due reward of our deeds; but this Man has done nothing wrong." Then he said to Jesus, "Lord, remember me when You come into Your kingdom." And Jesus said to him, "Assuredly, I say to you, today you will be with Me in Paradise." * Now I saw a new heaven and a new earth, for the first heaven and the first earth had passed away. Also there was no more sea. Then I, John, saw the holy city, New Jerusalem, coming down out of heaven from God, prepared as a bride adorned for her husband. And I heard a loud voice from heaven saying, "Behold, the tabernacle of God is with men, and He will dwell with them, and they shall be His people. God Himself will be with them and be their God. And God will wipe away every tear from their eyes; there shall be no more death, nor sorrow, nor crying. There shall be no more pain, for the former things have passed away." * He who overcomes shall inherit all things, and I will be his God and he shall be My son. * Amen and Amen.

Matthew 5:5 NKJV * Matthew 27:12-14 NKJV * Matthew 27:27-31 NKJV * Luke 23:36-43 NKJV * Revelation 21:1-4 NKJV * Revelation 21:7 NKJV * Psalm 72:19b NKJV

AUGUST

25 . . . .

**The strength of Jesus Christ is witnessed in
His demeanor under trial.**

20 _____ *

---

20 _____ *

---

20 _____ *

AUGUST 26

Blessed are those who hunger and thirst for righteousness, for they shall be satisfied. * Now as they went on their way, Jesus entered a village. And a woman named Martha welcomed him into her house. And she had a sister called Mary, who sat at the Lord's feet and listened to his teaching. But Martha was distracted with much serving. And she went up to him and said, "Lord, do you not care that my sister has left me to serve alone? Tell her then to help me." But the Lord answered her, "Martha, Martha, you are anxious and troubled about many things, but one thing is necessary. Mary has chosen the good portion, which will not be taken away from her." * And while he was at Bethany in the house of Simon the leper, as he was reclining at a table, a woman came with an alabaster flask of ointment of pure nard, very costly, and she broke the flask and poured it over his head. There were some who said to themselves indignantly, "Why was the ointment wasted like that? For this ointment could have been sold for more than three hundred denarii and given to the poor." And they scolded her. But Jesus said, "Leave her alone. Why do you trouble her? She has done a beautiful thing to me. For you always have the poor with you, and whenever you want, you can do good for them. But you will not always have me. She has done what she could; she has anointed my body beforehand for burial. And truly, I say to you, wherever the gospel is proclaimed in the whole world, what she has done will be told in memory of her." * But grow in the grace and knowledge of our Lord and Savior Jesus Christ. To him be the glory both now and to the day of eternity. Amen.

Matthew 5:6 ESV * Luke 10:38-42 ESV * Mark 14:3-9 ESV *
2 Peter 3:18 ESV

AUGUST

26 ....

**Praying hungry hearts are satisfied,
and thirsty souls are filled.**

20 _____ *

20 _____ *

20 _____ *

AUGUST 27

Blessed are the merciful, for they shall receive mercy. * Jesus replied and said, "A man was going down from Jerusalem to Jericho, and fell among robbers, and they stripped him and beat him, and went away leaving him half dead. And by chance a priest was going down on that road, and when he saw him, he passed by on the other side. Likewise a Levite also, when he came to the place and saw him, passed by on the other side. But a Samaritan, who was on a journey, came upon him; and when he saw him, he felt compassion, and came to him and bandaged up his wounds, pouring oil and wine on them; and he put him on his own beast, and brought him to an inn and took care of him. On the next day he took out two denarii and gave them to the innkeeper and said, 'Take care of him; and whatever more you spend, when I return I will repay you.' Which of these three do you think proved to be a neighbor to the man who fell into the robbers' hands?" And he said, "The one who showed mercy toward him." Then Jesus said to him, "Go and do the same." * And He said to him, " 'YOU SHALL LOVE THE LORD YOUR GOD WITH ALL YOUR HEART, AND WITH ALL YOUR SOUL, AND WITH ALL YOUR MIND.' This is the great and foremost commandment. The second is like it, 'YOU SHALL LOVE YOUR NEIGHBOR AS YOURSELF.'" * Amen, and Amen.

Matthew 5:7 NASB * Luke 10:30-37 NASB * Matthew 22:37-39 NASB * Psalm 72:19b NASB

AUGUST

27 . . . .

The merciful are filled with more than good intentions.

20 _____ *

_____

20 _____ *

20 _____ *

AUGUST 28

Blessed are the pure in heart, for they shall see God. * Then this Daniel distinguished himself above the governors and satraps, because an excellent spirit was in him; and the king gave thought to setting him over the whole realm. So the governors and satraps sought to find some charge against Daniel concerning the kingdom; but they could not find no charge or fault, because he was faithful; nor was there any error or fault found in him. Then these men said, "We shall not find any charge against Daniel unless we find it against him concerning the law of his God." So these governors and satraps thronged before the king, and said thus to him: "King Darius, live forever! All the governors of the kingdom, the administrators and satraps, the counselors and advisors, have consulted together to establish a royal statute and to make a firm decree, that whoever petitions any god or man for thirty days, except you, O king, shall be cast into the den of lions. * Therefore King Darius signed the written decree. Now when Daniel knew that the writing was signed, he went home. And in his upper room, with his windows open toward Jerusalem, he knelt down on his knees three times that day, and prayed and gave thanks before his God, as was his custom since early days. Then these men assembled and found Daniel praying and making supplication before his God. * And the king, when he heard these words, was greatly displeased with himself, and set his heart on Daniel to deliver him; and he labored till the going down of the sun to deliver him. Then the men approached the king, and said to the king, "Know, O king, that it is the law of the Medes and Persians that no decree or statute which the king establishes may be changed." So the king gave the command, and they brought Daniel and cast him into the den of lions. But the king spoke, saying to Daniel, "Your God, whom you serve continually, He will deliver you." * Now the king went to his palace and spent the night fasting; and no musicians were brought before him. Also his sleep went from him. Then the king arose very early in the morning and went in haste to the den of lions. And when he came to the den, he cried out with a lamenting voice to Daniel. The king spoke, saying to Daniel, "Daniel, servant of the living God, has your God, whom you serve continually, been able to deliver you from the lions?" Then Daniel said to the king, "O king, live forever! My God sent His angel and shut the lions' mouths, so that they have not hurt me, because I was found innocent before Him; and also, O king, I have done no wrong before you." * Amen and Amen.

Matthew 5:8 NKJV * Daniel 6:3-7 NKJV * Daniel 6:9-11 NKJV * Daniel 6:14-16 NKJV * Daniel 6:18-22 NKJV * Psalm 72:19b NKJV

AUGUST

28 . . . .

The pure in heart have vision.

20 _____ *

_____

_____

_____

_____

_____

_____

_____

20 _____ *

_____

_____

_____

_____

_____

_____

_____

20 _____ *

_____

_____

_____

_____

_____

_____

_____

AUGUST 29

Blessed are the peacemakers, for they shall be called sons of God. * For God does not show favoritism. * And now I want to plead with those two women, Euodia and Syntyche. Please, because you belong to the Lord, settle your disagreement. And I ask you, my true teammate, to help these women, for they worked hard with me in telling others the Good News. And they worked with Clement and the rest of my co-workers, whose names are written in the Book of Life. * For He Himself is our peace, who has made both one, and has broken down the middle wall of separation. * He who says he is in the light, and hates his brother, is in darkness until now. He who loves his brother abides in the light, and there is no cause for stumbling in him. But he who hates his brother is in darkness and walks in darkness, and does not know where he is going, because the darkness has blinded his eyes. * If someone says, "I love God," and hates his brother, he is a liar; for he who does not love his brother whom he has seen, how can he love God whom he has not seen? And this commandment we have from Him: that he who loves God must love his brother also. * Finally, all of you should be of one mind, full of sympathy toward each other, loving one another with tender hearts and humble minds. Don't repay evil for evil. Don't retaliate when people say unkind things about you. Instead, pay them back with a blessing. That is what God wants you to do, and he will bless you for it. For the Scriptures say, "If you want a happy life and good days, keep your tongue from speaking evil, and keep your lips from telling lies. Turn away from evil and do good. Work hard at living in peace with others. The eyes of the Lord watch over those who do right, and his ears are open to their prayers. But the Lord turns his face against those who do evil. * Do your part to live in peace with everyone, as much as possible. * Amen and Amen.

Matthew 5:9 NKJV * Romans 2:11 NLT * Philippians 4:2-3 NLT * Ephesians 2:14 NKJV * 1 John 2:9-11 NKJV * 1 John 4:20-21 NKJV * 1 Peter 3:8-12 NLT * Romans 12:18 NLT * Psalm 72:19b NLT

AUGUST

29 . . . .

Disunity destroys testimony.

20 _____ *

20 _____ *

20 _____ *

AUGUST 30

Blessed are those who are persecuted for righteousness sake, for theirs is the kingdom of heaven. * Bless those who persecute you; bless and do not curse. * And Stephen, full of faith and power did great wonders and signs among the people. Then there arose some from what is called the Synagogue of the Freedmen (Cyrenians, Alexandrians, and those from Cilicia and Asia), disputing with Stephen. And they were not able to resist the wisdom and the Spirit by which he spoke. * And they stirred up the people, the elders, and the scribes; and they came upon him, seized him, and brought him to the council. They also set up false witnesses who said, "This man does not cease to speak blasphemous words against this holy place and the law; for we have heard him say that this Jesus of Nazareth will destroy this place and change the customs which Moses delivered to us." And all who sat in the council, looking steadfastly at him, saw his face as the face of an angel. * Then the high priest said, "Are these things so?" * You stiff necked and uncircumcised in heart and ears! You always resist the Holy Spirit; as your fathers did, so do you. Which of the prophets did your fathers not persecute? And they killed those who foretold the coming of the Just One, of whom you now have become betrayers and murderers, who have received the law by the direction of angels and have not kept it. When they heard these things they were cut to the heart, and they gnashed at him with their teeth. But he, being full of the Holy Spirit, gazed into heaven and saw the glory of God, and Jesus standing at the right hand of God, and said, "Look! I see the heavens opened and the Son of Man standing at the right hand of God." They cried out with a loud voice, stopped their ears, and ran at him with one accord; and they cast him out of the city and stoned him. And the witnesses laid down their clothes at the feet of a young man named Saul. And they stoned Stephen as he was calling on God and saying, "Lord Jesus, receive my spirit." Then he knelt down and cried out with a loud voice, "Lord, do not charge them with this sin." And when he had said this, he fell asleep. * Amen and Amen.

Matthew 5:10 NKJV * Romans 12:14 NKJV * Acts 6:8-10 NKJV * Acts 6:12-15 NKJV * Acts 7:1 NKJV * Acts 7:51-60 NKJV * Psalm 72:19b NKJV

AUGUST

30 . . . .

Every flame of persecution has its own temperature.

20 _____ *

_____
_____
_____
_____
_____
_____
_____

20 _____ *

_____
_____
_____
_____
_____
_____
_____

20 _____ *

_____
_____
_____
_____
_____
_____
_____

AUGUST 31

Blessed are you when people insult you and persecute you, and falsely say all kinds of evil against you because of Me. Rejoice and be glad, for your reward in heaven is great; for in the same way they persecuted the prophets who were before you. * Now about that time Herod the king laid hands on some who belonged to the church in order to mistreat them. And he had James the brother of John put to death with a sword. When he saw that it pleased the Jews, he proceeded to arrest Peter also. Now it was during the days of Unleavened Bread. When he had seized him, he put him in prison, delivering him to four squads of soldiers to guard him, intending after the Passover to bring him out before the people. So Peter was kept in the prison, but prayer for him was being made fervently by the church to God. On the very night when Herod was about to bring him forward, Peter was sleeping between two soldiers, bound with two chains, and guards in front of the door were watching over the prison. And behold, an angel of the Lord suddenly appeared and a light shone in the cell; and he struck Peter's side and woke him up, saying, "Get up quickly." And his chains fell off his hands. And the angel said to him, "Gird yourself and put on your sandals." And he did so. And he said to him, "Wrap your cloak around you and follow me." And he went out and continued to follow, and he did not know that what was being done by the angel was real, but thought he was seeing a vision. When they had passed the first and second guard, they came to the iron gate that leads into the city, which opened for them by itself; and they went out and went along one street, and immediately the angel departed from him. When Peter came to himself, he said, "Now I know for sure that the Lord has sent forth His angel and rescued me from the hand of Herod and from all that the Jewish people were expecting." * Blessed is a man who perseveres under trial; for once he has been approved, he will receive the crown of life which the Lord has promised to those who love Him. * Amen, and Amen.

Matthew 5:11-12 NASB * Acts 12:1-11 NASB * James 1:12 NASB * Psalm 72:19b NASB

AUGUST

31 . . . .

When you suffer for Christ's name,
He rescues you in a special way.

20 ____ *

_____
_____
_____
_____
_____
_____
_____

20 ____ *

_____
_____
_____
_____
_____
_____
_____

20 ____ *

_____
_____
_____
_____
_____
_____
_____

SEPTEMBER

SEPTEMBER 1

You are the salt of the earth; but if the salt loses its flavor, how shall it be seasoned? It is then good for nothing but to be thrown out and trampled underfoot by men. * Behold what manner of love the Father has bestowed on us, that we should be called children of God! Therefore the world does not know us, because it did not know Him. Beloved, now we are children of God; and it has not yet been revealed what we shall be, but we know that when He is revealed, we shall be like Him, for we shall see Him as He is. And everyone who has this hope in Him purifies himself, just as He is pure. * Repent therefore and be converted, that your sins may be blotted out, so that times of refreshing may come from the presence of the Lord, and that He may send Jesus Christ, who was preached to you before, whom heaven must receive until the times of restoration of all things, which God has spoken by the mouth of all His holy prophets since the world began. * Since you have purified your souls in obeying the truth through the Spirit in sincere love of the brethren, love one another fervently with a pure heart, having been born again, not of the corruptible seed but incorruptible, through the word of God which lives and abides forever, because "All flesh is as grass, and all the glory of a man as the flowers of the grass. The grass withers, and its flowers fall away, but the word of the LORD endures forever." Now this is the word which by the gospel was preached to you. * Blessed be the LORD forevermore! Amen and Amen.

Matthew 5:13 NKJV * 1 John 3:1-3 NKJV * Acts 3:19-21 NKJV *
1 Peter 1:22-25 NKJV * Psalm 89:52 NKJV

SEPTEMBER

1

Purity is the salt preserving the church.

20 _____

_____
_____
_____
_____
_____
_____

20 _____

_____
_____
_____
_____
_____
_____

20 _____

_____
_____
_____
_____
_____
_____

SEPTEMBER 2

You are the light of the world. A city that is set on a hill cannot be hidden. Nor do they light a lamp and put it under a basket, but on a lamp stand, and it gives light to all who are in the house. Let your light so shine before men, that they may see your good works and glorify your Father in heaven. * For You, O God, have tested us; You have refined us as silver is refined. You brought us into the net; You laid affliction on our backs. You have caused men to ride over our heads; we went through fire and through water; but You brought us out to rich fulfillment. * God be merciful to us and bless us, and cause His face to shine upon us, that Your way may be known on earth, Your salvation among all nations. * Then those who feared the LORD spoke to one another, and the LORD listened and heard them; so a book of remembrance was written before Him for those who fear the LORD and who meditate on His name. "They shall be Mine," says the LORD of hosts, "On the day that I make them My jewels. And I will spare them as a man spares his own son who serves him." * Therefore, if anyone is in Christ, he is a new creation; old things have passed away; behold, all things have become new. Now all things are of God, who has reconciled us to Himself through Jesus Christ, and has given us the ministry of reconciliation, that is, that God was in Christ reconciling the world to Himself, not inputting their trespasses to them, and has committed to us the word of reconciliation. Now then, we are ambassadors for Christ, as though God were pleading through us: we implore you on Christ's behalf, be reconciled to God. For He made Him who knew no sin to be sin for us, that we might become the righteousness of God in Him. * The grace of the Lord Jesus Christ, and the love of God, and the communion of the Holy Spirit be with you all. Amen.

Matthew 5:14-16 NKJV * Psalm 66:10-12 NKJV * Psalm 67:1-2 NKJV * Malachi 3:16-17 NKJV * 2 Corinthians 5:17-21 NKJV * 2 Corinthians 13:14 NKJV

SEPTEMBER

2 . . . .

Your light guides the steps of those in the dark.

20 _____ *

_____

_____
_____
_____
_____
_____
_____

20 _____ *

_____
_____
_____
_____
_____
_____

20 _____ *

_____
_____
_____
_____
_____
_____

SEPTEMBER 3

But I am like a green olive tree in the house of God; I trust in the mercy of God forever and ever. I will praise You forever, because You have done it; and in the presence of Your saints I will wait on Your name, for it is good. * Blessed is the man who walks not in the counsel of the ungodly, nor stands in the path of sinners, nor sits in the seat of the scornful; but his delight is in the law of the LORD, and in His law he meditates day and night. He shall be like a tree planted by the rivers of water, that brings forth its fruit in its season, whose leaf also shall not wither; and whatever he does shall prosper. * That our sons may be as plants grown up in their youth; that our daughters may be as pillars, sculptured in palace style. * The righteous shall flourish like a palm tree, he shall grow like a cedar in Lebanon. Those who are planted in the house of the LORD shall flourish in the courts of our God. * When you eat the labor of your hands, you shall be happy, and it shall be well with you. Your wife shall be like a fruitful vine in the very heart of your house, your children like olive plants all around your table. Behold, thus shall the man be blessed who fears the LORD. * Behold, children are a heritage from the LORD, the fruit of the womb is a reward. Like arrows in the hand of a warrior, so are the children of one's youth. Happy is the man who has his quiver full of them; they shall not be ashamed, but shall speak with their enemies in the gate. * I will worship toward Your holy temple, and praise Your name for Your lovingkindness and Your truth; for You have magnified Your word above all Your name. In the day when I cried out, You answered me, and made me bold with strength in my soul. * Amen and Amen.

Psalm 51:8-9 NKJV * Psalm 1:1-3 NKJV * Psalm 144:12 NKJV * Psalm 92:12-13 NKJV * Psalm 128:2-4 NKJV * Psalm 127:3-5 NKJV * Psalm 138:2-3 NKJV * Psalm 72:19b NKJV

SEPTEMBER

3 . . . .

God's word invites constant growth.

20 _____ *

_____
_____
_____
_____
_____
_____
_____

20 _____ *

_____
_____
_____
_____
_____
_____
_____

20 _____ *

_____
_____
_____
_____
_____
_____
_____

SEPTEMBER 4

The LORD has heard my supplication; the LORD will receive my prayer. * The LORD also will be a refuge for the oppressed. A refuge in times of trouble. And those who know Your name will put their trust in You; for You, LORD, have not forsaken those who seek You. * My defense is of God, who saves the upright in heart. * When my enemies turn back, they shall fall and perish at Your presence. For You have maintained my right and my cause; You sat on the throne judging in righteousness. * LORD, You have heard the desire of the humble; You will prepare their heart; You will cause Your ear to hear, to do justice to the fatherless and the oppressed, that the man of the earth may oppress no more. * But I have trusted in Your mercy; My heart shall rejoice in Your salvation. * You will show me the path of life; in Your presence is fullness of joy; at Your right hand are pleasures forevermore. * I will sing to the LORD, because He has dealt bountifully with me. * Let all those who seek You rejoice and be glad in You; and let those who love Your salvation say continually, "Let God be magnified!" But I am poor and needy; make haste to me, O God! You are my help and my deliverer; O LORD, do not delay. * O God, You are more awesome than Your holy places. The God of Israel is He who gives strength and power to His people. Blessed be God! * And blessed be His glorious name forever! And let the whole earth be filled with His glory. Amen and Amen.

Psalm 6:9 NKJV * Psalm 9:9-10 NKJV * Psalm 7:10 NKJV * Psalm 9:3-4 NKJV * Psalm 10:17-18 NKJV * Psalm 13:5 NKJV * Psalm 16:11 NKJV * Psalm 13:6 NKJV * Psalm 70:4-5 NKJV * Psalm 68:35 NKJV * Psalm 72:19 NKJV

SEPTEMBER

4

God loves dialogue.

20 _____ *

_____
_____
_____
_____
_____
_____
_____

20 _____ *

_____
_____
_____
_____
_____
_____
_____

20 _____ *

_____
_____
_____
_____
_____
_____
_____

SEPTEMBER 5

I have written to you, children, because you have known the Father. I have written to you who are mature because you know Christ, the one who is from the beginning. I have written to you who are young because you are strong with God's word living in your hearts, and you have won your battle with Satan. * Use every piece of God's armor to resist the enemy in the time of evil, so that after the battle you will still be standing firm. Stand your ground, putting on the sturdy belt of truth and the body armor of God's righteousness. For shoes, put on the peace that comes with the Good News, so that you will be fully prepared. In every battle you will need faith as your shield to stop the fiery arrows aimed at you by Satan. Put on salvation as your helmet, and take the sword of the Spirit, which is the word of God. Pray at all times and on every occasion in the power of the Holy Spirit. Stay alert and be persistent in your prayers for all Christians everywhere. * For we are not fighting against people made of flesh and blood, but against evil rulers and authorities of the unseen world, against those mighty powers of darkness who rule this world, and against wicked spirits in the heavenly realms. * We are human, but we don't wage war with human plans and methods. We use God's mighty weapons, not mere worldly weapons, to knock down the Devil's strongholds. With these weapons we break down every proud argument that keeps people from knowing God. With these weapons we conquer their rebellious ideas, and we teach them to obey Christ. * And now, all glory to God, who is able to keep you from stumbling, and who will bring you into his glorious presence innocent of sin and with great joy. All glory to him, who alone is God our Savior, through Jesus Christ our Lord. Yes, glory, majesty, power, and authority belong to him, in the beginning, now, and forevermore. Amen.

1 John 2:14 NLT * Ephesians 6:13-18 NLT * Ephesians 6:12 NLT * 2 Corinthians 10:3-5 NLT * Jude 1:24-25 NLT

SEPTEMBER

5 . . . .

Spiritual maturity comes from knowledge of Christ.

20 _____ *

_____

_____
_____
_____
_____
_____
_____

20 _____ *

_____

_____
_____
_____
_____
_____
_____

20 _____ *

_____

_____
_____
_____
_____
_____
_____

SEPTEMBER 6

How wonderful it is, how pleasant, when brothers live together in harmony! For harmony is as precious as the fragrant anointing oil that was poured over Aaron's head, that ran down his beard and onto the border of his robe. Harmony is as refreshing as the dew from Mount Hermon that falls on the mountains of Zion. And the LORD has pronounced his blessing, even life forevermore. * So why do you condemn another Christian? Why do you look down on another Christian? Remember, each one of us will stand personally before the judgment seat of God. For the Scriptures say, "As surely as I live," says the Lord, "every knee will bow to me and every tongue will confess allegiance to God." Yes, each of us will have to give a personal account to God. So don't condemn each other anymore. Decide instead to live in such a way that you will not put an obstacle in another Christian's path. * Another reason for right living is that you know how late the time is; time is running out. Wake up, for the coming of our salvation is nearer now than when we first believed. The night is almost gone; the day of salvation will soon be here. So don't live in darkness. Get rid of your evil deeds. Shed them like dirty clothes. Clothe yourselves with the armor of right living, as those who live in the light. We should be decent and true in everything we do, so that everyone can approve of our behavior. Don't participate in wild parties and getting drunk, or in adultery and immoral living, or in fighting and jealousy. But let the Lord Jesus Christ take control of you, and don't think of ways to indulge your evil desires. * But the Kingdom of God is not a matter of what we eat or drink, but of living a life of goodness and peace and joy in the Holy Spirit. If you serve Christ with this attitude, you will please God. And other people will approve of you, too. So then, let us aim for harmony in the church and try to build each other up. * We should please others. If we do what helps them, we will build them up in the Lord. * May God, who gives this patience and encouragement, help you live in complete harmony with each other—each with the attitude of Christ Jesus toward the other. Then all of you can join together with one voice, giving praise and glory to God, the Father of our Lord Jesus Christ. So accept each other just as Christ has accepted you; then God will be glorified. * Amen and amen!

Psalm 133 NLT * Romans 14:10-13 NLT * Romans 13:11-14 NLT * Romans 14:17-19 NLT * Romans 15:2 NLT * Romans 15:5-7 NLT * Psalm 72:19b NLT

SEPTEMBER

6 . . . .

The cross is the secret to a unified group of sinners.

20 _____ *

_____

_____
_____
_____
_____
_____
_____
_____

20 _____ *

_____
_____
_____
_____
_____
_____
_____

20 _____ *

_____
_____
_____
_____
_____
_____
_____

SEPTEMBER 7

So then, my beloved brethren, let every man be swift to hear, slow to speak, slow to wrath, for the wrath of man does not produce the righteousness of God. Therefore lay aside all filthiness and overflow of wickedness, and receive with meekness the implanted word, which is able to save your souls. But be doers of the word, and not hearers only, deceiving yourselves. For if anyone is a hearer of the word and not a doer, he is like a man observing his natural face in a mirror; for he observes himself, goes away, and immediately forgets what kind of man he was. But he who looks into the perfect law of liberty and continues in it, and is not a forgetful hearer but a doer of the work, this one will be blessed in what he does. * Repay no one evil for evil. Have regard for good things in the sight of all men. If it is possible, as much as depends on you, live peaceably with all men. Beloved do not avenge yourselves, but rather give place to wrath; for it is written, "Vengeance is Mine, I will repay," says the Lord. * Be angry, and do not sin: do not let the sun go down on your wrath, nor give place to the devil. * Let all bitterness, wrath, anger, clamor, and evil speaking be put away from you, with all malice. And be kind to one another, tenderhearted, forgiving one another, even as God in Christ forgave you. * Be humble and gentle. Be patient with each other, making allowance for each other's faults because of your love. * To Him be the glory and the dominion forever and ever. Amen.

James 1:19-25 NKJV * Romans 12:17-19 NKJV * Ephesians 4:26-27 NKJV * Ephesians 4:31-32 NKJV * Ephesians 4:2 NLT * 1 Peter 5:11 NKJV

SEPTEMBER

7

Be swift to hear the word of God.

20 _____ *

20 _____ *

20 _____ *

SEPTEMBER 8

The Lord is merciful and gracious, slow to anger, and abounding in mercy. * So rend your heart, and not your garments; return to the LORD your God, for He is gracious and merciful, slow to anger, and of great kindness; and He relents from doing harm. Who knows if He will turn and relent, and leave a blessing behind Him—a grain offering and a drink offering for the LORD your God? * God is jealous, and the LORD avenges; the LORD avenges and is furious. The LORD will take vengeance on His adversaries, and He reserves wrath for His enemies; the LORD is slow to anger and great in power, and will not at all acquit the wicked. The LORD has His way in the whirlwind and in the storm, and the clouds are the dust of His feet. * Who can stand before His indignation? And who can endure the fierceness of His anger? His fury is poured out like fire, and the rocks are thrown down by Him. The LORD is good, a stronghold in the day of trouble; and He knows those who trust in Him. * Who is a God like You, pardoning iniquity and passing over the transgression of the remnant of His heritage? He does not retain His anger forever, because He delights in mercy. He will again have compassion on us, and will subdue our iniquities. You will cast all our sins into the depths of the sea. * Amen and Amen.

Psalm 103:8 NKJV * Joel 2:13-14 NKJV * Nahum 1:2-3 NKJV * Nahum 1:6-7 NKJV * Micah 7:18-19 NKJV * Psalm 72:19b NKJV

SEPTEMBER

8 . . . .

God is slow to anger.

20 _____ *

_____
_____
_____
_____
_____
_____
_____
_____

20 _____ *

_____
_____
_____
_____
_____
_____
_____
_____

20 _____ *

_____
_____
_____
_____
_____
_____
_____
_____

SEPTEMBER 9

You are of purer eyes than to behold evil, and cannot look on wickedness. Why do You look on those who deal treacherously, and hold Your tongue when the wicked devours a person more righteous than he? * Righteous are You, O LORD, when I plead with You; You let me talk with You about Your judgments. Why does the way of the wicked prosper? Why are those happy who deal treacherously? * Lord, how long will You look on? Rescue me from their destructions, my precious life from the lions. I will give You thanks in the great assembly; I will praise You among many people. Let them not rejoice over me who are wrongfully my enemies; nor let them wink with the eye who hate me without cause. For they do not speak peace, but they devise deceitful matters against the quiet ones in the land. They also opened their mouth wide against me, and said, "Aha, aha! Our eyes have seen it." This You have seen, O LORD; do not keep silence. O Lord, do not be far from me. Stir up Yourself, and awake to my vindication, to my cause, my God, according to Your righteousness; and let them not rejoice over me. Let them not say in their hearts, "Ah, so we would have it!" Let them not say, "We have swallowed him up." Let them be ashamed and brought to mutual confusion who rejoice at my hurt; let them be clothed with shame and dishonor who exalt themselves against me. Let them shout for joy and be glad, who favor my righteous cause; and let them say continually, "Let the LORD be magnified, who has pleasure in the prosperity of His servant." And my tongue shall speak of Your righteousness and of Your praise all the day long. * Blessed be the LORD forevermore! Amen and Amen.

Habakkuk 1:13 NKJV * Jeremiah 12:1 NKJV * Psalm 35:17-28 NKJV * Psalm 89:52 NKJV

SEPTEMBER

9 . . . .

God is waiting for you to cry out to Him.

20 _____ *

_____

_____
_____
_____
_____
_____
_____

20 _____ *

_____

_____
_____
_____
_____
_____
_____

20 _____ *

_____

_____
_____
_____
_____
_____
_____

SEPTEMBER 10

Be pleased, O LORD, to deliver me; O LORD, make haste to help me! * LORD, I cry out to You; make haste to me! Give ear to my voice when I cry out to You. Let my prayer be set before You as incense, the lifting up of my hands as the evening sacrifice. * Now a certain man was sick, Lazarus of Bethany, the town of Mary and her sister Martha. * Therefore the sisters sent to Him, saying, "Lord, behold, he whom You love is sick." When Jesus heard that, He said, "This sickness is not unto death, but for the glory of God, that the Son of God may be glorified through it." Now Jesus loved Martha and her sister and Lazarus. So, when He heard that he was sick, He stayed two more days in the place where He was. Then after this He said to the disciples, "Let us go to Judea again." * Then Jesus said to them plainly, "Lazarus is dead. And I am glad for your sakes that I was not there, that you may believe. Nevertheless let us go to him." * Now Martha, as soon as she heard that Jesus was coming, went and met Him, but Mary was sitting in the house. Now Martha said to Jesus, "Lord, if You had been here, my brother would not have died. But even now I know that whatever You ask of God, God will give You." Jesus said to her, "Your brother will rise again." Martha said to Him, "I know that he will rise again in the resurrection at the last day." Jesus said to her, "I am the resurrection and the life. He who believes in Me, though he may die, he shall live. And whoever lives and believes in Me shall never die. Do you believe this?" She said to Him, "Yes, Lord, I believe that You are the Christ, the Son of God, who is to come into the world. * Then, when Mary came where Jesus was, and saw Him, she fell down at His feet, saying to Him, "Lord, if You had been here, my brother would not have died." Therefore, when Jesus saw her weeping, and the Jews who came with her weeping, He groaned in the spirit and was troubled. And He said, "Where have you laid him?" They said to Him, "Lord, come and see." Jesus wept. Then the Jews said, "See how He loved him!" * Jesus said, "Take away the stone." Martha, the sister of him who was dead, said to Him, "Lord, by this time there is a stench, for he has been dead four days." Jesus said to her, "Did I not say to you that if you would believe you would see the glory of God?" * Blessed be the LORD forevermore! Amen and Amen.

Psalm 40:13 NKJV * Psalm 141:1-2 NKJV * John 11:1 NKJV * John 11:3-7 NKJV * John 11:14-15 NKJV * John 11:20-27 NKJV * John 11:32-36 NKJV * John 11:39-40 NLT * Psalm 89:52 NKJV

SEPTEMBER

10 ....

It's not over until God says it's over.

20 _____ *

_____

_____

_____

_____

_____

_____

_____

20 _____ *

_____

_____

_____

_____

_____

_____

_____

20 _____ *

_____

_____

_____

_____

_____

_____

_____

SEPTEMBER 11

Thus says the LORD: "Let not the wise man glory in his wisdom, let not the mighty man glory in his might, nor let the rich man glory in his riches; but let him who glories glory in this, that he understands and knows Me, that I am the LORD, exercising lovingkindness, judgment, and righteousness in the earth. For in these I delight," says the LORD. * My soul shall make its boast in the LORD; the humble shall hear of it and be glad. Oh magnify the LORD with me, and let us exalt His name together. I sought the LORD and He heard me, and delivered me from all my fears. * In God we boast all day long, and praise Your name forever. * And Hannah prayed and said: "My heart rejoices in the LORD; my horn is exalted in the LORD. I smile at my enemies, because I rejoice in Your salvation. No one is holy like the LORD, for there is none besides You, nor is there any rock like our God. Talk no more so very proudly; let no arrogance come from your mouth, for the LORD is the God of knowledge; and by Him actions are weighed. The bows of mighty men are broken, and those who stumbled are girded with strength. * He raises the poor from the dust and lifts the beggar from the ash heap, to set them among princes and make them inherit the throne of glory. For the pillars of the earth are the LORD's and He has set the world upon them. He will guard the feet of His saints, but the wicked shall be silent in darkness. For by strength no man shall prevail. The adversaries of the LORD shall be broken in pieces; from heaven He will thunder against them. The LORD will judge the ends of the earth. He will give strength to His king, and exalt the horn of His anointed. * Now to the King eternal, immortal, invisible, to God who alone is wise, be honor and glory forever and ever. Amen.

Jeremiah 9:23-24 NKJV * Psalm 34:2-4 NKJV * Psalm 44:8 NKJV * 1 Samuel 2:1-4 NKJV * 1 Samuel 2:8-10 NKJV * 1 Timothy 1:17 NKJV

SEPTEMBER

11 ·

**To God who is alone wise,
be honor and glory forever and ever!**

20 _____ *

20 _____ *

20 _____ *

SEPTEMBER 12

Let your garments always be white, and let your head lack no oil. * You have a few names even in Sardis who have not defiled their garments; and they shall walk with Me in white, for they are worthy. * Therefore they are before the throne of God, and serve Him day and night in His temple. And He who sits on the throne will dwell among them. They shall neither hunger anymore nor thirst anymore; the sun shall not strike them, nor any heat; for the Lamb who is in the midst of the throne will shepherd them and lead them to living fountains of waters. And God will wipe away every tear from their eyes. * Blessed are the pure in heart for they shall see God. * Let us be glad and rejoice and give Him glory, for the marriage of the Lamb has come, and His wife has made herself ready. And to her it was granted to be arrayed in fine linen, clean and bright, for the fine linen is the righteous acts of the saints. * I know your works. See, I have set before you an open door, and no one can shut it; for you have a little strength, have kept My word, and have not denied My name. * I will extol You, my God, O King; and I will bless Your name forever and ever. Everyday I will bless You, and I will praise Your name forever and ever. Great is the LORD, and greatly to be praised; and His greatness is unsearchable. One generation shall praise Your works to another, and shall declare Your mighty acts. * You prepare a table before me in the presence of my enemies; You anoint my head with oil; my cup runs over. * Now to Him who is able to do exceedingly abundantly above all that we ask or think, according to the power that works in us, to Him be glory in the church by Christ Jesus to all generations, forever and ever. Amen.

Ecclesiastes 9:8 NKJV * Revelation 3:4 NKJV * Revelation 7:15-17 NKJV * Matthew 5:8 NKJV * Revelation 19:7-8 NKJV * Revelation 3:8 NKJV * Psalm 145:1-4 NKJV * Psalm 23:5 NKJV * Ephesians 3:20-21 NKJV

SEPTEMBER

12 . . . .

God anoints.

20 _____ *

_____
_____
_____
_____
_____
_____
_____

20 _____ *

_____
_____
_____
_____
_____
_____
_____

20 _____ *

_____
_____
_____
_____
_____
_____
_____

SEPTEMBER 13

This I recall to my mind, therefore I have hope. Through the LORD's mercies we are not consumed, because His compassions fail not. They are new every morning; great is Your faithfulness. "The LORD is my portion," says my soul, "Therefore I hope in Him!" The LORD is good to those who wait for Him, to the soul who seeks Him. It is good that one should hope and wait quietly for the salvation of the LORD. * Why are you cast down, O my soul? And why are you disquieted within me? Hope in God, for I shall yet praise Him for the help of His countenance. * Then He said to them, "My soul is exceedingly sorrowful, even to death. Stay here and watch with Me." He went a little farther and fell on His face, and prayed, saying, "O My Father, if it is possible, let this cup pass from Me; nevertheless, not as I will, but as You will." Then He came to the disciples and found them sleeping, and said to Peter, "What! Could you not watch with Me one hour? Watch and pray, lest you enter into temptation. The spirit indeed is willing, but the flesh is weak." * My flesh and my heart fail; but God is the strength of my heart and my portion forever. * Grace be with you all. Amen.

Lamentations 3:21-25 NKJV * Psalm 42:5 NKJV * Matthew 26:38-41 NKJV * Psalm 73:26 NKJV * Hebrews 13:25 NKJV

SEPTEMBER

13 . . . .

Hope in God!

20 _____ *

_____
_____
_____
_____
_____
_____
_____

20 _____ *

_____
_____
_____
_____
_____
_____
_____

20 _____ *

_____
_____
_____
_____
_____
_____
_____

SEPTEMBER 14

And seek the peace of the city where I have caused you to be carried away captive, and pray to the LORD for it; for in its peace you will have peace. * Therefore I exhort first of all that supplications, prayers, intercessions, and giving of thanks be made for all men, for kings and all who are in authority, that we may lead a quiet and peaceable life in all godliness and reverence. For this is good and acceptable in the sight of God our Savior, who desires all men to be saved and to come to the knowledge of the truth. * I desire therefore that all men pray everywhere, lifting up holy hands, without wrath and doubting; in like manner also, that the women adorn themselves in modest apparel, with propriety and moderation, not with braided hair or gold or pearls or costly clothing, but, which is proper for women professing godliness, with good works. * Holding the mystery of the faith with a pure conscience. * Let no one despise your youth, but be an example to the believers in word, in conduct, in love, in spirit, in faith, in purity. * Do not rebuke an older man, but exhort him as a father, younger men as brothers, older women as mothers, younger women as sisters, with all purity. * Cast away from you all the transgressions which you have committed, and get yourselves a new heart and a new spirit. For why should you die, O house of Israel? * "Do I have any pleasure at all that the wicked should die?" says the Lord God, "and not that he should turn from his ways and live?" * "For I have no pleasure in the death of one who dies," says the Lord God. "Therefore turn and live!" * Blessed be the LORD forevermore! Amen and Amen.

Jeremiah 29:7 NKJV * 1 Timothy 2:1-4 NKJV * 1 Timothy 3:8-10 NKJV * 1 Timothy 3:9 NKJV * 1 Timothy 4:12 NKJV * 1 Timothy 5:1-2 NKJV * Ezekiel 18:31 NKJV * Ezekiel 18:23 NKJV * Ezekiel 18:32 NKJV * Psalm 89:52 NKJV

SEPTEMBER

14 . . . .

How will you seek peace?

20 _____ *

_____

_____

_____

_____

_____

_____

_____

20 _____ *

_____

_____

_____

_____

_____

_____

_____

20 _____ *

_____

_____

_____

_____

_____

_____

_____

SEPTEMBER 15

Every branch in Me that does not bear fruit He takes away, and every branch that bears fruit He prunes, that it may bear more fruit. * As His divine power has given to us all things that pertain to life and godliness, through the knowledge of Him who called us by glory and virtue, by which have been given to us exceedingly great and precious promises, that through these you may be partakers of the divine nature, having escaped corruption that is in the world through lust. But also for this very reason, giving all diligence, add to your faith virtue, to virtue knowledge, to knowledge self-control, to self-control perseverance, to perseverance godliness, to godliness brotherly kindness, and to brotherly kindness love. For if these things are yours and abound, you will be neither barren nor unfruitful in the knowledge of our Lord Jesus Christ. * He also spoke this parable: "A certain man had a fig tree planted in his vineyard, and he came seeking fruit on it and found none. Then he said to the keeper of his vineyard, 'Look, for three years I have come seeking fruit on this fig tree and find none. Cut it down; why does it use up the ground?' But he answered and said to him, 'Sir, let it alone this year also, until I dig around it and fertilize it. And if it bears fruit, well. But if not, after that you can cut it down.'" * But He, because He continues forever, has an unchangeable priesthood. Therefore He is able to save to the uttermost those who come to God through Him, since He always lives to make intercession for them. * The grace of the Lord Jesus Christ, and the love of God, and the communion of the Holy Spirit be with you all. Amen.

John 15:2 NKJV * 2 Peter 1:3-8 NKJV * Luke 13:6-9 NKJV * Hebrews 7:24-25 NKJV * 2 Corinthians 13:14 NKJV

SEPTEMBER

15 . . . .

Escape corruption by seeking God through Jesus Christ.

20 _____ *

20 _____ *

20 _____ *

SEPTEMBER 16

You are already clean because of the word which I have spoken to you. * If you abide in Me, and My words abide in you, you will ask what you desire, and it shall be done for you. * Jesus answered and said to him, "What I am doing you do not understand now, but you will know after this." Peter said to Him, "You shall never wash my feet!" Jesus answered him, "If I do not wash you, you have no part with Me." Simon Peter said to Him, "Lord, not my feet only, but also my hands and my head!" Jesus said to him, "He who is bathed needs only to wash his feet, but is completely clean; and you are clean, but not all of you." For He knew who would betray Him; therefore He said, "You are not all clean." So when He had washed their feet, taken His garments, and sat down again, He said to them, "Do you know what I have done to you? You call Me Teacher and Lord, and you say well, for so I am. If I then, your Lord and Teacher, have washed your feet, you also ought to wash one another's feet. For I have given you an example, that you should do as I have done to you. Most assuredly, I say to you, a servant is not greater than his master; nor is he who is sent greater than he who sent him. If you know these things, blessed are you if you do them. * Grace be with all those who love our Lord Jesus Christ in sincerity. Amen.

John 15:3 NKJV * John 15:7 NKJV * John 13:7-17 NKJV *
Ephesians 6:24 NKJV

SEPTEMBER

16 ....

Jesus teaches his disciples with perfect communication.

20 _____ *

_____
_____
_____
_____
_____
_____
_____

20 _____ *

_____
_____
_____
_____
_____
_____
_____

20 _____ *

_____
_____
_____
_____
_____
_____
_____

SEPTEMBER 17

And even now the ax is laid to the root of the trees. Therefore every tree that does not bear good fruit is cut down and thrown into the fire. * For a good tree does not bear bad fruit, nor does a bad tree bear good fruit. For every tree is known by its own fruit. For men do not gather figs from thorns, nor do they gather grapes from a bramble bush. A good man out of the good treasure of his heart brings forth good; and an evil man out of the evil treasure of his heart brings forth evil. For out of the abundance of the heart the mouth speaks. * I tell you, on the day of judgment people will give an account for every careless word they speak, for by your words you will be justified, and by your words you will be condemned. * Now the next day, when they had come out from Bethany, He was hungry. And seeing from afar a fig tree having leaves, He went to see if perhaps He would find something on it. When He came to it, He found nothing but leaves, for it was not the season for figs. In response Jesus said to it, "Let no one eat fruit from you ever again." And His disciples heard it. * Now in the morning, as they passed by, they saw the fig tree dried up from the roots. And Peter, remembering, said to Him, "Rabbi, look! The fig tree which You cursed has withered away." * I charge you therefore before God and the Lord Jesus Christ, who will judge the living and the dead at His appearance and His kingdom: Preach the word! Be ready in season and out of season. Convince, rebuke, exhort, with all long-suffering and teaching. * Those who are planted in the house of the LORD shall flourish in the courts of our God. They shall still bear fruit in old age; they shall be fresh and flourishing. * Amen and Amen.

Matthew 3:10 NKJV * Luke 6:43-45 NKJV * Matthew 12:36-37 ESV * Mark 11:12-14 NKJV * Mark 11:20-21 NKJV * 2 Timothy 4:1-2 NKJV * Psalm 92:13-14 NKJV * Psalm 72:19b NKJV

SEPTEMBER

17 . . . .

**A growing Christian will have fruit
in their speech to feed the hungry.**

20 ____ *

_____
_____
_____
_____
_____
_____

20 ____ *

_____
_____
_____
_____
_____
_____

20 ____ *

_____
_____
_____
_____
_____
_____

SEPTEMBER 18

Hope deferred makes the heart sick, but when the desire comes, it is a tree of life. * Now behold, two of them were traveling that same day to a village called Emmaus, which was seven miles from Jerusalem. And they talked together of all these things which had happened. So it was, while they conversed and reasoned, that Jesus Himself drew near and went with them. But their eyes were restrained, so that they did not know Him. And He said to them, "What kind of conversation is this that you have with one another as you walk and are sad?" Then the one whose name was Cleopas answered and said to Him, "Are You the only stranger in Jerusalem, and have You not known the things which happened there in these days?" * And how the chief priests and our rulers delivered Him to be condemned to death, and crucified Him. But we were hoping that it was He who was going to redeem Israel. Indeed, besides all this, today is the third day since these things happened. * Then He said to them, "O foolish ones, and slow of heart to believe in all that the prophets have spoken! Ought not the Christ to have suffered these things and to enter into His glory?" And beginning at Moses and all the Prophets, He expounded to them in all the Scriptures the things concerning Himself. Then they drew near to the village where they were going, and He indicated that He would have gone farther. But they constrained Him, saying, "Abide with us, for it is toward evening, and the day is far spent." And He went to stay with them. Now it came to pass, as He sat at the table with them, that He took bread, blessed and broke it, and gave it to them. Then their eyes were opened and they knew Him; and He vanished from their sight. And they said to one another, "Did not our heart burn within us while He talked with us on the road, and while He opened the Scriptures to us?" * My love be with you all in Christ Jesus. Amen.

Proverbs 13:12 NKJV * Luke 24:13-18 NKJV * Luke 24:20-21 NKJV * Luke 24:25-32 NKJV * 1 Corinthians 16:24 NKJV

SEPTEMBER

18 . . . .

Have you ever had a road to Emmaus conversation, where your once saddened heart turned to joyful excitement?

20 _____ *

_____
_____
_____
_____
_____
_____
_____

20 _____ *

_____
_____
_____
_____
_____
_____
_____

20 _____ *

_____
_____
_____
_____
_____
_____
_____

SEPTEMBER 19

Others, testing Him, sought from Him a sign from heaven. But He, knowing their thoughts, said to them: "Every kingdom divided against itself is brought to desolation, and a house divided against a house falls." * Then some of the scribes and Pharisees answered, saying, "Teacher, we want to see a sign from You." But He answered and said to them, "An evil and adulterous generation seeks after a sign, and no sign will be given to it except the sign of the prophet Jonah. For as Jonah was three days and three nights in the belly of the great fish, so will the Son of Man be three days and three nights in the heart of the earth." * Then the Pharisees and Sadducees came, and testing Him asked that He would show them a sign from heaven. He answered and said to them, "When it is evening and you say, 'It will be fair weather, for the sky is red'; and in the morning, 'It will be foul weather today, for the sky is red and threatening.' Hypocrites! You know how to discern the face of the sky, but you cannot discern the signs of the times. A wicked and adulterous generation seeks after a sign, and no sign shall be given to it except the sign of the prophet Jonah." And He left them and departed. * Your word is a lamp to my feet and a light to my path. * Grace be with you all. Amen.

Luke 11:16-17 NKJV * Matthew 12:38-40 NKJV * Matthew 16:1-4 NKJV * Psalm 119:105 NKJV * Hebrews 13:25 NKJV

September

19 . . . .

Any sign from heaven is wrapped in God's word.

20 _____ *

_____
_____
_____
_____
_____
_____
_____

20 _____ *

_____
_____
_____
_____
_____
_____
_____

20 _____ *

_____
_____
_____
_____
_____
_____
_____

SEPTEMBER 20

Then Jesus said to the crowds and to his disciples, "The teachers of religious law and the Pharisees are the official interpreters of the Scriptures. So practice and obey whatever they say to you, but don't follow their example. For they don't practice what they teach. They crush you with impossible religious demands and never lift a finger to help ease the burden." * How terrible it will be for you teachers of religious law and you Pharisees. Hypocrites! For you are careful to tithe even the tiniest part of your income, but you ignore the important things of the law—justice, mercy, and faith. You should tithe, yes, but you should not leave undone the more important things. * How terrible it will be for you teachers of religious law and you Pharisees. Hypocrites! You are so careful to clean the outside of the cup and the dish, but inside you are filthy—full of greed and self-indulgence! Blind Pharisees! First wash the inside of the cup, and then the outside will become clean, too. How terrible it will be for you teachers of religious law and you Pharisees. Hypocrites! You are like whitewashed tombs—beautiful on the outside but filled on the inside with dead people's bones and all sorts of impurity. You try to look like upright people outwardly, but inside your hearts are filled with hypocrisy and lawlessness. * If we say we have no sin, we are only fooling ourselves, and refusing to accept the truth. But if we confess our sins to him, he is faithful and just to forgive us and to cleanse us from every wrong. * Amen and Amen.

Matthew 23:1-4 NLT * Matthew 23:23 NLT * Matthew 23:25-28 NLT * 1 John 1:8-9 NLT * Psalm 72:19b NLT

SEPTEMBER

20 ....

God sees your heart with perfect clarity.

20 _____ *

_____
_____
_____
_____
_____
_____
_____

20 _____ *

_____
_____
_____
_____
_____
_____
_____

20 _____ *

_____
_____
_____
_____
_____
_____
_____

SEPTEMBER 21

But we urge you, brethren, that you increase more and more; that you also aspire to lead a quiet life, to mind your own business, and to work with your own hands, as we commanded you, that you may walk properly toward those who are outside, and that you may lack nothing. * What dainty morsels rumors are—but they sink deep into one's heart. * Any story sounds true until someone sets the record straight. * There are "friends" who destroy each other, but a real friend sticks closer than a brother. * A gossip tells secrets, so don't hang around with someone who talks too much. * People may think they are doing what is right, but the LORD examines the heart. * Those who plant seeds of injustice will harvest disaster, and their reign of terror will end. * Though good advice lies deep within a person's heart, the wise will draw it out. * Do not rob the poor because they are poor or exploit the needy in court. For the LORD is their defender. He will injure anyone who injures them. * Don't try to avoid responsibility by saying you didn't know about it. For God knows all hearts, and he sees you. He keeps watch over your soul, and he knows you knew! And he will judge all people according to what they have done. * It is an honor to receive an honest reply. * Just because you see something, don't be in a hurry to go to court. You might go down before your neighbors in shameful defeat. So discuss the matter with them privately. Don't tell anyone else, or others may accuse you of gossip. Then you will never again regain your good reputation. * Telling lies about others is as harmful as hitting them with an ax, wounding them with a sword, or shooting them with an arrow. * And so, dear brothers and sisters, we can boldly enter heaven's Most Holy Place because of the blood of Jesus. * For all have sinned; all fall short of God's glorious standard. Yet now God in his gracious kindness declares us not guilty. He has done this through Christ Jesus, who has freed us by taking away our sins. For God sent Jesus to take the punishment for our sins and to satisfy God's anger against us. We are made right with God when we believe that Jesus shed his blood, sacrificing his life for us. * Amen and Amen.

1 Thessalonians 4: 10b-12 NKJV * Proverbs 18:8 NLT * Proverbs 18:17 NLT * Proverbs 18:24 NLT * Proverbs 20:19 NLT * Proverbs 21:2 NLT * Proverbs 22:8 NLT * Proverbs 20:5 NLT * Proverbs 22:22-23 NLT * Proverbs 24:12 NLT * Proverbs 24:26 NLT * Proverbs 25:7b-10 NLT * Proverbs 25:18 NLT * Hebrews 10:19 NLT * Romans 3:23-25a NLT * Psalm 72:19b NLT

SEPTEMBER

21 . . . .

**Do you lead a quiet life, minding your own business,
while working with your hands?**

20 _____ *

_____
_____
_____
_____
_____
_____
_____

20 _____ *

_____
_____
_____
_____
_____
_____
_____

20 _____ *

_____
_____
_____
_____
_____
_____
_____

SEPTEMBER 22

When people work, their wages are not a gift. Workers earn what they receive. * It is pleasant to see dreams come true. * Whoever walks with the wise will become wise; whoever walks with fools will suffer harm. * A king rejoices in servants who know what they are doing; he is angry with those who cause trouble. * The wise person makes learning a joy. * A wise person is hungry for truth, while the fool feeds on trash. * A lazy person has trouble all through life; the path of the upright is easy! * Everyone enjoys a fitting reply; it is wonderful to say the right thing at the right time! * If you listen to constructive criticism, you will be at home among the wise. If you reject criticism, you only harm yourself; but if you listen to correction, you grow in understanding. Fear of the LORD teaches a person to be wise; humility precedes honor. * Commit your work to the LORD, and then your plans will succeed. * We can make our plans, but the LORD determines our steps. * A truly wise person uses few words; a person with understanding is even tempered. * A person's words can be life-giving water; words of true wisdom are as refreshing as a bubbling brook. * Intelligent people are always open to new ideas. In fact, they look for them. * Words satisfy the soul as food satisfies the stomach; the right words on a person's lips bring satisfaction. * You can make many plans, but the LORD's purpose will prevail. * Bless his glorious name forever! Let the whole earth be filled with his glory. Amen and Amen!

Romans 4:4 NLT * Proverbs 13:19a NLT * Proverbs 13:30 NLT * Proverbs 14:35 NLT * Proverbs 15:2a NLT * Proverbs 15:14 NLT * Proverbs 15:19 NLT * Proverbs 15:23 NLT * Proverbs 15:31-33 NLT * Proverbs 16:3 NLT * Proverbs 16:9 NLT * Proverbs 17:27 NLT * Proverbs 18:4 NLT * Proverbs 18:15 NLT * Proverbs 18:20 NLT * Proverbs 19:21 NLT * Psalm 72:19 NLT

SEPTEMBER

22 . . . .

A wise person is hungry for truth.

20 _____ *

_____
_____
_____
_____
_____
_____
_____

20 _____ *

_____
_____
_____
_____
_____
_____
_____

20 _____ *

_____
_____
_____
_____
_____
_____
_____

SEPTEMBER 23

Your law remains true today, for everything serves Your plans. * No matter what happens, always be thankful, for this is God's will for you who belong to Christ Jesus. * And the Holy Spirit helps us in our distress. For we don't even know what we should pray for, nor how we should pray. But the Holy Spirit prays for us with groanings that cannot be expressed in words. And the Father who knows all hearts knows what the Spirit is saying, for the Spirit pleads for us believers in harmony with God's own will. And we know that God causes everything to work together for the good of those who love God and are called according to his purpose for them. For God knew his people in advance, and he chose them to become like his Son, so that his Son would be the firstborn, with many brothers and sisters. * When you bow down before the Lord and admit your dependence on him, he will lift you up and give you honor. * And you will always give thanks for everything to God the Father in the name of our Lord Jesus Christ. * And now may God, who gives us his peace, be with you all. Amen.

Psalm 119:91 NLT * 1 Thessalonians 5:18 NLT * Romans 8:26-29 NLT * James 4:10 NLT * Ephesians 5:20 NLT * Romans 15:33 NLT

SEPTEMBER

23 . . . .

**The Helper in your distress,
prays for you in perfect harmony with God's will.**

20 _____ *

_____

_____
_____
_____
_____
_____
_____

20 _____ *

_____
_____
_____
_____
_____
_____

20 _____ *

_____
_____
_____
_____
_____
_____

SEPTEMBER 24

Then Abraham lifted his eyes and looked, and there behind him was a ram caught in a thicket by its horns. So Abraham went and took the ram, and offered it up for a burnt offering instead of his son. And Abraham called the name of the place, The- LORD-Will-Provide; as it is said to this day, "In the Mount of the LORD it shall be provided." * Then the LORD said to Moses, "Write this for a memorial in the book and recount it in the hearing of Joshua, that I will utterly blot out the remembrance of the Amalek from under heaven." And Moses built an altar and called its name, The- LORD-Is-My-Banner; for he said, "Because the LORD has sworn: the LORD will have war with Amalek from generation to generation." * Now Gideon perceived that He was the Angel of the LORD. So Gideon said, "Alas, O Lord God! For I have seen the Angel of the LORD face to face." Then the LORD said to him, "Peace be with you; do not fear, you shall not die." So Gideon built an altar there to the LORD, and called it The- LORD-Is-Peace. To this day it is still in Ophrah of the Abiezrites. * All the way around shall be eighteen thousand cubits; and the name of the city from that day shall be: THE LORD IS THERE. * Blessed be the LORD forevermore! Amen and Amen.

Genesis 22:13-14 NKJV * Exodus 17:14-15 NKJV * Judges 6:22-24 NKJV * Ezekiel 48:35 NKJV * Psalm 89:52 NKJV

SEPTEMBER

24 . . . .

Significant moments of God's presence.

20 _____ *

_____
_____
_____
_____
_____
_____
_____
_____

20 _____ *

_____
_____
_____
_____
_____
_____
_____
_____

20 _____ *

_____
_____
_____
_____
_____
_____
_____
_____

SEPTEMBER 25

As far as the east is from the west, so does he remove our transgressions from us. * Who is a God like you, pardoning iniquity and passing over transgression for the remnant of his inheritance? He does not retain his anger forever, because he delights in steadfast love. He will again have compassion on us; he will tread our iniquities underfoot. You will cast all our sins into the depths of the sea. * What shall we say then? Are we to continue in sin that grace may abound? By no means! How can we who died to sin still live in it? Do you not know that all of us who have been baptized into Christ Jesus were baptized into his death? We were buried therefore with him by baptism into death, in order that, just as Christ was raised from the dead by the glory of the Father, we too might walk in newness of life. * We know that our old self was crucified with him in order that the body of sin might be brought to nothing, so that we would no longer be enslaved to sin. For one who has died has been set free from sin. * So you also must consider yourselves dead to sin and alive in God in Christ Jesus. Let not sin therefore reign in your mortal body, to make you obey its passions. * For sin will have no dominion over you, since you are not under law but under grace. What then? Are we to sin because we are not under law but under grace? By no means! * But what fruit were you getting at that time from the things of which you are now ashamed? For the end of those things is death. But now that you have been set free from sin and have become slaves of God, the fruit you get leads to sanctification and its end, eternal life. For the wages of sin is death, but the free gift of God is eternal life in Christ Jesus our Lord. * To the only wise God be glory forevermore through Christ Jesus! Amen.

Psalm 103:12 ESV * Micah 7:18-19 ESV * Romans 6:1-4 ESV * Romans 6:6-7 ESV * Romans 6:11-12 ESV * Romans 6:14-15 ESV * Romans 6:21-23 ESV * Romans 16:27 ESV

SEPTEMBER

25 . . . .

Don't take advantage of grace, be thankful it's given.

20 _____ *

---

20 _____ *

---

20 _____ *

SEPTEMBER 26

Why have You broken down her hedges, so that all who pass by the way pluck her fruit? * "Everyone will deceive his neighbor, and will not speak the truth; they have taught their tongue to speak lies; they weary themselves to commit iniquity. Your dwelling place is in the midst of deceit; through deceit they refuse to know Me," says the Lord. * You, therefore, who teach another, do you not teach yourself? You who preach that a man should not steal, do you steal? * Then the scribes and Pharisees who were from Jerusalem came to Jesus, saying, "Why do Your disciples transgress the tradition of the elders? For they do not wash their hands when they eat bread." He answered and said to them, "Why do you transgress the commandment of God because of your tradition? * Do not lay up for yourselves treasures on earth, where moth and rust destroy and where thieves break in and steal; but lay up for yourselves treasure in heaven, where neither moth nor rust destroys and where thieves do not break in and steal. For where your treasure is, there your heart will be also. * Now may the God of peace who brought up our Lord Jesus from the dead, that great Shepherd of the sheep, through the blood of the everlasting covenant, make you complete in every good work to do His will, working in you what is well pleasing in His sight, through Jesus Christ, to whom be glory forever and ever. Amen.

Psalm 80:12 NKJV * Jeremiah 9:5-6 NKJV * Romans 2:21 NKJV * Matthew 15:1-3 NKJV * Matthew 6:19-21 NKJV * Hebrews 13:20-21 NKJV

SEPTEMBER

26 . . . .

**When God allows a wall to be broken down,
what's your response?**

20 _____ *

_____

_____

_____

_____

_____

_____

_____

20 _____ *

_____

_____

_____

_____

_____

_____

_____

20 _____ *

_____

_____

_____

_____

_____

_____

_____

SEPTEMBER 27

Do you not know that those who run in a race all run, but only one receives the prize? Run in such a way that you may win. Everyone who competes in the games exercises self-control in all things. They then do it to receive a perishable wreath, but we an imperishable. Therefore I run in such a way, as not without aim; I box in such a way, as not beating the air; but I discipline my body and make it my slave, so that, after I have preached to others, I myself will not be disqualified. * I have fought the good fight, I have finished the course, I have kept the faith; in the future there is laid up for me the crown of righteousness, which the Lord, the righteous Judge, will award to me on that day; and not only to me, but also to all who have loved His appearing. * But we, brethren, having been taken away from you for a short while—in person, not in spirit—were all the more eager with great desire to see your face. For we wanted to come to you—I, Paul, more than once—and yet Satan hindered us. For who is our hope or joy or crown of exultation? Is it not even you, in the presence of our Lord Jesus at His coming? For you are our glory and joy. * The fruit of the righteous is a tree of life, and he who is wise wins souls. * Shepherd the flock of God among you, exercising oversight not under compulsion, but voluntarily, according to the will of God; and not for sordid gain, but with eagerness; nor yet as lording it over those allotted to your charge, but proving to be examples to the flock. And when the Chief Shepherd appears, you will receive the unfading crown of glory. You younger men, likewise, be subject to your elders; and all of you, clothe yourselves with humility toward one another, for GOD IS OPPOSED TO THE PROUD, BUT GIVES GRACE TO THE HUMBLE. Therefore humble yourselves under the mighty hand of God, that He may exalt you at the proper time, casting all your anxiety on Him, because He cares for you. * Blessed is a man who perseveres under trial; for once he has been approved, he will receive the crown of life which the Lord has promised to those who love Him. * Do not fear what you are about to suffer. Behold, the devil is about to cast some of you into prison, so that you will be tested, and you will have tribulation for ten days. Be faithful until death, and I will give you the crown of life. * Blessed be the LORD forever! Amen and Amen.

1 Corinthians 9:24-27 NASB * 2 Timothy 4:7-8 NASB * 1 Thessalonians 2:17-20 NASB * Proverbs 11:30 NASB * 1 Peter 5:2-7 NASB * James 1:12 NASB * Revelation 2:10 NASB * Psalm 89:52 NASB

SEPTEMBER

27 . . . .

**I long for the day,
I get to cast that crown Christ's way.**

20 _____ *

_____

_____

_____

_____

_____

_____

_____

20 _____ *

_____

_____

_____

_____

_____

_____

_____

20 _____ *

_____

_____

_____

_____

_____

_____

_____

SEPTEMBER 28

Faithful are the wounds of a friend, but the kisses of an enemy are deceitful. * Then Satan entered into Judas called Iscariot, who was of the number of the twelve. He went away and conferred with the chief priests and officers how he might betray him to them. And they were glad, and agreed to give him money. So he consented and sought an opportunity to betray him to them in the absence of a crowd. * Then Jesus went with them to a place called Gethsemane, and he said to his disciples, "Sit here, while I go over there and pray." * Then He came to His disciples and said to them, "Are you still sleeping and resting? Behold, the hour is at hand, and the Son of Man is being betrayed into the hands of sinners. Rise, let us be going. See, My betrayer is at hand." And while He was still speaking, behold, Judas, one of the twelve, with a great multitude with swords and clubs, came from the chief priests and elders of the people. Now His betrayer had given them a sign, saying, "Whomever I kiss, He is the One; seize Him." Immediately he went up to Jesus and said, "Greetings, Rabbi!" and kissed Him. But Jesus said to him, "Friend, why have you come?" Then they came and laid hands on Jesus and took Him. * Then Judas, His betrayer, seeing that He had been condemned, was remorseful and brought back the thirty pieces of silver to the chief priests and elders, saying, "I have sinned by betraying innocent blood." And they said, "What is that to us? You see to it!" Then he threw down the pieces of silver in the temple and departed, and went and hanged himself. * For the wages of sin is death, but the gift of God is eternal life in Christ Jesus our Lord. * Prove by the way that you live that you have really turned from your sins and turned to God. * Amen and Amen!

Proverbs 27:6 NKJV * Luke 22:3-6 ESV * Matthew 26:36 ESV * Matthew 26:45-50 NKJV * Matthew 27:3-5 NKJV * Romans 6:23 NKJV * Matthew 3:8 NLT * Psalm 72:19b ESV

SEPTEMBER

28 . . . .

**Don't give up on people.
Jesus gave a second chance: "Friend, why have you come?"**

20 _____ *

_____

_____

_____

_____

_____

_____

20 _____ *

_____

_____

_____

_____

_____

_____

20 _____ *

_____

_____

_____

_____

_____

_____

SEPTEMBER 29

Loyalty makes a person attractive. And it is better to be poor than dishonest. * For the eyes of the LORD run to and fro throughout the whole earth, to show Himself strong on behalf of those whose heart is loyal to Him. * O LORD God Almighty! Where is there anyone as mighty as you, LORD? Faithfulness is your very character. * Your unfailing love will last forever. Your faithfulness is as enduring as the heavens. * If we are unfaithful, he remains faithful, for he cannot deny himself. * True, some of them were unfaithful; but just because they broke their promises, does that mean God will break his promises? Of course not! Though everyone else in the world is a liar, God is true. As the Scriptures say, "He will be proved right in what he says, and he will win his case in court." * Now you have every spiritual gift you need as you eagerly wait for the return of our Lord Jesus Christ. He will keep you strong right up to the end, and he will keep you free from all blame on the great day when our Lord Jesus Christ returns. God will surely do this for you, for he always does just what he says, and he is the one who invited you into this wonderful friendship with his Son, Jesus Christ our Lord. * May he be given glory in the church and in Christ Jesus forever and ever through endless ages. Amen.

Proverbs 19:22 NLT * 2 Chronicles 16:9a NKJV * Psalm 89:8 NLT * Psalm 89:2 NLT * 2 Timothy 2:13 NLT * Romans 3:3-4 NLT * 1 Corinthians 1:7-9 NLT * Ephesians 3:21 NLT

SEPTEMBER

29 ·

**Will you share your friendship with Jesus Christ,
with your friends?**

20 _____ *

_____

_____
_____
_____
_____
_____
_____

20 _____ *

_____

_____
_____
_____
_____
_____
_____

20 _____ *

_____

_____
_____
_____
_____
_____
_____

SEPTEMBER 30

When a man's ways please the LORD, He makes even his enemies be at peace with him. * So they taught in Judah, and had the Book of the Law of the LORD with them; they went throughout all the cities of Judah and taught the people. And the fear of the LORD fell on all the kingdoms of the lands that were around Judah, so that they did not make war against Jehoshaphat. * Then Abimelech came to him from Gerar with Ahuzzath, one of his friends, and Phichol the commander of his army. And Isaac said to them, "Why have you come to me, since you hate me and have sent me away from you?" But they said, "We have certainly seen that the LORD is with you. So we said, 'Let there now be an oath between us, between you and us; and let us make a covenant with you, that you will do us no harm, since we have not touched you, and since we have done nothing to you but good and have sent you away in peace. You are now the blessed of the LORD.'" So he made them a feast, and they ate and drank. Then they arose early in the morning and swore an oath with one another; and Isaac sent them away, and they departed from him in peace. * Amen and Amen.

Proverbs 16:7 NKJV * 2 Chronicles 17:9-10 NKJV * Genesis 26:26-31 NKJV * Psalm 72:19b NKJV

SEPTEMBER

30 . . . .

Seek to please God.

20 _____ *

_____
_____
_____
_____
_____
_____
_____

20 _____ *

_____
_____
_____
_____
_____
_____
_____

20 _____ *

_____
_____
_____
_____
_____
_____
_____

OCTOBER

OCTOBER 1

He permitted no one to do them wrong; yes, He rebuked kings for their sakes, saying, "Do not touch My anointed ones, and do My prophets no harm." * And Abraham journeyed from there to the South, and dwelt between Kadesh and Shur, and stayed in Gerar. Now Abraham said of Sarah his wife, "She is my sister." And Abimelech king of Gerar sent and took Sarah. But God came to Abimelech in a dream by night, and said to him, "Indeed you are a dead man because of the woman whom you have taken, for she is a man's wife." But Abimelech had not come near her; and he said, "Lord, will You slay a righteous nation also? Did he not say to me, 'She is my sister'? And she, even she herself said, 'He is my brother.' In the integrity of my heart and innocence of my hands I have done this." And God said to him in a dream, "Yes, I know that you did this in the integrity of your heart. For I also withheld you from sinning against Me; therefore I did not let you touch her. Now therefore, restore the man's wife; for he is a prophet, and he will pray for you and you shall live. But if you do not restore her, know that you shall surely die, you and all who are yours." * And Abimelech called Abraham and said to him, "What have you done to us? How have I offended you, that you have brought on me and on my kingdom a great sin? You have done deeds to me that ought not to be done." Then Abimelech said to Abraham, "What did you have in view, that you have done this thing?" And Abraham said, "Because I thought, surely the fear of God is not in this place; and they will kill me on account of my wife." * Then Abimelech took sheep, oxen, and male and female servants, and gave them to Abraham; and he restored Sarah his wife to him. * So Abraham prayed to God; and God healed Abimelech, his wife, and his female servants. Then they bore children; for the LORD had closed up all the wombs of the house of Abimelech because of Sarah, Abraham's wife. * The grace of our Lord Jesus Christ be with you all. Amen.

Psalm 105:14-15 NKJV * Genesis 20:1-7 NKJV * Genesis 20:9-11 NKJV * Genesis 20:14 NKJV * Genesis 20:17-18 NKJV * 2 Thessalonians 3:18 NKJV

OCTOBER

1 . . . .

God has a protective hedge around you.

20 _____ *

_____

_____

_____

_____

_____

_____

_____

20 _____ *

_____

_____

_____

_____

_____

_____

_____

20 _____ *

_____

_____

_____

_____

_____

_____

_____

OCTOBER 2

So be careful not to jump to conclusions before the Lord returns as to whether or not someone is faithful. When the Lord comes, he will bring our deepest secrets to light and will reveal our private motives. And then God will give to everyone whatever praise is due. * Peter turned around and saw the disciple Jesus loved following them—the one who had leaned over to Jesus during supper and asked, "Lord, who among us will betray you?" Peter asked Jesus, "What about him, Lord?" Jesus replied, "If I want him to remain alive until I return, what is that to you? You follow me." * Stop judging others, and you will not be judged. For others will treat you as you treat them. Whatever measure you use in judging others, it will be used to measure how you are judged. And why worry about a speck in your friend's eye when you have a log in your own? How can you think of saying, "Let me help you get rid of that speck in your eye," when you can't see past the log in your own eye? Hypocrite! First get rid of the log from your own eye; then perhaps you will see well enough to deal with the speck in your friend's eye. * You may be saying, "What terrible people you have been talking about!" But you are just as bad, and you have no excuse! When you say they are wicked and should be punished, you are condemning yourself, for you do these very same things. And we know that God, in his justice, will punish anyone who does such things. Do you think that God will judge and condemn others for doing them and not judge you when you do them, too? Don't you realize how kind, tolerant, and patient God is with you? Or don't you care? Can't you see how kind he has been in giving you time to turn from your sin? But no, you won't listen. So you are storing up terrible punishment for yourself because of your stubbornness in refusing to turn from your sin. For there is going to come a day of judgment when God, the just judge of all the world, will judge all people according to what they have done. * The day will surely come when God, by Jesus Christ, will judge everyone's secret life. This is my message. * Amen and Amen.

1 Corinthians 4:5 NLT * John 21:20-22 NLT * Matthew 7:1-5 NLT * Romans 2:1-6 NLT * Romans 2:16 NLT * Psalm 72:19b NLT

OCTOBER

2 . . . .

How is your own life doing?

20 ____ *

_____
_____
_____
_____
_____
_____
_____

20 ____ *

_____
_____
_____
_____
_____
_____
_____

20 ____ *

_____
_____
_____
_____
_____
_____
_____

OCTOBER 3

Oh, that my actions would consistently reflect your principles! * The steps of the godly are directed by the LORD, He delights in every detail of their lives. * The LORD is good and does what is right; he shows the proper path to those who go astray. He leads the humble in what is right, teaching them the way. The LORD leads with unfailing love and faithfulness all those who keep his covenant and obey his decrees. For the honor of your name, O LORD, forgive my many, many sins. Who are those who fear the LORD? He will show them the path they should choose. * Friendship with the LORD is reserved for those who fear him. With them he shares the secrets of his covenant. * The LORD says, "I will guide you along the best pathway for your life. I will advise you and watch over you." * For the word of the LORD holds true, and everything he does is worthy of our trust. * I have hidden your word in my heart, that I might not sin against you. * I am overwhelmed continually with a desire for your laws. You rebuke those cursed proud ones who wander from your commands. Don't let them scorn or insult me, for I have obeyed your decrees. Even princes sit and speak against me, but I will meditate on your principles. Your decrees please me; they give me wise advice. * I have chosen to be faithful; I have determined to live by your laws. I cling to your decrees. LORD, don't let me be put to shame! * Teach me, O LORD, to follow every one of your principles. Give me understanding and I will obey your law; I will put it into practice with all my heart. Make me walk along the path of your commands, for that is where my happiness is found. * I will walk in freedom, for I have devoted myself to your commandment. I will speak to kings about your decrees, and I will not be ashamed. How I delight in your commands! How I love them! I honor and love your commands. I meditate on your principles. * Your principles have been the music of my life throughout the years of my pilgrimage. I reflect at night on who you are, O LORD, and I obey your law because of this. This is my happy way of life: obeying your commandments. * Amen and Amen.

Psalm 119:5 NLT * Psalm 37:23 NLT * Psalm 25:8-12 NLT * Psalm 25:14 NLT * Psalm 32:8 NLT * Psalm 33:4 NLT * Psalm 119:11 NLT * Psalm 119:20-24 NLT * Psalm 119:30-31 NLT * Psalm 119:33-35 NLT * Psalm 119:45-47 NLT * Psalm 119:54-56 NLT * Psalm 72:19b NLT

OCTOBER

3 . . . .

Your steps today determine your tomorrows.

20_____ *

_____
_____
_____
_____
_____
_____
_____

20_____ *

_____
_____
_____
_____
_____
_____
_____

20_____ *

_____
_____
_____
_____
_____
_____
_____

OCTOBER 4

Please guarantee a blessing for me. Don't let those who are arrogant oppress me! My eyes strain to see your deliverance, to see the truth of your promise fulfilled. I am your servant; deal with me in unfailing love, and teach me your principles. Give discernment to me, your servant; then I will understand your decrees. LORD, it is time for you to act, for these evil people have broken your law. * Arrogant people have made up lies about me, but in truth I obey your commandments with all my heart. Their hearts are dull and stupid, but I delight in your law. * O God, whom I praise, don't stand aloof while the wicked slander me and tell lies about me. They are all around me with their hateful words, and they fight against me for no reason. I love them, but they try to destroy me—even as I am praying for them! They return evil for good, and hatred for my love. * I am an object of mockery to people everywhere; when they see me, they shake their heads. * But deal well with me, O Sovereign LORD, for the sake of your own reputation! Rescue me because you are faithful and good. For I am poor and needy, and my heart is full of pain. * Help me, O LORD my God! Save me because of your unfailing love. Let them see that this is your doing, that you yourself have done it, LORD. Then let them curse me if they like, but you will bless me! When they attack me, they will be disgraced! But I, your servant, will go right on rejoicing! Make their humiliation obvious to all; clothe my accusers with disgrace. But I will give repeated thanks to the LORD, praising him to everyone. For he stands beside the needy, ready to save them from those who condemn them. * Blessed be the LORD forever! Amen and Amen.

Psalm 119:122-126 NLT * Psalm 119:69-70 NLT * Psalm 109:1-5 NLT * Psalm 109:25 NLT * Psalm 109:21-22 NLT * Psalm 109:26-31 NLT * Psalm 89:52 NLT

OCTOBER

4 . . . .

**Don't rely on your natural perception;
ask God for discernment.**

20 _____ *

_____

_____
_____
_____
_____
_____
_____

20 _____ *

_____

_____
_____
_____
_____
_____
_____

20 _____ *

_____

_____
_____
_____
_____
_____
_____

OCTOBER 5

This is the day the LORD has made; we will rejoice and be glad in it. * The stone which the builders rejected has become the chief cornerstone. This was the LORD's doing; it is marvelous in our eyes. * Then Peter, filled with the Holy Spirit, said to them, "Rulers of the people and elders of Israel: If we this day are judged for a good deed done to a helpless man, by what means he has been made well, let it be known to you all, and to all the people of Israel, that by the name of Jesus Christ of Nazareth, whom you crucified, whom God raised from the dead, by Him this man stands here before you whole. This is the 'stone which was rejected by you builders, which has become the chief cornerstone.' Nor is there salvation in any other, for there is no other name under heaven given among men by which we must be saved. * Coming to Him as to a living stone, rejected indeed by men, but chosen by God and precious, you also, as living stones, are being built up a spiritual house, a holy priesthood, to offer up spiritual sacrifices acceptable to God through Jesus Christ. Therefore it is also contained in the Scripture, "Behold, I lay in Zion a chief cornerstone, elect, precious, and he who believes on Him will by no means be put to shame." Therefore, to you who believe, He is precious; but to those who are disobedient, "The stone which the builders rejected has become the chief cornerstone," and "a stone of stumbling and a rock of offense." They stumble, being disobedient to the word, to which they also were appointed. But you are a chosen generation, a royal priesthood, a holy nation, His own special people, that you may proclaim the praises of Him who called you out of darkness into His marvelous light; who once were not a people but are now the people of God, who had not obtained mercy but now have obtained mercy. * To Him be the glory and the dominion forever and ever. Amen.

Psalm 118:24 NKJV * Psalm 118:22-23 NKJV * Acts 4:8-12 NKJV * 1 Peter 2:4-10 NKJV * 1 Peter 5:11 NKJV

OCTOBER

5 . . . .

This is the day the Lord has made!

20 _____ *

_____
_____
_____
_____
_____
_____
_____

20 _____ *

_____
_____
_____
_____
_____
_____
_____

20 _____ *

_____
_____
_____
_____
_____
_____
_____

OCTOBER 6

Now when they saw the boldness of Peter and John, and perceived that they were uneducated and untrained men, they marveled. And they realized that they had been with Jesus. * And Jesus, walking by the Sea of Galilee , saw two brothers, Simon called Peter, and Andrew his brother, casting a net into the sea; for they were fishermen. Then He said to them, "Follow Me, and I will make you fishers of men." They immediately left their nets and followed Him. Going on from there, He saw two other brothers, James the son of Zebedee, and John his brother, in the boat with Zebedee their father, mending their nets. He called them, and immediately they left the boat and their father, and followed Him. * And seeing the multitudes, He went up on a mountain, and when He was seated His disciples came to Him. Then He opened His mouth and taught them, saying: "Blessed are the poor in spirit, for theirs is the kingdom of heaven. Blessed are those who mourn, for they shall be comforted. Blessed are the meek, for they shall inherit the earth. Blessed are those who hunger and thirst for righteousness, for they shall be filled. Blessed are the merciful, for they shall obtain mercy. Blessed are the pure in heart, for they shall see God. Blessed are the peacemakers, for they shall be called sons of God. Blessed are those who are persecuted for righteousness' sake, for theirs is the kingdom of heaven. Blessed are you when they revile and persecute you, and say all kinds of evil against you falsely for My sake. Rejoice and be exceedingly glad, for great is your reward in heaven, for so they persecuted the prophets who were before you. You are the salt of the earth; but if the salt loses its flavor, how shall it be seasoned? It is then good for nothing but to be thrown out and trampled underfoot by men. You are the light of the world. A city that is set on a hill cannot be hidden. Nor do they light a lamp and put it under a basket, but on a lamp stand, and it gives light to all who are in the house. Let your light so shine before men, that they may see your good works and glorify your Father in heaven. * "Go therefore and make disciples of all nations, baptizing them in the name of the Father and of the Son and of the Holy Spirit, teaching them to observe all things that I have commanded you; and lo, I am with you always, even to the end of the age." Amen.

Acts 4:13 NKJV * Matthew 4:18-22 NKJV * Matthew 5:1-16 NKJV * Matthew 28:19-20 NKJV

OCTOBER

6 . . . .

Have you spent quality and quantity time with Jesus?

20 _____ *

_____

_____

_____

_____

_____

_____

_____

20 _____ *

_____

_____

_____

_____

_____

_____

_____

20 _____ *

_____

_____

_____

_____

_____

_____

_____

OCTOBER 7

This is my comfort in my affliction, for Your word has given me life. * Your word I have hidden in my heart, that I might not sin against You. * For the wages of sin is death, but the gift of God is eternal life in Christ Jesus our Lord. * In the beginning was the Word, and the Word was with God, and the Word was God. He was in the beginning with God. * And the Word became flesh and dwelt among us, and we beheld His glory, the glory as of the only begotten of the Father, full of grace and truth. * Jesus said to him, "I am the way, the truth, and the life. No one comes to the Father except through Me." * "If you love Me, keep My commandments. And I will pray the Father, and He will give you another Helper, that He may abide with you forever—the Spirit of truth, whom the world cannot receive, because it neither sees Him nor knows Him; but you know Him, for He dwells with you and will be in you. * Likewise the Spirit also helps in our weaknesses. For we do not know what we should pray for as we ought, but the Spirit Himself makes intercession for us with groaning which cannot be uttered. Now He who searches the hearts knows what the mind of the Spirit is, because He makes intercession for the saints according to the will of God. * Bless the LORD, O my soul; and all that is within me, bless His holy name! * Who redeems your life from destruction, who crowns you with lovingkindness and tender mercies. * I will never forget Your precepts, for by them You have given me life. * And I will walk at liberty, for I seek Your precepts. * The grace of the Lord Jesus Christ, and the love of God, and the communion of the Holy Spirit be with you all. Amen.

Psalm 119:50 NKJV * Psalm 119:11 NKJV * Romans 6:23 NKJV * John 1:1-2 NKJV * John 1:14 NKJV * John 14:6 NKJV * John 14:15-17 NKJV * Romans 8:26-27 NKJV * Psalm 103:1 NKJV * Psalm 103:4 NKJV * Psalm 119:93 NKJV * Psalm 119:45 NKJV * 2 Corinthians 13:14 NKJV

OCTOBER

7

God's word brings life alive.

20 _____ *

20 _____ *

20 _____ *

OCTOBER 8

For wisdom is a defense as money is a defense, but the excellence of knowledge is that wisdom gives life to those who have it. * Happy is the man who finds wisdom, and the man who gains understanding; for her proceeds are better than the profits of silver, and her gain than fine gold. She is more precious than rubies, and all the things you may desire cannot compare with her. Length of days is in her right hand, in her left hand riches and honor. Her ways are ways of pleasantness, and all her paths are peace. She is a tree of life to those who take hold of her, and happy are all who retain her. * The fruit of the righteous is a tree of life, and he who wins souls is wise. * Hope deferred makes the heart sick, but when the desire comes, it is a tree of life. * A wholesome tongue is a tree of life, but perverseness in it breaks the spirit. * And out of the ground the LORD God made every tree grow that is pleasant to the sight and good for food. The tree of life was also in the midst of the garden, and the tree of knowledge of good and evil. * He who has an ear, let him hear what the Spirit says to the churches. To him who overcomes I will give to eat from the tree of life, which is in the midst of the Paradise of God. * And he showed me a pure river of water of life, clear as crystal, proceeding from the throne of God and of the Lamb. In the middle of its street, and on either side of the river, was the tree of life, which bore twelve fruits, each tree yielding its fruit every month. The leaves of the tree were for the healing of the nations. * The grace of our Lord Jesus Christ be with you all. Amen.

Ecclesiastes 7:12 NKJV * Proverbs 3:13-18 NKJV * Proverbs 11:30 NKJV * Proverbs 13:12 NKJV * Proverbs 15:4 NKJV * Genesis 2:9 NKJV * Revelation 2:7 NKJV * Revelation 22:1-2 NKJV * Revelation 22:21 NKJV

OCTOBER

8 . . . .

**Wisdom is a tree of life, with healing in its leaves;
bearing fruit to feed, all those in need.**

20 _____ *

_____
_____
_____
_____
_____
_____
_____

20 _____ *

_____
_____
_____
_____
_____
_____
_____

20 _____ *

_____
_____
_____
_____
_____
_____
_____

OCTOBER 9

I have no greater joy than to hear that my children walk in truth. * Looking for the blessed hope and glorious appearing of our great God and Savior Jesus Christ, who gave Himself for us, that He might redeem us from every lawless deed and purify for Himself His own special people, zealous for good works. * We then, as workers together with Him also plead with you not to receive the grace of God in vain. For He says: "In an acceptable time I have heard you, and in the day of salvation I have helped you." Behold, now is the accepted time; behold, now is the day of salvation. We give no offense in anything, that our ministry may not be blamed. But in all things we commend ourselves as ministers of God: in much patience, in tribulations, in needs, in distresses, in stripes, in imprisonments, in tumults, in labors, in sleeplessness, in fastings; by purity, by knowledge, by long-suffering, by kindness, by the Holy Spirit, by sincere love, by the word of truth, by the power of God, by the armor of righteousness on the right hand and on the left, by honor and dishonor, by evil report and good report; as deceivers, and yet true; as unknown, and yet well known; as dying, and behold we live; as chastened, and yet not killed; as sorrowful, yet always rejoicing; as poor, yet making many rich; as having nothing, and yet possessing all things. * Now to Him who is able to do exceedingly abundantly above all that we ask or think, according to the power that works in us, to Him be glory in the church by Christ Jesus to all generations, forever and ever. Amen.

3 John 4 NKJV * Titus 2:13-14 NKJV * 2 Corinthians 6:1-10 NKJV * Ephesians 3:20-21 NKJV

OCTOBER

9 . . . .

I have no greater joy than to hear that my children walk in truth.

20 _____ *

_____

_____
_____
_____
_____
_____
_____

20 _____ *

_____

_____
_____
_____
_____
_____
_____

20 _____ *

_____

_____
_____
_____
_____
_____
_____

OCTOBER 10

Behave courageously, and the LORD will be with the good. * Arise, for this matter is your responsibility. We also are with you. Be of good courage, and do it. * As for you, my son Solomon, know the God of your father, and serve Him with a loyal heart and with a willing mind; for the LORD searches all hearts and understands all the intent of the thoughts. If you seek Him, He will be found by you; but if you forsake Him, He will cast you off forever. Consider now, for the LORD has chosen you to build a house for the sanctuary; be strong and do it. * Have I not commanded you? Be strong and of good courage; do not be afraid, nor be dismayed, for the LORD your God is with you wherever you go. * Let your heart therefore be loyal to the LORD our God, to walk in His statutes and keep His commandments, as at this day. * To Him be the glory and the dominion forever and ever. Amen.

2 Chronicles 19:11b NKJV * Ezra 10:4 NKJV * 1 Chronicles 28:9-10 NKJV * Joshua 1:9 NKJV * 1 Kings 8:61 NKJV * 1 Peter 5:11 NKJV

OCTOBER

10 ....

**Courage and strength characterize
Christians reliant on the LORD.**

20 _____ *

_____
_____
_____
_____
_____
_____
_____
_____

20 _____ *

_____
_____
_____
_____
_____
_____
_____

20 _____ *

_____
_____
_____
_____
_____
_____
_____
_____

OCTOBER 11

Blessed be the God and Father of our Lord Jesus Christ, who according to His abundant mercy has begotten us again to a living hope through the resurrection of Jesus Christ from the dead. * Therefore, gird up the loins of your mind, be sober, and rest your hope fully upon the grace that is to be brought to you at the revelation of Jesus Christ. * Be sober, be vigilant; because your adversary the devil walks about like a roaring lion, seeking whom he may devour. Resist him, steadfast in the faith, knowing that the same sufferings are experienced by your brotherhood in the world. * But the end of all things is at hand; therefore be serious and watchful in your prayers. * And do this, knowing the time, that now it is high time to awake out of sleep; for now our salvation is nearer than when we first believed. The night is far spent, the day is at hand. Therefore let us cast off the works of darkness, and let us put on the armor of light. * Then I heard a loud voice saying in heaven, "Now salvation, and strength, and the kingdom of our God, and the power of His Christ have come, for the accuser of our brethren, who accused them before our God day and night, has been cast down. And they overcame him by the blood of the Lamb and by the word of their testimony, and they did not love their lives to the death. * Grace be with you all. Amen.

1 Peter 1:3 NKJV * 1 Peter 1:13 NKJV * 1 Peter 5:8 NKJV * 1 Peter 4:7 NKJV * Romans 13:11-12 NKJV * Revelation 12:10-11 NKJV * Hebrews 13:25 NKJV

OCTOBER

11 . . . .

**Rest your hope on the grace that is brought to you
at the revelation of Jesus Christ.**

20 _____ *

_____
_____
_____
_____
_____
_____

20 _____ *

_____
_____
_____
_____
_____
_____

20 _____ *

_____
_____
_____
_____
_____
_____

OCTOBER 12

Finally, all of you, having unity of mind, sympathy, brotherly love, a tender heart, and a humble mind. * By this all people will know that you are my disciples, if you have love for one another. * For whatever was written in former days was written for our instruction, that through endurance and through the encouragement of the Scriptures we might have hope. May the God of endurance and encouragement grant you to live in such harmony with one another, in accord with Christ Jesus, that together you may with one voice glorify the God and Father of our Lord Jesus Christ. * Complete my joy by being of the same mind, having the same love, being in full accord and of one mind. Do nothing from rivalry or conceit, but in humility count others more significant than yourselves. Let each of you look not only to his own interests, but also to the interests of others. * For the eyes of the Lord are on the righteous, and his ears are open to their prayer. But the face of the Lord is against those who do evil. Now who is there to harm you if you are zealous for what is good? But even if you should suffer for righteousness' sake, you will be blessed. Have no fear of them, nor be troubled, but in your hearts honor Christ the Lord as holy, always being prepared to make a defense to anyone who asks you for a reason for the hope that is in you; yet do it with gentleness and respect, having a good conscience, so that, when you are slandered, those who revile your good behavior in Christ may be put to shame. For it is better to suffer for doing good, if that should be God's will, than for doing evil. * But grow in the grace and knowledge of our Lord and Savior Jesus Christ. To him be the glory both now and to the day of eternity. Amen.

1 Peter 3:8 ESV * John 13:35 ESV * Romans 15:4-6 ESV * Philippians 2:2-4 ESV * 1 Peter 3:12-17 ESV * 2 Peter 3:18 ESV

OCTOBER

12 . . . .

The steadfast truth of Scripture gives us hope every day.

20 _____ *

_____

_____

_____

_____

_____

_____

_____

20 _____ *

_____

_____

_____

_____

_____

_____

_____

20 _____ *

_____

_____

_____

_____

_____

_____

_____

OCTOBER 13

But now, thus says the LORD, who created you, O Jacob, and He who formed you, O Israel: "Fear not, for I have redeemed you; I have called you by your name; you are Mine." * Since you were precious in My sight, you have been honored, and I have loved you; therefore I will give men for you, and people for your life. * And they brought Him to the place Golgotha, which is translated, Place of a Skull. Then they gave Him wine mingled with myrrh to drink, but He did not take it. And when they crucified Him, they divided His garments, casting lots for them to determine what every man should take. Now it was the third hour, and they crucified Him. And the inscription of His accusation was written above: THE KING OF THE JEWS. * And those who passed by blasphemed Him, wagging their heads and saying, "Aha! You who destroy the temple and build it in three days, save Yourself, and come down from the cross!" Likewise the chief priests also, mocking among themselves with the scribes, said, "He saved others; Himself He cannot save. Let the Christ, the King of Israel, descend now from the cross, that we may see and believe." Even those who were crucified with Him reviled Him. Now when the sixth hour had come, there was darkness over the whole land until the ninth hour. And at the ninth hour Jesus cried out with a loud voice, saying, "Eloi, Eloi, lama sabachthani?" which translated, "My God, My God, why have You forsaken Me?" * Amen and Amen.

Isaiah 43:1 NKJV * Isaiah 43:4 NKJV * Mark 15:22-26 NKJV * Mark 15:29-33 NKJV * Psalm 72:19b NKJV

OCTOBER

13 . . . .

**In His love for you—
God gave up His Son for your life.**

20 _____ *

_____
_____
_____
_____
_____
_____
_____

20 _____ *

_____
_____
_____
_____
_____
_____
_____

20 _____ *

_____
_____
_____
_____
_____
_____
_____

OCTOBER 14

I have fought the good fight, I have finished the race, I have kept the faith. * For we walk by faith, not by sight. We are confident, yes, well pleased rather to be absent from the body and to be present with the Lord. Therefore we make it our aim, whether present or absent, to be well pleasing to Him. For we must all appear before the judgment seat of Christ, that each one may receive the things done in the body, according to what he has done, whether good or bad. Knowing, therefore, the terror of the Lord, we persuade men; but we are well known to God, and I also trust are well known in your consciences. * Blessed is the man who fears the LORD, who delights greatly in His commandments. His descendants will be mighty on earth; the generation of the upright will be blessed. Wealth and riches will be in his house, and his righteousness endures forever. Unto the upright there arises light in the darkness; he is gracious, and full of compassion, and righteous. * Surely he will never be shaken; the righteous will be in everlasting remembrance. * He has dispersed abroad, he has given to the poor; his righteousness endures forever; his horn will be exalted with honor. * When the Son of Man comes in His glory, and all the holy angels with Him, then He will sit on the throne of His glory. * And He will set the sheep on His right hand, but the goats on the left. Then the King will say to those on His right hand, "Come, you blessed of My Father, inherit the kingdom prepared for you from the foundation of the world: for I was hungry and you gave Me food; I was thirsty and you gave Me drink; I was a stranger and you took Me in; I was naked and you clothed Me; I was sick and you visited Me; I was in prison and you came to Me." * To Him be glory in the church by Christ Jesus to all generations, forever and ever. Amen.

2 Timothy 4:7 NKJV * 2 Corinthians 5:7-11 NKJV * Psalm 112:1-4 NKJV * Psalm 112:6 NKJV * Psalm 112:9 NKJV * Matthew 25:31 NKJV * Matthew 25:33-36 NKJV * Ephesians 3:21 NKJV

OCTOBER

14 . . . .

You are well known to God.

20 _____ *

_____

_____
_____
_____
_____
_____
_____
_____

20 _____ *

_____
_____
_____
_____
_____
_____
_____

20 _____ *

_____
_____
_____
_____
_____
_____
_____

OCTOBER 15

"Go in peace," the priest replied. "For the Lord will go ahead of you on your journey." * May the Lord bless you and protect you. May the Lord smile on you and be gracious to you. May the Lord show you his favor and give you his peace. * The cloud of the Lord rested on the Tabernacle during the day, and at night there was a fire in the cloud so all the people of Israel could see it. This continued throughout all their journeys. * And He said to them, "It is not for you to know times or seasons which the Father has put in His own authority. But you shall receive power when the Holy Spirit has come upon you; and you shall be witnesses to Me in Jerusalem, and in all Judea and Samaria, and to the end of the earth." * Then they returned to Jerusalem from the mount called Olivet, which is near Jerusalem, a Sabbath day's journey. * But Peter, standing up with the eleven, raised his voice and said to them, "Men of Judea and all who dwell in Jerusalem, let this be known to you, and heed my words." * "But this is what was spoken by the prophet Joel: 'And it shall come to pass in the last days, says God, that I will pour out My Spirit on all flesh; your sons and your daughters shall prophesy, your young men shall see visions, your old men shall dream dreams. And on My menservants and on My maidservants, I will pour out My Spirit in those days; and they shall prophesy.'" * "And it shall come to pass that whoever calls on the name of the Lord shall be saved." "Men of Israel, hear these words: Jesus of Nazareth, a Man attested by God to you by miracles, wonders, and signs which God did through Him in your midst, as you yourselves also know— Him, being delivered by the determined purpose and foreknowledge of God, you have taken by lawless hands, have crucified, and put to death; whom God raised up, having loosed the pains of death, because it was not possible that He should be held by it. For David says concerning Him: 'I foresaw the Lord always before my face, for He is at my right hand, that I may not be shaken. Therefore my heart rejoiced, and my tongue was glad; moreover my flesh also will rest in hope. For You will not leave my soul in Hades, nor will You allow Your Holy One to see corruption. You have made known to me the ways of life; You will make me full of joy in Your presence.'" * My love be with you all in Christ Jesus. Amen.

Judges 18:6 NLT * Numbers 6:24-26 NLT * Exodus 40:38 NLT * Acts 1:7-8 NKJV * Acts 1:12 NKJV * Acts 2:14 NKJV * Acts 2:16-18 NKJV * Acts 2:21-28 NKJV * 1 Corinthians 16:24 NKJV

OCTOBER

15 . . . .

May the Lord smile on you.

20 _____ *

---

20 _____ *

---

20 _____ *

OCTOBER 16

Then Philip said, "If you believe with all your heart, you may." And he answered and said, "I believe that Jesus Christ is the Son of God." * Blessed is she who believed, for there will be a fulfillment of those things which were told her from the Lord. * The nobleman said to Him, "Sir, come down before my child dies!" Jesus said to him, "Go your way; your son lives." So the man believed the word that Jesus spoke to him, and he went his way. * She said to Him, "Yes, Lord, I believe that you are the Christ, the Son of God, who is to come into the world." * Then it happened, as He was coming near Jericho, that a certain blind man sat by the road begging. * And he cried out, saying, "Jesus, Son of David, have mercy on me!" Then those who went before warned him that he should be quiet; but he cried out all the more, "Son of David, have mercy on me!" So Jesus stood still and commanded him to be brought to Him. And when he had come near, He asked him, saying, "What do you want Me to do for you?" He said, "Lord, that I may receive my sight." Then Jesus said to him, "Receive your sight; your faith has made you well." And immediately he received his sight, and followed Him, glorifying God. And all the people, when they saw it, gave praise to God. * Then one of the crowd answered and said, "Teacher, I brought You my son, who has a mute spirit. * Jesus said to him, "If you can believe, all things are possible to him who believes." Immediately the father of the child cried out and said with tears, "Lord, I believe help my unbelief!" * Now this is the confidence that we have in Him, that if we ask anything according to His will, He hears us. And if we know that He hears us, whatever we ask, we know that we have the petitions that we have asked of Him. * To God our Savior, who alone is wise, be glory and majesty, dominion and power, both now and forever. Amen.

Acts 8:37 NKJV * Luke 1:45 NKJV * John 4:49-50 NKJV * John 11:27 NKJV * Luke 18:35 NKJV * Luke 18:38-43 NKJV * Mark 9:17 NKJV * Mark 9:23-24 NKJV * 1 John 5:14-15 NKJV * Jude 1:25 NKJV

OCTOBER

16 ....

Do you believe God will do what He has already promised?

20 _____ *

_____
_____
_____
_____
_____
_____
_____

20 _____ *

_____
_____
_____
_____
_____
_____
_____

20 _____ *

_____
_____
_____
_____
_____
_____
_____

OCTOBER 17

Therefore the sisters sent to Him, saying, "Lord, behold, he whom You love is sick." When Jesus heard that, He said, "This sickness is not unto death, but for the glory of God, that the Son of God may be glorified through it." * Then as He entered a certain village, there met Him ten men who were lepers, who stood afar off. And they lifted up their voices and said, "Jesus, Master, have mercy on us!" So when He saw them, He said to them, "Go, show yourselves to the priests." And so it was that as they went, they were cleansed. And one of them, when he saw that he was healed, returned, and with a loud voice, glorified God, and fell down on his face at His feet, giving Him thanks. And he was a Samaritan. So Jesus answered and said, "Were there not ten cleansed? But where are the nine? Were there not any found who returned to give glory to God except this foreigner?" And He said to him, "Arise, go your way. Your faith has made you well." * "Now My soul is troubled, and what shall I say? 'Father, save Me from this hour'? But for this purpose I came to this hour. Father, glorify Your name." Then a voice came from heaven saying, "I have both glorified it and will glorify it again." * The grace of our Lord Jesus Christ be with you all. Amen.

John 11:3-4 NKJV * Luke 17:12-19 NKJV * John 12:27 NKJV * Philippians 4:23 NKJV

OCTOBER

17 . . . .

How is God's name glorified in your situation?

20 _____ *

_____

20 _____ *

_____

20 _____ *

_____

OCTOBER 18

And immediately, coming up from the water, He saw the heavens parting and the Spirit descending upon Him like a dove. Then a voice came from heaven, "You are My beloved Son, in whom I am well pleased." * As He prayed, the appearance of His face was altered, and His robe became white and glistening. * But Peter and those with him were heavy with sleep; and when they were fully awake, they saw His glory and the two men who stood with Him. * While he was saying this, a cloud came and overshadowed them; and they were fearful as they entered the cloud. And a voice came out of the cloud, saying, "This is My beloved Son. Hear Him!" * "He who loves his life will lose it, and he who hates his life in this world will keep it for eternal life. If anyone serves Me, let him follow Me; and where I am, there My servant will be also. If anyone serves Me, him My Father will honor. * Then Jesus said to His disciples, "If anyone desires to come after Me, let him deny himself, and take up his cross, and follow Me. For whoever desires to save his life will lose it, but whoever loses his life for My sake will find it. For what profit is it to a man if he gains the whole world, and loses his own soul? Or what will a man give in exchange for his soul? For the Son of Man will come in the glory of His Father with His angels, and then He will reward each according to his works." * To God, alone wise, be glory through Jesus Christ forever. Amen.

Mark 1:10-11 NKJV * Luke 9:29 NKJV * Luke 9:32 NKJV * Luke 9:34-35 NKJV * John 12:25-26 NKJV * Matthew 16:24-27 NKJV * Romans 16:27 NKJV

OCTOBER

18 . . . .

God the Father affirmed His Son.

20 _____ *

_____
_____
_____
_____
_____
_____
_____

20 _____ *

_____
_____
_____
_____
_____
_____
_____

20 _____ *

_____
_____
_____
_____
_____
_____
_____

OCTOBER 19

Blessed is the man who walks not in the counsel of the ungodly, nor stands in the path of sinners, nor sits in the seat of the scornful. * My son, do not walk in the way of them, keep your foot from their path. * For the LORD gives wisdom; from His mouth come knowledge and understanding; He stores up sound wisdom for the upright; He is a shield to those who walk uprightly; He guards the paths of justice, and preserves the way of His saints. Then you will understand righteousness and justice, equity and every good path. When wisdom enters your heart, and knowledge is pleasant to your soul, discretion will preserve you; understanding will keep you, to deliver you from the way of evil, from the man who speaks perverse things, from those who leave the paths of uprightness to walk in the ways of darkness. * The fear of the LORD is the beginning of wisdom, and the knowledge of the Holy One is understanding. * Hear, my son, and receive my sayings, and the years of your life will be many. I have taught you in the way of wisdom; I have led you in right paths. When you walk, your steps will not be hindered, and when you run, you will not stumble. Take firm hold of instruction, do not let go; keep her, for she is your life. Do not enter the path of the wicked, and do not walk in the way of evil. Avoid it, do not travel on it; turn away from it and pass on. * Get wisdom! Get understanding! Do not forget, nor turn away from the words of my mouth. Do not forsake her, and she will preserve you; love her, and she will keep you. * Exalt her, and she will promote you; she will bring you honor, when you embrace her. She will place on your head an ornament of grace; a crown of glory she will deliver to you. * My son, give attention to my words; incline your ear to my sayings. Do not let them depart from your eyes; keep them in the midst of your heart; for they are life to those who find them, and health to all their flesh. Keep your heart with all diligence, for out of it spring the issues of life. * Ponder the path of your feet, and let all your ways be established. * I have no greater joy than to hear that my children walk in truth. * To God our Savior, who alone is wise, be glory and majesty, dominion and power, both now and forever. Amen.

Psalm 1:1 NKJV * Proverbs 1:15 NKJV * Proverbs 2:6-13 NKJV * Proverbs 9:10 NKJV * Proverbs 4:10-15 NKJV * Proverbs 4:5-6 NKJV * Proverbs 4:8-9 NKJV * Proverbs 4:20-23 NKJV * Proverbs 4:26 NKJV * 3 John 1:4 NKJV * Jude 1:25 NKJV

OCTOBER

19 . . . .

Mine the gems of wisdom.

20 _____ *

_____

_____

_____

_____

_____

_____

_____

20 _____ *

_____

_____

_____

_____

_____

_____

_____

20 _____ *

_____

_____

_____

_____

_____

_____

_____

OCTOBER 20

But his delight is in the law of the LORD, and in His law he meditates day and night. * For by one offering He has perfected forever those who are being sanctified. * My eyes fail from searching Your word, saying, "When will you comfort me?" For I have become like a wineskin in smoke, yet I do not forget Your statutes. How many are the days of Your servant? When will You execute judgment on those who persecute me? The proud have dug pits for me, which is not according to Your law. * Unless Your law had been my delight, I would have perished in my affliction. I will never forget Your precepts, for by them You have given me life. * Forever, O LORD, Your word is settled in heaven. * "For My thoughts are not your thoughts, nor are your ways My ways," says the LORD. "For as the heavens are higher than the earth, so are My ways higher than your ways, and My thoughts than your thoughts." * So shall My word be that goes forth from My mouth; it shall not return to Me void, but it shall accomplish what I please, and it shall prosper in the things for which I sent it. * Then the brethren immediately sent Paul and Silas away by night to Berea. When they arrived, they went into the synagogue of the Jews. These were more fair-minded than those in Thessalonica, in that they received the word with all readiness, and searched the Scriptures daily to find out whether these things were so. * Blessed are those who hunger and thirst for righteousness, for they shall be filled. * And Jesus said to them, I am the bread of life. He who comes to Me shall never hunger, and he who believes in Me shall never thirst. * Amen and Amen.

Psalm 1:2 NKJV * Hebrews 10:14 NKJV * Psalm 119:82-85 NKJV * Psalm 119:92-93 NKJV * Psalm 119:89 NKJV * Isaiah 55:8-9 NKJV * Isaiah 55:11 NKJV * Acts 17:10-12 NKJV * Matthew 5:6 NKJV * John 6:35 NKJV * Psalm 72:19b NKJV

OCTOBER

20 . . . .

**The word of God sustains every soul,
perfecting forever those being sanctified.**

20 _____ *

_____

_____

_____

_____

_____

_____

_____

20 _____ *

_____

_____

_____

_____

_____

_____

_____

20 _____ *

_____

_____

_____

_____

_____

_____

_____

OCTOBER 21

He shall be like a tree planted by the rivers of water, that brings forth its fruit in its season, whose leaf also shall not wither; and whatever he does shall prosper. * The words of the LORD are pure words, like silver tried in a furnace of earth, purified seven times. * As for God, His way is perfect; the word of the LORD is proven; He is a shield to all who trust in Him. * Blessed is the man who trusts in the LORD, and whose hope is in the LORD. For he shall be like a tree planted by the waters, which spreads out its roots by the river, and will not fear when heat comes; but its leaf will be green, and will not be anxious in the year of drought, nor will cease from yielding fruit. * For a good tree does not bear bad fruit, nor does a bad tree bear good fruit. For every tree is known by its own fruit. For men do not gather figs from thorns, nor do they gather grapes from a bramble bush. A good man out of the good treasure of his heart brings forth good; and an evil man out of the evil treasure of his heart brings forth evil. For out of the abundance of the heart the mouth speaks. * The heart is deceitful above all things, and desperately wicked; who can know it. I, the LORD, search the heart, I test the mind, even to give every man according to his ways, according to the fruit of his doings. * Then Jesus answered and said: "A certain man went down from Jerusalem to Jericho, and fell among thieves, who stripped him of his clothing, wounded him, and departed, leaving him half dead. Now by chance a certain priest came down the road. And when he saw him, he passed by on the other side. Likewise a Levite, when he arrived at the place, came and looked, and passed by on the other side. But a certain Samaritan, as he journeyed, came where he was. And when he saw him, he had compassion." * "So which of these three do you think was neighbor to him who fell among the thieves?" * Who is wise and understanding among you? Let him show by good conduct that his works are done in the meekness of wisdom. * To Him be the glory and the dominion forever and ever. Amen.

Psalm 1:3 NKJV * Psalm 12:6 NKJV * 2 Samuel 22:31 NKJV * Jeremiah 17:7-8 NKJV * Luke 6:43-45 NKJV * Jeremiah 17:9-10 NKJV * Luke 10:30-33 NKJV * Luke 10:36 NKJV * James 3:13 NKJV * 1 Peter 5:11 NKJV

OCTOBER

21 . . . .

When your roots are deep,
you nourish those in need.

20 _____ ⁎

---

20 _____ ⁎

---

20 _____ ⁎

OCTOBER 22

But this is not true of the wicked. They are like worthless chaff, scattered by the wind. They will be condemned at the time of judgment. Sinners will have no place among the godly. * But God shows his anger from heaven against all sinful, wicked people who push the truth away from themselves. For the truth about God is known to them instinctively. God has put this knowledge in their hearts. From the time the world was created, people have seen the earth and sky and all that God made. They can clearly see his invisible qualities— his eternal power and divine nature. So they have no excuse whatsoever for not knowing God. Yes, they knew God, but they wouldn't worship him as God or even give him thanks. And they began to think up foolish ideas of what God was like. The result was that their minds became dark and confused. Claiming to be wise, they became utter fools instead. * So God let them go ahead and do whatever shameful things their hearts desired. As a result, they did vile and degrading things with each other's bodies. * Their lives became full of every kind of wickedness, sin, greed, hate, envy, murder, fighting, deception, malicious behavior, and gossip. They are backstabbers, haters of God, insolent, proud, and boastful. They are forever inventing new ways of sinning and are disobedient to their parents. They refuse to understand, break their promises, and are heartless and unforgiving. They are fully aware of God's death penalty for those who do these things, yet they go right ahead and do them anyway. And worse, they encourage others to do them, too. * If we say we have no sin, we are only fooling ourselves and refusing to accept the truth. But if we confess our sins to him, he is faithful and just to forgive us and to cleanse us from every wrong. If we claim we have not sinned, we are calling God a liar and showing that his word has no place in our hearts. * Dear children, keep away from anything that might take God's place in your hearts. * Amen and Amen.

Psalm 1:4-5 NLT * Romans 1:18-22 NLT * Romans 1:24 NLT * Romans 1:29-32 NLT * 1 John 1:8-10 NLT * 1 John 5:21 NLT * Psalm 72:19b NLT

OCTOBER

22 . . . .

**Do you care that those who refuse to repent,
will stand condemned at the time of judgment?**

20 _____ *

_____
_____
_____
_____
_____
_____

20 _____ *

_____
_____
_____
_____
_____
_____

20 _____ *

_____
_____
_____
_____
_____
_____

OCTOBER 23

For the LORD knows the way of the righteous, but the way of the ungodly shall perish. * The spirit of a man is the lamp of the LORD, searching all the inner depths of his heart. * For what man knows the things of a man except the spirit of the man which is in him? Even so no one knows the things of God except the Spirit of God. * For as the body without the spirit is dead, so faith without works is dead also. * Also He said to them, "Is a lamp brought to be put under a basket or under a bed? Is it not to be set on a lamp stand? For there is nothing hidden which will not be revealed, nor has anything been kept secret but that it should come to light. * Then He said to them, "Take heed what you hear. With the same measure you use, it will be measured to you; and to you who hear, more will be given. * The hearing ear and the seeing eye, the LORD has made them both. * Whoever curses his father or his mother, his lamp will be put out in deep darkness. * "Honor your father and mother," which is the first commandment with promise: "that it may be well with you and you may live long on the earth." * The Lord knows the days of the upright; and their inheritance shall be forever. They shall not be ashamed in the evil time, and in the days of famine they shall be satisfied. But the wicked shall perish; and the enemies of the LORD, like the splendor of the meadows, shall vanish. Into smoke they shall vanish away. * But the salvation of the righteous is from the LORD; He is their strength in the time of trouble. And the LORD shall help them and deliver them; He shall deliver them from the wicked, and save them, because they trust in Him. * Grace be with all those who love our Lord Jesus Christ in sincerity. Amen.

Psalm 1:6 NKJV * Proverbs 20:27 NKJV * 1 Corinthians 2:11 NKJV * James 2:26 NKJV * Mark 4:21-22 NKJV * Mark 4:24 NKJV * Proverbs 20:12 NKJV * Proverbs 20:20 NKJV * Ephesians 6:2-3 NKJV * Psalm 37:18-20 NKJV * Psalm 37:39-40 NKJV * Ephesians 6:24 NKJV

OCTOBER

23 . . . .

God always helps.
He always delivers.

20 ____ *

_____
_____
_____
_____
_____
_____
_____

20 ____ *

_____
_____
_____
_____
_____
_____
_____

20 ____ *

_____
_____
_____
_____
_____
_____
_____

OCTOBER 24

But they lie in wait for their own blood, they lurk secretly for their own lives. So are the ways of everyone who is greedy for gain; it takes away the life of its owners. * Now godliness with contentment is great gain. For we brought nothing into this world, and it is certain we can carry nothing out. And having food and clothing, with these we shall be content. But those who desire to be rich fall into temptation and a snare, and into many foolish and harmful lusts which drown men in destruction and perdition. For the love of money is a root of all kinds of evil, for which some have strayed from the faith in their greediness, and pierced themselves through with many sorrows. But you, O man of God, flee these things and pursue righteousness, godliness, faith, love, patience, gentleness. * Guard what was committed to your trust. * Thorns and snares are in the way of the perverse; he who guards his soul will be far from them. * Do not rob the poor because he is poor, nor oppress the afflicted at the gate; for the LORD will plead their cause, and plunder the soul of those who plunder them. * The way of a guilty man is perverse; but as for the pure, his work is right. * To God, alone wise, be glory through Jesus Christ forever. Amen.

Proverbs 1:18-19 NKJV * 1 Timothy 6:6-11 NKJV * 1 Timothy 6:20a NKJV * Proverbs 22:5 NKJV * Proverbs 22:22-23 NKJV * Proverbs 21:8 NKJV * Romans 16:27 NKJV

OCTOBER

24 . . . .

**Those greedy for gain, rob themselves of life.
Contentment enjoys life.**

20 _____ *

_____

_____

_____

_____

_____

_____

_____

20 _____ *

_____

_____

_____

_____

_____

_____

_____

20 _____ *

_____

_____

_____

_____

_____

_____

_____

OCTOBER 25

Be angry, and do not sin. Meditate within your heart on your bed and be still. * I call to remembrance my song in the night; I meditate within my heart, and my spirit makes diligent search. * The LORD will command His lovingkindness in the daytime, and in the night His song shall be with me— a prayer to the God of my life. * "Be angry, and do not sin": do not let the sun go down on your wrath, nor give place to the devil. * Therefore, take up the whole armor of God, that you may be able to withstand in the evil day, and having done all, to stand. Stand therefore, having girded your waist with truth, having put on the breastplate of righteousness, and having shod your feet with the preparation of the gospel of peace, above all, taking the shield of faith with which you will be able to quench all the fiery darts of the wicked one. And take the helmet of salvation, and the sword of the spirit, which is the word of God; praying always with all prayer and supplication in the Spirit, being watchful to this end with all perseverance and supplication for all the saints— * So then, my beloved brethren, let every man be swift to hear, slow to speak, slow to wrath; for the wrath of man does not produce the righteousness of God. * Cease from anger, and forsake wrath; do not fret—it only causes harm. * I desire therefore that the men pray everywhere, lifting up holy hands, without wrath and doubting. * Now may the God of peace who brought up our Lord Jesus from the dead, that great Shepherd of the sheep, through the blood of the everlasting covenant, make you complete in every good work to do His will, working in you what is well pleasing in His sight, through Jesus Christ, to whom be glory forever and ever. Amen.

Psalm 4:4 NKJV * Psalm 77:6 NKJV * Psalm 42:8 NKJV * Ephesians 4:26-27 NKJV * Ephesians 6:13-18 NKJV * James 1:19-20 NKJV * Psalm 37:8 NKJV * 1 Timothy 2:8 NKJV * Hebrews 13:20-21 NKJV

OCTOBER

25 . . . .

**The armor of God protects you,
from the anger that tries to destroy you.**

20 _____ *

_____

_____
_____
_____
_____
_____
_____

20 _____ *

_____

_____
_____
_____
_____
_____
_____

20 _____ *

_____

_____
_____
_____
_____
_____
_____

OCTOBER 26

Now, therefore, why are you putting God to the test by placing a yoke on the neck of the disciples that neither our fathers nor we have been able to bear? * For you were called to freedom, brothers. Only do not use your freedom as an opportunity for the flesh, but through love serve one another. For the whole law is fulfilled in one word: "You shall love your neighbor as yourself." But if you bite and devour one another, watch out that you are not consumed by one another. But I say, walk by the Spirit, and you will not gratify the desires of the flesh. * For since the law has but a shadow of the good things to come instead of the true form of these realities, it can never, by the same sacrifices that are continually offered every year, make perfect those who draw near. * But when Christ had offered for all time a single sacrifice for sins, he sat down at the right hand of God, waiting from that time until his enemies should be made a footstool for his feet. For by a single offering he has perfected for all time those who are being sanctified. * Therefore, brothers, since we have confidence to enter the holy places by the blood of Jesus, * let us draw near with a true heart in full assurance of faith, with our hearts sprinkled clean from an evil conscience and our bodies washed with pure water. Let us hold fast the confession of our hope without wavering, for he who promised is faithful. And let us consider how to stir up one another to love and good works. * But recall the former days when, after you were enlightened, you endured a hard struggle with sufferings, sometimes being publicly exposed to reproach and affliction, and sometimes being partners with those so treated. For you had compassion on those in prison, and you joyfully accepted the plundering of your property, since you knew that you yourselves had a better possession and an abiding one. * Then Jesus said to the crowds and to his disciples, "The scribes and the Pharisees sit on Moses' seat, so practice and observe whatever they tell you—but not what they do. For they preach, but do not practice. They tie up heavy burdens, hard to bear, and lay them on people's shoulders, but they themselves are not willing to move them with their finger. * We put no obstacle in anyone's way, so that no fault may be found with our ministry. * Blessed be the LORD forever! Amen and Amen.

Acts 15:10 ESV * Galatians 5:13-16 ESV * Hebrews 10:1 ESV * Hebrews 10:12-14 ESV * Hebrews 10:19 ESV * Hebrews 10:22-24 ESV * Hebrews 10:32-34 ESV * Matthew 23:1-4 ESV * 2 Corinthians 6:3 ESV * Psalm 89:52 ESV

OCTOBER

26 . . . .

**You are perfect for your calling,
because Jesus Christ is perfected in you.**

20 _____ *

_____
_____
_____
_____
_____
_____
_____

20 _____ *

_____
_____
_____
_____
_____
_____
_____

20 _____ *

_____
_____
_____
_____
_____
_____
_____

OCTOBER 27

Faithfulness springs up from the ground, and righteousness looks down from the sky. * The righteous who walks in his integrity— blessed are his children after him! * Praise the LORD! Blessed is the man who fears the LORD, who greatly delights in his commandments! His offspring will be mighty in the land; the generation of the upright will be blessed. Wealth and riches are in his house, and his righteousness endures forever. Light dawns in the darkness for the upright; he is gracious, merciful, and righteous. It is well with the man who deals generously and lends; who conducts his affairs with justice. For the righteous will never be moved; he will be remembered forever. * Trust in the LORD, and do good; dwell in the land and befriend faithfulness. Delight yourself in the LORD, and he will give you the desires of your heart. Commit your way to the LORD; trust in him, and he will act. * To you, O LORD, I lift up my soul. * Make me to know your ways, O LORD; teach me your paths. Lead me in your truth and teach me, for you are the God of my salvation; for you I wait all the day long. * For your steadfast love is before my eyes, and I walk in your faithfulness. * He leads the humble in what is right, and teaches the humble his way. All the paths of the LORD are steadfast love and faithfulness, for those who keep his covenant and his testimonies. * Who is the man who fears the LORD? Him will he instruct in the way that he should choose. His soul shall abide in well-being, and his offspring shall inherit the land. * The grace of the Lord Jesus be with all. Amen.

Psalm 85:11 ESV * Proverbs 20:7 ESV * Psalm 112:1-6 ESV * Psalm 37:3-5 ESV * Psalm 25:1 ESV * Psalm 25:4-5 ESV * Psalm 26:3 ESV * Psalm 25:8-10 ESV * Revelation 22:21 ESV

OCTOBER

27 . . . .

Befriend faithfulness.

20_____ *

_____

_____

_____

_____

_____

_____

_____

20_____ *

_____

_____

_____

_____

_____

_____

_____

20_____ *

_____

_____

_____

_____

_____

_____

_____

OCTOBER 28

Then the Pharisees and scribes asked Him, "Why do Your disciples not walk according to the tradition of the elders, but eat bread with unwashed hands?" He answered and said to them, "Well did Isaiah prophesy of you hypocrites, as it is written: 'This people honors Me with their lips, but their heart is far from Me. And in vain they worship Me, teaching as doctrines the commandments of men.' For laying aside the commandment of God, you hold the tradition of men—the washing of pitchers and cups, and many other such things you do." He said to them, "All too well you reject the commandment of God, that you may keep your tradition." * And God spoke all these words, saying: * You shall have no other gods before Me. You shall not make for yourself a carved image—any likeness of anything that is in heaven above, or that is in the earth beneath, or that is in the water under the earth; you shall not bow down to them nor serve them. For I, the LORD your God, am a jealous God, visiting the iniquity of the fathers upon the children to the third and fourth generations of those who hate Me, but showing mercy to thousands, to those who love Me and keep My commandments. You shall not take the name of the LORD your God in vain, for the LORD will not hold him guiltless who takes His name in vain. Remember the Sabbath day, to keep it holy. * Honor your father and your mother, that your days may be long upon the land which the LORD your God is giving you. You shall not murder. You shall not commit adultery. You shall not steal. You shall not bear false witness against your neighbor. You shall not covet your neighbor's house; you shall not covet your neighbor's wife, nor his male servant, nor his female servant, nor his ox, nor his donkey, nor anything that is your neighbor's. * Wisdom rests in the heart of him who has understanding, but what is in the heart of fools is made known. * All the ways of a man are pure in his own eyes, but the LORD weighs the spirits. * To Him be glory in the church by Christ Jesus to all generations, forever and ever. Amen.

Mark 7:5-9 NKJV * Exodus 20:1 NKJV * Exodus 20:3-8 NKJV * Exodus 20:12-17 NKJV * Proverbs 14:33 NKJV * Proverbs 16:2 NKJV * Ephesians 3:21 NKJV

OCTOBER

28 . . . .

God's commandments declare what He cares about.

20 _____ *

_____
_____
_____
_____
_____
_____
_____

20 _____ *

_____
_____
_____
_____
_____
_____
_____

20 _____ *

_____
_____
_____
_____
_____
_____
_____

OCTOBER 29

But Joseph told them, "Don't be afraid of me. Am I God, to judge and punish you? As far as I am concerned, God turned into good what you meant for evil. He brought me to the high position I have today so I could save the lives of many people." * For God does not show favoritism. * And so, dear brothers and sisters, I plead with you to give your bodies to God. Let them be a living and holy sacrifice—the kind he will accept. When you think of what he has done for you, is this too much to ask? Don't copy the behavior and customs of this world, but let God transform you into a new person by changing the way you think. Then you will know what God wants you to do, and you will know how good and how pleasing and perfect his will really is. As God's messenger, I give each of you this warning: Be honest in your estimate of yourselves, measuring your value by how much faith God has given you. * We should be decent and true in everything we do, so that everyone can approve of our behavior. Don't participate in wild parties and getting drunk, or in adultery and immoral living, or in fighting and jealousy. But let the Lord Jesus Christ take control of you, and don't think of ways to indulge your evil desires. * Pay all your debts, except the debt of love for others. You can never finish paying that! If you love your neighbor, you will fulfill all the requirements of God's law. * Love does no wrong to anyone, so love satisfies all of God's requirements. * Blessed be the LORD forever! Amen and amen!

Genesis 50:19-20 NLT * Romans 2:11 NLT * Romans 12:1-3 NLT * Romans 13:13-14 NLT * Romans 13:8 NLT * Romans 13:10 NLT * Psalm 89:52 NLT

OCTOBER

29 . . . .

A transformed mind invites peace of mind.

20 ____ *

_____

_____
_____
_____
_____
_____
_____
_____

20 ____ *

_____

_____
_____
_____
_____
_____
_____
_____

20 ____ *

_____

_____
_____
_____
_____
_____
_____
_____

OCTOBER 30

Abraham never wavered in believing God's promise. In fact, his faith grew stronger, and in this he brought glory to God. He was absolutely convinced that God was able to do anything he promised. And because of Abraham's faith, God declared him to be righteous. * When people take an oath, they call on someone greater than themselves to hold them to it. And without question that oath is binding. God also bound himself with an oath, so that those who received the promise could be perfectly sure that he would never change his mind. So God has given us both his promise and his oath. These two things are unchangeable because it is impossible for God to lie. Therefore, we who have fled to him for refuge can take new courage for we can hold on to his promise with confidence. This confidence is like a strong and trustworthy anchor for our souls. It leads us through the curtain of heaven into God's inner sanctuary. * You are worthy O Lord our God, to receive glory and honor and power. For you created everything, and it is for your pleasure that they exist and were created. * And now, all glory to God, who is able to keep you from stumbling, and who will bring you into his glorious presence innocent of sin and with great joy. All glory to him, who alone is God our Savior, through Jesus Christ our Lord. Yes, glory, majesty, power, and authority belong to him, in the beginning, now, and forevermore. Amen.

Romans 4:20-222 NLT * Hebrews 6:16-19 NLT * Revelation 4:11 NLT * Jude 1:24-25 NLT

OCTOBER

30 ....

Walk confidently in the promises of God.

20 _____ *

_____
_____
_____
_____
_____
_____
_____

20 _____ *

_____
_____
_____
_____
_____
_____
_____

20 _____ *

_____
_____
_____
_____
_____
_____
_____

OCTOBER 31

He will swallow up death forever, and the LORD God will wipe away tears from all faces; the rebuke of His people He will take away from all the earth; for the LORD has spoken. * "For the Lamb who is in the midst of the throne will shepherd them and lead them to living fountains of water. And God will wipe away every tear from their eyes." * And I heard a loud voice from heaven saying, "Behold, the tabernacle of God is with men, and He will dwell with them, and they shall be His people. God Himself will be with them and be their God. And God will wipe away every tear from their eyes; there shall be no more death, nor sorrow, nor crying. There shall be no more pain, for the former things have passed away. * Blessed be the God and Father of our Lord Jesus Christ, the Father of mercies and God of all comfort, who comforts us in all our tribulation, that we may be able to comfort those who are in any trouble, with the comfort with which we ourselves are comforted by God. For as the sufferings of Christ abound in us, so our consolation also abounds through Christ. Now if we are afflicted, it is for your consolation and salvation, which is effective for enduring the same sufferings which we also suffer. Or if we are comforted, it is for your consolation and salvation. And our hope for you is steadfast, because we know that as you are partakers of the sufferings, so also you will partake of the consolation. * Grace be with you all. Amen.

Isaiah 25:8 NKJV * Revelation 7:17 NKJV * Revelation 21:3-4 NKJV * 2 Corinthians 1:3-7 NKJV * Hebrews 13:25 NKJV

31 ·

How has God comforted you?

20 _____ *

_____
_____
_____
_____
_____
_____
_____

20 _____ *

_____
_____
_____
_____
_____
_____
_____

20 _____ *

_____
_____
_____
_____
_____
_____
_____

NOVEMBER

NOVEMBER 1

Instead of believing what they knew was the truth about God, they deliberately chose to believe lies. So they worshipped the things God made but not the Creator himself, who is to be praised forever. Amen. That is why God abandoned them to their shameful desires. Even the women turned against the natural way to have sex and instead indulged in sex with each other. And the men, instead of having normal sexual relationships with women, burned with lust for each other. Men did shameful things with other men and, as a result, suffered within themselves the penalty they so richly deserved. When they refused to acknowledge God, he abandoned them to their evil minds and let them do things that should never be done. * Run away from sexual sin! No other sin so clearly affects the body as this one does. For sexual immorality is a sin against your own body. Or don't you know that your body is the temple of the Holy Spirit, who lives in you and was given to you by God? You do not belong to yourself, for God bought you with a high price. So you must honor God with your body. * For he himself has said, "You must be holy because I am holy." * Don't you know that those who do wrong will have no share in the Kingdom of God? Don't fool yourselves. Those who indulge in sexual sin, who are idol worshippers, adulterers, male prostitutes, homosexuals, thieves, greedy people, drunkards, abusers, and swindlers—none of these will have a share in the Kingdom of God. There was a time when some of you were just like that, but now your sins have been washed away, and you have been set apart for God. You have been made right with God because of what the Lord Jesus Christ and the Spirit of our God have done for you. * Give honor to marriage, and remain faithful to one another in marriage. God will surely judge people who are immoral and those who commit adultery. * For God so loved the world that he gave his only Son, so that everyone who believes in him will not perish but have eternal life. God did not send his Son into the world to condemn it, but to save it. * Prove by the way that you live that you have really turned from your sins and turned to God. * Bless his glorious name forever! Let the whole earth be filled with his glory. Amen and amen!

Romans 1:25-28 NLT * 1 Corinthians 6:18-20 NLT * 1 Peter 1:16 NLT * 1 Corinthians 6:9-11 NLT * Hebrews 13:4 NLT * John 3:16-17 NLT * Matthew 3:8 NLT * Psalm 72:19 NLT

NOVEMBER

1 . . . .

God's Word will never change.

20_____ *

_____
_____
_____
_____
_____
_____
_____

20_____ *

_____
_____
_____
_____
_____
_____
_____

20_____ *

_____
_____
_____
_____
_____
_____
_____

NOVEMBER 2

O Lord God Almighty! Where is there anyone as mighty as you, Lord? Faithfulness is your very character. * The unfailing love of the Lord never ends! By his mercies we have been kept from complete destruction. Great is his faithfulness; his mercies begin afresh each day. I say to myself, "The Lord is my inheritance; therefore, I will hope in him!" * Give thanks to the Lord, for he is good! His faithful love endures forever. Give thanks to the God of gods. His faithful love endures forever. Give thanks to the Lord of Lords. His faithful love endures forever. Give thanks to him who alone does mighty miracles. His faithful love endures forever. Give thanks to him who made the heavens so skillfully. His faithful love endures forever. Give thanks to him who made the heavenly lights— His faithful love endures forever. The sun to rule the day, His faithful love endures forever. And the moon and stars to rule the night. His faithful love endures forever. * Give thanks to him who parted the Red Sea. His faithful love endures forever. * He remembered our utter weakness. His faithful love endures forever. He saved us from our enemies. His faithful love endures forever. He gives food to every living thing. His faithful love endures forever. Give thanks to the God of heaven. His faithful love endures forever. * Amen and Amen!

Psalm 89:8 NLT * Lamentations 3:22-24 NLT * Psalm 136:1-9 NLT * Psalm 136:13 NLT * Psalm 136:23-26 NLT * Psalm 72:19b NLT

NOVEMBER

2

$\cdot \cdot \cdot \cdot \cdot \cdot \cdot \cdot \cdot \cdot \cdot \cdot \cdot \cdot \cdot \cdot \cdot \cdot \cdot \cdot \cdot \cdot \cdot \cdot \cdot \cdot \cdot \cdot \cdot \cdot \cdot \cdot$

The eternal weight of faithfulness is seen in Jesus Christ.

20 _____ *

_____
_____
_____
_____
_____
_____
_____
_____

20 _____ *

_____
_____
_____
_____
_____
_____
_____
_____

20 _____ *

_____
_____
_____
_____
_____
_____
_____
_____

NOVEMBER 3

After two days it was the Passover and the Feast of Unleavened Bread. And the chief priests and the scribes sought how they might take Him by trickery to put Him to death. * Nevertheless even among the rulers many believed in Him, but because of the Pharisees they did not confess Him, lest they should be put out of the synagogue; for they loved the praise of men more than the praise of God. * "If the world hates you, you know that it hated Me before it hated you. If you were of the world, the world would love its own. Yet because you are not of the world, but I chose you out of the world, therefore the world hates you. Remember the word that I said to you, 'A servant is not greater than his master.' If they persecuted Me, they will also persecute you. If they kept My word, they will keep yours also. But all these things they will do to you for My name's sake, because they do not know Him who sent Me. If I had not come and spoken to them, they would have no sin, but now they have no excuse for their sin." * "But this happened that the word might be fulfilled which is written in their law, 'They hated Me without a cause.'" * "These things I have spoken to you, that you should not be made to stumble. They will put you out of the synagogues; yes, the time is coming that whoever kills you will think that he offers God service. And these things they will do to you because they have not known the Father nor Me." * Until now you have asked nothing in My name. Ask, and you will receive, that your joy may be full. * To God, alone wise, be glory through Jesus Christ forever. Amen.

Mark 14:1 NKJV * John 12:42-43 NKJV * John 15:18-22 NKJV * John 15:25 NKJV * John 16:1-3 NKJV * John 16:24 NKJV * Romans 16:27 NKJV

NOVEMBER

3 . . . .

May I rejoice to suffer for Your name!

20 _____ *

_____

_____

_____

_____

_____

_____

_____

20 _____ *

_____

_____

_____

_____

_____

_____

_____

20 _____ *

_____

_____

_____

_____

_____

_____

_____

NOVEMBER 4

Then Jesus cried out and said, "He who believes in Me, believes not in Me but in Him who sent Me. And he who sees Me sees Him who sent Me. I have come as a light into the world, that whoever believes in Me should not abide in darkness." * For God so loved the world that He gave His only begotten Son, that whoever believes in Him should not perish but have everlasting life. For God did not send His Son into the world to condemn the world, but that the world through Him might be saved. He who believes in Him is not condemned; but he who does not believe is condemned already, because he has not believed in the name of the only begotten Son of God. And this is the condemnation, that the light has come into the world, and men loved the darkness rather than light, because their deeds were evil. For everyone practicing evil hates the light and does not come to the light, lest his deeds should be exposed. But he who does the truth comes to the light, that his deeds may be clearly seen, that they have been done in God. * Therefore, beloved, looking forward to these things, be diligent to be found by Him in peace, without spot and blameless. * Grace be with all those who love our Lord Jesus Christ in sincerity. Amen.

John 12:44-46 NKJV * John 3:16-21 NKJV * 2 Peter 3:14 NKJV * Ephesians 6:24 NKJV

NOVEMBER

4 . . . .

**Jesus has come as a light to the world.
The lost world is saved through Him alone.**

20 _____ *

_____
_____
_____
_____
_____
_____
_____

20 _____ *

_____
_____
_____
_____
_____
_____
_____

20 _____ *

_____
_____
_____
_____
_____
_____
_____

NOVEMBER 5

"And if anyone hears My words and does not believe, I do not judge him; for I did not come to judge the world but to save the world. He who rejects Me, and does not receive My words, has that which judges him—the word that I have spoken will judge him in the last day. For I have not spoken on My own authority; but the Father who sent Me gave Me a command, what I should say and what I should speak. And I know that His command is everlasting life. Therefore, whatever I speak, just as the Father has told Me, so I speak." * Jesus said to her, "I am the resurrection and the life. He who believes in Me, though he may die, he shall live. And whoever lives and believes in Me shall never die. Do you believe this?" * Jesus spoke these words, lifted up His eyes to heaven, and said, "Father, the hour has come. Glorify Your Son, that Your Son also may glorify You, as You have given Him authority over all flesh, that He should give eternal life to as many as You have given Him. And this is eternal life, that they may know You, the only true God, and Jesus Christ whom You have sent. I have glorified You on the earth. I have finished the work which You have given Me to do. And now, O Father, glorify Me together with Yourself, with the glory which I had with You before the world was. * Blessed be the LORD God of Israel from everlasting to everlasting! Amen and Amen.

John 12:47-50 NKJV * John 11:25-26 NKJV * John 17:1-5 NKJV * Psalm 41:13 NKJV

NOVEMBER

5 . . . .

**This is eternal life—
Knowing God.**

20 _____ *

_____
_____
_____
_____
_____
_____
_____

20 _____ *

_____
_____
_____
_____
_____
_____
_____

20 _____ *

_____
_____
_____
_____
_____
_____
_____

NOVEMBER 6

Take heed that you do not despise one of these little ones, for I say to you that in heaven their angels always see the face of My Father who is in heaven. * Therefore whoever humbles himself as this little child is the greatest in the kingdom of heaven. Whoever receives one little child like this in My name receives Me. * He who finds his life will lose it, and he who loses his life for My sake will find it. He who receives you receives Me, and he who receives Me receives Him who sent Me. * Because you have made the Lord, who is my refuge, even the Most High, your dwelling place, no evil shall befall you, nor shall any plague come near your dwelling; for He shall give His angels charge over you, to keep you in all your ways. In their hands they shall bear you up, lest you dash your foot against a stone. * His name shall endure forever; His name shall continue as long as the sun. And men shall be blessed in Him; all nations shall call Him blessed. Blessed be the Lord God, the God of Israel, who only does wondrous things! And blessed be His glorious name forever! And let the whole earth be filled with His glory. Amen and Amen.

Matthew 18:10 NKJV * Matthew 18:4-5 NKJV * Matthew 10:39-40 NKJV * Psalm 91:9-12 NKJV * Psalm 72:17-19 NKJV

NOVEMBER

6 . . . .

Will you humble yourself?

20 _____ *

_____

_____

_____

_____

_____

_____

_____

20 _____ *

_____

_____

_____

_____

_____

_____

_____

20 _____ *

_____

_____

_____

_____

_____

_____

_____

NOVEMBER 7

But if anyone causes one of these little ones who trusts in me to lose faith, it would be better for that person to be thrown into the sea with a large millstone tied around the neck. How terrible it will be for anyone who causes others to sin. Temptation to do wrong is inevitable, but how terrible it will be for the person who does the tempting. * In the same way, it is not my heavenly Father's will that even one of these little ones should perish. * For the grace of God has been revealed, bringing salvation to all people. And we are instructed to turn from godless living and sinful pleasures. We should live in this evil world with self-control, right conduct, and devotion to God, while we look forward to that wonderful event when the glory of our great God and Savior, Jesus Christ, will be revealed. He gave his life to free us from every kind of sin, to cleanse us, and to make us his very own people, totally committed to doing what is right. * He generously poured out the Spirit upon us because of what Jesus Christ our Savior did. He declared us not guilty because of his great kindness. And now we know that we will inherit eternal life. Blessed be the LORD forever. Amen and amen!

Matthew 18:6-7 NLT * Matthew 18:14 NLT * Titus 2:11-14 NLT * Titus 3:6-7 NLT * Psalm 89:52 NLT

NOVEMBER

7 ....

Are you committed to doing what is right?

20 _____ *

_____

_____

_____

_____

_____

_____

_____

20 _____ *

_____

_____

_____

_____

_____

_____

_____

20 _____ *

_____

_____

_____

_____

_____

_____

_____

NOVEMBER 8

What do you think? If a man has a hundred sheep, and one of them goes astray, does he not leave the ninety-nine and go to the mountains to seek the one that is straying? * So He came to a city of Samaria which is called Sychar, near the plot of ground that Jacob gave to his son Joseph. Now Jacob's well was there. Jesus therefore, being wearied from His journey, sat thus by the well. It was about the sixth hour. A woman of Samaria came to draw water. Jesus said to her, "Give Me a drink." * Then the woman of Samaria said to Him, "How is it that You, being a Jew, ask a drink from me, a Samaritan woman?" For Jews have no dealings with Samaritans. Jesus answered and said to her, "If you knew the gift of God, and who it is who says to you, 'Give Me a drink,' you would have asked Him, and He would have given you living water." * See then that you walk circumspectly, not as fools but as wise, redeeming the time, because the days are evil. Therefore do not be unwise, but understand what the will of the Lord is. And do not be drunk with wine, in which is dissipation; but be filled with the Spirit, speaking to one another in psalms and hymns and spiritual songs, singing and making melody in your heart to the Lord, giving thanks always for all things to God the Father in the name of our Lord Jesus Christ, submitting to one another in the fear of God. * The grace of our Lord Jesus Christ be with you. My love be with you all in Christ Jesus. Amen.

Matthew 18:12 NKJV * John 4:5-7 NKJV * John 4: 9-10 NKJV * Ephesians 5:15-21 NKJV * 1 Corinthians 16:23-24 NKJV

NOVEMBER

8 . . . .

Will you go the extra mile?

20 _____ *

_____

_____

_____

_____

_____

_____

_____

20 _____ *

_____

_____

_____

_____

_____

_____

_____

20 _____ *

_____

_____

_____

_____

_____

_____

_____

NOVEMBER 9

"I have called you back from the ends of the earth so you can serve me. For I have chosen you and will not throw you away. Don't be afraid, for I am with you. Do not be dismayed, for I am your God. I will strengthen you. I will help you. I will uphold you with my victorious right hand. * "I am the Alpha and the Omega—the beginning and the end," says the Lord God. "I am the one who is, who always was, and who is still to come, the Almighty One." * When I saw him, I fell at his feet as dead. But he laid his right hand on me and said, "Don't be afraid! I am the First and the Last. I am the living one who died. Look, I am alive forever and ever! And I hold the keys of death and the grave." * I am John, your brother. In Jesus we are partners in suffering and in the Kingdom and in patient endurance. I was exiled to the island of Patmos for preaching the word of God and speaking about Jesus. It was the Lord's Day, and I was worshipping in the Spirit. Suddenly, I heard a loud voice behind me, a voice that sounded like a trumpet blast. It said, "Write down what you see, and send it to the seven churches: Ephesus, Smyrna, Pergamum, Thyatira, Sardis, Philadelphia, and Laodicea." * Ears to hear and eyes to see—both are gifts from the LORD. * Amen and Amen!

Isaiah 41:9-10 NLT * Revelation 1:8 NLT * Revelation 1:17-18 NLT * Revelation 1:9-11 NLT * Proverbs 20:12 NLT * Psalm 72:19b NLT

NOVEMBER

9 ·

God is with you.

20 _____ *

_____

20 _____ *

_____

20 _____ *

_____

NOVEMBER 10

When I turned to see who was speaking to me, I saw seven gold lamp-stands. And standing in the middle of the lampstands was the Son of Man. He was wearing a long robe with a gold sash across his chest. * Make special clothing for Aaron to show his separation to God—beautiful garments that will lend dignity to his work. Instruct all those who have special skills as tailors to make the garments that will set Aaron apart from everyone else, so he may serve me as a priest. They are to make a chestpiece, an ephod, a robe, an embroidered tunic, a turban, and a sash. They will also make special garments for Aaron's sons to wear when they serve as priests before me. * Earlier, during the first year of King Belshazzar's reign in Babylon, Daniel had a dream and saw visions as he lay in his bed. He wrote the dream down, and this is what he saw. In my vision that night, I Daniel, saw a great storm churning the surface of a great sea, with strong winds blowing from every direction. * As my vision continued that night, I saw someone who looked like a man coming with the clouds of heaven. He approached the Ancient One and was led into his presence. He was given authority, honor, and royal power over all the nations of the world, so that people of every race and nation and language would obey him. His rule is eternal—it will never end. His kingdom will never be destroyed. * Jesus replied, "Yes, it is as you say. And in the future you will see Me, the Son of Man, sitting at God's right hand in the place of power and coming back on the clouds of heaven." * For I, the Son of Man, will come in the glory of My Father with his angels and will judge all people according to their deeds. * That is why we have a great High Priest who has gone to heaven, Jesus the Son of God. Let us cling to him and never stop trusting him. This High Priest of ours understands our weaknesses, for he faced all of the same temptations we do, yet he did not sin. * Amen and Amen.

Revelation 1:12-13 NLT * Exodus 28:2-4 NLT * Daniel 7:1-2 NLT * Daniel 7:13-14 NLT * Matthew 26:64 NLT * Matthew 16:27 NLT * Hebrews 4:14-15 NLT * Psalm 89:52b NLT

NOVEMBER

10 . . . .

Our great High Priest's rule is eternal.

20 _____ *

_____
_____
_____
_____
_____
_____
_____

20 _____ *

_____
_____
_____
_____
_____
_____
_____

20 _____ *

_____
_____
_____
_____
_____
_____
_____

NOVEMBER 11

His head and his hair were white like wool, as white as snow. And his eyes were bright like flames of fire. * In my vision that night, I, Daniel, saw a great storm churning the surface of a great sea, with strong winds blowing from every direction. * I watched as thrones were put in place and the Ancient One sat down to judge. His clothing was as white as snow, his hair like whitest wool . He sat on a fiery throne with wheels of blazing fire. * "Come now, let us argue this out," says the LORD. "No matter how deep the stain of your sins, I can remove it. I can make you as clean as freshly fallen snow. Even if you are stained as red as crimson, I can make you as white as wool. * But now you must be holy in everything you do, just as God—who chose you to be his children—is holy. For he himself has said, "You must be holy because I am holy." * And you husbands must love your wives with the same love Christ showed the church. He gave up his life for her to make her holy and clean, washed by baptism and God's word. * But there is going to come a time of testing at the judgment day to see what kind of work each builder has done. Everyone's work will be put through the fire to see whether or not it keeps its value. If the work survives the fire, that builder will receive a reward. But if the work is burned up, the builder will suffer great loss. The builders themselves will be saved, but like someone escaping through a wall of flames. * Nothing in all creation can hide from him. Everything is naked and exposed before his eyes. This is the God to whom we must explain all that we have done. * Amen and Amen!

Revelation 1:14 NLT * Daniel 7:2 NLT * Daniel 7:9 NLT * Isaiah 1:18 NLT * 1 Peter 1:15-16 NLT * Ephesians 5:25-26 NLT * 1 Corinthians 3:13-15 NLT * Hebrews 4:13 NLT * Psalm 72:19b NLT

NOVEMBER

11 . . . .

Everything is exposed before Jesus' loving eyes.

20 _____ *

_____
_____
_____
_____
_____
_____
_____
_____

20 _____ *

_____
_____
_____
_____
_____
_____
_____
_____

20 _____ *

_____
_____
_____
_____
_____
_____
_____
_____

NOVEMBER 12

His feet were as bright as bronze refined in the furnace, and his voice thundered like mighty ocean waves. * The altar for burning animal sacrifices also was constructed of acacia wood. It was 7 ½ feet square at the top and 4 ½ feet high. There were four horns, one at each of the four corners, all of one piece with the rest. This altar was overlaid with bronze. * But only the high priest goes into the Most Holy Place, and only once a year, and always with blood, which he offers to God to cover his own sins and the sins the people have committed in ignorance. * This is an illustration pointing to the present time. For the gifts and sacrifices that the priests offer are not able to cleanse the consciences of the people who bring them. * So Christ has now become the High Priest over all the good things that have come. He has entered that great, perfect sanctuary in heaven, not made by human hands and not part of this created world. Once for all time he took blood into that Most Holy Place, but not the blood of goats and calves. He took his own blood, and with it he secured our salvation forever. Under the old system, the blood of goats and bulls and the ashes of a young cow could cleanse people's bodies from ritual defilement. Just think how much more the blood of Christ will purify our hearts from deeds that lead to death so that we can worship the living God. For by the power of the eternal Spirit, Christ offered himself to God as a perfect sacrifice for our sins. * The Lord said to my Lord, "Sit in honor at my right hand until I humble your enemies, making them a footstool under your feet." * Long ago God spoke many times and in many ways to our ancestors through the prophets. But now in these final days, he has spoken to us through his Son. God promised everything to the Son as an inheritance, and through the Son he made the universe and everything in it. The Son reflects God's own glory, and everything about him represents God exactly. He sustains the universe by the mighty power of his command. After he died to cleanse us from the stain of sin, he sat down in the place of honor at the right hand of the majestic God of heaven. * Amen and Amen.

Revelation 1:15 NLT * Exodus 38:1-2 NLT * Hebrews 9:7 NLT * Hebrews 9:9 NLT * Hebrews 9:11-14 NLT * Psalm 110:1 NLT * Hebrews 1:1-3 NLT * Psalm 89:52b NLT

NOVEMBER

12 . . . .

**The blood of Christ purifies our hearts;
defeating the enemy, humbled beneath His feet.**

20 _____ *

_____

_____

_____

_____

_____

_____

20 _____ *

_____

_____

_____

_____

_____

_____

20 _____ *

_____

_____

_____

_____

_____

_____

NOVEMBER 13

He held seven stars in his right hand, and a sharp two-edged sword came from his mouth. And his face was as bright as the sun in all its brilliance. * This is the meaning of the seven stars you saw in my right hand and the seven gold lampstands: The seven stars are the angels of the seven churches, and the seven lampstands are the seven churches. * For the word of God is full of living power. It is sharper than the sharpest knife, cutting deep into our innermost thoughts and desires. It exposes us for what we really are. * As the men watched, Jesus' appearance changed so that his face shone like the sun, and his clothing became a dazzling white. * For God, who said, "Let there be light in the darkness," has made us understand that this light is the brightness of the glory of God that is seen in the face of Jesus Christ. But this precious treasure—this light and power that now shine within us—is held in perishable containers, that is, in our weak bodies. So everyone can see that our glorious power is from God and is not our own. * Amen and Amen!

Revelation 1:16 NLT * Revelation 1:20 NLT * Hebrews 4:12 NLT * Matthew 17:2 NLT * 2 Corinthians 4:6-7 NLT * Psalm 72:19b NT

NOVEMBER

13 . . . .

The word of God is full of living power meeting every need.

20 _____ *

_____

_____
_____
_____
_____
_____
_____
_____

20 _____ *

_____

_____
_____
_____
_____
_____
_____
_____

20 _____ *

_____

_____
_____
_____
_____
_____
_____
_____

NOVEMBER 14

My little children, let us not love in word or in tongue, but in deed and truth. And by this we know that we are of the truth, and shall assure our hearts before Him. * For I say, through the grace given to me, to everyone who is among you, not to think of himself more highly than he ought to think, but to think soberly, as God has dealt to each one a measure of faith. For as we have many members in one body, but all the members do not have the same function, so we, being many, are one body in Christ, and individually members of one another. Having then gifts differing according to the grace that is given to us, let us use them: if prophecy, let us prophesy in proportion to our faith; or ministry, let us use it in our ministering; he who teaches, in teaching; he who exhorts, in exhortation; he who gives, with liberality; he who leads, with diligence; he who shows mercy, with cheerfulness. * Be doers of the word, and not hearers only, deceiving yourselves. For if anyone is a hearer of the word and not a doer, he is like a man observing his natural face in a mirror; for he observes himself, goes away, and immediately forgets what kind of man he was. But he who looks into the perfect law of liberty and continues in it, and is not a forgetful hearer but a doer of the work, this one will be blessed in what he does. * For as the body without the spirit is dead, so faith without works is dead also. * Therefore, to him who knows to do good and does not do it, to him it is a sin. * To Him be the glory and the dominion forever and ever. Amen.

1 John 3:18-19 NKJV * Romans 12:3-8 NKJV * James 1:22-25 NKJV * James 2:26 NKJV * James 4:17 NKJV * 1 Peter 3:11 NKJV

NOVEMBER

14 . . . .

**There is a time to pray,
And a time to put feet to your faith.**

20 _____ *

_____
_____
_____
_____
_____
_____
_____

20 _____ *

_____
_____
_____
_____
_____
_____
_____

20 _____ *

_____
_____
_____
_____
_____
_____
_____

NOVEMBER 15

I thank my God, making mention of you always in my prayers, hearing of your love and faith which you have toward the Lord Jesus and toward all the saints, that the sharing of your faith may become effective by the acknowledgement of every good thing which is in you in Christ Jesus. For we have a great joy and consolation in your love, because the hearts of the saints have been refreshed by you, brother. * For this reason we also, since the day we heard it, do not cease to pray for you, and to ask that you may be filled with the knowledge of His will in all wisdom and spiritual understanding; that you may walk worthy of the Lord, fully pleasing Him, being fruitful in every good work and increasing in the knowledge of God; strengthened with all might, according to His glorious power, for all patience and longsuffering with joy; giving thanks to the Father who has qualified us to be partakers of the inheritance of the saints in the light. He has delivered us from the power of darkness and conveyed us into the kingdom of the Son of His love, in whom we have redemption through His blood, the forgiveness of sins. * As you therefore have received Christ Jesus the Lord, so walk in Him, rooted and built up in Him and established in the faith, as you have been taught, abounding in it with thanksgiving. * And whatever you do, do it heartily, as to the Lord and not to men, knowing that from the Lord you will receive the reward of the inheritance; for you serve the Lord Christ. * Continue earnestly in prayer, being vigilant in it with thanksgiving. * Walk in wisdom toward those who are outside, redeem the time. Let your speech always be with grace, seasoned with salt, that you may know how you ought to answer each one. * Now to Him who is able to do exceedingly abundantly above all that we ask or think, according to the power that works in us, to Him be glory in the church by Christ Jesus to all generations, forever and ever. Amen.

Philemon 1:4-7 NKJV * Colossians 1:9-14 NKJV * Colossians 2:6-7 NKJV * Colossians 3:23-24 NKJV * Colossians 4:2 NKJV * Colossians 4:5-6 NKJV * Ephesians 3:20-21 NKJV

NOVEMBER

15 . . . .

Who are you praying for today?

20 _____ *

_____
_____
_____
_____
_____
_____
_____

20 _____ *

_____
_____
_____
_____
_____
_____
_____

20 _____ *

_____
_____
_____
_____
_____
_____
_____

NOVEMBER 16

Therefore, though I might be very bold in Christ to command you what is fitting, yet for love's sake I rather appeal to you—being such as one as Paul, the aged, and now also a prisoner of Jesus Christ—I appeal to you for my son Onesimus, whom I have begotten while in my chains, who once was unprofitable to you and to me. * Therefore, as the elect of God, holy and beloved, put on tender mercies, kindness, humility, meekness, longsuffering; bearing with one another, and forgiving one another, if anyone has a complaint against another; even as Christ forgave you, so you also must do. But above all things put on love, which is the bond of perfection. And let the peace of God rule in your hearts, to which also you were called in one body; and be thankful. * Masters, give your bondservants what is just and fair, knowing that you also have a Master in heaven. * And whatever you do in word or deed, do all in the name of the Lord Jesus, giving thanks to God the Father through Him. * Brethren, if a man is overtaken in any trespass, you who are spiritual restore such a one in a spirit of gentleness, considering yourself lest you also be tempted. Bear one another's burdens, and so fulfill the law of Christ. * The grace of our Lord Jesus Christ be with you all. Amen.

Philemon 1:8-11 NKJV * Colossians 3:12-15 NKJV * Colossians 4:1 NKJV * Colossians 3:17 NKJV * Galatians 6:1-2 NKJV * 2 Thessalonians 3:18 NKJV

NOVEMBER

16 . . . .

Above all things put on love.

20_____ *

_____
_____
_____
_____
_____
_____
_____

20_____ *

_____
_____
_____
_____
_____
_____
_____

20_____ *

_____
_____
_____
_____
_____
_____
_____

NOVEMBER 17

I am sending him back to you, and with him comes my own heart. I really wanted to keep him here with me while I am in these chains for preaching the Good News, and he would have helped me on your behalf. But I didn't want to do anything without your consent. And I didn't want you to help because you were forced to do it but because you wanted to. Perhaps you could think of it this way: Onesimus ran away for a little while so you could have him back forever. He is no longer just a slave; he is a beloved brother, especially to me. Now he will mean much more to you, both as a slave and as a brother in the Lord. * What this means is that those who become Christians become new persons. They are not the same anymore, for the old life is gone. A new life has begun! All this newness of life is from God, who brought us back to himself through what Christ did. And God has given us the task of reconciling people to him. For God was in Christ, reconciling the world to himself, no longer counting people's sins against them. This is the wonderful message he has given us to tell others. We are Christ's ambassadors, and God is using us to speak to you. We urge you, as though Christ himself were here pleading with you, "Be reconciled to God!" For God made Christ, who never sinned, to be the offering for our sin, so that we could be made right with God through Christ. * For I want you to understand what really matters, so that you may live pure and blameless lives until Christ returns. May you always be filled with the fruit of your salvation—those good things that are produced in your life by Jesus Christ—for this will bring much glory and praise to God. * And I am sure that God, who began the good work within you, will continue his work until it is finally finished on that day when Christ Jesus comes back again. * Bless his glorious name forever! Let the whole earth be filled with his glory. Amen and amen!

Philemon 1:12-16 NLT * 2 Corinthians 5:17-21 NLT * Philippians 1:10-11 NLT * Philippians 1:6 NLT * Psalm 72:19 NLT

NOVEMBER

17 . . . .

May you always be filled with the fruit of your salvation.

20 ____ *

_____
_____
_____
_____
_____
_____
_____

20 ____ *

_____
_____
_____
_____
_____
_____
_____

20 ____ *

_____
_____
_____
_____
_____
_____
_____

NOVEMBER 18

If then you count me as a partner, receive him as you would me. But if he has wronged you or owes anything, put that on my account. * Greater love has no one than this, than to lay down one's life for his friends. * "Be angry, and do not sin": do not let the sun go down on your wrath, nor give place to the devil. Let him who stole steal no longer, but rather let him labor, working with his hands what is good, that he may have something to give him who has need. * There is therefore now no condemnation to those who are in Christ Jesus, who do not walk according to the flesh, but according to the Spirit. * For as many as are led by the Spirit of God, these are sons of God. For you did not receive the spirit of bondage again to fear, but you received the Spirit of adoption by whom we cry out, "Abba, Father." The Spirit Himself bears witness with our spirit that we are children of God, and if children, then heirs—heirs of God and joint heirs with Christ, if indeed we suffer with Him, that we may also be glorified together. For I consider that the sufferings of this present time are not worthy to be compared with the glory which shall be revealed in us. * Therefore, since we have this ministry, as we have received mercy, we do not lose heart. * For we do not preach ourselves, but Christ Jesus the Lord, and ourselves your bondservants for Jesus' sake. For it is the God who commanded light to shine out of darkness, who has shone in our hearts to give the light of the knowledge of the glory of God in the face of Jesus Christ. * We are confident of all of this because of our great trust in God through Christ. It is not that we think we can do anything of lasting value by ourselves. Our only power and success come from God. * And we know that all things work together for good to those who love God, to those who are the called according to His purpose. For whom He foreknew, He also predestined to be conformed to the image of His Son, that He might be the firstborn among many brethren. * Therefore I, a prisoner for serving the Lord, beg you to lead a life worthy of your calling, for you have been called by God. Be humble and gentle. Be patient with each other, making allowance for each other's faults because of your love. Always keep yourselves united in the Holy Spirit, and bind yourselves together with peace. * Blessed be the LORD forevermore! Amen and Amen.

Philemon 1:17-18 NKJV * John 15:13 NKJV * Ephesians 4:26-28 NKJV * Romans 8:1 NKJV * Romans 8:14-18 NKJV * 2 Corinthians 4:1 NKJV * 2 Corinthians 4:5-6 NKJV * 2 Corinthians 3:4-5 NLT * Romans 8:28-29 NKJV * Ephesians 4:1-3 NLT * Psalm 89:52 NKJV

NOVEMBER

18 . . . .

Do not lose heart.

20 _____ *

_____

_____

_____

_____

_____

_____

_____

20 _____ *

_____

_____

_____

_____

_____

_____

_____

20 _____ *

_____

_____

_____

_____

_____

_____

_____

NOVEMBER 19

The statutes of the LORD are right, rejoicing the heart; the commandment of the LORD is pure, enlightening the eyes; the fear of the LORD is clean, enduring forever; the judgments of the LORD are true and righteous altogether. * Righteousness will go before Him, and shall make His footsteps our pathway. * Teach me, O LORD, the way of Your statutes, and I shall keep it to the end. * Your word is very pure; therefore Your servant loves it. * Your word is a lamp to my feet and a light to my path. * You will show me the path of life; in Your presence is fullness of joy; at Your right hand are pleasures forevermore. * Teach me Your way, O LORD; I will walk in truth; unite my heart to fear Your name. I will praise You, O Lord my God, with all my heart, and I will glorify Your name forevermore. * Surely His salvation is near to those who fear Him, that glory may dwell in our land. * All nations whom You have made shall come and worship before You, O Lord, and shall glorify Your name. For You are great, and do wondrous things; You alone are God. * Let Your work appear to Your servants, and Your glory to their children. And let the beauty of the LORD our God be upon us, and establish the work of our hands for us; yes, establish the work of our hands. * Let the words of my mouth and the meditation of my heart be acceptable in Your sight, O LORD, my strength and my Redeemer. * To Him be glory in the church by Christ Jesus to all generations, forever and ever. Amen.

Psalm 19:8-9 NKJV * Psalm 85:13 NKJV * Psalm 119:33 NKJV * Psalm 119:140 NKJV * Psalm 119:105 NKJV * Psalm 16:11 NKJV * Psalm 86:11-12 NKJV * Psalm 85:9 NKJV * Psalm 86:9-10 NKJV * Psalm 90:16-17 NKJV * Psalm 19:14 NKJV * Ephesians 3:21 NKJV

NOVEMBER

19 . . . .

Let the words of my mouth be pleasing to You, O Lord.

20 _____ *

_____

_____

_____

_____

_____

_____

20 _____ *

_____

_____

_____

_____

_____

_____

20 _____ *

_____

_____

_____

_____

_____

_____

NOVEMBER 20

You will keep in perfect peace all who trust in you, whose thoughts are fixed on you! Trust in the LORD always, for the LORD GOD is the eternal Rock. He humbles the proud and brings the arrogant city to the dust. It's walls come crashing down! The poor and oppressed trample it underfoot. * All night long I search for you; earnestly I seek for God. For only when you come to judge the earth will people turn from wickedness and do what is right. * The LORD has said to me in the strongest terms: "Do not think like everyone else does. Do not be afraid that some plan conceived behind closed doors will be the end of you. Do not fear anything except the LORD Almighty. He alone is the Holy One. If you fear him, you need fear nothing else. He will keep you safe." * God has given gifts to each of you from his great variety of spiritual gifts. Manage them well so that God's generosity can flow through you. Are you called to be a speaker? Then speak as though God himself were speaking through you. Are you called to help others? Do it with all the strength and energy that God supplies. Then God will be given glory in everything through Jesus Christ. All glory and power belong to him forever and ever. Amen.

Isaiah 26:3-6 NLT * Isaiah 26:9 NLT * Isaiah 9:11-14a NLT *
1 Peter 4:10-11 NLT

NOVEMBER

20 . . . .

Do not fear anything except the LORD Almighty.

20 _____ *

_____
_____
_____
_____
_____
_____

20 _____ *

_____
_____
_____
_____
_____
_____

20 _____ *

_____
_____
_____
_____
_____
_____

NOVEMBER 21

Seek the LORD while He may be found, call upon Him while He is near. Let the wicked forsake his way, and the unrighteous man his thoughts; let him return to the LORD, and He will have mercy on him; and to our God, for He will abundantly pardon. * Therefore be imitators of God as dear children. And walk in love as Christ also has loved us and given Himself for us, an offering and a sacrifice to God for a sweet-smelling aroma. * And be kind to one another, tenderhearted, forgiving one another, even as God in Christ forgave you. * See then that you walk circumspectly, not as fools but as wise, redeeming the time, because the days are evil. * O God, You are my God; early will I seek You; my soul thirsts for You; my flesh longs for You in a dry and thirsty land where there is no water. * For a thousand years in Your sight are like yesterday when it is past, and like a watch in the night. * You have set our iniquities before You, our secret sins in the light of Your countenance. * So teach us to number our days, that we may gain a heart of wisdom. * Now it came to pass, as He was praying in a certain place, when He ceased, that one of His disciples said to Him, "Lord, teach us to pray, as John also taught his disciples." So He said to them, "When you pray, say: Our Father in heaven, hallowed be Your name. Your kingdom come. Your will be done on earth as it is in heaven. Give us day by day our daily bread. And forgive us our sins, for we also forgive everyone who is indebted to us. And do not lead us into temptation, but deliver us from the evil one." * Amen and Amen.

Isaiah 55:6-7 NKJV * Ephesians 5:1-2 NKJV * Ephesians 4:32 NKJV * Ephesians 5:15-16 NKJV * Psalm 63:1 NKJV * Psalm 90:4 NKJV * Psalm 90:8 NKJV * Psalm 90:12 NKJV * Luke 11:1-4 NKJV * Psalm 72:19b NKJV

NOVEMBER

21 . . . .

Pray first.

20 _____ *

_____
_____
_____
_____
_____
_____
_____

20 _____ *

_____
_____
_____
_____
_____
_____
_____

20 _____ *

_____
_____
_____
_____
_____
_____
_____

NOVEMBER 22

But do not forget to do good and to share, for with such sacrifices God is well pleased. * May He grant you according to your heart's desire, and fulfill all your purpose. We will rejoice in your salvation, and in the name of our God we will set up our banners! May the LORD fulfill all your petitions. Now I know that the LORD saves His anointed; He will answer him from His holy heaven with the saving strength of His right hand. * Trust in the LORD, and do good; dwell in the land, and feed on His faithfulness. Delight yourself also in the LORD, and He shall give you the desires of your heart. Commit your way to the LORD, trust also in Him, and He shall bring it to pass. He shall bring forth your righteousness as the light, and your justice as the noonday. * LORD, will you grant us peace, for all we have accomplished is really from you. O LORD our God, others have ruled us, but we worship You alone. * God be merciful to us and bless us, and cause His face to shine upon us, that Your way may be known on earth, Your salvation among all nations. * Those who are wise shall shine like the brightness of the firmament, and those who turn many to righteousness like the stars forever and ever. * The fruit of the righteous is a tree of life, and he who wins souls is wise. * And so we have the prophetic word confirmed, which you do well to heed as a light that shines in a dark place, until the day dawns and the morning star rises in your hearts; knowing this first, that no prophecy of Scripture is of any private interpretation, for prophecy never came by the will of man, but holy men of God spoke as they were moved by the Holy Spirit. * Behold what manner of love the Father has bestowed on us, that we should be called children of God! Therefore the world does not know us, because it did not know Him. Beloved, now we are children of God; and it has not yet been revealed what we shall be, but we know that when He is revealed, we shall be like Him, for we shall see Him as He is. And everyone who has this hope in Him purifies himself, just as He is pure. * And so, dear friends, while you are waiting for these things to happen, make every effort to live a pure and blameless life. And be at peace with God. * He who testifies to these things says, "Surely I am coming quickly." Amen. Even so, come, Lord Jesus!

Hebrews 13:16 NKJV * Psalm 20:4-6 NKJV * Psalm 37:3-6 NKJV * Isaiah 26:12-13 NLT * Psalm 67:1-2 NKJV * Daniel 12:3 NKJV * Proverbs 11:30 NKJV * 2 Peter 1:19-21 NKJV * 1 John 3:1-3 NKJV * 2 Peter 3:14 NLT * Revelation 22:20 NKJV

NOVEMBER

22 . . . .

What is your heart's desire?

20_____ *

_____

_____

_____

_____

_____

_____

20_____ *

_____

_____

_____

_____

_____

_____

20_____ *

_____

_____

_____

_____

_____

_____

NOVEMBER 23

"I create the fruit of the lips: Peace, peace to him who is far off and to him who is near," says the LORD, "And I will heal him." * Therefore by Him let us continually offer the sacrifice of praise to God, that is, the fruit of our lips, giving thanks to His name. * Let the words of my mouth and the meditation of my heart be acceptable in Your sight, O LORD, my strength and my Redeemer. * For since the beginning of the world men have not heard nor perceived by the ear, nor has the eye seen any God besides You, who acts for the one who waits for Him. * Then the seventh angel sounded: And there were loud voices in heaven, saying, "The kingdoms of this world have become the kingdoms of our Lord and of His Christ, and He shall reign forever and ever!" And the twenty-four elders who sat before God on their thrones fell on their faces and worshipped God, saying: "We give You thanks, O Lord God Almighty, the One who is and who was and who is to come, because You have taken Your great power and reigned. The nations were angry, and Your wrath has come, and the time of the dead, that they should be judged, and that You should reward Your servants the prophets and the saints, and those who fear Your name, small and great, and should destroy those who destroy the earth." * The grace of our Lord Jesus Christ be with you. Amen.

Isaiah 57:19 NKJV * Hebrews 13:15 NKJV * Psalm 19:14 NKJV * Revelation 11:15-18 NKJV * 1 Thessalonians 5:28 NKJV

NOVEMBER

23 ....

What are you thanking God for?

20 _____ *

_____
_____
_____
_____
_____
_____

20 _____ *

_____
_____
_____
_____
_____
_____

20 _____ *

_____
_____
_____
_____
_____
_____

NOVEMBER 24

Oh, give thanks to the LORD, for He is good! For His mercy endures forever. * For the grace of God that brings salvation has appeared to all men, teaching us that, denying ungodliness and worldly lusts, we should live soberly, righteously, and godly in the present age, looking for the blessed hope and glorious appearing of our great God and Savior Jesus Christ, who gave Himself for us, that He might redeem us from every lawless deed and purify for Himself His own special people, zealous for good works. * Now may the Lord direct your hearts into the love of God and into the patience of Christ. * And whatever you do in word or deed, do all in the name of the Lord Jesus, giving thanks to God the Father through Him. * We give thanks to the God and Father of our Lord Jesus Christ, praying always for you, since we heard of your faith in Christ Jesus and of your love for all the saints; because of the hope which is laid up for you in heaven, of which you heard before in the word of the truth of the gospel, which has come to you, as it has also in all the world, and is bringing forth fruit, as it is also among you since the day you heard and knew the grace of God in truth. * To Him be the glory and the dominion forever and ever. Amen.

Psalm 136:1 NKJV * Titus 2:11-14 NKJV * 2 Thessalonians 3:5 NKJV
* Colossians 3:17 NKJV * Colossians 1:3-6 NKJV * 1 Peter 5:11 NKJV

NOVEMBER

24 . . . .

Give thanks.

20 _____ *

_____

_____
_____
_____
_____
_____
_____
_____

20 _____ *

_____

_____
_____
_____
_____
_____
_____
_____

20 _____ *

_____

_____
_____
_____
_____
_____
_____
_____

NOVEMBER 25

Look a righteous king is coming! And honest princes will rule under him. He will shelter Israel from the storm and the wind. He will refresh her as a river in the desert and as the cool shadow of a large rock in a hot and weary land. Then everyone who can see will be looking for God, and those who can hear will listen to his voice. Even the hotheads among them will be full of sense and understanding. Those who stammer in uncertainty will speak out plainly. * Everyone will recognize ungodly fools for what they are. They spread lies about the LORD; they deprive the hungry of food and give no water to the thirsty. The smooth tricks of evil people will be exposed, including all the lies they use to oppress the poor in the courts. * Those who make the innocent guilty by their false testimony will disappear. And those who use trickery to pervert justice and tell lies to tear down the innocent will be no more. * But good people will be generous to others and will be blessed for all they do. * And this righteousness will bring peace. Quietness and confidence will fill the land forever. My people will live in safety, quietly at home. They will be at rest. * God will greatly bless his people. Wherever they plant seed, bountiful crops will spring up. Their flocks and herds will graze in green pastures. * That is why the LORD, who redeemed Abraham, says to the people of Israel, "My people will no longer pale with fear or be ashamed. For when they see their many children and material blessings, they will recognize the holiness of the Holy One of Israel. They will stand in awe of the God of Israel. Those in error will then believe the truth, and those who constantly complain will accept instruction. * Blessed be the LORD forever! Amen and amen!

Isaiah 32:1-4 NLT * Isaiah 32:6-7 NLT * Isaiah 29:21 NLT * Isaiah 32:8 NLT * Isaiah 32:17-18 NLT * Isaiah 32:20 NLT * Isaiah 29:22-24 NLT * Psalm 89:52 NLT

NOVEMBER

25 . . . .

Righteousness brings peace.

20 _____ *

_____

_____

_____

_____

_____

_____

_____

20 _____ *

_____

_____

_____

_____

_____

_____

_____

20 _____ *

_____

_____

_____

_____

_____

_____

_____

NOVEMBER 26

Jesus felt genuine love for this man as he looked at him. "You lack one thing," he told him. "Go, and sell all you have and give the money to the poor, and you will have treasure in heaven. Then come follow me." At this, the man's face fell, and he went sadly away because he had many possessions. * And Jesus replied, "I assure you that everyone who has given up house or brothers or sisters or mother or father or children or property, for my sake and for the Good News, will receive now in return, a hundred times over, houses, brothers, sisters, mothers, children, and property—with persecutions. And in the world to come they will have eternal life. But many who seem to be important now will be the least important then, and those who are considered least here will be the greatest then." * For everyone will be purified by fire. * So be careful not to jump to conclusions before the Lord returns as to whether or not someone is faithful. When the Lord comes, he will bring our deepest secrets to light and will reveal our private motives. And then God will give to everyone whatever praise is due. * You must each make up your own mind as to how much you should give. Don't give reluctantly or in response to pressure. For God loves the person who gives cheerfully. And God will generously provide all you need. Then you will always have everything you need and plenty left over to share with others. * Do for others as you would like them to do for you. * Giving thanks always for all things to God the Father in the name of our Lord Jesus Christ. * Amen and amen!

Mark 10:21-22 NLT * Mark 10:29-31 NLT * Mark 9:49 NLT *
1 Corinthians 4:5 NLT * 2 Corinthians 9:7-8 NLT * Luke 6:31 NLT *
Ephesians 5:20 NKJV * Psalm 72:19b NLT

NOVEMBER

26 . . . .

**Everyone is being purified by a flame of fire.
What can you do to help?**

20 _____ *

20 _____ *

20 _____ *

NOVEMBER 27

If you give, you will receive. Your gift will return to you in full measure, pressed down, shaken together to make room for more, and running over. Whatever measure you use in giving—large or small—it will be used to measure what is given back to you. * Then a poor widow came by and dropped in two pennies. "I assure you," he said, "this poor widow has given more than all the rest of them. For they have given a tiny part of their surplus, but she, poor as she is, has given everything she has. * Suddenly, a terrible storm came up, with waves breaking into the boat. But Jesus was sleeping. The disciples went to him and woke him up, shouting, "Lord, save us! We're going to drown!" And Jesus answered, "Why are you afraid? You have so little faith!" Then he stood up and rebuked the wind and waves, and suddenly all was calm. The disciples just sat there in awe. "Who is this?" they asked themselves. "Even the wind and waves obey him!" * Then turning to his disciples, Jesus said, "So I tell you, don't worry about everyday life—whether you have enough food to eat or clothes to wear. For life consists of more than food and clothing. Look at the ravens. They don't need to plant or harvest or put food in the barns because God feeds them. And you are far more valuable to him than any birds! Can all your worries add a single moment to your life? Of course not! And if worry can't do little things like that, what's the use of worrying over bigger things. * Amen and amen!

Luke 6:38 NLT * Luke 21:2-4 NLT * Matthew 8:24-27 NLT * Luke 12:22-26 NLT * Psalm 72:19b NLT

NOVEMBER

27 . . . .

God has already out-given you.

20 ____ *

---

20 ____ *

---

20 ____ *

NOVEMBER 28

But know that the LORD has set apart for Himself him who is godly; the LORD will hear when I call to Him. * I cried to the LORD with my voice, and He heard me from His holy hill. * I sought the LORD, and He heard me, and delivered me from all my fears. * The LORD also will be a refuge for the oppressed, a refuge in times of trouble. And those who know Your name will put their trust in You; for You, LORD, have not forsaken those who seek You. * I will both lie down in peace, and sleep; for You alone, O LORD, make me dwell in safety. * You are my hiding place; You shall preserve me from trouble; You shall surround me with songs of deliverance. * The LORD shall preserve you from all evil; He shall preserve your soul. The LORD shall preserve your going out and your coming in from this time forth, and even forevermore. * Blessed be the LORD forevermore! Amen and Amen.

Psalm 4:3 NKJV * Psalm 3:4 NKJV * Psalm 34:4 NKJV * Psalm 9:9-10 NKJV * Psalm 4:8 NKJV * Psalm 32:7 NKJV * Psalm 121:7-8 NKJV * Psalm 89:52 NKJV

NOVEMBER

28 ·

The Lord delivered me from all my fears.

20 ____ *

20 ____ *

20 ____ *

NOVEMBER 29

A student is not greater than the teacher. But the student who works hard will become like the teacher. * Then Jesus said, "Come to me all you who are weary and carry heavy burdens, and I will give you rest. Take my yoke upon you. Let me teach you, because I am humble and gentle, and you will find rest for your souls. For my yoke fits perfectly, and the burden I give you is light." * He will not fight or shout; he will not raise his voice in public. He will not crush those who are weak, or quench the smallest hope, until he brings full justice with his final victory. And his name will be the hope of all the world. * The LORD is my shepherd; I have everything I need. He lets me rest in green meadows; he leads me beside peaceful streams. He renews my strength. He guides me along right paths, bringing honor to his name. Even when I walk through the dark valley of death, I will not be afraid, for you are close beside me. Your rod and your staff protect and comfort me. You prepare a feast for me in the presence of my enemies. You welcome me as a guest, anointing my head with oil. My cup overflows with blessings. Surely your goodness and unfailing love will pursue me all the days of my life, and I will live in the house of the LORD forever. * Bless his glorious name forever! Let the whole earth be filled with his glory. Amen and amen!

Luke 6:40 NLT * Matthew 11:28-30 NLT * Matthew 12:19-21 NLT * Psalm 23:1-6 NLT * Psalm 72:19 NLT

NOVEMBER

29 . . . .

God knows exactly what you need.

20 _____ *

_____
_____
_____
_____
_____
_____
_____

20 _____ *

_____
_____
_____
_____
_____
_____
_____

20 _____ *

_____
_____
_____
_____
_____
_____
_____

NOVEMBER 30

I tell you, her sins—and they are many—have been forgiven, so she has shown me much love. But a person who is forgiven little shows only little love. Then Jesus said to this woman, "Your sins are forgiven." * After breakfast Jesus said to Simon Peter, "Simon son of John, do you love me more than these?" "Yes, Lord," Peter replied, "you know I love you." "Then feed my lambs," Jesus told him. Jesus repeated the question: "Simon son of John, do you love me?" "Yes, Lord," Peter said, "you know I love you." "Then take care of my sheep," Jesus said. Once more he asked him, "Simon son of John, do you love me?" Peter was grieved that Jesus asked the question a third time. He said, "Lord, you know everything. You know I love you." Jesus said, "Then feed my sheep. * Then Mary took a twelve-ounce jar of expensive perfume made from essence of nard, and she anointed Jesus' feet with it and wiped his feet with her hair. And the house was filled with fragrance. But Judas Iscariot, one of his disciples—the one who would betray him—said, "That perfume was worth a small fortune. It should have been sold and the money given to the poor." Not that he cared for the poor—he was a thief who was in charge of the disciples' funds, and he often took some for his own use. Jesus replied, "Leave her alone. She did it in preparation for my burial. You will always have the poor among you, but I will not be here with you much longer." * "I assure you, wherever the Good News is preached throughout the world, this woman's deed will be talked about in her memory." * Amen and amen!

Luke 8:47-48 NLT * John 21:15-17 NLT * John 12:3-8 NLT * Mark 14:9 NLT * Psalm 72:19b NLT

NOVEMBER

30 ....

**Have you heard these very personal words?
Your sins are forgiven.**

20 _____ *

_____
_____
_____
_____
_____
_____
_____

20 _____ *

_____
_____
_____
_____
_____
_____
_____

20 _____ *

_____
_____
_____
_____
_____
_____
_____

DECEMBER

DECEMBER 1

For the time has come for me to avenge my people, to ransom them from their oppressors. I looked, but no one came to help my people. I was amazed and appalled at what I saw. So I executed vengeance alone; unaided, I passed down judgment. I crushed the nations in my anger and made them stagger and fall to the ground. * For I, the LORD, love justice. I hate robbery and wrongdoing. I will faithfully reward my people for their suffering and make an everlasting covenant with them. Their descendants will be known and honored among the nations. Everyone will realize that they are a people the LORD has blessed. * In all their suffering he also suffered, and he personally rescued them. In his love and mercy he redeemed them. He lifted them up and carried them through all the years. * For a child is born to us, a son is given to us. And the government will rest on his shoulders. These will be his royal titles: Wonderful Counselor, Mighty God, Everlasting Father, Prince of Peace. His ever expanding, peaceful government will never end. He will rule forever with fairness and justice from the throne of his ancestor David. The passionate commitment of the LORD Almighty will guarantee this! * Bless the LORD God of Israel, who lives forever from eternal ages past. Amen and amen!

Isaiah 63:4-6 NLT * Isaiah 61:8-9 NLT * Isaiah 63:9 NLT * Isaiah 9:6-7 NLT * Psalm 41:13 NLT

DECEMBER

1 . . . .

When you suffered, He suffered.

20 _____ *

_____
_____
_____
_____
_____
_____
_____

20 _____ *

_____
_____
_____
_____
_____
_____
_____

20 _____ *

_____
_____
_____
_____
_____
_____
_____

DECEMBER 2

In Caesarea there lived a Roman army officer named Cornelius, who was a captain of the Italian Regiment. He was a devout man who feared the God of Israel, as did his entire household. He gave generously to charity and was a man who regularly prayed to God. One afternoon about three o'clock, he had a vision in which he saw an angel of God coming toward him. "Cornelius!" the angel said. Cornelius stared at him in terror. "What is it, sir?" he asked the angel. And the angel replied, "Your prayers and gifts to the poor have not gone unnoticed by God!" * The smoke of the incense, mixed with the prayers of the saints, ascended up to God from the altar where the angel had poured them out. * For God is not unfair. He will not forget how hard you have worked for him and how you have shown your love to him by caring for other Christians, as you still do. Our great desire is that you will keep right on loving others as long as life lasts, in order to make certain that what you hope for will come true. Then you will not become spiritually dull and indifferent. Instead you will follow the example of those who are going to inherit God's promises because of their faith and patience. * Amen and amen!

Acts 10:1-4 NLT * Revelation 8:4 NLT * Hebrews 6:10-12 NLT * Psalm 72:19b NLT

DECEMBER

2 . . . .

**Your prayers and gifts to the poor have not gone
unnoticed by God.**

20 _____ *

_____
_____
_____
_____
_____
_____
_____

20 _____ *

_____
_____
_____
_____
_____
_____
_____

20 _____ *

_____
_____
_____
_____
_____
_____
_____

DECEMBER 3

At that time you won't need to ask me for anything. The truth is, you can go directly to the Father and ask him, and he will grant your request because you use my name. You haven't done this before. Ask, using my name, and you will receive, and you will have abundant joy. * You didn't choose me. I chose you. I appointed you to go and produce fruit that will last, so that the Father will give you whatever you ask for, using my name. * I am leaving you with a gift—peace of mind and heart. And the peace I give isn't like the peace the world gives. So don't be troubled or afraid. * The truth is, anyone who believes in me will do the same works I have done, and even greater works, because I am going to be with the Father. You can ask for anything in my name, and I will do it, because the work of the Son brings glory to the Father. Yes, ask anything in my name, and I will do it! * Amen and amen!

John 16:23-24 NLT * John 15:16 NLT * John 14:27 NLT * John 14:12-14 NLT * Psalm 89:52b NLT

DECEMBER

3 ....

When you ask God, using Jesus Christ's name—
He will give you fruit to feed more than one season.

20_____ *

20_____ *

20_____ *

DECEMBER 4

Truly, anyone who welcomes my messenger is welcoming me, and anyone who welcomes me is welcoming the Father who sent me. * So Peter went down and said, "I'm the man you are looking for. Why have you come?" They said, "We were sent by Cornelius, a Roman officer. He is a devout man who fears the God of Israel and is well respected by all the Jews. A holy angel instructed him to send for you so you can go to his house and give him a message." * They arrived in Caesarea the following day. Cornelius was waiting for him and had called together his relatives and close friends to meet Peter. As Peter entered the home, Cornelius fell to the floor before him in worship. But Peter pulled him up and said, "Stand up! I'm a human being like you!" So Cornelius got up, and they talked together and went inside where the others were assembled. Peter told them, "You know it is against the Jewish laws for me to come into a Gentile home like this. But God has shown me that I should never think of anyone as impure. So I came as soon as I was sent for. Now tell me why you sent for me." Cornelius replied, "Four days ago I was praying in my house at three o'clock in the afternoon. Suddenly, a man in dazzling clothes was standing in front of me. He told me, 'Cornelius, your prayers have been heard, and your gifts to the poor have been noticed by God! Now send some men to Joppa and summon Simon Peter. He is staying in the home of Simon, a leatherworker who lives near the shore.' So I sent for you at once, and it was good of you to come. Now here we are, waiting before God to hear the message the Lord has given you. Then Peter replied, "I see very clearly that God doesn't show partiality. In every nation he accepts those who fear him and do what is right. * Amen and amen!

John 13:20 NLT * Acts 10:21-22 NLT * Acts 10:24-35 NLT * Psalm 89:52b NLT

December

4

· ·

God has no favorites.

20 _____ *

_____

_____
_____
_____
_____
_____
_____

20 _____ *

_____

_____
_____
_____
_____
_____
_____

20 _____ *

_____

_____
_____
_____
_____
_____
_____

DECEMBER 5

"O Lord, God of my master," he prayed. "Give me success and show kindness to my master, Abraham. Help me to accomplish the purpose of my journey. See, here I am, standing beside this spring, and the young women of the village are coming out to draw water. This is my request, I will ask one of them for a drink. If she says, 'Yes, certainly, and I will water your camels, too!' –let her be the one you have appointed as Isaac's wife. By this I will know that you have shown kindness to my master." As he was still praying, a young woman named Rebekah arrived with a water jug on her shoulder. Her father was Bethuel, who was the son of Abraham's brother Nahor and his wife, Milcah. Now Rebekah was very beautiful, and she was a virgin; no man had ever slept with her. She went down to the spring, filled her jug, and came up again. Running over to her, the servant asked, "Please give me a drink." "Certainly, sir," she said, and she quickly lowered the jug for him to drink. When she had finished, she said, "I'll draw water for your camels, too, until they have had enough!" * The servant watched her in silence, wondering whether or not she was the one the Lord intended him to meet. Then at last, when the camels had finished drinking, he gave her a gold ring for her nose and two large gold bracelets for her wrists. * Then supper was served. But Abraham's servant said, "I don't want to eat until I told you why I have come." "All right," Laban said, "tell us your mission." * "So this afternoon when I came to the spring I prayed this prayer: 'O Lord, the God of my master, Abraham, if you are planning to make my mission a success, please guide me in a special way.'" * I love the Lord because he hears and answers my prayers. Because he bends down and listens, I will pray as long as I have breath! * Blessed be the Lord forever! Amen and amen!

Genesis 24:12-19 NLT * Genesis 24:21-22 NLT * Genesis 24:33 NLT * Genesis 24:42 NLT * Psalm 116:1-2 NLT * Psalm 89:52 NLT

DECEMBER

5 . . . .

This is my request . . .

20 _____ *

_____
_____
_____
_____
_____
_____

20 _____ *

_____
_____
_____
_____
_____
_____

20 _____ *

_____
_____
_____
_____
_____
_____

DECEMBER 6

Then the Pharisees came out and began to dispute with Him, seeking from Him a sign from heaven, testing Him. But He sighed deeply in His spirit, and said, "Why does this generation seek a sign? Assuredly, I say to you, no sign shall be given to this generation." * Then Jesus said to those Jews who believed in Him, "If you abide in My word, you are My disciples indeed. And you shall know the truth, and the truth shall make you free." * Then Jesus spoke to them again, saying, "I am the light of the world. He who follows Me shall not walk in darkness, but have the light of life." * Now the Lord is the Spirit; and where the Spirit of the Lord is, there is liberty. But we all, with unveiled face, beholding as in a mirror the glory of the Lord, are being transformed into the same image from glory to glory, just as by the Spirit of the Lord. * For we know that if our earthly house, this tent, is destroyed, we have a building from God, a house not made with hands, eternal in the heavens. For in this we groan, earnestly desiring to be clothed with our habitation which is from heaven, if indeed, having been clothed, we shall not be found naked. For we who are in this tent groan, being burdened, not because we want to be unclothed, but further clothed, that mortality may be swallowed up by life. Now He who has prepared us for this very thing is God, who also has given us the Spirit as a guarantee. So we are always confident, knowing that while we are at home in the body we are absent from the Lord. For we walk by faith, not by sight. * For we must all appear before the judgment seat of Christ, that each one may receive the things done in the body, according to what he has done, whether good or bad. Knowing, therefore, the terror of the Lord, we persuade men; but we are well known to God, and I also trust are well known in your consciences. * Amen and Amen!

Mark 8:11-12 NKJV * John 8:31-32 NKJV * John 8:12 NKJV * 2 Corinthians 3:17-18 NKJV * 2 Corinthians 5:1-7 NKJV * 2 Corinthians 5:10-11 NKJV * Psalm 72:19b NKJV

DECEMBER

6 . . . .

If you follow the Light, you will never walk in darkness.

20 _____ *

_____

_____

_____

_____

_____

_____

_____

20 _____ *

_____

_____

_____

_____

_____

_____

_____

20 _____ *

_____

_____

_____

_____

_____

_____

_____

DECEMBER 7

Wives, submit to your own husbands, as to the Lord. For the husband is head of the wife, as also Christ is head of the church; and He is the Savior of the body. Therefore, just as the church is subject to Christ, so let the wives be to their own husbands in everything. * The heart of her husband safely trusts her; so he will have no lack of gain. She does him good and not evil all the days of her life. * She considers a field and buys it; from her profits she plants a vineyard. She girds herself with strength, and strengthens her arms. * Strength and honor are her clothing; she shall rejoice in time to come. She opens her mouth with wisdom, and on her tongue is the law of kindness. She watches over the ways of her household, and does not eat the bread of idleness. Her children rise up and call her blessed; her husband also, and he praises her: "Many daughters have done well, but you excel them all." * Wives, likewise, be submissive to your own husbands, that even if some do not obey the word, they, without a word, may be won by the conduct of their wives, when they observe your chaste conduct accompanied by fear. Do not let your adornment be merely outward—arranging the hair, wearing gold, or putting on fine apparel—rather let it be the hidden person of the heart, with the incorruptible beauty of a gentle and quiet spirit, which is very precious in the sight of God. * Praying always with all prayer and supplication in the Spirit, being watchful to this end with all perseverance and supplication for all the saints. * Let us be glad and rejoice and give Him glory, for the marriage of the Lamb has come, and His wife has made herself ready. * Greet one another with a kiss of love. Peace to you all who are in Christ Jesus. Amen.

Ephesians 5:22-24 NKJV * Proverbs 31:11-12 NKJV * Proverbs 31:16-17 NKJV * Proverbs 31:25-29 NKJV * 1 Peter 3:1-4 NKJV * Ephesians 6:18 NKJV * Revelation 19:7 NKJV * 1 Peter 5:14 NKJV

DECEMBER

7 . . . .

She opens her mouth with wisdom.

20 _____ *

_____
_____
_____
_____
_____
_____
_____

20 _____ *

_____
_____
_____
_____
_____
_____
_____

20 _____ *

_____
_____
_____
_____
_____
_____
_____

DECEMBER 8

Husbands love your wives, just as Christ also loved the church and gave Himself for her, that He might sanctify and cleanse her with the washing of water by the word, that He might present her to Himself a glorious church, not having spot or wrinkle or any such thing, but that she should be holy and without blemish. * But as He who called you is holy, you also be holy in all your conduct, because it is written, "Be holy, for I am holy. * Since you have purified your souls in obeying the truth through the Spirit in sincere love of the brethren, love one another with a pure heart, having been born again, not of corruptible seed but incorruptible, through the word of God which lives and abides forever. * So husbands ought to love their own wives as their own bodies; he who loves his wife loves himself. * Husbands, likewise dwell with them with understanding, giving honor to the wife, as to the weaker vessel, and as being heirs together of the grace of life, that your prayers may not be hindered. * Finally, brethren, whatever things are true, whatever things are noble, whatever things are just, whatever things are pure, whatever things are lovely, whatever things are of good report, if there is any virtue and if there is anything praiseworthy—meditate on these things. * Become complete. Be of good comfort, be of one mind, live in peace; and the God of love and peace will be with you. * Rejoice in the Lord always. Again I will say, rejoice! Let your gentleness be known to all men. The Lord is at hand. * The grace of the Lord Jesus Christ, and the love of God, and the communion of the Holy Spirit be with you all. Amen.

Ephesians 5:25-27 NKJV * 1 Peter 1:15-16 NKJV * 1 Peter 1:22-23 NKJV * Ephesians 5:28 NKJV * Philippians 4:8 NKJV * 2 Corinthians 13:11b NKJV * 1 Peter 3:7 NKJV * Philippians 4:4-5 NKJV * 2 Corinthians 13:14 NKJV

DECEMBER

8 ·

Be holy.

20 _____ *

_____
_____
_____
_____
_____
_____
_____
_____

20 _____ *

_____
_____
_____
_____
_____
_____
_____
_____

20 _____ *

_____
_____
_____
_____
_____
_____
_____
_____

DECEMBER 9

Likewise you younger people, submit yourselves to your elders. Yes, all of you be submissive to one another, and be clothed with humility, for "God resists the proud, but gives grace to the humble." Therefore humble yourselves under the mighty hand of God, that He may exalt you in due time. * Servants, be submissive to your masters with all fear, not only to the good and gentle, but also to the harsh. For this is commendable, if because of your conscience toward God one endures grief, suffering wrongfully. For what credit is it if, when you are beaten for your faults, you take it patiently? But when you do good and suffer, if you take it patiently, this is commendable before God. For to this you were called, because Christ also suffered for us, leaving us an example that you should follow His steps. * Coming to Him as to a living stone, rejected indeed by men, but chosen by God and precious, you also, as living stones, are being built up a spiritual house, a holy priesthood, to offer up spiritual sacrifices acceptable to God through Jesus Christ. * Therefore submit yourselves to every ordinance of man for the Lord's sake, whether to the king as supreme, or to governors, as to those who are sent by him for the punishment of evildoers, and for the praise of those who do good. For this is the will of God, that by doing good you may put to silence the ignorance of foolish men—as free, yet not using liberty as a cloak for vice, but as bondservants of God. * But let none of you suffer as a murderer, a thief, an evildoer, or as a busybody in other people's matters. Yet if anyone suffers as a Christian, let him not be ashamed, but let him glorify God in this matter. For the time has come for judgment to begin at the house of God; and if it begins with us first, what will be the end of those who do not obey the gospel of God? * But grow in the grace and knowledge of our Lord and Savior Jesus Christ. To Him be the glory both now and forever. Amen.

1 Peter 5:5-6 NKJV * 1 Peter 2:18-21 NKJV * 1 Peter 2:4-5 NKJV * 1 Peter 2:13-16 NKJV * 1 Peter 4:15-17 NKJV * 2 Peter 3:18 NKJV

DECEMBER

9 . . . .

What is your example?

20 _____ *

20 _____ *

20 _____ *

DECEMBER 10

The Sovereign LORD has given me his words of wisdom, so that I know what to say to all these weary ones. Morning by morning he wakens me and he opens my understanding to his will. * Because the Sovereign LORD helps me, I will not be dismayed. Therefore, I have set my face like a stone, determined to do his will. And I know that I will triumph. * The end of the world is coming soon. Therefore, be earnest and disciplined in your prayers. Most important of all, continue to show deep love for each other, for love covers a multitude of sins. * This is real love. It is not that we loved God, but that he loved us and sent his Son as a sacrifice to take away our sins. * For by that one offering he perfected forever all those whom he is making holy. * Without the shedding of blood there is no forgiveness of sins. * This is the message he has given us to announce to you: God is light and there is no darkness in him at all. So we are lying if we say we have fellowship with God but go on living in spiritual darkness. We are not living in the truth. But if we are living in the light of God's presence, just as Christ is, then we have fellowship with each other, and the blood of Jesus, his Son, cleanses us from every sin. If we say we have no sin, we are only fooling ourselves and refusing to accept the truth. But if we confess our sins to him, he is faithful and just to forgive us and to cleans us from every wrong. If we claim we have not sinned, we are calling God a liar and showing that his word has no place in our hearts. * Prove by the way that you live that you have really turned from your sins and turned to God. * God blesses those whose hearts are pure; for they will see God. * Amen and Amen!

Isaiah 50:4 NLT * Isaiah 50:7 NLT * 1 Peter 4:7-8 NLT * 1 John 4:10 NLT * Hebrews 10:14 NLT * Hebrews 9:22b NLT * 1 John 1:5-10 NLT * Matthew 3:8 NLT * Matthew 5:8 NLT * Psalm 72:19b NLT

DECEMBER

10 ....

Are you determined to do God's will?

20 _____ *

_____
_____
_____
_____
_____
_____
_____

20 _____ *

_____
_____
_____
_____
_____
_____
_____

20 _____ *

_____
_____
_____
_____
_____
_____
_____

DECEMBER 11

Christ is the visible image of the invisible God. He existed before God made anything at all and is supreme over all creation. Christ is the one through whom God created everything in heaven and earth. He made the things we can see and the things we can't see—kings, kingdoms, rulers, and authorities. Everything has been created through him and for him. He existed before everything else began, and he holds all creation together. Christ is the head of the church, which is his body. He is the first of all who will rise from the dead, so he is first in everything. For God in all his fullness was pleased to live in Christ and by him God reconciled everything to himself. He made peace with everything in heaven and on earth by means of his blood on the cross. This includes you who were once so far away from God. You were enemies, separated from him by your evil thoughts and actions, yet now he has brought you back as his friends. He has done this through his death on the cross in his own human body. As a result, he has brought you into the very presence of God, and you are holy and blameless as you stand before him without a single fault. * Long ago God spoke many times and in many ways to our ancestors through the prophets. But now in these final days, he has spoken to us through his Son. God promised everything to the Son as an inheritance, and through the Son he made the universe and everything in it. The Son reflects God's own glory, and everything about him represents God exactly. He sustains the universe by the mighty power of his command. After he died to cleanse us from the stain of sin, he sat down in the place of honor at the right hand of the majestic God of heaven. This shows that God's Son is far greater than the angels, just as the name God gave him is far greater than their names. * Bless his glorious name forever! Let the whole earth be filled with his glory. Amen and amen!

Colossians 1:15-22 NLT * Hebrews 1:1-4 NLT * Psalm 72:19 NLT

DECEMBER

11 . . . .

Jesus Christ is the head of the church.

20 _____ *

_____
_____
_____
_____
_____
_____
_____

20 _____ *

_____
_____
_____
_____
_____
_____
_____

20 _____ *

_____
_____
_____
_____
_____
_____
_____

DECEMBER 12

I thank my God upon every remembrance of you, always in every prayer of mine making request for you all with joy. * That the God of our Lord Jesus Christ, the Father of glory, may give to you the spirit of wisdom and revelation in the knowledge of Him, the eyes of your understanding being enlightened; that you may know what is the hope of His calling, what are the riches of the glory of His inheritance in the saints and what is the exceeding greatness of His power toward us who believe, according to the working of His mighty power which He worked in Christ when He raised Him from the dead and seated Him at His right hand in the heavenly places, far above all principality and power and might and dominion, and every name that is named, not only in this age but also in that which is to come. * For this reason we also, since the day we heard it, do not cease to pray for you, and to ask that you may be filled with the knowledge of His will in all wisdom and spiritual understanding, that you may walk worthy of the Lord, fully pleasing Him, being fruitful in every good work and increasing in the knowledge of God; strengthened with all might, according to His glorious power, for all patience and long-suffering with joy; giving thanks to the Father who has qualified us to be partakers of the inheritance of the saints in the light. * That Christ may dwell in your hearts through faith: that you, being rooted and grounded in love, may be able to comprehend with all the saints what is the width and length and depth and height—to know the love of Christ which passes knowledge; that you may be filled with all the fullness of God. * He has delivered us from the power of darkness and conveyed us into the kingdom of the Son of His love, in whom we have redemption through His blood, the forgiveness of sins. * All who are with me greet you. Greet those who love us in the faith. Grace be with you all. Amen.

Philippians 1:3-4 NKJV * Ephesians 1:17-21 NKJV * Colossians 1:9-12 NKJV * Ephesians 3:17-19 NKJV * Colossians 1:13-14 NKJV * Titus 3:15 NKJV

DECEMBER

12 ....

Pray for the church.
Revival of the hearts.

20 _____ *

_____
_____
_____
_____
_____
_____
_____

20 _____ *

_____
_____
_____
_____
_____
_____
_____

20 _____ *

_____
_____
_____
_____
_____
_____
_____

DECEMBER 13

Therefore, holy brethren, partakers of a heavenly calling, consider Jesus, the Apostle and High Priest of our confession; He was faithful to Him who appointed Him, as Moses also was in all His house. For He has been counted worthy of more glory than Moses, by just so much as the builder of the house has more honor than the house. For every house is built by someone, but the builder of all things is God. Now Moses was faithful in all His house as a servant, for a testimony of those things which were to be spoken later; but Christ was faithful as a Son over His house—whose house we are, if we hold fast our confidence and the boast of our hope firm until the end. * Then speak to him, saying, "Thus says the LORD of hosts, saying: 'Behold, the Man whose name is the BRANCH! From His place He shall branch out, and He shall build the temple of the LORD; yes, He shall build the temple of the LORD. He shall bear the glory, and shall sit and rule on His throne; so He shall be a priest on His throne, and the counsel of peace shall be between them both.'" * There shall come forth a Rod from the stem of Jesse, and a Branch shall grow out of his roots. The Spirit of the LORD shall rest upon Him, the Spirit of wisdom and understanding, the Spirit of counsel and might, the Spirit of knowledge and of the fear of the LORD. * He who testifies to these things says, "Surely I am coming quickly." Amen. Even so, come, Lord Jesus!

Hebrews 3:1-6 NASB * Zechariah 6:12-13 NKJV * Isaiah 11:1-2 NKJV * Revelation 22:20 NKJV

DECEMBER

13 ....

All nourishment in the house comes from Jesus Christ.

20 _____ *

_____
_____
_____
_____
_____
_____
_____

20 _____ *

_____
_____
_____
_____
_____
_____

20 _____ *

_____
_____
_____
_____
_____
_____

DECEMBER 14

Now in the sixth month the angel Gabriel was sent by God to a city of Galilee named Nazareth, to a virgin betrothed to a man whose name was Joseph, of the house of David. The virgin's name was Mary. And having come in, the angel said to her, "Rejoice, highly favored one, the Lord is with you; blessed are you among women!" * Then Simeon blessed them, and said to Mary His mother, "Behold, this Child is destined for the fall and rising of many in Israel, and for a sign which will be spoken against (yes, a sword will pierce through your own soul also), that the thoughts of many hearts may be revealed. * In that hour Jesus rejoiced in the Spirit and said, "I thank You, Father, Lord of heaven and earth, that You have hidden these things from the wise and prudent and revealed them to babes. Even so, Father, for so it seemed good in Your sight. All things have been delivered to Me by My Father, and no one knows who the Son is except the Father, and who the Father is except the Son, and the one to whom the Son wills to reveal Him." Then He turned to His disciples and said privately, "Blessed are the eyes which see the things you see; for I tell you that many prophets and kings have desired to see what you see, and have not seen it, and to hear what you hear, and have not heard it." * Of this salvation the prophets have inquired and searched carefully, who prophesied of the grace that would come to you, searching what, or what manner of time, the Spirit of Christ who was in them was indicating when He testified beforehand the sufferings of Christ and the glories that would follow. To them it was revealed that, not to themselves, but to us they were ministering the things which now have been reported to you through those who have preached the gospel to you by the Holy Spirit sent from heaven—things which angels desire to look into. * To Him be the glory and the dominion forever and ever. Amen.

Luke 1:26-28 NKJV * Luke 2:34-35 NKJV * Luke 10:21-24 NKJV * 1 Peter 1:10-12 NKJV * 1 Peter 5:11 NKJV

DECEMBER

14 . . . .

Blessed are the eyes that see prophecy fulfilled.

20 _____ *

_____
_____
_____
_____
_____
_____
_____

20 _____ *

_____
_____
_____
_____
_____
_____
_____

20 _____ *

_____
_____
_____
_____
_____
_____
_____

DECEMBER 15

But when she saw him, she was troubled at his saying, and considered what manner of greeting this was. Then the angel said to her, "Do not be afraid, Mary, for you have found favor with God. And behold, you will conceive in your womb and bring forth a Son, and shall call His name JESUS. He will be great, and will be called the Son of the Highest; and the Lord God will give Him the throne of His father David. And He will reign over the house of Jacob forever, and of His kingdom there will be no end." * And when He was twelve years old, they went up to Jerusalem according to the custom of the feast. When they had finished the days, as they returned, the Boy Jesus lingered behind in Jerusalem. And Joseph and His mother did not know it. * Now so it was that after three days they found Him in the temple, sitting in the midst of the teachers, both listening to them and asking them questions. And all who heard Him were astonished at His understanding and answers. So when they saw Him, they were amazed; and His mother said to Him, "Son, why have You done this to us? Look, Your father and I have sought You anxiously." And He said to them, "Why did you seek Me? Did you not know that I must be about My Father's business?" * Then He went down with them and came to Nazareth, and was subject to them, but His mother kept all these things in her heart. And Jesus increased in wisdom and stature, and in favor with God and men. * Now both Jesus and His disciples were invited to the wedding. And when they ran out of wine, the mother of Jesus said to Him, "They have no wine." Jesus said to her, "Woman, what does your concern have to do with Me? My hour has not yet come." His mother said to the servants, "Whatever He says to you, do it." * Now there stood by the cross of Jesus His mother, and His mother's sister, Mary the wife of Clopas, and Mary Magdalene. When Jesus therefore saw His mother and the disciple whom he loved standing by, He said to His mother, "Woman, behold your son!" And from that hour that disciple took her to his own home. * Grace be with you all. Amen.

Luke 1:29-33 NKJV * Luke 2:42-43 NKJV * Luke 2:46-49 NKJV * Luke 2:51-52 NKJV * John 2:2-5 NKJV * John 19:25-27 NKJV * Hebrews 13:25 NKJV

DECEMBER

15 . . . .

She bore the Son that rescued her.

20 _____ *

_____
_____
_____
_____
_____
_____
_____
_____

20 _____ *

_____
_____
_____
_____
_____
_____
_____
_____

20 _____ *

_____
_____
_____
_____
_____
_____
_____
_____

DECEMBER 16

Then Mary said to the angel, "How can this be, since I do not know a man?" And the angel answered and said to her, "The Holy Spirit will come upon you, and the power of the Highest will overshadow you; therefore, also, the Holy One who is to be born will be called the Son of God. Now indeed, Elizabeth your relative has also conceived a son in her old age; and this is now the sixth month for her who was called barren. For with God nothing will be impossible." * Now faith is the substance of things hoped for, the evidence of things not seen. * But without faith it is impossible to please Him, for he who comes to God must believe that He is, and that He is a rewarder of those who diligently seek Him. * Blessed are the pure in heart, for they shall see God. * For You formed my inward parts; You covered me in my mother's womb. I will praise You, for I am fearfully and wonderfully made; marvelous are Your works, and that my soul knows very well. My frame was not hidden from You, when I was made in secret, and skillfully wrought in the lowest parts of the earth. Your eyes saw my substance, being yet unformed. And in Your book they were all written, the days fashioned for me, when as yet there were none of them. How precious also are Your thoughts to me, O God! How great is the sum of them! If I should count them, they would be more in number than the sand; when I awake, I am still with You. * Amen and Amen.

Luke 1:34-37 NKJV * Hebrews 11:1 NKJV * Hebrews 11:6 NKJV * Matthew 5:8 NKJV * Psalm 139:13-18 NKJV * Psalm 72:19b NKJV

DECEMBER

16 ....

God knows the details of every child.

20 _____ *

---

20 _____ *

---

20 _____ *

DECEMBER 17

Then Mary said, "Behold the maidservant of the Lord! Let it be to me according to your word." And the angel departed from her. * And it happened, when Elizabeth heard the greeting of Mary, that the babe leaped in her womb; and Elizabeth was filled with the Holy Spirit. Then she spoke out with a loud voice and said, "Blessed are you among women, and blessed is the fruit of your womb! But why is this granted to me, that the mother of my Lord should come to me? For indeed, as soon as the voice of your greeting sounded in my ears, the babe leaped in my womb for joy. Blessed is she who believed, for there will be fulfillment of those things which were told her from the Lord." * The people who walked in darkness have seen a great light; those who dwelt in the land of the shadow of death, upon them a light has shined. You have multiplied the nation and increased its joy; they rejoice before You according to the joy of harvest, as men rejoice when they divide the spoil. For You have broken the yoke of his burden and the staff of his shoulder, the rod of his oppressor, as in the day of Midian. * For unto us a Child is born, unto us a Son is given; and the government will be upon His shoulder. And His name will be called Wonderful, Counselor, Mighty God, Everlasting Father, Prince of Peace. Of the increase of His government and peace there will be no end, upon the throne of David and over His kingdom, to order it and establish it with judgment and justice from that time forward, even forever. The zeal of the LORD of hosts will perform this. * Then Jesus spoke to them again, saying, "I am the light of the world. He who follows Me shall not walk in darkness, but have the light of life. * The city had no need of the sun or of the moon to shine in it, for the glory of God illuminated it. The Lamb is its light. And the nations of those who are saved shall walk in its light, and the kings of the earth bring their glory and honor into it. * Blessed be the LORD forevermore! Amen and Amen.

Luke 1:38 NKJV * Luke 1:41-45 NKJV * Isaiah 9:2-4 NKJV * Isaiah 9:6-7 NKJV * John 8:12 NKJV * Revelation 21:23-24 NKJV * Psalm 89:52 NKJV

DECEMBER

17 ·

Jesus' birth broke the yoke of every burden.

20 _____ *

_____
_____
_____
_____
_____
_____
_____

20 _____ *

_____
_____
_____
_____
_____
_____
_____

20 _____ *

_____
_____
_____
_____
_____
_____
_____

DECEMBER 18

And Mary said: "My soul magnifies the Lord, and my spirit has rejoiced in God my Savior. For He has regarded the lowly state of His maidservant; for behold, henceforth all generations will call me blessed. For He who is mighty has done great things for me, and holy is His name. And His mercy is on those who fear Him from generation to generation. He has shown strength with His arm; He has scattered the proud in the imagination of their hearts. He has put down the mighty from their thrones, and exalted the lowly. He has filled the hungry with good things, and the rich He has sent away empty. He has helped His servant Israel, in remembrance of His mercy, as He spoke to our fathers, to Abraham and to his seed forever." * Now the LORD had said to Abram: "Get out of your country, from your family and from your father's house, to a land that I will show you. I will make you a great nation; I will bless you and make your name great; and you shall be a blessing. I will bless those who bless you, and I will curse him who curses you; and in you all the families of the earth shall be blessed. * The king's heart is in the hand of the LORD, like rivers of water; he turns it wherever He wishes. * And it came to pass in those days that a decree went out from Caesar Augustus that all the world should be registered. * So all went to be registered, everyone to his own city. Joseph also went up from Galilee, out of the city of Nazareth, into Judea, to the city of David, which is called Bethlehem, because he was of the house and lineage of David, to be registered with Mary, his betrothed wife, who was with child. So it was, that while they were there, the days were completed for her to be delivered. And she brought forth her first born Son, and wrapped Him in swaddling cloths, and laid Him in a manger, because there was no room for them in the inn. * Blessed be the LORD God of Israel from everlasting to everlasting! Amen and Amen.

Luke 1:46-55 NKJV * Genesis 12:1-3 NKJV * Proverbs 21:1 NKJV * Luke 2:1 NKJV * Luke 2:3-7 NKJV * Psalm 42:13 NKJV

DECEMBER

18 . . . .

My spirit rejoices in God my Savior.

20 _____ *

_____
_____
_____
_____
_____
_____
_____

20 _____ *

_____
_____
_____
_____
_____
_____
_____

20 _____ *

_____
_____
_____
_____
_____
_____
_____

DECEMBER 19

Lord, You have been our dwelling place in all generations. Before the mountains were brought forth, or ever You had formed the earth and the world, even from everlasting to everlasting, You are God. * As for me, I will see Your face in righteousness; I shall be satisfied when I awake in Your likeness. * For You are my hope, O Lord GOD; You are my trust from my youth. * I have become as a wonder to many, but You are my strong refuge. Let my mouth be filled with Your praise and with Your glory all the day. * The grass withers, the flower fades, but the word of our God stands forever. * Have you not known? Have you not heard? The everlasting God, the LORD, the Creator of the ends of the earth, neither faints nor is weary. His understanding is unsearchable. He gives power to the weak, and to those who have no might He increases strength. Even the youths shall faint and be weary, and the young men shall utterly fall, but those who wait on the LORD shall renew their strength; they shall mount up with wings like eagles, they shall run and not be weary, they shall walk and not faint. * "Even them I will bring to My holy mountain, and make them joyful in My house of prayer. Their burnt offerings and their sacrifices will be accepted on My altar; for My house shall be called a house of prayer for all nations." * To God, alone wise, be glory through Jesus Christ forever. Amen.

Psalm 90:1-2 NKJV * Psalm 17:15 NKJV * Psalm 71:5 NKJV * Psalm 71:7-8 NKJV * Isaiah 40:8 NKJV * Isaiah 40:28-31 NKJV * Isaiah 56:7 NKJV * Romans 16:27 NKJV

December

19 . . . .

**When you patiently persevere in prayer—
Your heart is strengthened.**

20 _____ *

_____
_____
_____
_____
_____
_____
_____

20 _____ *

_____
_____
_____
_____
_____
_____
_____

20 _____ *

_____
_____
_____
_____
_____
_____
_____

DECEMBER 20

Not that I seek the gift, but I seek the fruit that abounds to your account. * I have been crucified with Christ; it is no longer I who live, but Christ lives in me; and the life which I now live in the flesh I live by faith in the Son of God, who loved me, and gave Himself for me. * For by grace you have been saved through faith, and that not of yourselves; it is the gift of God, not of works, lest anyone should boast. For we are His workmanship, created in Christ Jesus for good works, which God prepared beforehand that we should walk in them. * And He Himself gave some to be apostles, some prophets, some evangelists, and some pastors and teachers, for the equipping of the saints for the work of ministry, for the edifying of the body of Christ, till we all come to the unity of the faith and of the knowledge of the Son of God, to a perfect man, to the measure of the stature of the fullness of Christ. * Also I heard the voice of the Lord, saying: "Whom shall I send, and who will go for Us?" Then I said, "Here I am! Send me." * He must increase, but I must decrease. * We then, as workers together with Him also plead with you not to receive the grace of God in vain. For He says: "In an acceptable time I have heard you, and in the day of salvation I have helped you." Behold, now is the accepted time; behold, now is the day of salvation. We give no offense in anything, that our ministry may not be blamed. But in all things we commend ourselves as ministers of God: in much patience, in tribulations, in needs, in distresses, in stripes, in imprisonments, in tumults, in labors, in sleeplessness, in fastings; by purity, by knowledge, by longsuffering, by kindness, by the Holy Spirit, by sincere love, by the word of truth, by the power of God, by the armor of righteousness on the right hand and on the left, by honor and dishonor, by evil report and good report; as deceivers, and yet true; as unknown, and yet well known; as dying, and behold we live; as chastened, and yet not killed; as sorrowful, yet always rejoicing; as poor, yet making many rich; as having nothing, and yet possessing all things. * But none of these things move me; nor do I count my life dear to myself, so that I may finish my race with joy, and the ministry which I received from the Lord Jesus, to testify to the gospel of the grace of God. * The Lord Jesus Christ be with your spirit. Grace be with you. Amen.

Philippians 4:17 NKJV * Galatians 2:20 NKJV * Ephesians 2:8-10 NKJV * Ephesians 4:11-13 NKJV * Isaiah 6:8 NKJV * John 3:30 NKJV * 2 Corinthians 6:1-10 NKJV * Acts 20:24 NKJV * 2 Timothy 4:22 NKJV

DECEMBER

20 . . . .

**He must increase,
But I must decrease.**

20 _____ *

_____
_____
_____
_____
_____
_____
_____

20 _____ *

_____
_____
_____
_____
_____
_____
_____

20 _____ *

_____
_____
_____
_____
_____
_____
_____

DECEMBER 21

Now there were in the same country shepherds living out in the fields, keeping watch over their flock by night. And behold, an angel of the Lord stood before them, and the glory of the Lord shone around them, and they were greatly afraid. Then the angel said to them, "Do not be afraid, for behold, I bring you good tidings of great joy which will be to all people. For there is born to you this day in the city of David a Savior, who is Christ the Lord. And this will be the sign to you: You will find a Babe wrapped in swaddling cloths, lying in a manger." And suddenly there was with the angel a multitude of heavenly host praising God and saying: "Glory to God in the highest, and on earth peace, goodwill toward men!" So it was, when the angels had gone away from them into heaven, that the shepherds said to one another, "Let us now go to Bethlehem and see this thing that has come to pass, which the Lord has made known to us." And they came with haste and found Mary and Joseph, and the Babe lying in a manger. Now when they had seen Him, they made widely known the saying which was told them concerning this Child. And all those who heard it marveled at those things which were told them by the shepherds. But Mary kept all these things and pondered them in her heart. * Oh, taste and see that the LORD is good; blessed is the man who trusts in Him! Oh, fear the LORD, you His saints! There is no want to those who fear Him. * For the LORD God is a sun and shield; the LORD will give grace and glory; no good thing will He withhold from those who walk uprightly. * Blessed be the LORD forevermore! Amen and Amen.

Luke 2:8-19 NKJV * Psalm 34:8-9 NKJV * Psalm 84:11 NKJV * Psalm 89:52 NKJV

DECEMBER

21 ....

Glory to God in the Highest!

20 _____ *

_____
_____
_____
_____
_____
_____
_____

20 _____ *

_____
_____
_____
_____
_____
_____
_____

20 _____ *

_____
_____
_____
_____
_____
_____
_____

DECEMBER 22

And behold, there was a man in Jerusalem whose name was Simeon, and this man was just and devout, waiting for the Consolation of Israel, and the Holy Spirit was upon him. And it had been revealed to him by the Holy Spirit that he would not see death before he had seen the Lord Christ. So he came by the Spirit into the temple. And when the parents brought in the Child Jesus, to do for Him according to the custom of the law, he took Him up in his arms and blessed God and said: "Lord, now You are letting Your servant depart in peace, according to Your word; for my eyes have seen Your salvation which You have prepared before the face of all peoples, a light to bring revelation to the Gentiles, and the glory of Your people Israel." And Joseph and His mother marveled at those things which were spoken of Him. * I, the LORD, have called You in righteousness, and will hold Your hand; I will keep You and give You as a covenant to the people, as a light to the Gentiles, to open blind eyes, to bring out prisoners from the prison, those who sit in darkness from the prison house. I am the LORD, that is My name; and My glory I will not give to another, nor My praise to carved images. Behold, the former things have come to pass, and new things I declare; before they spring forth I tell you of them." * They shall see His face, and His name shall be on their foreheads. * The grace of our Lord Jesus Christ be with you all. Amen.

Luke 2:25-33 NKJV * Isaiah 42:6-9 NKJV * Revelation 22:4 NKJV * Revelation 22:21 NKJV

DECEMBER

22 . . . .

What promise has God given to you?

20 _____ *

_____

_____
_____
_____
_____
_____
_____

20 _____ *

_____
_____
_____
_____
_____
_____
_____

20 _____ *

_____
_____
_____
_____
_____
_____

DECEMBER 23

Because he holds fast to Me in love, I will deliver him; I will protect him, because he knows My name. When he calls to me, I will answer him; I will be with him in trouble; I will rescue him and honor him. With long life I will satisfy him and show him My salvation. * Offer to God a sacrifice of thanksgiving, and perform your vows to the Most High, and call upon Me in the day of trouble; I will deliver you, and you shall glorify Me. * The one who offers thanksgiving as his sacrifice glorifies Me; to one who orders his way rightly I will show the salvation of God! * And now my head shall be lifted up above my enemies all around me, and I will offer in his tent sacrifices with shouts of joy; I will sing and make melody to the LORD. Hear, O LORD, when I cry aloud; be gracious to me and answer me! You have said, "Seek my face." My heart says to you, "Your face, LORD, do I seek." * Through him let us continually offer up a sacrifice of praise to God, that is, the fruit of lips that acknowledge his name. Do not neglect to do good and to share what you have, for such sacrifices are pleasing to God. * Now may the God of peace who brought again from the dead our Lord Jesus, the great shepherd of the sheep, by the blood of the eternal covenant, equip you with everything good that you may do his will, working in us that which is pleasing in his sight, through Jesus Christ, to whom be glory forever and ever. Amen.

Psalm 91:14-16 ESV * Psalm 50:14-15 ESV * Psalm 50:23 ESV * Psalm 27:6-8 ESV * Hebrews 13:15-16 ESV * Hebrews 13:20-21 ESV

DECEMBER

23 . . . .

Do you hold fast to Jesus Christ?

20 _____ *

_____
_____
_____
_____
_____
_____
_____

20 _____ *

_____
_____
_____
_____
_____
_____
_____

20 _____ *

_____
_____
_____
_____
_____
_____
_____

DECEMBER 24

And she brought forth her firstborn Son, and wrapped Him in swaddling cloths, and laid Him in a manger, because there was no room for them in the inn. * And when they had come to the place called Calvary, there they crucified Him, and the criminals, one on the right hand and the other on the left. Then Jesus said, "Father, forgive them, for they do not know what they do." And they divided His garments and cast lots. And the people stood looking on. But even the rulers with them sneered, saying, "He saved others; let Him save Himself if He is the Christ, the chosen of God." The soldiers also mocked Him, coming and offering Him sour wine, and saying, "If You are the King of the Jews, save Yourself. And an inscription also was written over Him in letters of Greek, Latin, and Hebrew: THIS IS THE KING OF THE JEWS. Then one of the criminals who were hanged blasphemed Him, saying, "If You are the Christ, save Yourself and us." But the other, answering, rebuked him, saying, "Do you not even fear God, seeing you are under the same condemnation? And we indeed justly, for we receive the due reward of our deeds; but this Man has done nothing wrong." Then he said to Jesus, "Lord, remember me when You come into Your kingdom." And Jesus said to him, "Assuredly, I say to you, today you will be with Me in Paradise." * When Jesus therefore saw His mother and the disciple whom he loved standing by, He said to His mother, "Woman, behold your son!" Then He said to the disciple, "Behold your mother!" And from that hour that disciple took her to his own home. * Now when the sixth hour had come, there was darkness over the whole land until the ninth hour. And at the ninth hour Jesus cried out with a loud voice, saying, "Eloi, Eloi, lama sabachthani?" which is translated, "My God, My God, why have You forsaken Me?" * After this, Jesus, knowing that all things were now accomplished, that the Scripture might be fulfilled, said, "I thirst!" Now a vessel full of sour wine was sitting there; and they filled a sponge with sour wine, put it on hyssop, and put it to His mouth. So when Jesus had received the sour wine, He said, "It is finished!" And bowing His head, He gave up His spirit. * And when Jesus had cried out with a loud voice, He said, "Father, 'into Your hands I commit My spirit.'" Having said this, He breathed His last. * Grace be with you all. Amen.

Luke 2:7 NKJV * Luke 23:33-43 NKJV * John 19:26-27 NKJV * Mark 15:33-34 NKJV * John 19:28-30 NKJV * Luke 23:46 NKJV * Hebrews 13:25 NKJV

DECEMBER

24 . . . .

**He was born to die,
To save mankind.**

20 _____

---

20 _____

---

20 _____

DECEMBER 25

Now this is how Jesus the Messiah was born. His mother, Mary, was engaged to be married to Joseph. But while she was still a virgin, she became pregnant by the Holy Spirit. Joseph, her fiancé, being a just man, decided to break the engagement quietly, so as not to disgrace her publicly. As he considered this, he fell asleep, and an angel of the Lord appeared to him in a dream. "Joseph, son of David," the angel said, "do not be afraid to go ahead with your marriage to Mary. For the child within her has been conceived by the Holy Spirit. And she will have a son, and you are to name him Jesus, for he will save his people from their sins." All of this happened to fulfill the Lord's message through his prophet: "Look! The virgin will conceive a child! She will give birth to a son, and he will be called Immanuel (meaning, God is with us)." When Joseph woke up, he did what the angel of the Lord commanded. He brought Mary home to be his wife, but she remained a virgin until her son was born. And Joseph named him Jesus. * Jesus was born in the town of Bethlehem in Judea, during the reign of King Herod. About that time some wise men from eastern lands arrived in Jerusalem asking, "Where is the newborn king of the Jews? We have seen his star as it arose, and we have come to worship him." * After this interview the wise men went their way. Once again the star appeared to them, guiding them to Bethlehem. It went ahead of them and stopped over the place where the child was. When they saw the star, they were filled with joy! They entered the house where the child and his mother, Mary, were, and they fell down before him and worshiped him. Then they opened their treasure chests and gave him gifts of gold, frankincense, and myrrh. * For we have all sinned; all fall short of God's glorious standard. * But God showed his great love for us by sending Christ to die for us while we were still sinners. * For the wages of sin is death, but the free gift of God is eternal life through Christ our Lord. * Salvation that comes from trusting Christ—which is the message we preach—is already within easy reach. In fact, the Scriptures say, "The message is close at hand; it is on your lips and in your heart." For if you confess with your mouth that Jesus is Lord and believe in your heart that God raised him from the dead, you will be saved. For it is by believing in your heart that you are made right with God, and it is by confessing with your mouth that you are saved. As the Scriptures tell us, "Anyone who believes in him will not be disappointed." * Amen and Amen!

Matthew 1:18-25 NLT * Matthew 2:1-2 NLT * Matthew 2:9-11 NLT * Romans 3:23 NLT * Romans 5:8 NLT * Romans 6:23 NLT * Romans 10:8-11 NLT * Psalm 72:19b NLT

DECEMBER

25 . . . .

What gift are you giving to Jesus this year?

20 _____ *

_____
_____
_____
_____
_____
_____
_____

20 _____ *

_____
_____
_____
_____
_____
_____
_____

20 _____ *

_____
_____
_____
_____
_____
_____
_____

DECEMBER 26

Shepherd the flock of God that is among you, exercising oversight, not under compulsion, but willingly, as God would have you; not for shameful gain, but eagerly; not domineering over those in your charge, but being examples to the flock. And when the chief Shepherd appears, you will receive the unfading crown of glory. * Do you not know that those who run in a race all run, but one receives the prize? Run in such a way that you may obtain it. And everyone who competes for the prize is temperate in all things. Now they do it to obtain a perishable crown, but we for an imperishable crown. Therefore I run thus: not with uncertainty. Thus I fight: not as one who beats the air. But I discipline my body and bring it into subjection, lest, when I have preached to others, I myself should become disqualified. * Do no fear what you are about to suffer. Behold the devil is about to throw some of you into prison, that you may be tested, and for ten days you will have tribulation. Be faithful unto death, and I will give you the crown of life. * Blessed is the man who remains steadfast under trial, for when he has stood the test he will receive the crown of life, which God has promised to those who love him. * Henceforth there is laid up for me the crown of righteousness, which the Lord, the righteous judge, will award to me on that Day, and not only to me but also to all who have loved his appearing. * For what is our hope or joy or crown of boasting? Is it not you? For you are our glory and joy. * Now may the God of peace who brought again from the dead our Lord Jesus, the great shepherd of the sheep, by the blood of the eternal covenant, equip you with everything good that you may do his will, working in us that which is pleasing in his sight, through Jesus Christ, to whom be glory forever and ever. Amen.

1 Peter 5:2-4 ESV * 1 Corinthians 9:24-27 NKJV * Revelation 2:10 ESV * James 1:12 ESV * 2 Timothy 4:8 ESV * 1 Thessalonians 2:19-20 ESV * Hebrews 13:20-21 ESV

DECEMBER

26 . . . .

Why are crowns important?

20 _____ *

_____
_____
_____
_____
_____
_____
_____

20 _____ *

_____
_____
_____
_____
_____
_____
_____

20 _____ *

_____
_____
_____
_____
_____
_____
_____

DECEMBER 27

Pursue love, and earnestly desire the spiritual gifts, especially that you may prophesy. For one who speaks in a tongue speaks not to men but to God; for no one understands him, but he utters mysteries in the Spirit. On the other hand, the one who prophesies speaks to people for their upbuilding and encouragement and consolation. * Love builds up. * Beloved, let us love one another, for love is from God, and whoever loves has been born of God and knows God. Anyone who does not love does not know God, because God is love. In this the love of God was made manifest among us, that God sent his only Son into the world, so that we might live through him. In this is love, not that we have loved God but that he loved us and sent his Son to be the propitiation for our sins. Beloved, if God so loved us, we also ought to love one another. No one has ever seen God; if we love one another, God abides in us and his love is perfected in us. * So we have come to know and to believe the love that God has for us. God is love, and whoever abides in love abides in God, and God abides in him. By this is love perfected with us, so that we may have confidence for the day of judgment, because as he is so also are we in this world. There is no fear in love, but perfect love casts out fear. For fear has to do with punishment, and whoever fears has not been perfected in love. We love because He first loved us. If anyone says, "I love God," and hates his brother, he is a liar; for he who does not love his brother whom he has seen cannot love God whom he has not seen. And this commandment we have from him: whoever loves God must also love his brother. * I therefore, a prisoner for the Lord, urge you to walk in a manner worthy of the calling to which you have been called, with all humility and gentleness, with patience, bearing with one another in love, eager to maintain unity of the Spirit in the bond of peace. * But grace was given to each one of us according to the measure of Christ's gift. * And he gave the apostles, the prophets, the evangelists, the shepherds and teachers, to equip the saints for the work of ministry for building up the body of Christ, until we all attain to the unity of the faith and of the knowledge of the Son of God, to mature manhood, to the measure of the stature of the fullness of Christ. * Speaking the truth in love, we are to grow up in every way into him who is the head, into Christ, from whom the whole body, joined and held together by every joint with which it is equipped, when each part is working properly, makes the body grow so that it builds itself up in love. * Amen and Amen.

1 Corinthians 14:1-3 ESV * 1 Corinthians 8:1b ESV * 1 John 4:7-12 ESV * 1 John 4:16-21 ESV * Ephesians 4:1-3 ESV * Ephesians 4:7 ESV * Ephesians 4:11-13 ESV * Ephesians 4:15-16 ESV * Psalm 72:19b ESV

DECEMBER

27 . . . .

Love builds up the church.

20 _____ *

_____
_____
_____
_____
_____
_____
_____

20 _____ *

_____
_____
_____
_____
_____
_____
_____

20 _____ *

_____
_____
_____
_____
_____
_____
_____

DECEMBER 28

"You are my witnesses," declares the LORD, "and my servant whom I have chosen, that you may know and believe me and understand that I am he. Before me no god was formed, nor shall there be any after me. I, I am the LORD, and beside me there is no savior. I declared and saved and proclaimed, when there was no strange god among you; and you are my witnesses," declares the LORD, "and I am God." * On God rests my salvation and my glory; my mighty rock, my refuge is God. * Salvation belongs to the LORD; your blessing be on your people! * The salvation of the righteous is from the LORD; he is their stronghold in the time of trouble. The LORD helps them and delivers them; he delivers them from the wicked and saves them, because they take refuge in him. * When my life was fainting away, I remembered the LORD, and my prayer came to you, into your holy temple. Those who pay regard to vain idols forsake their hope and steadfast love. But I with the voice of thanksgiving will sacrifice to you; what I have vowed I will pay. Salvation belongs to the LORD! * "Hallelujah! Salvation and glory and power belong to our God." * The grace of the Lord Jesus be with all. Amen.

Isaiah 43:10-12 ESV * Psalm 62:7 ESV * Psalm 3:8 ESV * Psalm 37:39-40 ESV * Jonah 2:7-9 ESV * Revelation 19:1b ESV * Revelation 22:21 ESV

DECEMBER

28 . . . .

How has your knowledge of God grown?

20 _____ *

20 _____ *

20 _____ *

DECEMBER 29

Worship God. * And we know that the Son of God has come and has given us an understanding, that we may know Him who is true; and we are in Him who is true, in His Son Jesus Christ. This is the true God and eternal life. * And this is eternal life, that they may know You, the only true God, and Jesus Christ whom You have sent. * For God did not send His Son into the world to condemn the world, but that the world through Him might be saved. * "And to the angel of the church in Philadelphia write, 'These things says He who is holy, He who is true, "He who has the key of David, He who opens and no one shuts, and shuts and no one opens": "I know your works. See, I have set before you an open door, and no one can shut it; for you have a little strength, have kept My word, and have not denied My name.'" * I will betroth you to Me forever; yes, I will betroth you to Me in righteousness and justice, in lovingkindness and mercy; I will betroth you to Me in faithfulness, and you shall know the LORD. * Let us know, let us pursue the knowledge of the LORD. His going forth is established as the morning; He will come to us like the rain, like the latter and former rain to the earth. * Grace and peace be multiplied to you in the knowledge of God and of Jesus our Lord, as His divine power has given to us all things that pertain to life and godliness, through the knowledge of Him who called us by glory and virtue. * Little children, keep yourselves from idols. Amen.

Revelation 22:9b NKJV * 1 John 5:20 NKJV * John 17:3 NKJV * John 3:17 NKJV * Revelation 3:7-8 NKJV * Hosea 2:19-20 NKJV * Hosea 6:3 NKJV * 2 Peter 1:2-3 NKJV * 1 John 5:21 NKJV

December

29 . . . .

God has opened a door for you that no man can shut.

20 _____ *

_____

_____

_____

_____

_____

_____

_____

20 _____ *

_____

_____

_____

_____

_____

_____

_____

20 _____ *

_____

_____

_____

_____

_____

_____

_____

DECEMBER 30

All the ways of a man are pure in his own eyes, but the LORD weighs the spirit. * Every way of man is right in his own eyes, but the LORD weighs the heart. * Even a child makes himself known by his acts, by whether his conduct is pure and upright. * You will recognize them by their fruits. Are grapes gathered from thorn bushes, or figs from thistles? So, every healthy tree bears good fruit, but the diseased tree bears bad fruit. A healthy tree cannot bear bad fruit, nor can a diseased tree bear good fruit. Every tree that does not bear good fruit is cut down and thrown into the fire. Thus you will recognize them by their fruits. * What good is it, my brothers, if someone says he has faith but does not have works? Can that faith save him? If a brother or sister is poorly clothed and lacking in daily food, and one of you says to them, "Go in peace, be warmed and filled," without giving them the things needed for the body, what good is that? So also faith by itself, if it does not have works, is dead. But someone will say, "You have faith and I have works." Show me your faith apart from your works, and I will show you my faith by my works. * But grow in the grace and knowledge of our Lord and Savior Jesus Christ. To him be the glory both now and to the day of eternity. Amen.

Proverbs 16:2 ESV * Proverbs 21:2 ESV * Proverbs 20:11 ESV * Matthew 7:16-20 ESV * James 2:14-18 ESV * 2 Peter 3:18 ESV

DECEMBER

30 . . . .

What is the vision on your heart for next year?

20 _____ *

_____
_____
_____
_____
_____
_____
_____

20 _____ *

_____
_____
_____
_____
_____
_____
_____

20 _____ *

_____
_____
_____
_____
_____
_____
_____

DECEMBER 31

Trust in the LORD, and do good; dwell in the land and befriend faithfulness. * Trust in the LORD with all your heart, and do not lean on your own understanding. In all your ways acknowledge him, and he will make straight your paths. Be not wise in your own eyes; fear the LORD, and turn away from evil. It will be healing to your flesh and refreshment to your bones. * Trust in the LORD forever, for the LORD GOD is an everlasting rock. * Trust in him at all times, O people; pour out your heart before him; God is a refuge for us. * Delight yourself in the LORD, and he will give you the desires of your heart. * But seek first the kingdom of God and his righteousness, and all these things will be added to you. * Rejoice in the Lord always; again I will say, Rejoice. * Commit your way to the LORD; trust in him, and he will act. * Commit your work to the LORD, and your plans will be established. * My love be with you all in Christ Jesus. Amen.

Psalm 37:3 ESV * Proverbs 3:5-8 ESV * Isaiah 26:4 ESV * Psalm 62:8 ESV * Psalm 37:4 ESV * Matthew 6:33 ESV * Philippians 4:4 ESV * Psalm 37:5 ESV * Proverbs 16:3 ESV * 1 Corinthians 16:24 ESV

DECEMBER

31 . . . .

Trust in the Lord forever.
May He guide your every endeavor.

20 _____ *

_____

_____

_____

_____

_____

_____

_____

20 _____ *

_____

_____

_____

_____

_____

_____

_____

20 _____ *

_____

_____

_____

_____

_____

_____

_____

ABOUT THE AUTHOR

A lysa VanderWeerd is also the author of the poetry book, *Life*. She has written bible study curriculums for the Jr. High ministry at Harvest Christian Fellowship—Pastor Greg Laurie on: Psalm 16:11, the book of James, and the book of Revelation.

She has her Bachelors in History with a minor in English from the University of California- Irvine. She has her Master of Arts in History from the University of California- Riverside; and is currently working on her Doctorate in Education in Community Care and Counseling: Family and Marriage from Liberty University.

Alysa lives in Southern California. She loves camping at the beach with her family, running, and working on wood projects.

For more about Alysa, visit relentlessprayer.org.

CPSIA information can be obtained
at www.ICGtesting.com
Printed in the USA
FFOW02n1159220518
46819969-49003FF